A Dream Unfinished

A Dream Unfinished

Theological Reflections on America from the Margins

Eleazar S. Fernandez
and
Fernando F. Segovia,
Editors

Maryknoll, New York 10545

The Catholic Foreign Mission Society of America (Maryknoll) recruits and trains people for overseas missionary service. Through Orbis Books, Maryknoll aims to foster the international dialogue that is essential to mission. The books published, however, reflect the opinions of their authors and are not meant to represent the official position of the Society.

To obtain more information about Maryknoll and Orbis Books, please visit our website at www.maryknoll.org.

Manufactured in the United States of America

Manuscript editing and typesetting by Joan Weber Laflamme

Lbrary of Congress Cataloging-in-Publication Data

A dream unfinished : theological reflections on America from the margins / Eleazar S. Fernandez and Fernando F. Segovia, editors.
     p. cm.
    Includes bibliographical references and index.
    ISBN 1-57075-367-9 (pbk.)
     1. Theology, Doctrinal—United States. 2. Church and minorities—United States. 3. Minorities—Religious life—United States. I. Fernandez, Eleazar S. II. Segovia, Fernando F.

BT30.U6D74 2001
277.3'083'08—dc21

                                             00-047848

Contents

PART I
AFRICAN-AMERICAN VOICES

PART II
ASIAN-AMERICAN VOICES

Preface

The last decades of the twentieth century witnessed the explosion of non-Western theological studies—broadly conceived as Christian Studies—both outside the West, among the children of the colonized in the Two-Thirds World, and inside the West, among ethnic and racial minorities in the United States. Outside the West, such studies first developed in Latin America, in the form of liberation theology, and it was not long before the movement had spread in a variety of shapes and forms to Africa, Asia and the Pacific, and the Caribbean. Inside the West, such studies first came to the fore among African Americans, by way of black theology, and later spread to Hispanic Americans as well as Asian Americans.

Yet, collaboration among the different regions and groups has differed considerably. Outside the West, theologians from the various geographical areas of the Two-Thirds World have, for a long time now, participated in a variety of common projects and endeavors, while continuing to address the particular concerns of each major region. Inside the West, theologians from the various minority groups have kept, for the most part, to their own respective circles and discussions and, as a result, have failed not only to engage one another but also to develop any sense of common agenda or discourse. Thus, while dialogue and collaboration have been quite common in the Two-Thirds World, atomization and dispersion have prevailed instead among ethnic and racial minorities in the West.

Given the ever-growing numbers and strength of minorities in theological studies within the United States, however, we believe that the time has come for a fundamental change in this regard. Indeed, we are of the opinion that a sustained and systematic conversation among the various groups has become imperative. Our present fragmentation not only works against our cause, both as a whole and as individual groups, ultimately reinforcing our marginalization in the country, but also makes it easier for the forces of closure—the forces of racism and discrimination, injustice and oppression, always at work in the land—to have their way. The present volume, therefore, is meant as a first attempt at such a conversation. As such, we wanted both project and volume to be broadly inclusive, bringing together a proper balance of theologians from the major groups in question (African Americans, Asian Americans, Hispanic Americans), a proper balance of women and men theologians, and a proper balance of theologians from the Catholic and Protestant traditions. Such is the diversity of our groups, and such must be the diversity of any conversation among us. Our only regret in this regard is that the volume did not turn out to be as diversified as originally intended, due to a number of factors endemic in any project of publication and simply beyond our control.

For a conversation as multicentered and multilingual as the one envisioned, a central issue of interest to all as point of departure proves essential. We opted for the concept of the "American Dream." We thus asked the various contributors to offer theological reflections on the country in general and the American Dream in particular from their respective positions in the margins as members and voices of minority groups.

Such a choice we deemed most appropriate, given both the centrality of this concept in the life of the country and the highly conflicted experience of minorities in this regard. On the one hand, the vision of the Dream is beyond question: a long-standing and much-cherished view of the country as an open land of freedom, justice, and opportunity, not only for all of its born citizens but also for all those who enter the country as immigrants. On the other hand, the underside of the Dream is also beyond question. Although some Americans of non-European descent have "made it" in the country—have attained a measure of the American Dream—ethnic and racial minorities have, by and large, remained marginal participants in this dream. Indeed, for many such a dream has become, at best, a deferred vision, and, at worst, a terrible nightmare. Yet, America remains dear to ethnic and racial minorities insofar as they refuse to relinquish the America of their hearts. It was this conflict of promise and experience, therefore—this sense of "a dream unfinished"—that we wanted to address in unison, as a theological exercise in common, and so we asked all participants to do so, in whatever way they saw fit, from within the context of their own respective communities in the country. The result proved a success beyond all expectations—a veritable cornucopia of theological reflections on dream and country alike.

We conclude with a threefold hope. First, that this project prove but a beginning for protracted conversation among minorities in the United States. Second, that such dialogue lead us beyond the fragmentation we have experienced thus far, much to our detriment and that of the country as well as that of theological studies in general. Finally, that this dialogue in and from the margins ultimately lead us beyond marginalization itself, toward a very different conception and practice of theological studies and, most important, toward the eventual fulfillment of our unfinished dream in the country.

Acknowledgments

The editors would like to express their profound gratitude to all those individuals who have made this volume possible:

First and foremost, to Robert Ellsberg, editor-in-chief of Orbis Books, for his undivided support and encouragement.

Second, to the Rev. Tan Yak-Hwee, a doctoral student in the Graduate Department of Religion at Vanderbilt University, for her invaluable work in all aspects of the editorial task.

Third, to the editorial staff of Orbis Books who guided the volume to a successful completion with its usual mixture of expert and gracious supervision. A special word of thanks in this regard is due Ms. Catherine Costello, the production coordinator.

Finally, to those scholars and friends who kindly answered our invitation to serve as contributors to this project and whose works are represented in these pages.

Introduction

Minority Studies and Christian Studies

FERNANDO F. SEGOVIA

Over the course of the last three decades, the face of the United States has been changing, and drastically so. Periodic reports from the U.S. Bureau of the Census serve as sharp reminders of what its own long-range projections have now envisioned for some time regarding the ethnic-racial composition of the country in the twenty-first century. A review of these projections proves most telling.[1] In the following table I list the middle-series projections (for July 1 of each year) according to five categories:

A=White (not Hispanic)
B=Black (not Hispanic)
C=American Indian, Eskimo, Aleut (not Hispanic)
D=Asian and Pacific Islander (not Hispanic)
E=Hispanic (of any race)

	2000	2005	2010	2030	2050
A	71.8%	69.9%	68.0%	60.5%	52.8%
B	12.2%	12.4%	12.6%	13.1%	13.6%
C	0.7%	0.8%	0.8%	0.8%	0.9%
D	3.9%	4.4%	4.8%	6.6%	8.2%
E	11.4%	12.6%	13.8%	18.9%	24.5%

Such projections clearly point to a decline in the country's population of European origins relative to a rise in its population of non-European origins: from a ratio of 71.8 percent to 28.2 percent in the year 2000 to 52.8 percent to 47.2 percent in 2050. This is a demographic shift of massive proportions.

---

[1] See U.S. Bureau of the Census, Current Population Reports, Series P25-1130, "Population Projections of the United States by Age, Sex, Race, and Hispanic Origin: 1995-2050." The projections are given in three series: high, middle, and low. I have chosen the middle-series projections as neither the most conservative nor the most radical.

Such figures prove even more telling when two other factors are taken into consideration. On the one hand, this projected shift is in keeping with the results of the last two national censuses: the 1980 Census listed the non-Western population of the country at approximately 20 percent (one out of five); the 1990 Census listed that population at 25 percent (one out of four). Following the projections above, the percentage of the non-Western population will reach 33 percent around 2015 (one out of three) and 50 percent shortly after 2050 (one out of two). On the other hand, the periodic reports issued by the Bureau indicate that its ongoing population estimates are running ahead—slightly rather than sharply—of its middle-series projections, so that in the long run this ethnic-racial demographic shift will take place at a somewhat faster pace than anticipated.[2] Consequently, the change at work in the country since the 1960s, profound as it has already been, pales by comparison to what lies in store in the decades ahead.

This ongoing transformation in the visage of the country has already had profound repercussions in every aspect of its life and discourse, and these are only bound to deepen and multiply as this demographic shift follows its projected path in the years to come. Such has certainly been the case already, and will continue to be so, in both the academy and the church, as minority groups of non-Western origins or descent continue to join the ranks of both institutions, bringing with them their histories and experiences, their concerns and interests, their perspectives and positions. In the process the ways of life and discursive frameworks of such institutions are not only directly affected but also significantly altered. I should like to pursue this question by bringing together two fields of study: minority studies and Christian studies. In effect, I propose to examine the relationship between the academic study of the Christian religion and the academic study of minority formations. In other words, what happens when ethnic-racial minorities—African Americans, Asian Americans, Hispanic Americans, and Native Americans—begin to reflect on their religious past, present, and future within the Christian tradition? I shall begin by placing the demographic shift in question in the context of U.S. immigration history; continue with an overview of minority studies, its nature and contours; and conclude with reflections on the impact of such discourse on the study of Christianity.

IMMIGRATION HISTORY: PATTERNS AND POLICIES

The present shift is by no means the first time that the face of the country has undergone a drastic change; in point of fact, it is but the latest in a series of such

---

[2] See, e.g., U.S. Census Bureau, Population Estimates Program, "Resident Population Estimates of the United States by Sex, Race, and Hispanic Origin: April 1, 1990 to August 1, 1999" (October 1, 1999). The categories for August 1999 are reported as follows: White (not Hispanic), 71.8%; Black (not Hispanic), 12.1%; American Indian, Eskimo, and Aleut (not Hispanic), 0.7%; Asian and Pacific Islander (not Hispanic), 3.8%; Hispanic Origin (of any race), 11.5%. Thus, in effect, the projections for 2000 regarding the populations of Western and non-Western descent have already been reached.

transformations. To be sure, the narrative of such changes would have to begin with the impact of sustained European immigration on the native populations of the continent, the consequences of which proved both devastating and long-lasting for the latter. From a demographic point of view alone, such havoc is readily evident in the steady ratio projected for the American Indian, Eskimo, and Aleut population vis-à-vis the total population of the country (from .7 percent in 2000 to .9 percent in 2050). This is a segment of the population that, having experienced decimation and containment, can now barely hold its own within the country. As foundational as that story needs to be for all of us who follow later, regardless of origins, my focus here is on the phenomenon of immigration itself, its patterns of flow and policies of control.[3]

Looking Back

The point of departure is, at first sight, unmistakable. For the first two centuries of the country—that is to say, for the whole of its colonial history (1607-1775) and the early decades of its postcolonial experience (1776-1815)[4]—Great Britain served as the main source of population and culture, though by no means the only source.[5] The result was the formation of what has come to be known as the WASP phenomenon: a dominant "white, Anglo-Saxon, Protestant" presence and influence in the country at large. This Anglo-American beginning, however, would undergo radical changes in the course of the nineteenth and early twentieth centuries, yielding in the end a broad Euro-American complexion. I emphasize the phrase "at first sight," because it is clear that the population

---

[3] My discussion of this topic is much indebted to the history of immigration policy provided by W. S. Bernard, "Immigration: History of U.S. Policy," in *The Immigration Reader: America in a Multidisciplinary Perspective*, ed. David Jacobson (Malden-Oxford: Blackwell Publishers Ltd., 1998), 48-71.

[4] Bernard divides the history of U.S. immigration policy into five periods: Colonial Era (1609-1775); Open Door (1776-1881); Regulation (1882-1916); Restriction (1917-1964); and Liberalization (1965-present) (ibid., 48). Two comments are in order with regard to my own dates here: First, with regard to the colonial period, I use 1607, the actual date for the establishment of the Jamestown settlement, rather than 1609, the date given by Bernard for the first measure in immigration policy—the launching of a publicity drive in London by the Virginia Company. Second, with regard to the Open Door period, I use 1815 as a reference to the end of the Napoleonic Wars and the start of the real flow of "old" immigration.

[5] Ibid., 52-57. In the colonial period the main goal of immigration was the recruitment of labor—people who would settle and cultivate the lands of the New World. Within the imperial-colonial framework of Great Britain, the colonies would supply raw materials to the motherland, while the latter would provide manufactured goods to the former. Immigration policy was carried out at two levels of government, the imperial and the colonial. Within this framework, it was the colonies who were responsible for attracting people, which they proceeded to do in any number of ways, both throughout the British Isles and the European continent. As a result, by the War of Independence, more than a third of the country's white residents were of non-Anglo origin.

changes affecting this Anglo-American beginning were there from the very start, yielding a very different sort of foundation as well.

David Kennedy proves helpful in this regard.[6] He highlights two major developments in the history of U.S. immigration. To begin with, from the end of the fifteenth century to the end of the eighteenth century, the principal source of immigration for the whole of the New World—the two American continents as well as the Caribbean—was not Europe but Africa. Only in the early nineteenth century did the number of European settlers surpass that of Africans in the New World, by then approximately ten million. This massive presence was by no means voluntary, grounded as it was in the expansion of large-scale plantation agriculture and its need for large-scale commercial slavery. From the beginning, therefore, the dominant Anglocentric impulse in the country finds a counterbalance in a subordinate Afrocentric presence. Then, in the course of the nineteenth century, the great European migration takes place, involving the displacement of seventy million people in all, of whom thirty-five million found their way to the United States. This massive movement of people was also involuntary. On the one hand, Europe faced enormous population growth through the century as a result of improvements in diet, sanitation, and disease control. On the other hand, Europe also confronted the disruptions brought about by the Industrial Revolution—the rupture with traditional ways of life; the exodus from agriculture and countryside to factories and cities; the inability of the market at first to bear such movement of people. In time, therefore, the foundational Anglocentric impulse began to find itself under heavy and unremitting pressure from large-scale immigration from other parts of Europe.

Kennedy outlines and explains the path of such immigration: As the process of industrialization expanded from the British Isles in the late eighteenth century, to the Low Countries and Germany in the early and mid nineteenth century, to eastern and southern Europe in the late nineteenth century and early twentieth centuries, the source of emigration from Europe followed suit. Two major periods, traditionally characterized as "old" and "new" immigration can be readily distinguished in this regard. The difference between them is well captured by Arthur Schlesinger Jr., who uses the Civil War as a sort of natural divide between the two.[7] Prior to the Civil War, the "old" non-Anglo emigration came from western and northern Europe—Irish, Dutch, Germans, Scandinavians. As their numbers increased, so did the dislike of the Anglo-American population for the new arrivals—their personal characteristics, ways of life, religious practices. By the 1850s such antagonism had led to the formation of nativist organizations, like the Supreme Order of the Star-Spangled Banner, better known as the Know-Nothings, the force behind the American

---

[6] David Kennedy, "Can We Still Afford to Be a Nation of Immigrants?," *The Atlantic Monthly* 278/5 (November 1996): 52-68. Kennedy is the Donald J. McLachlan Professor of History at Stanford University.

[7] A. M. Schlesinger, *The Disuniting of America: Reflections on a Multicultural Society,* rev. and enl. ed. (New York and London: W. W. Norton & Company, 1998), 33-39.

Party. After the Civil War, the "new" non-Anglo emigration hailed from southern and eastern Europe—Italians and Greeks; Poles and Russians; Czechs, Hungarians, and Slovaks; Jews. As their numbers multiplied, so did prejudice on the part of the Anglo-American population against these newer arrivals, and on the very same grounds. By the turn of the century such hostility had led to the rise of new nativist organizations, like the American Protective Association in the late nineteenth century and the Ku Klux Klan in the early twentieth century.

Just as one can trace the actual beginning of the "old" wave of immigration to the cessation of the Napoleonic Wars in Europe (1815), with a formal beginning perhaps at the end of the War of Independence (1776), so can one point to the outbreak of World War I as the actual end of the "new" wave of immigration (1914), with a formal conclusion perhaps at the start of the Great Depression (1929). In the intervening period, extending from a century to a century and a half, the face of the country had undergone two drastic changes: the Anglocentric impulse had become broadly Eurocentric, as social forces in an "old" continent with an excess of population and a "new" continent with a dearth of population came together in the wake of the Industrial Revolution. Such transformations, as noted, had not come without demurral and resistance, although in this regard the opposition to the "new" wave proved far more severe and successful in the end.

Looking Forward

This broad Eurocentric complexion of the United States would remain firmly in place for the next fifty years or so, until the mid-1960s, when the face of the country would begin to undergo yet another drastic change, now toward a more global complexion, as immigration from the non-Western world began to pour in, above all from Asia and the Pacific as well as from Latin America and the Caribbean. Several developments account for this new transformation. Two of these reproduce the major factors at work behind the great European migration of the nineteenth century[8]: first, the rapid population growth experienced in the non-Western world through the course of the century, as a result of similar advancements in disease control, sanitation, and diet; and second, the gradual spread of industrialization to the non-Western world, with the same disruptive effects on traditional ways of life across the globe—internal migration from countryside and agriculture to cities and factories plus the inability of the market to absorb such migration. A third reason concerns immigration policy. The resentment caused by the "new" immigration brought about increasing calls for limits on the flow of immigration and ultimately a series of restrictive legislation, beginning in 1917 and continuing through the 1920s. These restrictions would not be lifted until the passage of the Immigration and Naturalization Act of 1965—the point of departure for the latest and ongoing shift.

To be sure, restrictions of an ethnic-racial character were nothing new in immigration policy. Indeed, the first such restrictions go back to the second half

---

[8] Kennedy, "Can We Still Afford to Be a Nation of Immigrants?," 3.

of the nineteenth century and have to do with immigration from China. Mounting numbers, largely as a result of contract labor destined for railroad construction, led to a series of state and federal measures that culminated with the Chinese Exclusion Act of 1882, which suspended the entry of Chinese workers into the country for ten years and barred all foreign-born Chinese from acquiring citizenship. In 1902 the 1882 Act was renewed indefinitely by Congress. By that time the Japanese had begun to arrive in great numbers as well, and a similar outcry erupted, leading to the Gentlemen's Agreement of 1907-1908 between the two countries, which called for voluntary regulation immigration on the part of the Japanese. With the Immigration Act of 1917 previous measures against the Chinese and the Japanese were extended to what was called the "Asiatic Barred Zone" and tightened: no laborers allowed from India, Indochina, Afghanistan, Arabia, the East Indies, and other smaller Asian countries. Immigration from Asia was thus not only the earliest but also, and by far, the most severely affected.

With the Immigration Act of 1917 the restrictions began to affect the "new" immigration from Europe as well. Here the point of departure is clear: In 1910 the Dillingham Commission—appointed by Congress and headed by Senator William Dillingham of Vermont, a moderate restrictionist—issued a massive report on immigration, underlining its detrimental effects for the welfare of the country. The report called for limits on immigration from southern and eastern Europe on the grounds that such peoples were racially inferior and incapable of assimilation as Americans. In its wake followed the Immigration Act of 1917, the Quota Act of 1921, the Immigration Act of 1924, and the National Origins System of 1927. The Immigration Act of 1917 was but the first salvo: besides the further restrictions placed on Asian immigration, a literacy test for all new arrivals over sixteen years of age was put into effect as a way of stemming the tide from the undesirable areas of Europe. When the latter failed to have its intended effect, a number of further measures followed:

- The Quota Act of 1921 limited the annual number of arrivals from each admissible country to 3 percent of the foreign-born of that nationality as recorded in the Census of 1910. Quotas were thus established for Europe, the Near East, Africa, Australia, and New Zealand; only the Western hemisphere was allowed free immigration.[9] The result was a sharp decline in the flow from southern and eastern Europe, since the annual quotas for all the countries in question represented less than 25 percent of the numbers admitted before World War I.
- The Immigration Act of 1924 reduced the admissible annual total to 165,000—less than 20 percent of the average level before World War I—and set the annual quota for each admissible nation at 2 percent of the foreign-born of

---

[9] The Quota Act of 1921 allowed for special preference in two other ways as well: (1) within the quota system, priority was given to family ties and family reunification; (2) outside of it, a "nonquota" category was introduced based on special skills.

that country as recorded in the 1890 Census.[10] The result was even sharper restriction of the flow from southern and eastern Europe, with the annual quotas for all countries now amounting to a mere 3 percent of the annual immigration average before World War I. In addition, the entry of all aliens ineligible for citizenship was barred, thus reaffirming the exclusion of the Chinese and the banning of many Asians.

- The Immigration Act of 1924 further provided for the establishment of a "national origins" system that would replace the formal quota system in 1927 and would favor northern and western European groups. The total annual quota from all nations was now fixed at 150,000, with each country receiving the percentage of that figure equal to the percentage of people from that country, by birth or descent, in the Census of 1920. A minimum quota of 100 was assigned every country, but aliens ineligible for citizenship (Chinese and Japanese) continued to be barred from the country. In the end, northern and western Europe, including the British Isles, received 82 percent of the annual quota; southern and eastern Europe, 16 percent; all other nations, 2 percent.

The intent of the national origins system was to prevent any further change in the ethnic-racial composition of U.S. society. In this it proved highly successful, although its effects also happened to coincide with a considerable drop in the flow of immigration due not only to the Great Depression of 1929 and its aftermath but also World War II and its surrounding upheaval, so much so that many of the quotas assigned went unfilled during this period. Indeed, the system was not to be dismantled until the 1960s, when the combination of a greater tolerance for diversity and a new sense of internationalism within the context of the Cold War made it increasingly objectionable and undesirable.[11] With the

---

[10] The 1924 Act further extended the principle of special preference: (a) with respect to family ties, wives and dependent children of U.S. citizens were now included in the nonquota category; (b) with respect to special skills, the nonquota category was expanded to cover all recognized learned professions as well as domestic servants.

[11] A number of alterations were made in the intervening years, however. First, in 1943 the Chinese Exclusion Act was repealed, though with minimal effect, since the quota for China remained barely above the minimum level. Second, in the postwar period a number of measures were passed to accept (a) the spouses and children of armed-forces personnel in the nonquota category and (b) refugees from the war under the quota system. Third, during the Cold War, a number of measures were again passed to accept refugees, now in the nonquota category. Finally, in 1952 Congress passed the Immigration and Nationality Act, which was meant to codify all previous legislation and which thus preserved the principle of national origins. Two provisions should be noted: (1) Asian immigration: the category of aliens ineligible for citizenship was abolished, thus opening immigration to both Japan and the "Asia-Pacific Triangle," though under minimal quotas; (2) the second affected the British West Indies: people from colonial territories would no longer qualify under the quotas of their mother countries but were to be assigned quotas of their own, again at a minimal level. The bill also retained special preferences both by way of the quota system (special skills) and the nonquota category (family ties).

Immigration and Naturalization Act of 1965, immigration policy underwent a complete rehauling, unleashing in the process major new forces in patterns of immigration and hence in the ethnic-racial makeup of the country. Its provisions, designed to take effect in 1968, included:

- Elimination of both the national origins system of quotas and the designation of the Asia-Pacific Triangle.
- Increase of total annual immigration to 290,000: 120,000 in the Western hemisphere, without limit for any one country; 170,000 for the Eastern hemisphere, with no more than 20,000 for any one country.
- Retention of nonquota admissions.
- Preferential treatment for certain quota immigrants (family members, special skills), though only for the Eastern hemisphere.[12]
- Allotment of few visas for refugees of both hemispheres, but no numerical limitations on admission under parole.

The result was a sharp increase in immigration from countries previously placed at a disadvantage under the earlier system of national origins.[13] By 1975 immigration from Europe accounted for 19 percent of total immigration, and by the 1980s that figure was down to 11 percent. The tectonic ramifications of the new policy could be felt already in the censuses of 1980 and 1990 and became ever more palpable in the population projections for 2000 and beyond. In the process the broad Eurocentric visage that had emerged by the 1910s as a result of both "old" and "new" waves of immigration from Europe and that was intended to be frozen in perpetuity by the restrictive agenda of the 1920s found itself, like the earlier Anglo-American foundation, under heavy and unremitting pressure from large-scale immigration from the whole of the non-Western world, gradually yielding to what could only be reasonably characterized as a cosmocentric complexion. In an ironic twist of history, the European presence in the country began to find itself, as at the beginning, facing a significant non-European component, now no longer solely from Africa but from every corner of the non-Western world.

As in the case of the previous demographic shifts, such a transformation could not but bring in its wake reactions and measures of a nativist sort, now on the part of the broad Eurocentric component of the country. Such signs of the times include calls for limits on the flow of immigration from the non-Western

---

[12] Subsequently, the Western Hemisphere Act of 1976 extended the preferential system to the Western hemisphere as well, with priority given to family ties and special skills, while the limit of no more than 20,000 for any one country was also put into effect.

[13] For the effects of such immigration, see R. Ueda, "The Changing Face of Post-1965 Immigration," in Jacobson, *The Immigration Reader*, 72-91. Ueda argues that the special preference given to family ties has been particularly responsible for the great increases in immigration from Asia and the Pacific as well as from the Caribbean and Latin America.

world; drives to make English the official language of the country; violence against individuals, institutions, and symbols of the groups in question; even a sense of doom regarding the future of the country in the face of such barbarian hordes. The new immigrants readily testify as well to encounters with prejudice and hostility on a sustained and systematic basis. If anything, in comparison to the previous waves of immigration, one should expect the fear of these newest arrivals, as both inferior and inassimilable, to be much sharper, given their origins outside the West—in fact, by and large in former colonies of the West—and the "tinting" of the country, physiologically as well as culturally, which they represent.

MINORITY STUDIES

As the numbers of such immigrants have swelled, their impact on the country's society and culture has also intensified. Actually, the way had already been prepared by the Civil Rights Movement of the 1960s, when ethnic-racial minorities—above all, African Americans and U.S. Hispanic Americans (Mexican Americans and U.S. Puerto Ricans)—began to make their voices heard with much greater confidence and vehemence than ever before. Following in such well-laid tracks from the time of its commencement in 1968, the newest wave of immigration would solidify and expand such earlier developments. An important consequence of this foregrounding of and by ethnic-racial minorities has been an increasing presence in the academy, with a resultant diversification of knowledges and discourses. Not only have the histories and experiences, the concerns and interests, the perspectives and positions of particular minority groups been introduced into the academy as proper areas of research and study, but also the very question of the relationship among such groups. It is the whole of this inquiry, encompassing the particular as well as the comparative, that I would characterize as "minority studies."

To be sure, this is not a phenomenon unique to the United States. As former colonial subjects of the European empires have flocked to the lands of their former imperial masters in the aftermath of the decolonization movement beginning after World War II, the question of minority groups, their practices and discourses, has come to the surface as well in European academic circles. Furthermore, since minorities represent neither a uniquely modern nor a uniquely Western development, the gaze of minority studies can be cast outward, outside the West, as well as backward, into the premodern period. Minority studies thus implies, and benefits from, an inherent global scope and perspective.

In an attempt to define the nature and scope of postcolonial studies, Georg Gugelberger provides a solid intellectual framework from which to understand the rise and position of minority studies.[14] Since the 1960s, he argues, a major

---

[14] G. M. Gugelberger, "Postcolonial Cultural Studies," in *The Johns Hopkins Guide to Literary Theory and Criticism*, ed. M. Groden and M. Kreiwirth (Baltimore and London: The Johns Hopkins University Press, 1994), 581-85. Interestingly, this massive guide contains no entry on minority studies.

revisionist project has taken hold in academia, in opposition to the hegemony of Western studies and in recognition of the fact that the other "minority" cultures are actually "majority" cultures in the world. This project has yielded a broad array of counter-discourses—"'tempests' in a postist world replacing *Prospero's Books* . . . with a Calibanic viewpoint"[15]—among which the following are cited: cultural studies, women's studies, gender studies, ethnic studies, third-world studies. It is in such company that Gugelberger places what he calls "Minority Discourse," with such examples as Chicano studies and African-American studies in the United States and *Gastarbeitsliteratur* (Guest Worker Literature) in Germany. Given their similar origins and aims as deliberate oppositional moves to inscribe the "other" bypassed and marginalized by the West, all such counter-discourses emerge as very much interrelated and interdependent—variations, as it were, on the "other" of the West. Minority studies is no exception in this regard. Thus, for example, the question of minority groups can be approached from the perspective of internal colonization and thus within the ambit of postcolonial studies or from the angle of displacement and exile and thus within the realm of diasporic studies.

This is a view of minority studies with which I find myself in full accord. As a counter-discourse in the postist world of the last four decades, its focus is on ethnic-racial groups that constitute a numerical as well as a disadvantaged minority in their respective social contexts, with the purpose in mind of inscribing their presence in such contexts. In what follows, then, I should like to trace certain key developments in the formation of minority studies.[16] In so doing I follow two basic principles. First, I confine myself to the discussion regarding minority studies as such, as an encompassing discursive formation, with no consideration of individual configurations within such studies. Second, I restrict myself to constructive articulations of such studies, leaving aside for now their critical reception. Such self-imposed limitations are due not only to the constraints of space but also to the nature of this overview as but an initial step on my part.

Toward a Minor Literature

As point of departure I turn to the definition of "minor" literature *(littérature mineure)* offered by Gilles Deleuze and Félix Guattari in their major study of

---

[15] Ibid., 581.

[16] For overviews of minority studies, see V. B. Leitch, *Cultural Criticism, Literary Theory, Poststructuralism* (New York and Oxford: Columbia University Press, 1992), 83-103; M. Sarup, *Identity, Culture, and the Postmodern World* (Athens, Ga.: University of Georgia Press, 1996), 1-13; B. Moore-Gilbert, G. Stanton, and W. Maley, "Introduction," in *Postcolonial Criticism*, ed. B. Moore-Gilbert, G. Stanton, and W. Maley, Longman Critical Readers (New York: Addison Wesley Longman, 1997), 1-72, esp. 47-57.

Franz Kafka, subtitled *Toward a Minor Literature (Pour une littérature mineure)*.[17] The volume, as the subtitle indicates, presents Kafka as a salient example of minor literature and uses him as entrée into the definition of such literature. For over twenty years Deleuze, a poststructuralist philosopher, and Guattari, a poststructuralist psychoanalyst, coauthored a series of works in which they sought to bring the fields of philosophy and psychoanalysis into dialogue. This collaboration began in 1972 with the publication of *Anti-Oedipus: Capitalism and Schizophrenia* and concluded in 1991 with the appearance of *What Is Philosophy?*, a summary of the project as a whole written not long before their respective deaths.[18] Central to this project was the notion of "deterritorialization," the process of breaking with limiting or coercive structures, social or intellectual, represented in geographical terms as "territory"—in effect, a variant of the decentering impulse at the heart of poststructuralism. The monograph on Kafka, originally published in 1975, comes early in the project; it constitutes, in effect, their second joint effort, coming three years after *Anti-Oedipus*. In its discussion of minor literature, the volume invokes the concept of deterritorialization to describe the rupture effected by such literature on the dominant structures of linguistic usage and literary production.[19]

---

[17] G. Deleuze and F. Guattari, "What Is a Minor Literature?," chap. 3 in *Kafka: Toward a Minor Literature*, Theory and History of Literature 30 (Minneapolis, Minn.: University of Minnesota Press, 1986), 16-27. Originally published as *Kafka: pour une littérature mineure*, Collection Critique (Paris: Les Éditions de Minuit, 1975).

[18] G. Deleuze and F. Guattari, *Anti-Oedipus: Capitalism and Schizophrenia* (New York: Viking, 1977) and *What Is Philosophy?* (London: Verso, 1994). Originally published as: *L'anti-Oedipe* (Paris: Les Éditions de Minuit, 1972) and *Qu'est-ce que la philosophie?* (Paris: Les Éditions de Minuit, 1991). Other works include *Rhizome* (Paris: Les Éditions de Minuit, 1976) and *Mille Plateaux* (Paris: Les Éditions de Minuit, 1980). The dates for both are as follows: Deleuze (1925-95); Guattari (1936-92).

[19] In his discussion of poststructuralism and its profound debt to Nietzscheanism, Madan Sarup (*Identity, Culture, and the Postmodern World*, 99-104) provides a good summary of the wider framework behind this notion of deterritorialization. For Deleuze and Guattari, he points out, human beings are desiring machines. This desire is at once personal and collective, so that its effects are psychological as well as political. Desire itself is of two types: paranoid, which emphasizes authoritarianism and corresponds to a fascist society, the realm of the symbolic (language, structure, society); and schizophrenic, which stresses libertarianism and corresponds to a revolutionary society, the realm of the imaginary (freedom). For Deleuze and Guattari, schizophrenia emerges as the important condition. Thus, the transition from the imaginary stage to the symbolic stage represents a tragic loss. Consequently, a return to the imaginary is imperative: a human freedom involving spontaneity and primitive, unmediated desire and signified by direct and fusional relationships. This realm of the imaginary is to be found among children, primitive peoples, and the mad. The condition of and option for minor literature represents, therefore, a return to the imaginary at the literary level, away from the limiting or coercive structures of linguistic usage and literary production.

This discussion is neither theoretical nor systematic. On the one hand, it is embedded within a critical study of Kafka and hence largely developed with direct reference to his work and his context. In other words, what is predicated of minor literature in general is arrived at by way of Kafka in particular. On the other hand, it is freeform in style, loose in structure and complex in expression, making for a rather disjointed and elusive reading altogether. As such, it represents an example of deterritorializing in its own right. Nevertheless, a basic outline of their response to the question of what constitutes a minor literature can be ultimately put together. In fact, such a response begins with a definition proper. While widely pursued, Deleuze and Guattari point out, attempts to define the concept of "marginal" literature, "popular" literature, or "proletarian" literature have proved futile, insofar as the criteria necessary for such a definition are difficult to establish. What is needed, they argue, is a more "objective" concept (18), for which they propose that of "minor" literature, defined as follows: literature written not in a minor language but rather produced by a minority within a major language. Such literature exhibits three fundamental traits: linguistic deterritorialization, political immediacy, and collective enunciation.

First, minor literature is written in a language marked by a high degree of "deterritorialization," a language with no direct or significant roots for the group that employs it. What this means is best approached by their own analysis of language in Kafka. Kafka, a Jew, writes in Prague German and, in so doing, signifies the impossibility of writing faced by the Jews of Prague, an impossibility in itself described as threefold: first, of not writing as such—since literature is essential for a national consciousness that is oppressed or uncertain; second, of writing other than in German—since Prague Jews find themselves at an unbridgeable distance from their former Czech territoriality; finally, the impossibility of writing in German—since this is the language of an oppressive minority, hence a language not only removed from the people but also of a minority to which the Prague Jews belong but from which they are excluded. Consequently, the Jews of Prague have no choice but to write; cannot but do so in German; but find it hard to do so, given that German is not the language of the masses but rather of a minority that excludes the Jews. Prague German thus constitutes an excellent example of deterritorialized language, quite appropriate for minor and strange uses.[20]

Second, minor literature is profoundly and inescapably political. In major literature individual concerns—such as of family or marriage—connect readily with other such concerns, while the social milieu functions simply as background or environment. Its space is large, so that individual concerns emerge as neither "specifically indispensable" nor "absolutely necessary" (17). In minor

---

[20] Such a situation is likened to that of the "blacks in America" and their use of the English language. Although not developed, one can readily infer the logic of the argumentation: (a) impossibility of not writing, as an oppressed national consciousness; (b) impossibility of writing in a language other than English, given the insurmountable difference from their former territoriality; (c) impossibility of writing in English, given its use by an oppressive majority.

literature, however, individual concerns are immediately and intrinsically tied to politics. Its space is cramped, so that individual concerns not only prove necessary and indispensable but also emerge as magnified, conveyors of another story altogether and thus signifiers of larger concerns, commercial, economic, bureaucratic, and/or juridical. That, according to Deleuze and Guattari, is certainly the case in Kafka, for whom politics impinges on everything in explicit and absorbing fashion.

Third, minor literature is collective rather than individuated. It is a literature lacking in abundance of talent, thereby making any individuated enunciation from a "master" impossible and rendering "a literature of masters" out of the question (17). Instead, what each author writes is necessarily collective and political. Thus, given a framework where national consciousness often finds itself in a state of inaction and always in a process of disintegration, literature turns into a collective and revolutionary enunciation, calling forth active solidarity within the minority and raising the possibility of a different community, with a different consciousness and sensibility, especially if the writer in question finds himself or herself marginalized within or excluded from the minority community itself. Such literature becomes, therefore, a "machine of expression" and the "people's concern" (18), and hence much more capable of addressing and developing its content. Thus, for Kafka, Deleuze and Guattari argue, the message belongs to neither the enunciating subject (the author or narrator) nor the subject of the enunciation (the hero or character), since there is no subject, only "collective assemblages of enunciation" (18). Kafka, like any other author, is locked into such an assemblage in his solitude, which in turn opens him up to all that goes in history.

In light of this definition, Deleuze and Guattari go on to speak of minor literature not in terms of specific bodies of literature but as the "revolutionary conditions" for every literature present at the heart of great literature (18). Given its framework of multiple deterritorializations of language and its character as a collective machine of expression, such literature may develop along two different lines, enrichment or sobriety. The two options are described by way of the problem confronting the Jews of Prague—a situation where the Czech language and the rural environment have been discarded and where the German language functions as an artificial language (19).[21] The first option is to enrich such German, "to swell it up through all the resources of symbolism, of oneirism, of esoteric sense, of a hidden signifier"; this was the route chosen by the Prague School, as exemplified in such writers as Gustav Meyrinck and Max Brod. Here the goal was to reterritorialize by way of symbolism "based in archetypes, Kabbala, and alchemy"; in the end, however, such a move only served to heighten

---

[21] These two options are further exemplified by way of Irish literature, with specific reference to James Joyce and Samuel Beckett. Both are said to confront, as Irish, the revolutionary conditions for minor literature. While Joyce proceeds "by exhilaration and overdetermination," engaging in a reterritorialization of English and every other language, Beckett opts for "dryness and sobriety," pushing a further deterritorialization of English and French.

its break with the people and found its political result in Zionism. The second option is to take such German as it is, "in its very poverty," and to denude it further, "to the point of sobriety," in opposition to any symbolic, significant, or even signifying use of it; this was the route invented by Kafka. Here the aim was to deterritorialize by way of intensification, "to make the language vibrate in its aridity with new intensity"; in the end, the result would be material intensity in expression.

Despite their evident focus on minorities in their approach to minor literature—most concretely on the Jews of Prague and their use of German, but also with reference to Irish authors and their use of English and other languages and African-American authors and their use of English—Deleuze and Guattari ultimately argue for minor literature as a universal possibility. Such a move is not at all surprising, given their definition of minor literature in terms of the "revolutionary conditions" present in every major language; in effect, such conditions can be grasped by both those who do not live in that language and those who do. To be sure, it is immigrants, especially the children of immigrants, and minorities who face the conditions that make for minor literature—living in a language that is not their own; perhaps no longer or not yet knowing their language; knowing poorly the language in which they presently live. At the same time, such conditions can be rendered universal by choice—"tearing" a minor literature away from its language, challenging the language as a result and leading it along a revolutionary path. Consequently, anyone who has "the misfortune of being born in the country of a great literature," who must write in its language, can become an immigrant or a minority, "finding his own point of underdevelopment, his own *patois*, his own third world, his own desert" (18).

In the end, given such potential for universalization, Deleuze and Guattari speak of minor literature as both an imperative and a vision. The imperative is clear: since only what is minor is truly major or revolutionary, one must "hate all languages of masters" (26). To do so, one must become a stranger in one's own language, whether by way of over-reterritorialization or ultra-deterritorialization. In this regard the way of Kafka, of ultra-deterritorialization, is evidently favored: making use of the "polylingualism" of language, of its character as a "schizophrenic mélange" of different functions and centers of power, by playing such functions and centers against one another; opting for an intensive use of language through creative lines of escape, especially from a syntactical point of view; opposing the oppressed quality of language to its oppressive quality—in sum, "finding points of nonculture or underdevelopment, linguistic Third World zones by which a language can escape" (27). The vision is similarly clear: a dream not of becoming-major, of aspiring to become an official language, but rather of becoming-minor. And here what is true of linguistic usage and literary production should be true of other such enterprises as psychoanalysis and philosophy—to engage in anti-psychiatry, against the desire of psychoanalysis to become a master "of the signifier, of metaphor, or wordplay," as well as in anti-philosophy, against its longstanding status as an "official, reverential genre" (27). In the process the problem of deterritorialization faced by immigrants and minorities is adopted as a must and a dream for all others as well—a veritable apotheosis of "minor" literature.

Critical Summary. Deleuze and Guattari establish a beginning field of vision for minority studies with a focus on literature and language. A series of dichotomies maps out its domain: that of minor and major literature functions as primary; the others follow in parallel and reinforcing fashion (deterritorialized and rooted; political and nonpolitical; collective and individual; of the people and of masters). Such sets of oppositions presuppose, as always, a superior and an inferior pole: minor literature stands for freedom from, while major literature represents subjection to linguistic and literary structures. The condition of minor literature is further defined in linguistic rather than social terms, as that which a minority constructs within a major language; as such, it is conceived as a universal option. Thus, while it is the natural province of immigrant and minority groups, it can also be chosen by the majority. The condition itself admits of two variations: the first, along the lines of overflowing richness; the second, along the lines of utter sobriety—the way chosen by Kafka and preferred by Deleuze and Guattari. In the end, therefore, minor literature emerges as a literature of revolution, open to minorities and majority alike. Following the logic of the argumentation, such literature constitutes anti-literature.

Such intent focus on and analysis of the minor in literature and language I find quite laudable; at the same time, however, a number of points strike me as rather problematic. First, the dichotomous nature of the distinction is far too restrictive, with its view of minor and major literature as a binary opposition: what one is, the other is not. I would favor a more convoluted view of this relationship, in which it is better to speak of orientations or inflections. Second, the definition of minor literature offered bears a number of debilitating limitations and stereotypes. The following come readily to mind: (1) minor literature is defined solely within the space of great literature—as a result, literature written in a language regarded as "minor" in the global scene is, by definition, ruled out of consideration; (2) minor literature is described as lacking in talent qua collective—in other words, little talent is to be had among minorities, given their collective disposition and orientation; (3) major literature emerges as a literature with little sense of the political—consequently, it remains a literature of the aesthetic realm, in which the social dimension is present only by way of non-intrusive background. Third, the two options deemed available to minor literature, which in themselves may be seen as constituting a further dichotomy, prove much too limiting as well. I would favor a wider spectrum of possibilities. Finally, language and literature are separated from their material conditions of existence, of which there is no analysis whatsoever. In other words, the textual overwhelms the contextual. This separation, moreover, allows the "major" to become as "minor" as the "minor" itself—the dominant can and must become minorities thereby, but without the historical and cultural oppression suffered by minorities, the heritage of injustice and discrimination.

A last point is in order. The purpose of becoming-minor, of breaking with the dominant structures of language and literature, remains nebulous. While the revolutionary path of the minor in the face of the major is readily comprehensible, the ultimate destination of this path is not as evident. In the end, one may reasonably ask: Where does this hatred of the masters' language lead? What lies beyond the revolution and the tearing? What is the point of not becoming an official language? An answer, I find, is not immediately forthcoming. In fact, one can even detect in the vision and imperative represented by this path traces of a certain romantic "first-worldism": an idealist option for the *patois*, for underdevelopment and nonculture, for the Third World. Despite such observations, this early moment in the formation of minority studies is immensely important, with its focus on the linguistic and literary conditions and problems faced by minorities.

Toward Minority Discourse

A further important step in the development of minority studies comes with the attempt on the part of Abdul JanMohamed and David Lloyd to define the character and contours of "minority discourse."[22] At the time, both were already widely known figures in postcolonial criticism, with a mutual interest in the colonial subject: JanMohamed, a native of Kenya, specialized in African literature and had argued for a Manichean division between colonizer and colonized; Lloyd, a native of Ireland, worked in Irish literature and had focused on modern Irish identity.[23] The project as a whole, as the preface explains (ix-xi), was undertaken with a twofold purpose in mind: to define a field of discourse among various minority cultures, and to intervene in the politics of cultural education in the United States. A basic principle at work behind the project is further identified: all minority groups share a common experience of domination and exclusion by the majority. Both aims are thus directly rooted in this principle: in the light of such experience, the project set out to provide a theoretical articulation of the political and cultural structures linking minority groups; in so doing, the project sought to marginalize the hegemonic discourse

---

[22] A. R. JanMohamed and D. Lloyd, "Introduction: Toward a Theory of Minority Discourse: What Is To Be Done?," in *The Nature and Context of Minority Discourse*, ed. A. R. JanMohamed and D. Lloyd (Oxford: Oxford University Press, 1990), 1-16. This collection of essays first appeared, under the same title, as special issues of *Cultural Critique* 6 and 7 (1987). Most of the essays proceed from a conference, again with the same title, held at the University of California at Berkeley in 1986; for publication a few additional essays were included.

[23] For JanMohamed, see *Manichean Aesthetics: The Politics of Literature in Colonial Africa* (Amherst, Mass.: University of Massachusetts Press, 1983) and "The Economy of Manichean Allegory: The Function of Racial Difference in Colonialist Literature," in *"Race," Writing, and Difference*, ed. H. L. Gates (Chicago: Chicago University Press, 1986), 79-106. For Lloyd, see *Nationalism and Minor Literature: James Clarence Morgan and the Emergence of Irish Cultural Nationalism* (Berkeley and Los Angeles: University of California Press, 1987); *Anomalous States: Irish Writing and the Postcolonial Moment* (Dublin and North Carolina: Lilliput/Duke University Press, 1993); and "Writing in the Shit: Beckett, Nationalism, and the Colonial Subject," in special issue *Narratives of Colonial Resistance*, ed. T. Brennan, *Modern Fiction Studies* 35/1 (1989): 71-86.

of the center and challenge its agenda of cultural education in the country. On both counts, the authors argue, it proved successful, though in varying degrees.[24]

Their own joint essay comes not only in the wake of but also in full knowledge of the definition of minor literature advanced by Deleuze and Guattari fifteen years earlier. While quite correct in their definition of minor literature as collective, JanMohamed and Lloyd point out, the reason adduced—lack of talent—is entirely off the mark. The collective nature of this literature is due, rather, to factors cultural and political. To begin with, such collective subjectivity is portrayed as a result of the damage inflicted upon minorities by the majority—societies left in fundamental transition from the oral, mythic, and collective values of traditional cultures to the literary, rational, and individualistic values of Western cultures. In such conditions the minority writer responds by turning established vehicles for the representation of individual experience, such as the novel, into new venues for the manifestation of collective experience. In addition, collective subjectivity is depicted as the result of the casting of minorities into negative, generic subject-positions by the majority. In such situations the minority writer responds by turning such experience into a positive, collective one. Although brief, partial, and in no way highlighted—indeed offered *in medias res* and almost by the way—this critique of Deleuze and Guattari, with its emphasis on the social context of minor literature, serves as point of departure for their own analysis of minority discourse.

This analysis begins with a critical account of the social dimensions of minority discourse, undertaken from a variety of different angles. First, while academics engaged in ethnic and feminist studies have produced much significant work, archival as well as theoretical, such studies are largely confined to special programs or centers and thus widely dispersed in the academy. As a result, they remain marginalized, paralleling the status of minority groups and cultures in society at large, and fragmented, unable to establish relations among themselves. Second, despite enormous differences, minority cultures stand in a similar relationship of antagonism and marginalization from the dominant culture. Consequently, discourses that should come together to examine such marginalization and to develop strategies for empowerment remain at considerable distance from each other. Third, such antagonism and marginalization are ultimately grounded in the highly negative evaluation of minority cultures at work in the agenda of the dominant Western, Eurocentric humanism. From the

---

[24] The authors describe (x) both conference and volume as a factor, alongside other publications and events, in the outbreak of the culture wars of the 1980s, what they describe as the "Western Cultures" or the "Canon Debate." Thus, while the conference proposal envisioned a dialogue among minorities as a way of expanding the challenge of dominant values, the official evaluation stereotyped the proposed dialogue as a babelian confusion of tongues. Similar attacks, they point out, would follow on similar projects, whether focused on multiculturalism, interdisciplinary or cultural studies, or the expansion of canons. On the whole, they conclude, the attempt to mark out a space for minority discourse proved more successful than the attempt to intervene in the politics of cultural education.

point of view of hegemonic discourse—"universalistic, univocal, and monologic" (1)—all such cultures and voices are regarded as "barbarians beyond the pale of civilization; . . . forever consigned to play the role of the ontological, political, economic, and cultural Other" (2). Fourth, minority discourses are regarded as having nothing in common and thus as incapable of communication with one another. As a result, such communication is either actively obstructed or considered possible only when routed through the dominant discourses.[25] Finally, minority discourses emerge as offspring of damage, systematic and multifrontal damage—affecting all modes of social formations, overturning functional economic systems, and uprooting if not eliminating entire peoples. The aftereffects of such damage, including all elements of cultural production, become in turn signifiers of underdevelopment and warrants for marginalization, with development possible only by way of assimilation to the Western model of development. Such, therefore, are the social dimensions of minority discourse— marginalization and fragmentation; perception as barbarian "other" and incoherent babble; mark of underdevelopment.

In the light of such conditions, overwhelmingly negative in tone, the task of minority discourse is elaborated as threefold: archival work, theoretical reflection by way of critique, and theoretical reflection by way of construction.

First, within a context of profound and pervasive "institutional forgetting," where the cultural practices and values of minorities remain out of sight and out of mind, it is essential for minority discourse to engage in "counter-memory," in the recuperation and mediation of such values and practices (6). Such archival work is fundamental: it breaks through the ideological horizons of the dominant culture by retrieving works rendered unavailable and alternatives rendered invisible within its scope of vision.[26] Given the sheer power of the dominant

---

[25] JanMohamed and Lloyd pointedly cite in this regard the rationale used by the National Endowment for the Humanities in its rejection of the 1986 proposal for the funding of an international conference on this topic (3). Out of six external reviews solicited, the NEH set a specific deadline for five reviewers and asked for a response from a sixth reviewer "ASAP." While the former were all positive in their recommendation, with minor reservations, the latter was unconditionally negative. In the end, the NEH followed the latter evaluation: such a conference could not but be quite diffuse and ultimately turn into "an academic tower of Babel," since the participants would have little to say to one another. Such objections, the authors add, would never surface in a comparative exercise involving the national literatures of Europe; to the contrary, such exercises are not only encouraged but institutionalized in departments of comparative literature.
[26] Given its focus on cultural practices, JanMohamed and Lloyd launch what is for all practical purposes a preemptive defense against a Marxist critique of the proposed minority discourse project (5-6). Such discourse, they readily grant, does represent a mode of ideology similar to that of religion—a sublimation or expression of misery. However, a critical difference should also be noted: minority discourse, unlike religious discourse (understood), constitutes both a strategy for physical survival and a strategy for political critique. For minority discourse, therefore, cultural practices do not represent a superstructure imposed by the dominant culture but an inherent weapon in the struggle against dominant culture. In other words, physical survival emerges as a fundamental mode of political critique.

culture, however, such work faces a constant danger: relegation to the margins of universal, human experience as exotica. Such retrieval could ultimately result, therefore, in a more sophisticated but no less repressive form of marginalization, whereby formerly occluded practices and values become fringe spectacles in the optic of universal humanism.

Second, given the possibility of exoticism, it is imperative for minority discourses to carry out a full-scale critique of the dominant culture, foregrounding in sustained and systematic fashion the historical reasons why and the formal ways in which its institutions have engaged in exclusion and marginalization. Such theoretical reflection is indispensable; it lays bare the ideological horizons of the dominant culture, exposing its own self-evaluation as well as its evaluation of minority cultures, and thus the inclusive and exclusive practices at work in a supposedly universalist, humanist project. Such critical reflection is not without its dangers, again given the force of the dominant culture: assimilation—selective integration of minority practices as examples of the achievement possible within the framework of the dominant culture, without regard for the politics at work in universal humanism; or pluralism—surface integration of minority practices within a framework of values established by the dominant culture, blind to issues of exploitation and discrimination.

A third task is thus in order. Together, archival retrieval and critical reflection serve to establish the presence and status of minority cultures. However, given the possibilities of cooptation, it is crucial for minority discourse to explore and reevaluate the alternative practices and values operative in minority cultures. Such theoretical reflection is invaluable; it rereads traditional signifiers of underdevelopment and warrants for marginalization as sites of radical opposition to the values and practices of the center. In such a move, to be sure, certain dangers do lurk as well, ultimately derived from the enormous influence of the dominant culture: a celebration of diversity as such or a turn toward a priori concepts of ethnicity and gender. Such constructive reflection must involve, therefore, the development of a minority discourse that brings together the great variety of minority groups and cultures. Through such linkage the solidarities at work among minorities are established in light of their similar relationship *as minorities* vis-à-vis the dominant culture. As a result, minority practices and values are approached not as a question of irreducible essence or festive diversity but as a question of position—the result of a constellation of measures (social, economic, political, cultural, ideological) deployed by the center. Thus, JanMohamed and Lloyd describe minority discourse as "a project of systematically articulating the implications of that subject-position—a project of exploring the strengths and weaknesses, the affirmations and negations that are inherent in that position" (9). It is precisely this subject-position, and not lack of talent, as Deleuze and Guattari would have it, that accounts for the collective character of "minor" literature, and hence it is the articulation of this subject-position that emerges as "*the* central task" of minority discourse (9).

The execution of this task, this project of becoming-minor, clearly demands radical transformation in cultural education, in the pedagogy of universal humanism. Such transformation involves changes in content as well as in form.

From the point of view of content, expansion by way of subject matter. Given the fact of marginalization, this expansion calls for the introduction of new courses into the curriculum and the addition of new material into the syllabi of existing offerings. From the point of view of form, expansion by way of disciplinary border-crossings. Given the fact of across-the-board damage, this expansion requires work across a number of disciplines. Such changes are designed to call into question the agenda of universal humanism, with its focus on aesthetic effects and essential values. Responsibility for such a transformation is placed squarely on the shoulders of minority intellectuals in the academy.[27]

In the end, JanMohamed and Lloyd posit three major goals behind the proposed critical articulation of minority discourse. First, minority discourse must work with a fluid rather than static view of domination—an approach to domination not in terms of ontological otherness, involving the reification of any one group's experience as privileged, but of constantly shifting configurations, involving constantly shifting counter-strategies with regard to both goals and solidarities. Consequently, minority discourse demands constant forming and re-forming of "ever-more-inclusive solidarities" (14) as well as constant review of the material and intellectual dimensions of minority formations. Second, minority discourse must strive toward a radical break at the discursive level, toward ever greater acceptance of difference and diversity in the academy. At the same time, minority discourse must be aware of its own limitations in this regard, since a true acceptance of difference and diversity within Western society is impossible until a radical transformation takes place in the material structures of exploitation. Finally, minority discourse must differentiate itself from the discourse of Western intellectuals, despite evident similarities with postmodernism and poststructuralism and frequent recourse to such methods and theories.[28] Especially so with regard to the dissolution of the (bourgeois) subject. While Western intellectuals set out to deconstruct identity formations from within, minority intellectuals begin from a position of nonidentity. Thus, what for the latter is a social given, a point of departure, becomes for the former a social project, a point of destination. For minorities, however, this given represents in no way a sign

---

[27] This is a task envisioned as quite difficult (11). First, insofar as minority intellectuals face double marginalization within the academy: (a) separation from the minority culture, given the privileges afforded by educational institutions of the dominant culture; (b) discrimination and marginalization within such institutions. Second, insofar as minority intellectuals can only overcome such alienation by means of actual attempts to transform the academy, involving a mixture of theoretical critique and practical struggle. Two such possibilities are described: (1) critique of both the traditional role of humanist intellectuals and disciplinary divisions in the academy; and (2) exposé of traditional humanism, its relations of dominance and the effects of such relations, alongside a commitment to a humanism that has as its main focus the victims of domination.

[28] A number of similarities are cited: working toward social and cultural formations tolerant of difference; challenging any representation of a single universal mode of being human; deployment of gender theory.

of liberation, as it does for Western intellectual discourse, but rather a call for struggle.

Critical Summary. JanMohamed and Lloyd significantly expand the field of vision in minority studies by turning from the focus of Deleuze and Guattari on the linguistic and literary characteristics of minor literature to the social conditions of minority discourse. Such conditions involve, for all minority groups and at a most fundamental level, antagonism and damage by the majority—a relationship of domination and exclusion leading to marginalization and fragmentation. It is a relationship marked by a view of minorities as undercivilized and underdeveloped. The task of minority discourse becomes, therefore, that of foregrounding this common experience of minority groups in order to move beyond marginalization and fragmentation, to expose this operative relationship of antagonism and damage on the part of the center, and to take steps toward a decentering of the center itself. This task demands a threefold front: archival retrieval of marginalized practices and values; critical analysis of the dominant culture and its project of liberal humanism, with its practices and values of domination and exclusion; and constructive reliance upon the minoritarian practices and values retrieved as grounds for alternative visions of society. Such a task must involve not only work across a variety of disciplines, given the multifrontal nature of the antagonism and damage at play, but also work across minority groups, given the common nature of their relationship to the majority. In the end, minority discourse emerges as a radical transformation of marginalization and fragmentation into opposition to the majority, its values, and its practices. Such opposition, JanMohamed and Lloyd add, is very different from that emerging from within the center itself, insofar as it finds in nonidentity, the fundamental condition of minorities, not a point of destination and sign of liberation but a point of departure and a call to struggle.

This turn to the social on the part of JanMohamed and Lloyd I find entirely felicitous, bringing to the fore a dimension of minority studies that had been completely overlooked by Deleuze and Guattari. In the process, however, it does seem to me that the linguistic and literary dimension so highlighted by the latter recedes far too much into the background. The contextual element now overwhelms the textual. This emphasis on the social also has important ramifications. With some of these I find myself in agreement; in the case of others, I must diverge.

Among the agreements, I would note the following two. On the one hand, the relationship between dominant discourse and minority discourse is presented as oppositional but not dichotomous. To be sure, JanMohamed and Lloyd posit a relationship of stark antagonism between the two: the damage inflicted by the majority on the minority is depicted as systematic and sustained. However, this relationship, while structurally similar vis-à-vis all minorities, is presented as varying from group to group, given the enormous differences among the groups themselves; in addition, it is presented as ever in flux, yielding shifting configurations of otherness with no one group as uniquely privileged in this regard. On the other hand, the political character of both discourses, majority and minority, is duly highlighted, given the hostile nature of the relationship at work. Thereby majority discourse emerges as political as minority discourse.

Among the disagreements, I would note two as well. On the one hand, one finds continued insistence on the collective nature of minority discourse. The rationale is much more sophisticated now: no longer a question of lack of talent but rather a matter of social context. In effect, the generic construction of the minority subject by the majority and the transitional character of minority cultures in the wake of damage lead minority writers to the deployment of a collective subjectivity. While perhaps more explicitly oriented toward the collective, I see minority discourse as nevertheless the product of individual authors with different and conflicting locations in and attitudes toward the collective they represent. As such, I would argue, minority discourse is best approached as a combination of the personal and the collective, a point that would hold true as well for majority discourse.

On the other hand, one finds undue emphasis on minoritarian sources of opposition to majority discourse. To be sure, while the value of oppositional sources within majority culture itself is properly acknowledged, as the links with postmodernism and poststructuralism amply demonstrate, it is the practices and values retrieved from minority cultures and works that are most heavily emphasized. I would favor the use of any source deemed helpful to the project of minority studies, regardless of provenance. Indeed, I would argue that the practices and values found in retrieved minority works should be subjected to the same kind of critical analysis as those of the dominant culture, for they may prove just as hostile and damaging.

Finally, the purpose behind minority discourse is in no way nebulous. Given the fundamental relationship of antagonism and damage between majority discourse and minority discourse, the goal of radical opposition assigned to the latter is readily manifest: piercing (via archival work), exploding (via critical theory), and bypassing (via constructive theory) the ideological scope of vision of the former—the project of universal humanism. Behind such opposition lies, in turn, a greater acceptance of difference and diversity, a fuller humanism that is to be incorporated throughout the academy but which must also look forward to the transformation of material conditions in the future. Needless to say, this second moment in the development of minority studies, with its focus on the social conditions of minority cultures and discourses, proves enormously significant as well.

Refining Minority Discourse

The last move I want to consider in the formation of minority studies is a subsequent refinement of the concept of minority discourse. Several years after the publication of *The Nature and Context of Minority Discourse* and its joint introduction by Abdul JanMohamed and David Lloyd on the nature and scope of such discourse, Lloyd returned, on his own, to this definition by way of a contribution to a collection of essays on issues of colony and empire.[29] This return, he explains, was made necessary by the criticism brought to bear against the earlier proposal. This criticism, left entirely undefined and undeveloped, he takes in a most positive vein, indeed as a learning experience, so that the return itself is portrayed "not so much [as] a defence" but as "an attempt at further elaboration and clarification of the concepts involved" (221). Such refinement, ironically hobbled by a forbidding style, frustratingly dense and at times down-right abstruse, advances a two-pronged revision: the introduction of a distinction now deemed necessary—between the concepts of "ethnic culture" and "minor-ity culture," applicable to individuals, groups, and discursive formations; and the elaboration of its ramifications in practice—the political consequences of the dynamics of "ethnic discourse" and "minority discourse," inside as well as outside the academy. Behind this refinement, Lloyd specifies, stands the goal of transforming the concept of minority discourse so that it can engage its own conditions of existence.[30]

The distinction itself is sharply drawn: ethnic culture faces inward—toward its own internal concerns and problems, its own traditions and histories, its own projects and dreams; minority culture faces outward—toward a dominant state formation, capable of bringing destruction upon it either by violence or by as-similation. Between the two cultures stands a "transitional moment or movement" (222) involving ethnic self-consciousness in the face of confrontation with the dominant culture. Out of this confrontation emerges minority discourse—an oppositional discourse marking the actual or potential destruction in question at the hands of the dominant culture, but also offering the grounds for a critique of this culture in terms of its own internal logic and projects. That logic is the logic of liberal pluralism, at the core of which lies a project of assimilation undergirded by the following principles: the abstraction of ethnic cultural practices from the material conditions of their existence; the appropriation of these practices at the level of aesthetic culture, removed from any sort of political or economic con-siderations and thus confined to the realm of recreation; and the ongoing exercise

---

[29] D. Lloyd, "Ethnic Cultures, Minority Discourse and the State," in *Colonial Dis-course/Postcolonial Theory*, ed. F. Barker, P. Hulme, and M. Iversen, The Essex Symposia (Manchester and New York: Manchester University Press, 1994). This essay thus fol-lows the publication of *The Nature and Context of Minority Discourse* in book form by four years (1990) and in *Cultural Critique* by seven (1987). Both essay and volume are also the result of a conference, under the same title, held at the University of Essex in 1991.

[30] This transformation, Lloyd points out (220), requires—in addition to the pro-posed distinction between ethnic culture and minority culture—acknowledgment of a twofold tension: (a) between minorities and the state; (b) between the minority subject and the ethnic subject, in itself consisting of two variations: between the minority sub-ject and the ethnic community; and between solidarity among different minority groups and the specificity of each group. Such tensions can, in turn, serve as the basis for a profound critique of the state formation and the function of culture in and for the state.

of homogenization and rationalization in the political and economic spheres. For Lloyd, therefore, minority discourse must go beyond liberal pluralism and engage in a radical critique of the dominant culture. This critique he undertakes from two different though related angles, that of culture and that of ethnicity.

The critique begins with the concept of culture in general and, in so doing, has a direct impact upon received definitions of culture. Within cultural studies as presently configured, Lloyd identifies three such definitions: the traditional conception of aesthetic culture and two longstanding counter-conceptions, that of Marxism and that of anthropology. The traditional definition, as anticipated above, posits the autonomy of aesthetic forms, from production to reception. Contrary to other realms of human practice, such as the political and the economic, where the heteronomy of need and interest rule, the aesthetic definition presents the cultural realm as free of all such constraints, thus allowing for the fullest realization of human freedom, "the free and harmonious development of the individual in conformity with a universal concept of the human" (223-24). In the first counter-conception, the Marxist critique, this claim to autonomy is challenged through analysis of the socioeconomic determination of aesthetic forms, variously conceived—a materialist view of culture. In the second counter-conception, the anthropological critique, the challenge is through analysis of culture as the totality of practices of any one society or grouping, variously conceived as well—a view of culture as everything.

Minority discourse finds all three formulations wanting, traditional conception and counter-conceptions alike. Against the former, it looks upon cultures and material conditions as inseparable; against the latter, it regards ethnic cultures and cultural forms as thoroughly determined in contradictions, indeed, of such character as to be beyond resolution.[31] Its impact on the study and representation of culture is thus decisive. In effect, minority discourse foregrounds the heteronomy of ethnic cultures, their relationship of antagonism and damage vis-à-vis the dominant culture, and the differentiation of spheres (religious, political, economic, cultural) within them, both in terms of their own interrelated internal development and their external relation to their counterparts as developed elsewhere, whether in the dominant culture or in other ethnic cultures.

The political consequences of this conception of culture are evident. The traditional definition of culture, with its emphasis on the human subject as universal,

---

[31] Both counter-conceptions, Lloyd argues (224-25), lessen the role of contradiction in cultural practices. In Marxism, the materialist conception of culture is accompanied, despite the emphasis on the ideological function of such practices, by a view of their distinct existence as a given. Two consequences are noted: (1) the cultural forms of the oppressed are regarded as pre-aesthetic, given their lack of autonomy; and (2) the role of contradiction in either the space between the work and its historical context or in the gaps and silences of the text itself—as emphasized by recent theoretical work—is bypassed. In anthropology, the conception of culture as everything leads, in the functionalist tradition, given its perception of society as a closed and integral reality, to a view of cultural practices as having a regulated and regulating role, and, in the structuralist tradition, to an emphasis on the resolution rather than the foregrounding of contradictions.

is oriented toward the state as the representative of universal rather than divided and interested humanity. Within this aesthetic framework, ethnic cultures, as cultures without an autonomous cultural sphere, emerge as deficient—"under-developed rather than differently developed," and hence in need of assimilation—development by "imitation or repetition of canonical cultural values" (227).[32] As such, they fall short of the state to which they are nonetheless subject. For minority discourse, however, ethnic cultures become signifiers of subordination vis-à-vis the dominant culture as well as grounds for resistance by way of alternative histories and formations. In the end, therefore, what minority discourse brings to the discussion of culture extends beyond archival work (the scholarly retrieval of marginalized ethnic cultures and works) and expansion of knowledge (the democratic inclusion of ethnic cultures as proper objects of study), crucial endeavors in their own right, to encompass a fundamental reconsideration of the "signifying difference of the ethnic space" (228).

The critique continues with the concept of ethnic culture in particular and, in so doing, acts directly as well upon the received definition of ethnicity. This traditional conception is presented as standard in the dominant culture, with no mention of counter-conceptions, and identified as that of the generic minority. This definition constructs individuals from the same ethnic culture as typical minorities, equal representatives of the community in question, which is denuded thereby of all diversity and contradiction. In the eyes of the dominant culture, therefore, ethnicity is but a stereotype, an embodiment of the "they are all the same" syndrome. The definition further constructs the movement from "ethnic culture" into "mainstream culture" as an ethical and developmental process. From the point of view of the dominant culture, the bounded individual becomes a free subject. Consequently, at the very same time that ethnic culture is constructed as local and limited, as something to be left behind, the ethnic subject is constructed as a minority, a typical representative of such a culture.

Minority discourse finds such a formulation wanting. It looks upon this traditional construction as an external and retrospective imposition on the part of the dominant culture, unknown to the minority itself outside of its own relationship to that culture. Against it, it presents ethnic culture as inassimilable. Its impact on the study and representation of ethnicity is thus fundamental. In effect, minority discourse foregrounds the heterodoxy of ethnic culture, which it portrays as marked by fundamental diversity—a diversity of differences and hierarchies along any number of lines (gender, sexuality, class, ethnicity) as well as diversity of criticism and transformation both within and across all such categories. In so doing, minority discourse foregrounds as well the problematic of totalization and representation inherent in the traditional conception of the generic minority.

---

[32] Within this framework, Lloyd points out (227), ethnic cultural writings are regarded as ethnographic sources or reactive protests. When viewed as autonomous, it is because they have been divorced from their material conditions of emergence or their dialogical relationship to a specific community.

The political consequences of this conception of ethnicity are clear. The traditional definition of ethnicity, with its emphasis on minorities as generic, is oriented toward the state, the democratic nation-state, and its formation of subjects by means of its various ideological apparatuses. Given its claim to legitimacy through a concept of government by popular participation, the state seeks consent by way not of active coercion but of cultural hegemony. Such hegemony operates with a concept of individuals as citizens—"formally equivalent subjects whose private interests are put in abeyance in free subordination to the will of the majority" (230).[33] Such hegemony has very definite consequences as well: on the one hand, it only allows for a singular form of public sphere, where autonomous ethical subjects, free of interest and formally equivalent, interact; on the other hand, it denies legitimacy to minority cultures, which it views as sites of possible resistance and seeks to dissolve.[34] Within such a framework, the process of citizenship demands the leaving behind of "ethnic culture" for "mainstream culture." Minority discourse highlights instead the power relations at work in this process and points to a fundamental contradiction in the relationship between the dominant culture and its minorities at the heart of the democratic nation-state. To wit, in the very process of assimilating bounded individuals from "ethnic cultures" into "mainstream cultures" as free subjects, such individuals experience a marked loss of individuality and a much diminished voice, given their construction as "typical minorities." In other words, for minority discourse, the process of citizenship could hardly be described in terms of development and freedom. In addition, minority discourse points to the alternative cultural formations present in ethnic cultures as modes of counter-hegemony. In the end, what minority discourse brings to the discussion of ethnicity goes beyond a view of it as "non-totalisable and anti-representational" (228)—crucial as this insight is—to include a revalorization of it as a site of opposition and transformation.

Needless to say, minority discourse offers, as envisioned, a radical critique of the dominant culture—its logic of liberal pluralism and its project of cultural assimilation. Indeed, this critique extends as well to the role of this culture in and for the state—its discourse of hegemony, its antagonism to alternative cultural formations, and its construction of minority subjects as generic rather than individualized citizens, representatives of their cultures of origin. This critique

---

[33] This formal equivalence of individuals, Lloyd specifies (230), is based on the principle, taken as self-evident, that all human beings are born equal and posited prior to and aside from any conditions of material existence.

[34] From this hegemonic perspective, Lloyd explains (230-31), subordinate cultures represent a lower level of development, from which individuals must be "educed" by a process of cultivation so that they can become proper human subjects. This process grants freedom: economic freedom from natural needs as well as moral freedom from the pressures, conformities, or limited horizons of the group. The survival of ethnic communities thus constitutes a threat to the state and its claim to legitimacy and brings forth continuing opposition.

yields a view of ethnic culture not as a prehistorical residue of the process of assimilation—"a pre-political space of the private sphere," but as a source of resistance against both process and mainstream—"an alternative kind of public sphere" (235). Since such resistance will vary from culture to culture, although it always has the dominant culture as its target, this critique must always involve constant interchange among the different minority groups. The move beyond liberal pluralism is unmistakable: the aim is not the traditional affirmation of civil rights within the state formation but rather a fundamental questioning of such a formation, so that the "the radical self-determination of various social formations [can] become possible" (235).[35]

Critical Summary. Lloyd further expands the field of vision in minority studies by bringing greater sharpness to minority discourse and its focus on the social conditions of minorities—the antagonism and damage experienced on a sustained and systematic basis at the hands of the majority. This he does through the introduction of a distinction between ethnic culture and minority culture, whereby minority discourse can address its own conditions of existence. It is a distinction based on orientation and attitude. On the one hand, ethnic culture looks to itself, with ethnic discourse revolving around the highly complex and highly conflicted internal dynamics of such culture. On the other hand, minority culture looks to the dominant culture and the state formation it serves, with minority discourse revolving around the external threat of destruction represented by this culture, a threat that it both records and resists. Given its focus and character, minority discourse is defined as oppositional discourse; in fact, ethnic discourse becomes minority discourse through confrontation with the state and its dominant culture.

Its task—previously defined in terms of foregrounding the common experience of minority groups on a threefold front (retrieval, critique, construction)—is now further specified in light of this distinction. First, with regard to its critique of dominant culture. This critique is extended to traditional conceptions of culture and ethnicity: ethnic culture as local and limited, to be superseded in the process of assimilation; minority culture as generic, emerging in the very process of assimilation. The former it regards as hegemonic, embodying developmental and ethical valuations; the latter, as bounded, lacking in voice and individuality. Instead, minority discourse posits ethnic culture as a site of alternative cultural formations and thus counter-hegemonic and minority culture as profoundly heterodox and hence anything but bounded. Second, with regard to its project of construction. In the face of assimilation by the dominant culture and hegemony by the state formation, both signifiers of antagonism and damage, minority discourse looks to such alternative formations and such heterodoxy as

---

[35] However, Lloyd cautions (235), it is impossible at this point to determine what such radical self-determination will yield. All one can do at this point is to bring down the dominant structures that continue "to legitimate a single mode of historical verisimilitude for humanity and to stem the force of those other histories even as they emerge" (235).

sources of opposition, signifiers of resistance and transformation, to the dominant culture and the state it serves. As a result, minority discourse emerges as
even more radical, calling into question traditional conceptions of culture and
ethnicity, while advancing revisionist conceptions of its own.

This refinement of minority discourse I find highly incisive and fruitful. To
begin with, the traditional conceptions of ethnic and minority culture are effectively challenged as contradictory: far more is lost in assimilation than is gained.
In the process, the projects of the dominant culture and the democratic nation-
state—such as the emphasis on the universal human subject with the state as
representative of universal humanity or the emphasis on the formation of citizens with the state as representing a singular form of public sphere—are radically
exposed and critiqued. In addition, such standard conceptions are given a fundamental recasting: the complexities and conflicts of ethnic cultures are duly
brought to the fore, as is the embattled and oppositional situation of minority
discourse. My main reservation continues to be with regard to the constructive
project envisioned. First of all, while such a vision should look, to be sure, to
the heterodoxy of ethnic cultures and the alternative cultural formations signified by such cultures, it should do so with the same spirit of critical analysis
brought to bear on the dominant culture, for again not all such formations will
prove worth retrieving. At the same time, such a vision should avail itself of
whatever weapons it can use from the dominant culture for its own purposes. In
the end, the purpose behind the refinement is far from nebulous. Given the standard approaches to the issues of culture and ethnicity and their resultant
constructions of ethnic and minority cultures, the goal of radical opposition
assigned to minority discourse is decidedly unambiguous: to bring down the
structures of assimilation and hegemony in order to pave the way for a variety
of cultural formations in a transformed state formation.

MINORITY STUDIES AND CHRISTIAN STUDIES: IMPACT

In light of this developing formation of minority studies, I conclude by offering some reflections on the impact of such studies on the academic study of
Christianity—what I shall refer to, for now, as minority Christian studies. In so
doing, I limit myself to what I see as direct consequences of the various positions outlined above. A more expansive vision of the nature and contours of
Christian studies from a minoritarian perspective must remain at present a task
for the future. The following remarks constitute, therefore, but a first sally in
this regard, indispensable as it is fundamental—a clearing of space, as it were.
These reflections are offered with ethnic-racial minorities of non-Western origins or descent engaged in Christian studies in the United States in mind. I
should think them valid as well not only for non-Western ethnic-racial minorities so occupied elsewhere in the West, from Canada to Europe, but also for
non-Western scholars of Christianity outside the West. As noted earlier, the
postist world of today is a thoroughly interrelated and interdependent world of
counter-discourses.

Minority Christian Studies as Minor Literature

The fundamental point of Gilles Deleuze and Félix Guattari certainly applies: we live in a language that is not our own. This is an insight that applies in twofold fashion: not only in terms of the common language in question, whether English or any other European language, but also of the specialized language at work, a combination of the religious language of Christianity, regardless of ecclesiastical tradition (Catholic, Protestant), and the theological language of Christian studies, regardless of academic specialization (biblical studies, historical studies, theological studies, moral studies, practical studies). This is a language inherited from Western Christianity and elaborated with reference to Western Christianity. It is a language in which non-Western Christians, inside or outside the West, find themselves inscribed but only by way of Western Christianity and not in their own terms, through their own eyes and in their own voices. It is a language, therefore, in which ethnic-racial minorities and non-Western Christians in general find themselves uprooted or deterritorialized.

It is also a language in which we do write, signifying thereby the impossibility of writing. First, because we must write, for, unless we do so, we cannot give expression, through our own eyes and in our own voices, to our religious worlds and perspectives, traditions and visions, practices and beliefs. Second, because we cannot write but in this language, for it is the language we have inherited for so doing. Given historical, social, and cultural developments, there is simply no other language to which we can have recourse for so doing. Third, because we find it quite difficult to write in this language, since it is the language of the center, a language where we find ourselves, our concerns and interests, relegated to the margins, whether by way of absence or presence.

Yet, following the line of Deleuze and Guattari, it is a language that we must leave behind as we write. The question, therefore, is how to do so. Their proposal, I find, provides an excellent point of departure. This is a task that calls for close attention to the characteristics of the literary production of minorities. Given my earlier critique of the proposal, I offer the following as guideposts in this regard:

- We must go beyond the alternatives drawn regarding mode of expression: over-determination by way of symbolic richness or ultra-determination by way of intensive sobriety. We must use this inherited and deterritorialized language in all sorts of ways, with all sorts of strategies and all kinds of goals, across a broad spectrum of possibilities. We must bend and mold, revision and envision, explode and construct—always with a profound and combined sense of suspicion and imagination. In so doing, we break down the opposition of territorialization and rootedness; we make the language our own, we territorialize it, in ever so many ways.
- We must foreground the political dimension of religious and theological language at all times, surfacing the grounds and ramifications, the contexts and agendas, of all formulations, whether of the dominant or of minorities. In so doing, we break down the opposition of political and nonpolitical; we

expose the ideological dimension of all Christian studies.

- We must highlight the fact that we do so as both individuals and members of collectives. While we give expression to the experiences, realities, and visions of our respective groupings, we do so as individual authors, with different locations and agendas within such groupings. In so doing, we break down the opposition of collective and personal: we emphasize the individual as well as the social components of our work. We break down as well the opposition of popular and masterly: we affirm that talent is to be had as much among minorities as in the majority.

- We must keep in mind throughout the material conditions of our production. It is simply not sufficient to focus on the literary characteristics of such production, essential as such work is. In so doing, we emphasize the close relationship that exists between literature and society: we engage in textual as well as contextual analysis.

Through such writing on our part, the primary opposition between major and minor begins to break down as well. Major and minor undergo thereby a gradual but inexorable process of *mestizaje*, whereby the major is reconstructed and decentered while the minor is constructed and inscribed. The result is an expansive view of Christian studies as a field of study—multipolar and multilingual, cacophonous and conflicted.

Minority Christian Studies and Minority Discourse

The fundamental observation of Abdul JanMohamed and David Lloyd certainly applies as well: we live in a context of antagonism and damage from the center. This is an insight that applies across the board, encompassing all dimensions of minority groups, and thus applies as well to the realm of religion. Here too a relationship of domination and exclusion, yielding marginalization and fragmentation, is evident. From an ecclesiastical point of view, the world of Christianity—regardless of tradition—is a world gestated and formed in the West, exported by the West through a missionary project with close links to the Western expansionism of the last five hundred years, implanted outside the West largely by force, and upheld throughout the non-Western world by means of external control and direction. From an academic point of view, the world of Christian studies—regardless of specialization—is a world that revolves resolutely around the Western tradition and that approaches, if at all, its non-Western expressions as extensions of the West. In both regards, the operative vision of the center regarding non-Western Christianity is one of undercivilization and under-development—standing somewhere between the apex of Western Christianity and the nadir of native religions. Given this vision, the world of ethnic-racial minorities, as indeed the world of non-Western Christians in general, is a world marked perforce by marginalization and fragmentation—a world at the periphery of the center, with a clear sense of its relationship to the center but no sense at all of its relationship to others in the periphery. It is a world, therefore, in which we breathe hostility and oppression.

Yet, following the line of JanMohamed and Lloyd, it is a world that we must leave behind. The issue, again, is how to proceed, and here I find their proposal very much on target. This is a task that must foreground the context of antagonism and damage in three-pronged fashion: pursuing archival work in marginalized religious practices and values; undertaking a critical analysis of Western Christianity and its missionary project of universal church and theology; drawing upon the marginalized religious practices and beliefs retrieved for alternative visions of church and theology. The following principles I offer as guideposts in this endeavor, in the light of my previous appraisal of the proposal:

- We must pursue this task by looking at the realm of religion and its study not in isolation from other realms but rather as deeply imbricated in all other realms, such as the cultural and the social, the economic and the political. The insight of JanMohamed and Lloyd is basic in this regard: the antagonism and damage emanating from the center are multifrontal and must be countered as such. For this purpose it is necessary for us to become well versed in a variety of other fields of study as presently conceptualized and practiced.
- We must pursue this task not only in terms of specific minority discourses but also in terms of a combined minority discourse. Again, the insight of JanMohamed and Lloyd is basic: while minority groups differ greatly from one another, they all stand in a similar structural relationship to the center, and, insofar as they do, such a relationship should be analyzed in as global a fashion as possible.
- We must keep in mind as well another basic insight of JanMohamed and Lloyd, namely, the use of "minority" to signify not ontological otherness but shifting configurations. Thereby we prevent the privileging of any one group as unique and allow for flux in minority discourse.
- We must not overlook critical analysis of the linguistic and literary traits of our production. These prove as essential to the project as the social dimensions of minority discourse. Again, we must see literature and society as closely related and engage in both textual and contextual work.
- We must not privilege unconditionally the practices and values retrieved through archival work. While the recuperation and rehabilitation of these constitute an essential part of the project, in the end we must subject such findings to the same kind of critical analysis applied to dominant discourse.

Through such foregrounding on our part, our condition of marginalization and fragmentation is gradually but inexorably turned into radical opposition to the center and its project of a universal Christianity. The result is a more expansive view of Christian studies—a transformed field of study in which the center, with its practices and values of domination and exclusion, undergoes decentering, minority discourses are integrated at every step of the way, and the situation of antagonism and damage begins to be corrected, awaiting the transformation of material conditions.

Minority Christian Studies and the Ethnic-Minority Distinction

The fundamental insight of David Lloyd most certainly applies as well: we live in a context of assimilation and hegemony, where the construction of ourselves as ethnics and minorities functions as a signifier of antagonism and damage from the center. This is an insight that applies across all dimensions of our representation, including that of religion. Here too we are constituted as typical or generic minorities, equal representatives of our respective ethnic communities, in themselves regarded as local and limited. From an ecclesiastical point of view, the world of non-Western Christianity—regardless of tradition—is a world cast in developmental and ethical terms: a bounded world in which freedom and development are to be found in assimilation to Western Christianity. It is a world with little to teach and much to learn from the Christianity that imposed it and that went on to mold, control, and direct it. From an academic point of view, the world of non-Western Christian studies—regardless of specialization—is a world cast in stereotypical terms: a world marked by simplicity and uniformity. It is a world of interest only to those who hail from that world, though it is a world that can be readily comprehended and competently imparted by those of Western Christianity. In both respects, the operative construction of the center regarding non-Western Christianity is one of boundedness and genericness. Given this vision, the world of ethnic-racial minorities, and in fact the world of non-Western Christians in general, is a world marked by confinement and sameness.

Yet, following the line of David Lloyd, it is a world that we must put behind. The question, once again, is how to do so, and here I find the proposal quite to the point. This is a task that calls for critique and construction with respect to concepts of culture and ethnicity. Drawing on my previous evaluation of the proposal, I offer the following as guideposts for such an enterprise:

- We must subject the construction of ourselves, our histories and formations, at work in the dominant religious and theological formations to a thoroughgoing exposé and critique. In so doing, we must examine as well the political dimensions of such formations, their relationship to the state formation in question.
- We must engage in full critical analysis of the religious histories and formations of our communities, highlighting at every step of the way the diversity of differences and of discourses to be found in such communities. In so doing, such diversity becomes part and parcel of our theological discourse, across all specializations.
- We must look to these formations and histories as possible sources of resistance against the dominant formations as well as grounds toward the transformation of such formations.

Through such oppositional discourse on our part, the standard conceptions of ourselves as bounded and generic from a religious as well as a theological perspective will be replaced, slowly but surely, by our own revisionist conceptions.

The result will be an even more expansive view of Christian studies—a transformed field of study in which a broad array of theological discourses is allowed to develop and flourish and interact.

CONCLUDING COMMENTS

As the number of non-Western ethnic-racial minorities in the United States continues to expand, as projected, through the twenty-first century, their power and influence shall increase as well, across every aspect of the nation's life and discourse. This will become increasingly evident in the world of the academy, as these groups continue to inscribe themselves—their histories and experiences, concerns and interests, perspectives and positions—across the entire disciplinary spectrum. Christian studies will prove no exception in this regard, as the numbers, influence, and power of ethnic-racial minorities make themselves felt in the world of the church as well, across the entire ecclesiastical spectrum. Moreover, what is true of the United States is ultimately true of the West in general, though by no means to the same extent.

Such studies stand to benefit greatly from a thorough knowledge of the counter-discourses at work in the contemporary postist world in general and of minority studies in particular. It was with such a goal in mind that I undertook a critical overview of key moments in the development of this discursive framework and proceeded to outline, in preliminary fashion, their ramifications for Christian studies. Needless to say, much remains to be done along these lines, both by way of further analysis of minority studies as such and further mapping of Christian studies from a minority perspective. The end result, though still very much beyond our comprehension at this point, will be a radically transformed field of Christian studies.

PART I

AFRICAN-AMERICAN VOICES

1

Critical Reflection on the Problems of History and Narrative in a Recent African-American Research Program

VICTOR ANDERSON

James H. Cone crystallized the debate on black sources for black liberation theology when he questioned the relevance of traditional Chalcedonian Christology for black existence in the United States.[1] He questioned its adequacy for interpreting black religious faith in order to make way for a research program in black religion that would take black sources as a fundamental canon of black theological reflection. The impact of Cone's question extends to the very meaning of history, narrative, religious identity, and moral consciousness in African-American theology. The importance of Cone's question lies not only in its rhetorical persuasiveness but also in its existential import. His question signaled a major research program in African-American theology. It enacted the radical departure of black liberation theology from everything white, European, and Western. Cone called for the possibility of a new black consciousness, the instantiation of a *New Being*: a powerful, struggling, surviving, resisting, and creative black consciousness. The new black consciousness, to which Cone sought to give ideological legitimacy as well as theological and moral justification, would have to be historical. It had to answer the question of its radical departure from white theology in historical terms. At the beginning of the black liberation theology program, the problem of history and narrative emerged as the burden of African-American constructive theology.

I formulated the problem of history and narrative in black liberation theology elsewhere as a dilemma of self-referential inconsistency.[2] The problem is whether black liberation theology can maintain a posture of radical alienation from the West and its textual traditions, while supporting black institutions such

---

[1] James H. Cone, *God of the Oppressed* (New York: Seabury Press, 1975), 5, 14.
[2] Victor Anderson, *Beyond Ontological Blackness* (New York: Continuum, 1995), 90ff.

as the black churches and the African-American theological academy, each of which owes its existence in part to Western colonial practices. I do not want to reduce the problem of self-referential inconsistency strictly to a logical status. To be sure, it is a logical problem, for the problem turns on the degree to which African-American theology is necessarily entailed in Western intellectual history. Like Cone's original question, however, the problem of self-referential inconsistency is also historical. Therefore, it requires historical answers on the part of African-American theologians.

In this essay I examine one such answer among contemporary African-American theologians. The problem of history and narrative is central to a research project proposed in a 1991 collection of essays entitled *Cut Loose Your Stammering Tongue: Black Theology in the Slave Narratives.*[3] My reading of this research program focuses on two concerns: (1) the black liberation theologian's alienated consciousness; and (2) a hermeneutics of narrative-return. In the first concern, I examine the slave-narrative program within the context of the apparent alienation of the black theological academy from much of contemporary black cultural life. In the second concern, I look at the ways that black theologians return narratively to historical black materials for grounding their contemporary constructive theologies. In my critique I focus on several ambiguities in the slave-narrative research program that I think test its persuasiveness, and I propose an alternative path for dealing with black sources of religious insight.

BLACK LIBERATION THEOLOGY'S ALIENATED CONSCIOUSNESS

During the late 1980s a group of young African-American scholars—particularly Dwight Hopkins, George Cummings, and Will Coleman—who were studying and teaching in the Berkeley, California, area met continually to discuss the future of black liberation theology in their Black Theology Forum.[4] They exchanged papers and engaged in an exploration of slave narratives as a source for contemporary black liberation theology. Behind their explorations was a set of problems that had plagued Cone's original formulation of black theology. These problems centered around the strained and often alienated relation of black theology to the black churches and black culture. Some black church theologians questioned whether black theology could be a theology of the black churches, if it disentangled itself from the creeds, confessions, and liturgical practices of the traditional churches. Others asked in what sense black theology could be black, if its theological method was derived from white, European theologians, such as Karl Barth and Paul Tillich, and European philosophers, such as Albert Camus and Jean-Paul Sartre. Still others wondered how black theology could be relevant to a culture of black radicalism and revolution and remain theologically and morally Christian. This was the question of

[3] Dwight N. Hopkins and George Cummings, eds., *Cut Loose Your Stammering Tongue: Black Theology in the Slave Narratives* (Maryknoll, N.Y.: Orbis Books, 1991).
[4] Hopkins, "Introduction," *CLST*, xx.

many who embraced the ideology of black power and associated Christianity with white oppression.

Cone addressed some of these questions in many of his subsequent writings.[5] Yet, the historical problem of alienated consciousness lies in his call for a radical departure of black liberation theology from white theology and European religious sources. If Cone maintained the posture of radical departure from European Christianity, he would have a difficult time showing how black theology is the theology of the black churches. And he would remain an alienated theologian. If he gave up his radical claims to black exceptionalism, then the claims that he wanted to make for the epistemic privilege of blackness in black theological reflection would be undercut, losing their critical weight. Cone tried to overcome this dilemma by emphasizing the commensurability of black sources for the construction of black Christian liberation theology. He turned to the spirituals and the blues as cultural sources of black theology. However, the spirituals and blues proved difficult sources from which to disclose the normal, routine religious beliefs of African-American peoples and render them regulative theological and moral judgments. To many, the spirituals appeared too other-worldly to be of much use for the purposes of black liberation theology and its claims for black radicalism, protest, and resistance.[6] And much of the blues was regarded by the black churches as degenerative, secular, and misogynist expressions of black hopelessness.

Several decades after beginning his research program, Cone would say, at a national conference held at Vanderbilt University in 1992, that, as he assessed the history of black liberation theology, if this theology failed to connect the theologian and the churches, then the failure belonged not only to black theologians but also to the black churches. He exclaimed that the black churches continued to be governed by the creeds and confession of white, European religious authorities and not by the indigenous sources of black life.[7] After several decades it appears that black liberation theology and many black theologians remain alienated from the regular life and practices of the black churches and much of black culture. Moreover, this alienation remains a major provocation behind the recent turn of some black theologians to slave narratives.

A source behind such alienation is the class differentiation of black theologians from others in the community. African-American theologians are an elite

---

[5] James H. Cone, *Spirituals and the Blues* (New York: Seabury Press, 1972; Maryknoll, N.Y.: Orbis Books, 1991); *God of the Oppressed*; "Christian Theology and Scripture as the Expression of God's Liberating Activity for the Poor" and "Sanctification and Liberation in the Black Religious Tradition, with Special Reference to Black Worship," in *Speaking the Truth* (Grand Rapids, Mich.: Eerdmans, 1986; Maryknoll, N.Y.: Orbis Books, 1999), 4-34.

[6] Anthony B. Pinn, *Why Lord?: Suffering and Evil in Black Theology* (New York: Continuum, 1995), 21-48.

[7] James H. Cone, "Black Theology and the Black Church," in *What Does It Mean to Be Black and Christian?*, ed. Forrest Harris et al. (Nashville, Tenn.: Townsend Press, 1995), 57.

class of educated intellectuals, often exhibiting bourgeois tendencies that alienate them from the underclass strata of life in both the black churches and black culture. As black theologians, committed to liberation politics and ethics as regulative ideals of black Christianity, they are often alienated from the churches for whom they desire to speak, but whose piety is characteristically evangelical, reformist, and liberal in disposition, doctrine, and political ideology. Such churches are not likely to be moved by the revisionist agenda that defines the constructive content of much of black liberation theology. Black theologians are also alienated by class from the strata of black society, the poor urban underclass, whose voices they want to evoke and whose desperation they now raise as the new rallying call for the advancement of black liberation and the mobilization of the black theological academy.

To be sure, the shift from race-dependent to class-dependent discourse is generational. In the early formulation of black liberation theology, the radical, revolutionary interests of liberation centered on the oppressive structures of legislative discrimination and poverty that were justified by a history of racist public policy in the United States. Now, at the beginning of the twenty-first century, black theologians are defending the cogency of their liberation project and its justification by race in a climate of greater class differentiation among blacks themselves than was experienced in the 1960s and 1970s. It is quite clear that in the late 1960s and 1970s race and racism galvanized black liberation theology, which proved to be a powerful site for amalgamating the diverse interests of African-American theologians around a radical, revolutionary liberation rhetoric. It forged widespread agreement among theologians and church persons on the meaning of God (the sociopolitical and economic liberator of the poor), Jesus (the one who walks with the poor and disinherited in their situation), and the church (the mediating spiritual and political institution of social justice).

However, at the beginning of a new century, it is not very clear that racial discourse will have the same effect. What is clear is that the fragility of black liberation theology in the United States is being tested by a class differentiation that is nonreducible to the racial categories of white over black. Rather, class differentiation cuts across the various levels of the black community itself, raising the question whether the black community may not be facing an incommensurability of values and interests among the various classes that now define the black community. Black life in the United States is differentiated by the wealthy, entrepreneurial, celebrity, and professional classes and the white-collar and blue-collar working middle and lower classes. It is also a community characterized by a desperate urban underclass that is constituted by the homeless, an undereducated and underemployed class of black youths, and a rising society of incarcerated black young males. The contemporary challenge to alienated black theologians is whether they can speak univocally for the poor and underclass and express the real interests of the black community today out of their internal resources.

Many of these concerns are being addressed by African-American theologians. In his recent systematic theology James H. Evans proposes that the theologian's alienation from the religious life of black people can be transcended when "black theology is rooted in the faith of the church and the faith of the church is given intellectual clarity and expression in black theology."[8] Evans finds the answer to the alienation of the black theologian in a hermeneutical return to a common black narrative. Here it is claimed that a return to African chattel slavery discloses values, commitments, teachings, and a wisdom that sustained blacks under the unprecedented experience of chattel slavery. Evans also contends that this wisdom can be brought forward into the present to challenge a black culture that is now struggling with the push and pull of a secular, materialistic, hedonistic, narcissistic, and pessimistic culture.[9] For Evans, then, the return of black theologians to narrative sources is sparked by the need to reground contemporary black culture in a morally nurturing myth.

In books such as *CLST* and *Shoes That Fit Our Feet*,[10] Hopkins also proposes that the forms of alienation separating black liberation theologians from the black churches and much of black culture can be challenged effectively by a hermeneutical return to distinctive black sources as the basis for contemporary black liberation theology. The hermeneutics of narrative-return connects contemporary black life to a historical life of creative resistance and communal focus that is capable of minimizing what Hopkins sees as a rabid individualism plaguing black culture. He turns to the slave narratives, or more appropriately, the ex-slave narratives.

THE SLAVE NARRATIVES AS A SOURCE
OF BLACK LIBERATION THEOLOGY

The slave-narrative program is a very ambitious research project for African-American theologians working in the trajectory of black liberation theology. The materials were collected between 1936 and 1938 under the auspices of the Folklore Division of the Federal Writers' Project and inaugurated by President Franklin D. Roosevelt as a division of the Federal Works Administration. The project was one means of keeping mostly white, white-collar workers employed during the depression years. The collection contains interviews depicting the experience of former slaves in the United States. Although the collection was mostly a federal project, some individual states, including Virginia and Louisiana, as well as the American Freedmen Inquiry Commission, had already begun collecting slave narratives as early as 1863. However, these were a very small number of cases. Personal journals and autobiographies tracing the rise of many free men and women from slavery to freedom are also regarded by Hopkins and his colleagues as sources for constructive black theology. There is a consensus

---

[8] James H. Evans, *We Have Been Believers* (Minneapolis, Minn.: Fortress Press, 1992), 1.

[9] Ibid., 5-6.

[10] Dwight N. Hopkins, *Shoes That Fit Our Feet: Sources of a Constructive Black Theology* (Maryknoll, N.Y.: Orbis Books, 1993).

among Hopkins, Cummings, Coleman, and Cheryl Sanders that the wealth of folk materials contained in the slave narratives ought to have an authoritative function in the development of contemporary black liberation theology. At least, their task is to make a case for their canonical standing.

A contributor to the research program, George Cummings makes the slave narratives central to the legitimacy of *CLST* and contemporary African-American theology. He writes:

> This collection of essays shares a common view that the slave narratives are a legitimate source of the experiences of black oppressed people in the USA, as well as of the theological interpretations of their experiences of enslavement. Concomitantly, the slave narratives provide a means to return to the religious genius of the ancestors, who were forcibly taken from Africa and made to serve in the brutal crucible of chattel slavery. The narratives provide us with insight concerning the religious and cultural world-views that informed black slaves' theological interpretation of the experience and can be the basis upon which contemporary black theologians can incorporate the "thematic universe" of the black oppressed into their discourse.[11]

Hopkins, the principal architect of the project, concurs with Cummings: "Drawing on their African traditional religions and the Bible, the Old Testament in particular, slaves could only comprehend total deliverance as including the individual and the community."[12] He further suggests that the lessons slaves inferred from these sources protected them cognitively from "fall[ing] prey to a white capitalist theological precept that glorifies individualism and private-property democracy."[13] Hopkins then challenges contemporary black theologians "to promote individuality and communalism, not individualism and selfish motivation."[14]

Among the collaborators of the slave-narrative program, the hermeneutics of narrative-return signals a *re-turn* of black liberation theology to indigenous historical and narrative sources for religious insight and moral guidance. For them, the slave narratives evoke a great cloud of witnesses whose heroic legacy of survival, resistance, and hope can mediate the fragility of African-American life today and bind together our present generation, so much in need of a heroic black faith. Each theologian regards the slave narratives as authentic historical representations of slave religion as it developed in the "invisible institution" of the antebellum South. According to Will Coleman, the invisible institution of slave religion was antecedent to the development of the independent African-American churches.[15] Consequently, the relationship between slave religion and

---

[11] George Cummings, "Slave Narratives, Black Theology of Liberation (USA), and the Future," *CLST*, 137-38.

[12] Hopkins, "Slave Theology," *CLST*, 44.

[13] Ibid.

[14] Ibid.

[15] Will Coleman, "Coming through 'Legion': Metaphor in Non-Christian and Christian Experiences with the Spirit(s) in African American Slave Narratives," *CLST*, 68.

the independent churches is defined in such a way that the former, the invisible institution, "was not so much an organization as it was an organic syncretism that enabled slaves to combine their Afrocentric religious beliefs with the Eurocentric ones of their masters. The consequence of this merger was their own unique form of African American Christianity."[16]

Hopkins, Cummings, Coleman, and Sanders argue that the ex-slave narratives not only authentically represent the religious beliefs and moral practices that constitute slave religion as practiced in the invisible institution, but also exhibit a religious unity that is subject to theological formulation and moral inferences. Hopkins has made the most of this possibility, not only in outline in *CLST* but more substantively in his constructive theology, *Shoes That Fit Our Feet*. He maps the ex-slaves' religious utterances around God, Jesus, and humanity. He argues:

> Enslaved Africans realized that God had created them originally with a free soul, heart, and mind. Yet white American Christians had re-created them in the demonic image of a distorted Christianity. Hence, for the slave, the purpose of humanity was to show fully the spark of God's created equality implanted deep within black breasts. To return to original creation, then, African American slaves pursued a resistance of politics and a culture of resistance.[17]

Hopkins's constructive task in *Shoes That Fit Our Feet* is to draw the appropriate theological and moral inferences that follow from the religious stories of African-American slaves. He highlights Jesus, the mediator of God's agapic love, friend and mother, king and priest, provider of hope to the oppressed, and setter of their path toward freedom and justice. This narrative, he declares, ought to challenge "the so-called secular black community representatives to dig within and rely on the same African American freedom impulse."[18] Cummings maps the religious utterances of the ex-slaves under the theology of the Spirit and eschatology. Ironically, for all their talk of Africanisms, Cummings and Hopkins structure the slaves' religious utterances under the traditional European loci of systematic theology: God, humanity, Jesus, Spirit, and eschatology.

Coleman approaches the narratives with a hermeneutical concern to elicit, by means of a linguistic-poetic method, the way the slaves created their own black existence, religion, and reality through the power of their interpretations, symbols, and metaphors. According to him, "Slave narratives speak to us through symbols and metaphors that redescribe the experiences of African American people under slavery. . . . Historically, the oral tradition of African American slaves placed a high value upon the power of speech. It was evocative, driving internal mental, emotional, and spiritual experiences into the exterior reality of the African American slave."[19] In other words, through interpretation the ex-slaves

---

[16] Ibid.

[17] Hopkins, *Shoes That Fit Our Feet*, 47.

[18] Ibid., 48.

[19] Coleman, "Coming through 'Legion,'" 97.

created an ontology of religious significance by making a reality of what they subjectively experienced.

Cheryl Sanders explores the ethical aspects of the ex-slaves' religious utterances. According to her, "The ex-slave interviews provide day-to-day moral data that can be used to analyze the ethical perspectives of the ex-slaves. Many of them testified of the experience of conversion, understood here as a conscious moral change from wrong to right, involving reorientation of the self from complacency or error to a state of right religious knowledge and action."[20] Sanders applies an interpretative structure to the narratives that she believes will elicit from them some description of the concrete situation of the slaves— their loyalties, norms of moral reasoning, and religious beliefs concerning God, humanity, and human destiny.[21] Her essay is revealing, because it shows the divergent ways in which ex-slaves remember their situation. Their attitudes range from nostalgia to abomination. According to Sanders, however, all of their moral estimations of slavery were based on the criterion of humane treatment.[22] Their loyalties—either to their ex-masters, whites, or others—were grounded in their own judgments of who were "good Christians" or exhibited Christian virtues.[23] Moreover, their norms of moral reflection were shaped by their sense of persons as good Christians, Bible believing, and obedient to God.[24]

Sanders also shows how theologically divergent the ex-slaves were in interpreting their recollection of emancipation. What they all had in common, she says, was the presumption that freedom was central to their overall interpretation of religion. Sanders draws this primary inference from her analysis of the ex-slave narratives that she examines:

> The conversion experience did not transform them [the ex-slaves] into adherents of the slave ethic taught and upheld by their oppressors, even if it did make them "better" slaves by bringing an increased measure of moral integrity and conscientiousness into their lives and labors as slaves. If there is any social ethic at all among the ex-slave converts, it is indeed an ethic of liberation and not one of submission to the institution of slavery or to the bondage of oppressive religious beliefs and ideas.[25]

In a more recent book, *Empowerment Ethics for a Liberated People*, Sanders reiterates the claims inferred from her initial studies of ex-slave narratives.[26] Here, however, her aim is to press more strongly than she does in *CLST* the ways in which the ex-slave narratives function as "testimony" to the present

---

[20] Cheryl J. Sanders, "Liberation Ethics in the Ex-Slave Interviews," *CLST*, 103.

[21] Ibid., 104.

[22] Ibid., 114.

[23] Ibid., 122-24.

[24] Ibid., 124-27.

[25] Ibid., 132.

[26] Cheryl J. Sanders, *Empowerment Ethics for a Liberated People* (Minneapolis, Minn.: Fortress Press, 1995).

generation of black Christians. For these ex-slaves, it was *Christian religion* that was central to their liberation ethics and that played a determinant role in forming the moral consciousness of African-American slaves of previous generations. The moral wisdom that she attempts to bring forward to the present from these testimonies is that "the religious testimony of the former slaves should be read as a graphic illustration of the most critical hermeneutical challenge facing Bible-believing Christians, namely, the struggle to be faithful to God's call to freedom and justice in the midst of a society that offers attractive compromises with the evils of oppression."[27]

To be sure, Hopkins, Cummings, Coleman, and Sanders acknowledge that there exists an inherent diversity in approaching and organizing the materials that constitute the slave narratives. Nevertheless, each also sees a thematic unity in the ex-slaves' religious utterances. As I understand their intention, these utterances substantively express the definitive, exceptional, and liberationist faith of African-American slaves in the United States. According to Hopkins, the slaves maintained faith in a "God [who] ruled with unquestioned omnipotence and realized release from total captivity. And Jesus assumed an intimate and kingly relationship with the poor black chattel."[28] Hopkins continues, "Slaves emphasized both the suffering humanity of Jesus as well as Jesus's warrior ability to set the downtrodden free. Moreover, the slaves distinguished their humanity from the white slave master. For blacks, God and Jesus called them to use all means possible to pursue religiously a human status of equality."[29] A similar configuration of themes is rehearsed by each theologian throughout the various essays. Other themes include the slaves' rejection of sacred and secular spaces, otherworldliness, affirmations of the intercession of spirits and Spirit possession, and privileging of community over individualism.

I think it is fair to say that Hopkins and his colleagues look upon the slave narratives as representing and expressing the African-American cultural world that slave religion had created. In slave culture, Hopkins argues, the slaves' "dogged and creative strength fashioned a new black collective self behind the closed doors in the slave quarters or deep in the woods late at night. Here slaves developed a culture of survival that included all the dimensions of a thriving but enchained community."[30] According to Hopkins, slave religion gave rise to and fulfilled the new black consciousness in history that Cone inscribed as the end of black liberation theology. It formed "a collective African American being, a new people in the hell of slavery, the most common bond among all who suffered as chattel was slave religion."[31] It is clear from these statements that, for the members of this research program, the slave narratives constitute unexplored and unmined sources for a distinctive, common spring upon which the nurturing of black liberation theology may depend for its vitality, substantive unity

---

[27] Ibid., 25.
[28] Hopkins, "Slave Theology," 2.
[29] Ibid.
[30] Hopkins, "Introduction," ix.
[31] Ibid., x.

with the historic black faith, and moral wisdom. In the hermeneutics of narrative-return, the alienation of black theology from traditional black Christian faith is overcome by a "traditioning" of slave religion and its moral consciousness as well as by admitting the slave narratives as an authoritative canon for constructive black liberation theology.

CRITIQUE

I do not want to get into the seemingly interminable problem of Africanisms, retentions, and so forth in African-American religion. For now, I leave such a problem to religious historians. As a philosophical and moral theologian, I am more interested in the inferences theologians want to draw from such arguments than I am in establishing their facticity. Thus, I want to confine myself to what I see as a problem of faulty equivalence operative throughout the slave-narrative research program. Stating this problem is not easy, however. I would put it as follows: when these researchers examine the religious utterances of the ex-slaves and correlate them with utterances typical of black liberation theology and liberation politics, this correlation is so strong that the ex-slaves' talk of freedom, human dignity, justice, and redemption is readily translated into the rhetoric of struggle-protest, survival, resistance, and hope in liberation or black radicalism. In other words, what appear as elements of evangelical-abolitionist theological rhetoric in the ex-slave narratives are rendered as instances of continuous liberation motifs from slave religion to the present. The ex-slaves' talk of freedom is thereby equated with liberation ideology. The result is clear: It is not so much black liberation theology that has to justify itself to a black church that is characteristically evangelical in faith, liberal in politics, and reformist in social action, but the black church that has to assess its practices in the light of a prior history of radicalism and subversion of Western ideology inscribed on slave religion.

The slave-narrative project not only draws an equivalence between nineteenth-century black evangelicalism and black liberation theology but also between slave religion and the ex-slave narratives, collapsing the one into the other. Hopkins, Coleman, Cummings, and Sanders argue that these narratives are authentic representations of slave religion. It is true that the narratives represent the religious understanding of late-nineteenth-century and early-twentieth-century ex-slaves, but it is what these narratives disclose theologically about slave religion (historically conceived) that is at issue. This problem, I believe, is linked rhetorically to equating ex-slave evangelicalism and black liberation.

What the theologians are working with are the narratives of ex-slaves whose utterances display the spirituality and piety of Second Great Awakening evangelical conversionist theology, abolitionist editing, and the formation of institutional black churches in the post–Civil War period. Their case for black theological exceptionalism depends on whether the ex-slaves interviewed do authentically recall the antebellum conditions of slave religion as practiced in the invisible institution, as distinct from the post–Civil War redaction that

abounds throughout the narratives. The question is what this historically specific evangelical theology among ex-slaves has to tell us about the religious
beliefs and worship of plantation slaves in the seventeenth- and eighteenth-
century antebellum slave plantation communities. That the ex-slaves maintained,
seventy-odd years removed from antebellum conditions, an authentic historical
memory of antebellum slave religion is to my mind doubtful.

My criticism is that these theologians fail to take adequately into account the
historical thresholds that occurred from the earliest formations of the invisible
institution of plantation religion to the formal conversion of slaves by evangelicals
and the abolitionist debates on the meaning of Christianity prior to and after the
Civil War, especially during reconstruction. These theologians see a direct correlation among black liberation theology, slave religion on the large plantations,
and the formal organization of the ex-slaves into Protestant churches prior to
and after emancipation. I do not think that such a correlation is self-evident
from the slave narratives. I have no doubt that the evangelical beliefs of the ex-
slaves are faithfully expressed in their narratives. However, Hopkins and his
colleagues assume—and I do not—that there is a direct correlation between
their own commitments to black liberation theology, the evangelical faith of the
ex-slaves, and antebellum slave religion. Hopkins equates them when he says:
"White theological proscriptions served as a negative incentive for slaves to
pursue their independent religious thinking. On the positive side, blacks felt the
powerful living presence of divinity in the midst of their daily burdens and
concentrated in the Invisible Institution. These radical religious experiences
colored their biblical interpretation; and thus, they produced a theology of liberation."[32] Although ex-slaves and black liberation theologians may favor the
idea of freedom in their theological understanding, equating black evangelical
religion and black liberation theology distorts what freedom and religion mean
in both historical contexts and traditions.

My criticism is intended to discourage such cognitive reductions in black
theology, if what remains is a distorted understanding of the worlds of difference in religious experience and theological thinking that provide black history
and black religion with multiple trajectories of religious protest, spiritual development, theological positions, and political engagement. I do not object to the
interest of these theologians in relating contemporary black religious thought
historically to the religious beliefs and patterns of worship or the moral consciousness developed by African slaves in the context of American slavery. I
am just not convinced that the twofold equivalence of black liberation theology
with black evangelicalism in the ex-slave narratives and ex-slave narratives with
slave religion will be very effective in their attempt to overcome the many forms
of alienation that characterize the relationship of the black theological academy
to the black churches and black culture.

Like these theologians, I also think that the adequacy of African-American
constructive theology ought to be tested by the weight of black religious experience and history. Therefore, I have no doubt that historical research into black

---

[32] Hopkins, *Shoes That Fit Our Feet*, 22.

cultural life is central for theological reflection. However, I am persuaded by other thinkers such as Charles Long, Theophus Smith, and Anthony Pinn that a more appropriate manner of approaching black sources of religious insight is not to conceal, for the sake of forging a monistic theological discourse predicated on race, the worlds of difference that African slaves and black Americans created. Theophus Smith stakes out a path that I think better comes to terms with black sources of religious insight.[33] He proposes that African-American theology can use another metaphor (conjuration/conjuring culture) for guiding research that will place at the center of hermeneutical understanding not only struggle and survival or resistance and liberation but also the creative, innovative, pharmacopeic, playful, and imaginative aspects of black religious experience. He writes:

> Out of Afro-America too, "always something new." [Conjuring Culture] disclose[s] something new out of Afro-America. Here the sacred text of Western culture, the Bible, comes to view as a magical formulary for African Americans; a book of ritual prescriptions for reenvisioning and therein, transforming history and culture. . . . The claim "something new out of Africa" is confirmed by a heretofore unacknowledged combination: the combining of (1) biblical interpretation with (2) magical transformation, as practiced by the descendants of Africans in North America.[34]

Smith realizes that discussions of magic in African Traditional Religion is not itself a novelty of religious research, but he adds: "What is innovative is a remarkably efficacious use of biblical figures, with historically transformative and therapeutic intent, in the social imagination and political performances of black North Americans."[35] For Smith, when the Bible is understood as a conjuring book in the development of black religion in the United States, the religious insights gained from the experience or performance of conjuration can open theologians to more of the innovations, creativity, play, tricks, light, and even dark aspects of black religion than seeking to establish linguistic correlations between slaves' narratives and liberation theology.

I do not want to deny that there exists a legitimate myth-making function in constructive theology. However, engaging black sources in such a way as to take advantage of not only the familiar sources of religious insight but also the unmined areas that may threaten the comfort of African-American theologians and the claims we make for black liberation is a regulative aspect of critical theology. Pinn speaks boldly to this point: "I believe that human liberation is more important than the maintenance of any religious symbol, sign, canon, or icon. It must be accomplished—both psychologically and physically—despite

---

[33] Theophus H. Smith, *Conjuring Culture: Biblical Formations of Black America* (New York: Oxford University Press, 1994), 177-248.

[34] Ibid., 3.

[35] Ibid.

the damage done to cherished religious principles and traditions."[36] I am not as sure as Pinn seems to be that traditional Christian theological judgments are as dispensable in the interests of human liberation. However, I agree with him that the adequacy of African-American theology, today, depends on its ability to take into itself the widest ranges of sources from black history and culture. Such sources include storytelling, myth-making, memory recovering, theologizing black culture, dancing, shouting in churches and fields, leaping on stage, engaging music that uplifts the spirit and music that evokes not only black tragedies but human ones in general, and making and watching films depicting both the struggles of blacks toward freedom and the often ironic and comedic realities of black life. The point I share with both Pinn and Smith is that black sources of religious insight can be as wide as black culture is expansive and open to new being.

I have argued elsewhere that being grotesquely open to the ways these sources of black religious insight disclose the powers and manifestations of black religious experience is fundamental to the adequacy of our theological judgments.[37] I also take it from Smith that, in the quest for adequate black, indigenous sources for constructive theology (whether the spirituals, blues, or slave narratives), the scriptures and Christian tradition stand in the fundamental hermeneutical situation for interpreting black religious experience in the United States. Under the metaphor of conjuration, the Christian scriptures and Christian tradition—including creeds and confessions, doctrines and liturgy—are also black sources of religious insight. They are not the particular possession of European and American Christianity. They are co-present in the hermeneutical situation of black religion. This is a perspective that Smith and I share with Charles Long.[38]

When discussing the Trinity in black religion, for instance, Long speaks of black religion as adaptive and inventive responses of black Americans to their historic situation of oppression and discrimination. Taking what was at hand not only from the depth of their West African spiritualities but also from the languages of Christian doctrine, black Americans interpreted their experiences of the power and manifestation of God in their religious experience. Long suggests that we ought not to think of their trinitarian beliefs as simply an effect of conversion, however. Rather, the process was far more fluid and inventive:

God for this community appears as an all-powerful and moral deity, though one hardly ever knows why he has willed this or that. God is never, or hardly ever, blamed for this situation of humanity, for somehow in an inscrutable manner there is a reason for all of this. By and large, a fundamental distinction is made between God and Jesus Christ. To the extent that the language of Christianity is used, black Americans have held to Trinitarian distinction, but adherence to this distinction has been for experiential rather

---

[36] Pinn, *Why Lord?*, 11.

[37] Anderson, *Beyond Ontological Blackness*, 161.

[38] Charles H. Long, *Significations: Signs, Symbols, and Images in the Interpretation of Religion* (Philadelphia: Fortress Press, 1986).

than dogmatic reasons. Historians of religion have known for a long time that the Supreme Being appears in differing forms. . . . It is not so much the Trinity which is important as it is the modalities of experience of the Trinity which are most important. The experience of God is thus placed within the context of the other images and experience of black religion.[39]

For Long, it is the experience of God, and therefore religious experience, that is the boundary condition for understanding, interpreting, and judging the adequacy of our theological judgments and languages.

As I think of it, black religion refracts worlds of difference. Ritual and dance, drama and stories, sermons and singing, scriptures and doctrines, and academic theology disclose the many sites and manners in which black religious experience is a taking hold of God and the world and a channeling of religious insight. However, what is taken up and refracted is not ever without its grotesqueries, that is, its unresolved ambiguities of light and dark, hope and tragedy, limits and openings to more religious experience and more insight. I think that the key to reformulating constructive black theology on black religious sources is openness to more religious knowledge not less, more criticism not less, more stories, poems, biographies and narratives, more myths and even better ones that take hold of the widest ranges of black religious experiences and interpret these experiences in the largest contexts of black history and culture.

CONCLUDING COMMENTS

To conclude, I know that grounding African-American theology on black history and culture can become quickly antiquarian and self-serving when our research programs fail to establish contemporary relevance to black public life. Establishing contemporary relevance is also the burden of the slave-narrative research program. As Hopkins puts it, the strength of the slave-narrative project "lies in literally developing a *black theology* from the actual voices of poor, enslaved African Americans." He further suggests that "learning from the liberating faith that comes out of the actual mouths of the poor" ought to remain one of the tasks of black liberation theology.[40] In a summary statement, Cummings reiterates the aim of their project as contributing "to contemporary black theology in the United States by engaging in the process of utilizing the slave narratives as a source for theological ideas and interpreting the significance of the Spirit and the eschatology in them."[41] For these theologians, the hermeneutical return to the slave narratives is a return to a deposit of faith that is not fraught with the conflicts of values and interests that now define contemporary black life in the United States. Rather, it is claimed that the narratives exhibit a fundamental

---

[39] Ibid., 179-80.
[40] Hopkins, "Introduction," xii, xv.
[41] Cummings, "Slaves Narratives," 146.

unity of black religious experience forged in the experience of African chattel slavery and the invisible institution.

Whether our research programs follow the methodologies of religious history, phenomenology, cultural studies, or black theology, the test of adequacy for both selecting and retrieving black sources is whether African-American theologians can also bring forward into the present the emancipatory and enlightening powers and manifestations of black religion. I hope that our various religious and theological research programs can establish their contemporary relevance. For the corresponding question to historical retrieval is one of historical reversal, that is, whether the retrievals correlate with the historical present. The historical question, today, is: What have African-American theologians to say to and do with the public lives of a growing poor, urban underclass whose lives are characterized by homelessness and pervasive poverty and who are themselves undereducated, underemployed, and overincarcerated?

The need is for livable and affordable homes, protection from black-on-black violence, effective education that yields employment, and justice in criminal prosecution. This is the historical and narrative structure that locates the wretched in much of African-American cultural life today. I suggest that whether African-American theology can be historically relevant to this culture constitutes a viable criterion for assessing our uses of black sources of religious insight. Satisfying such a criterion will require not only many more research programs and debates but also much creativity and inventiveness on the part of African-American theological thinkers.

2

To Be the Bridge

Voices from the Margin

DIANA L. HAYES

Within the history of every Christian community there comes the time when it reaches adulthood. This maturity brings with it the duty, the privilege and the joy to share with others the rich experience of the "Word of Life."[1]

These words, pronounced by the black bishops of the United States, foretell the coming of age of black Catholics in the United States. They ring true as well for all Catholics of color who have historically found themselves on the margins of the church in the United States, silenced and invisible to all around them. Today, black, Latino/a, Asian, and Native-American Catholics, as well as women of all races and ethnicities, are stepping forward and proclaiming their "coming of age" in voices not only richly evocative of their historical experience of oppression within both the Roman Catholic Church and U.S. society but also expressive of their own cultures and traditions, which consistently have been denied access through the front doors of church and society.

A major reason for our recognition of this majority has been the critical yet more inclusive atmosphere that has emerged in both church and society in the aftermath of the Second Vatican Council and the Civil Rights and Black Power/ Black Nationalism movements of the 1960s. These events tapped into a rich vein of frustration and anger at the slow pace of justice and equality for people of color. The result was the emergence of theologies of liberation, which arose from the very core of peoples once enslaved or in other ways dehumanized and degraded by the dominant society. A paradigm shift resulted in how we see

---

[1] *What We Have Seen and Heard: U.S. Black Bishops Pastoral Letter* (Cincinnati, Ohio: St. Anthony Messenger Press, 1984), 1.

ourselves, both as Catholics and as United Statesians.[2] Doors once shut against persons of color have been opened, though sometimes with resistance from those within, and leadership roles at every level of church and society have been made more accessible than before, albeit in limited fashion.

Today, at the start of the third millennium, we are reaching another definitive moment in the life of the church and society. The Roman Catholic Church, both local and global, is undergoing significant changes in terms of its racial and ethnic makeup, a shift that mirrors the changes taking place in the United States. Historically, the world as we know it has always been one where people of color were in the majority. Their numerical superiority, however, has been ignored and suppressed, especially in the last five hundred years, as those who have held positions of power in both the world and the Christian churches have come from one group, which defines itself as "white."[3] Initially comprised of persons from England as well as northern and western Europe, this group increased its numbers and authority by eventually including people from Ireland, eastern and southern Europe, and other countries who were seen to qualify as "whites." Excluded were all those of darker complexion from Africa, Asia and Oceania, Latin America, and the Caribbean.

Blessed by the grace of God—or so it seemed to them—with skills and knowledge that provided them with an edge over the lands and peoples that they conquered and/or colonized, they proceeded to develop an ideology, grounded in Christian scripture and law, with which to support their assumed positions of superiority. In so doing, those who modeled themselves after them were rewarded, while those who were different and sought to maintain their culture and traditions were usually condemned and dehumanized. At the same time, individual effort was encouraged, while community effort was seen as negative. The impact of their presence continues to the present day in what is now known as Western civilization—a social, cultural, religious, political, and economic hegemonic ideology that has been carried to the farthest corners of the world,

---

[2] I deliberately use this term rather than the more common *American* as more descriptive of reality, since the latter term includes persons from both continents of the Americas and the Caribbean.

[3] The term *white* has no scientific basis. It was developed as a result of slavery in the Americas in order to differentiate between enslaved Africans and those who enslaved them. The term expanded over the centuries into a description for racial purity. See T. W. Allen, *The Invention of the White Race,* vol. 1, *Racial Oppression and Social Control* (London and New York: Verso, 1994); idem, *The Invention of the White Race,* vol. 2, *The Origins of Racial Oppression in Anglo-America* (London and New York: Verso, 1997); M. Frye Jacobson, *Whiteness of a Different Color: European Immigrants and the Alchemy of Race* (Cambridge, Mass.: Harvard University Press, 1998). In the past decade a number of books on "whiteness" as race have appeared, and a new movement, white studies, has emerged (see, e.g., R. Delgado and J. Stefancic, eds., *Critical White Studies: Looking beyond the Mirror* [Philadelphia: Temple University Press, 1997]). For an interesting perspective on how a particular immigrant group changed in status, see N. Ignatiev, *How the Irish Became White* (London and New York: Routledge, 1995).

with beneficial as well as detrimental results. They saw themselves, for the most part, as standard bearers for Christ, engaged in the building of the New Jerusalem. However, their dream of a model "city on a hill" has never been fully realized, since they lost sight of their goals in confrontations, often deadly, with the indigenous peoples of the Americas and the African and Asian peoples brought over as laborers.

Charles Long analyzes this impact in religious terms, noting that wherever the English, Spanish, French, and other Western peoples came, they carried with them an ingrained bias against persons of color and of different religious beliefs. Often fleeing from religious persecution themselves, their bias was so unconscious by the time of the discovery of the Americas that it was not recognized as such, even by the church; it was simply seen as the "natural" way of living and acting toward persons of color. Thus, a revolutionary religion, Christianity, found itself reduced to a tool of oppression, mired in the quagmire of religious and racial prejudice. A nation with the "soul of a church" became a living hell for Native Americans, Latinos/as, Asians, and African peoples, as the country failed miserably to live up to its own self-proclamation of a land of justice and liberty for all. As Long affirms, American religion was never truly American in its most inclusive sense:

> If by American we mean the Christian European immigrants and their progeny, then we have overlooked American Indians and American blacks. And if religion is defined as revealed Christianity and its institutions, we have again overlooked much of the religion of American blacks, American Indians, and the Jewish communities. Even from the point of view of civil religions, it is not clear that from the perspective of the various national and ethnic communities . . . there has ever been a consistent meaning of the national symbols and meanings. In short, a great deal of the writings and discussions on the topic of American religion has been consciously or unconsciously ideological, serving to embrace, justify, and render sacred the history of European immigrants in this land.
>
> Indeed, this approach to American religion has rendered the religious reality of non-Europeans to a state of invisibility.[4]

The voices of which Long speaks are not just the voices of women, who were for so long considered only as appendages of their husbands or otherwise under the authority of other men, whether fathers, brothers, or uncles. He is referring more specifically to the voices of entire peoples who have lived within

---

[4] Charles H. Long, "Civil Rights–Civil Religion: Visible People and Invisible Religion," in *American Civil Religion*, ed. Russell B. Richey and Donald G. James (New York: Harper & Row, 1974), 212-13. As cited in D. L. Hayes, "Emerging Voices, Emerging Challenges: An American Contextual Theology," in *Theology toward the Third Millennium: Theological Issues for the Twenty-first Century*, ed. D. Schultenover, S.J. (Lewiston, N.Y.: Mellen Press, 1991), 43.

the borders of the United States from its earliest beginnings—namely, African, Native, Asian, and Hispanic/Latino Americans. All of these groups have cultures of which they are justifiably proud and which have been handed down from generation to generation, despite often deliberate efforts to deny them their histories and thus render them invisible, empty slates upon which others could draw vastly different and derogatory images of them.[5]

THE DISTORTION OF CHRISTIANITY

This understanding of religion, most particularly Christianity, which has denied humanity and human dignity to persons of color, represents a distorted understanding of true Christianity. It is one that has evolved over time and place, as all theologies evolve. It has done so, however, in isolation, giving rise thereby to a vision of universality that was in actuality parochial and exclusive of most of the world. In the United States, especially, this hegemonic perspective took on a particularly Protestant cast, so that Roman Catholics, of whatever race or ethnicity, were also seen as "others" and "aliens," therefore not truly American. Indeed, a national mythology persists in the United States to the present day. Fernando Segovia describes it as "a deeply ingrained and much cherished belief that the United States has been blessed and hence marked in a very distinctive and unique way by God (the Christian God)."[6] He continues:

> Given the Protestant background of the dominant and majority group of the country and the centrality of the Bible for this group, such a belief— what has come to be known as "American exceptionalism"—has traditionally been given expression in strong biblical terms. Drawing on the "Old Testament," for example, the United States is seen as a present-day counterpart to ancient Israel: a promised land given by God to a chosen people and hence not only a chosen nation but also a "light to the nations." Likewise, drawing on the "New Testament," the country is further seen as a counterpart to the early Christian church: a beginning presence of the Kingdom of God in the world with a duty to extend the message and confines of the kingdom to "all nations."[7]

---

[5] See, for example, C. Davis, O.S.B., *The History of Black Catholics in the United States* (New York: Crossroad Books, 1990); D. L. Hayes and C. Davis, eds., *Taking Down Our Harps: Black Catholics in the United States* (Maryknoll, N.Y.: Orbis Books, 1998); V. Deloria, *Custer Died for Your Sins: An Indian Manifesto* (New York: Macmillan, 1967); J. Treat, ed., *Native and Christian: Indigenous Voices of Religious Identity in the United States and Canada* (New York-London: Routledge, 1996); A. M. Isasi-Díaz and F. F. Segovia, eds., *Hispanic/Latino Theology: Challenge and Promise* (Minneapolis, Minn.: Fortress Press, 1996).

[6] F. F. Segovia, "Aliens in the Promised Land: The Manifest Destiny of U. S. Hispanic American Theology," in Isasi-Díaz and Segovia, *Hispanic/Latino Theology*, 21.

[7] Ibid., 22.

Somehow this understanding of a predestined chosenness went horribly wrong. A nation grounded in principles of justice, freedom, and equality lost sight of the universality of its calling and limited rights meant for all to only a few.

Early Christianity and Its Roots

We must look back at the roots of Christianity in Judaism and at early Christianity itself. In the Hebrew scriptures we find the constant admonition of God to the Israelites that they must care for the widowed and the orphaned as well as for the stranger in their midst, for they too were once strangers and sojourners in an alien land themselves. Obviously, the Hebrew scriptures can also be read to support the oppression of peoples,[8] but this harsher reading is consistently contradicted by the prophets, the voice of God, who urge justice and righteousness in the name of God as the model for the Israelites and for all who see themselves as the children of God. In the Christian scriptures this compassionate mandate is even more clearly expressed in Jesus' teachings, from his first sermon in Nazareth, to the Sermon on the Mount, to his very death, when he called not for vengeance but for forgiveness for any who had participated in his crucifixion.

From Inculturation to Assimilation

As we look at the early church, prior to Constantine and for several centuries thereafter, we find a different understanding of its mission and ministry. It soon becomes clear that the church did not spring full-blown from the mind of Jesus but was instead a divinely inspired yet very human institution that developed as a result of contacts and clashes with people of other nations and religions.

Christianity emerged in a time and place where cultures constantly merged and clashed, the crossroads of the Roman Empire found in the Middle East and Northern Africa. Here, people of all nations, creeds, and colors came together—rubbing elbows; exchanging ideas; learning from, teaching, and influencing each other socially, politically, economically, and religiously. In its first century the church was a sect of Judaism, gathering and spreading the message of Christ Crucified through Jewish rituals, symbols, gestures, and customs familiar to Jesus and his original followers. Yet, all such practices were also somehow different, subtly transformed through the understanding of who Jesus was for those who believed in him. Even today, many Christians are ignorant of the Jewish roots of Christianity, seeing Jesus and his first followers as Christians.

The histories and cultures of the people living around the Mediterranean Basin also influenced and transformed the infant Christian church. The disciples, seeking to follow Jesus' command of Matthew 28:19 ("Go ye therefore

---

[8] Native Americans, for example, clearly see a correlation between their treatment by Euro-Americans and the plundering and slaughtering of the Canaanites by the freed Hebrews. See R. A. Warrior, "Canaanites, Cowboys, and Indians: Deliverance, Conquest and Liberation Theology Today," in Treat, *Native and Christian*, 93-104.

and teach all nations"), traveled to Greek, Roman, and African territories, where Christianity not only spread but also evolved as it came into contact with new and different peoples. These new Christians received much from their teachers and gave much to them in return, becoming teachers themselves and bearers of the good news in new tongues and cultures, all of which helped to broaden our understanding of Jesus' life, death, and resurrection. At the same time, they enriched our liturgical and religious language with words and understandings from their own cultures: the alleluias and amens of the Jewish faithful; the language of epiphany, agape, eucharist, advent, lent, and eulogy from Greek and Roman worshipers; new formulas for prayer and baptism as well as new forms of spirituality and worship from eastern and northern African churches; new understandings of Jesus' own being along with increasing ceremonial ritual from the imperial court. All these influences helped to shape the new religion of Christianity in ways that are still familiar today.

Wherever the church traveled, wherever the seed of the gospel was planted, new and fertile growth took place—a growth always and everywhere established in and nurtured by the traditions and heritages of the peoples and cultures with which it came into contact. It was this ever-spreading cross-fertilization that nourished and sustained the infant church in its mission. The church was not only Jewish but also Greek, Roman, and African. Historically, it was always recognized, though often unconsciously so, that inculturation of the signs, symbols, and language, of the rites and rituals, of the very life of the faith, should and must reflect the culture of those participating, since otherwise they would not be able to communicate the message of salvation that they carried within them.

This period of inculturation and growth slowed after the church moved into Germanic, Celtic, and Anglo-Saxon lands. Christianity—threatened by the rise of Islam and the loss of contact with Spain, Africa, and the Middle East—turned into a religion very much turned in upon itself. The contributions and knowledge of peoples with different cultures and traditions and perspectives were forgotten, under the assumption that there was only one expression of Christianity possible, universal rather than merely cultural, to which all believers were required to adhere. A harsh and unbending rigor set in as a result, with a view of the church as set in stone, unchanging, unadapting, uniform, robotic, often seemingly mindless, unfeeling, and unfelt. The members of the laity were reduced to observers, becoming increasingly isolated as the life of the church centered on the daily mass said by a priest with only a serving boy in attendance. Its theology became restricted to those few who were educated, namely, the wealthy and the powerful. Such uniformity became even more pronounced after the Protestant Reformation, which set Catholic and Protestant Christians at odds for centuries to come.

It was this restricted and parochial understanding of the faith that was carried across the Atlantic to the Americas and that clashed with peoples whose cultures and traditions were a total antithesis to it. The Catholicism of the French, Spanish, and English missionaries who were instrumental in introducing the Catholic faith to the Indians, enslaved Africans, and Latinos/as was so intimately wed to their European culture that many of them could not easily distinguish the gospel they preached from their own particular and often biased expressions of it. As a result, the church in the Americas assumed that European cultures and the missionaries' particular expression of them were the only viable and valid cultures and found it difficult if not impossible to imagine or value cultures other than their own.

This "Old World" understanding was brought to the Americas and forcibly imposed on Africans, Native Americans, Asians, Hispanics/Latinos, and any and all others whose way of being in the world was in any way seen as different. The emphasis was no longer on inculturation but on assimilation, thus denying the individuality of each person's encounter with the divine. Yet, as Orlando Espín declares, "no experience of the divine occurs in a vacuum. . . . From the perspective of the human partner, the experience of the divine is possible only through cultural, social, and historical means."[9] It follows, therefore, that all religious experience is an inculturated one: "All possibility of a pure, a-cultural encounter with the divine is, therefore, excluded."[10] In sum, we all experience God in similar and different ways as a result of the cultural matrix in which we find ourselves. To deny this is to deny the mystery and infinitude of God.

> No religion, regardless of its type or history, has ever believed that what it affirms of the divine is all that can be affirmed of or about it. . . . The cultural idiom of an individual or group will shape the language, symbols and so on used by that individual or group in the process of interpreting religious experience, hereby shaping the experience itself as "religious" and the image(s) of the One encountered as "divine."[11]

THE AFRICAN-AMERICAN EXPERIENCE

All peoples have a particular experience of the divine that shapes them and enables them to make sense of the world around them. As a person of African descent, my understanding of God has been shaped by the way in which my community has experienced God in its life within the United States.[12] As a people

---

[9] O. Espín, "Popular Catholicism: Alienation or Hope?," in Isasi-Díaz and Segovia, *Hispanic/Latino Theology*, 310.

[10] Ibid.

[11] Ibid.

[12] Here I will be speaking specifically of African Americans, whom I define as those persons of African descent who trace their ancestry back to the period of slavery in the United States, whether their ancestors were free or slave. All who lived during that time were marked by that experience and therefore usually have a worldview somewhat different from that of other persons of African descent who would, with African Americans, fall under the nomenclature of black Americans. The latter include recent immigrants from Africa itself as well as from Central or South America and the Caribbean. The black community is extremely diverse in language, culture, skin color, and a variety of other ways but is usually looked upon by the dominant society as monolithic and monochromatic.

stolen from their homeland, African Americans encountered God from within an African worldview that was significantly influenced by their introduction, usually forced, to the God of Christianity and those who saw themselves as God's designated chosen ones. This encounter was in many ways harsh and often deliberately destructive of their self-understanding as a people with cultures, traditions, religions, and histories of their own passed down for centuries in their homeland. White Christianity contradicted everything that African peoples believed about themselves and the world around them. Manning Marable speaks of it as follows:

> The passion of white Christianity transfers critical thought to an idealist or supernatural plane, removing individual Christians from making moral decisions within the secular world, allowing the "sadistic extermination of the weak" to continue. The purpose of white Christianity as a popular philosophy, therefore, is not to change the world, but to offer the prejudices and emotions of those who dwell within the world to tolerate their real conditions. . . . White Christianity is limited to the realm of the pulpit and the pews; it would not nor could not take an aggressive stand on secular issues, such as human rights of blacks, Indians, or other ethnic minorities. . . . White racism became a faith in which millions subconsciously or willingly shared, because the orthodox religious institutions took *no positions* in favor of black humanity.[13]

African Americans were and still are, for the most part, a holistic, communitarian, joy-filled, spiritual, and life-sustaining people. Their understanding of God as a being transcendent and unapproachable yet also very much present and active in their lives through the intercession of the ancestors—those who had lived lives worthy of emulation—and lesser gods found resonance in the ideology of Christianity. Here too they came across a transcendent God, who created them, as he created all things, for good, and an immanent God in the being of Jesus the Christ, who was like them in their impoverished and perilous state. At the same time, however, white Christianity attempted to enforce a critically different understanding. In the words of Dwight Hopkins:

> White theology forced its domination upon black life by maintaining ruthless control and rendering slaves subservient to white humanity. . . . The practice of white slavemasters' Christianity restricted African Americans' access to an independent encounter with religion. . . . The white man believed he replaced the mediating and liberating role of Jesus Christ. As the anointed Jesus, the white man possessed omnipotent and salvific

---

[13] M. Marable, "Religion and Black Protest Thought in African American History," in *African American Religious Studies: An Interdisciplinary Anthology*, ed. G. S. Wilmore (Durham, N.C.: Duke University Press, 1989), 320.

capabilities. For black chattel to reach God, then, whites forced black chattel to accept the intermediary and divisive status of the white race.[14]

Yet, the slaves resisted this heretical distortion of the meaning and message of Jesus Christ and were instead able to embrace Christianity in a radically different and liberating form. They refused to accept a distorted Christianity from those who denied their humanity. They resisted their reduction to the state of animals without feelings or needs, other than the most rudimentary, and created a spiritual life of faith that sustained them in their physical life of degradation. As I have stated elsewhere, "Theirs was a defiant faith, born of the Spirit, which moved them to disobey their masters in order to obey their God."[15] Their stance was similar to that of their descendants centuries later, who refused to acknowledge the legality of Jim-Crow laws, insisting that the law of God superseded that of humanity and that only God's laws were truly just laws.

African Americans, for the most part, refused to accept their status as slaves or as second-class citizens in the United States. Those who were persecuted with them, Native Americans and other racial/ethnic minorities, did the same. They sought to build communities of faith in which they were able to develop lives of value, which enabled them to survive against all who opposed them. The ghettos, barrios, Chinatowns, Koreatowns, and reservations existed not because these communities sought to segregate themselves but rather because they were forced to do so in order to survive as a people. In these segregated communities they were able to retain their cultural traditions and pass them on. Shawn Copeland puts it this way:

> On the one hand, the moral integrity of Black Catholicism and the theology that would mediate it requires an unequivocal rejection of segregation in any form. As members of the Body of Christ, we too desire to live as Jesus lived, to put our communal and personal, cultural and social decisions at the service of the coming Reign of God. On the other hand, pastoral neglect and disregard by white clergy and hierarchy have forced black Catholics to seek out separate sites for the development of their own spiritual life.[16]

THE FAILURE OF THE "MELTING POT"

Native-American theologian Vine Deloria notes that, while African Americans and Asian Americans were seen as so different that they were denied even

---

[14] D. N. Hopkins, *Shoes That Fit Our Feet: Sources for a Constructive Black Theology* (Maryknoll, N.Y.: Orbis Books, 1993), 22.

[15] D. L. Hayes, "Through the Eyes of Faith: The Seventh Principle of the *Nguzo Saba* and the Beatitudes of Matthew," in Hayes and Davis, *Taking Down Our Harps*, 56.

[16] M. Shawn Copeland, "Method in Emerging Black Catholic Theology," in Hayes and Davis, *Taking Down Our Harps*, 134.

the possibility of ever achieving the status of true Americans, the opposite was often true of Native Americans and Hispanic Americans. These latter were, ironically, required to become as much like Euro-Americans as possible. They were forcibly stripped of their languages, cultures, traditions—everything that identified them as different.[17] For blacks and Asians, the impact was just as harsh, albeit different. Yet they too lost everything—languages, cultures, traditions.

Overall, these "patterns of dominance and repression" used against persons of color in the United States, which called for a "melting" of peoples in order to create a "common culture," were unsuccessful.[18] The "melting pot" of peoples from which would spring forth the new and true American, allegedly a mixture of all, was in actuality the transformation of all to fit the norm of the white, Anglo-Saxon, Protestant male, whose understanding of themselves as the new chosen people of God building the New Jerusalem led them to see themselves as the standard by which all other peoples were to be judged. As the late Supreme Court Justice Thurgood Marshall pointed out in a July 4 presentation, that "We the People"—the first three words of the Preamble to the Constitution, the foundational document for the United States—did not include, when first written, persons of African descent. Nor did these words include Latinos/as, Native Americans, persons of Asian descent, women of any race or ethnicity, or white men without property.

The call for a "common culture" has had, in actuality, the opposite effect— the alienation of many. True citizenship should not require the loss of self but should affirm rather than deny one's humanity and human dignity. Persons of color in the United States have had to endure such forms of oppression as "poverty, powerlessness and institutional chaos."[19] Harsh as these have been, the historically marginalized have suffered from an even broader system of oppression. Ismael García describes it as follows,

> The oppression . . . is defined as the social process through which society, institutionally and systematically, disregards, stereotypes, and denigrates the racial makeup, language, potentiality, capacities, heritage, customs, and traditional habits of [the particular] community. This negative projection . . . has had the consequence of devaluing and undermining the community's sense of self-worth and self-confidence as well as the moral and aesthetic value of its culture.[20]

The result is that "the lives of many African Americans [and other persons of color] are threatened daily by continued institutionalized oppressions, internal-

---

[17] See Deloria, *Custer Died for Your Sins*.

[18] D. L. Machado, "Kingdom Building in the Borderlands: The Church and Manifest Destiny," in Isasi-Díaz and Segovia, *Hispanic/Latino Theology*, 63.

[19] I. García, "A Theological-Ethical Analysis of Hispanic Struggles for Community Building in the United States," in Isasi-Díaz and Segovia, *Hispanic/Latino Theology*, 297.

[20] Ibid. Although García is speaking specifically of the Hispanic community here, his statement is equally applicable to all ethnic/racial minorities in the United States.

ized self-hatred, and nihilistic despair."[21] In effect, the "melting pot" assimilation in its harshest sense requires that, in order to become a part of the new American people, one must "abandon or give secondary importance to his or her traditional loyalties." The result is clear:

> Thus, individuals' ethnic, racial and national loyalties and even cultural and religious traditions must be relativized or abandoned altogether if they are to become new persons within the new nation. While the process of assimilation seemed to have worked fairly well for most Europeans, particularly the dominant Anglo-Saxon group, it has proven to be quite detrimental to people of African, Asian and Latin American descent.[22]

The Failure of Faith

These "others" have to this day not received the full rights of citizenship due to them as native-born United Statesians. Even when they have become economically successful, they remain second- and even third-class citizens in the eyes of their fellow citizens as well as in the eyes of their co-religionists. Indeed, the Christian churches, including the Roman Catholic Church, have participated fully in both the dehumanization of persons of color inside and outside of the church and in forced efforts at their assimilation. Machado makes this quite clear: "[The] desire for a consumer culture found in U.S. society was also adopted and legitimized by the church in its missionary efforts."[23] In fact,

> These efforts continue to the present day as persons of color, now increasingly the majority in states and local dioceses, still find themselves marginalized, misunderstood, and forced into an invisibility and voicelessness that denies the teachings of the church at every level. To differentiate among human beings based on the color of their skin or any other factor is a sin against God and must be condemned. "Whatever violates the integrity of the human person, . . . whatever insults human dignity, . . . all these things and others like them are infamous."[24]

The sin perdures as the church, consciously or unconsciously, continues to attempt to fit all of the people of God into one mold, causing serious psychological and spiritual harm to all concerned. The sin of forced assimilation does not affect only those so oppressed. It has a debilitating effect upon the oppressors as

---

[21] J. T. Phelps, O.P., "Inculturating Jesus: A Search for Dynamic Images for the Mission of the Church among African Americans," in Hayes and Davis, *Taking Down Our Harps*, 73.

[22] García, "Theological-Ethical Analysis," 298.

[23] Machado, "Kingdom Building," 64.

[24] D. L. Hayes, "Slavery," in *Rome Has Spoken . . . A Guide to Forgotten Papal Statements and How They Have Changed through the Centuries*, ed. Maureen Fiedler and Linda Rabben (New York: Crossroad, 1998), 89.

well, giving them a false sense of superiority that makes it difficult, if not at times impossible, for them to recognize the full humanity of those unlike themselves or to welcome them into their midst as they are.

Signs of the Times

However, the times are indeed changing. The signs can be found wherever the church finds itself gathered. The most significant change is demographic. As early as 1990, it became quite clear that by the twenty-first century U.S. society would be made up predominantly of persons of color who trace their ancestry "to Africa, Asia, the Hispanic world, the Pacific Islands, Arabia— almost anywhere but white Europe."[25] These changes are taking place even more rapidly within the church itself, as the number of Latinos/as, blacks, and Asians— both native-born and immigrant—increases within its ranks. They are changing the face of the church in the United States from white to brown and darker hues. At the same time, they are also turning to the church, their religious home for generations, for recognition of their continued presence within it.

Persons of African descent trace their catholicity back to the Ethiopian eunuch converted in Acts as well as to those Africans converted by the Portuguese and the Spanish beginning in the fifteenth century in Africa. Today, African immigrants come from every part of the African continent and bring their Catholic faith with them, with its richness of tradition, ritual, harmony, and spirituality. They also come from the Caribbean, along with the great tide of Spanish-speaking peoples coming from Latin America. Spanish-speaking peoples have an equally rich and long history in the church, first in Spain itself and subsequently in the Americas and the Caribbean. They bring with them a faith that has withstood traumatic oppression and the denial of the cultural expressions of their faith, just as their black sisters and brothers have. They also share with Asians the denial of their languages and traditions. Yet Asian Americans have also persisted, tracing their faith to the early missions in India, to the French in Southeast Asia, and other such contacts. They too have enriched Catholicism by inculturating it within their own cultures and heritages, as have Native Americans, who, forced from their lands, still maintain faith in a God who saves and also frees, both spiritually and physically.

These are not new Catholics but old ones; they have brought rich gifts to the church, gifts that have too often gone unrecognized or unappreciated. North- and East-African Catholics introduced monasticism to the church in its early years, while the people of Mexico revealed the glory of the mother of God as a peasant Indian girl, the face of the people. Asians teach us the value of seeing Jesus in myriad forms, both human and nonhuman; they speak of him as rice, the source of all life, without whom they would perish. This long history must be acknowledged and affirmed by the church of today, for people of color will not disappear but rather will grow stronger, both in numbers and in faith. We do

---

[25] W. Henry, "Beyond the Melting Pot," *Time* (April 9, 1990): 28.

not come empty-handed, seeking a token and marginalized life on the boundaries of the church, for that has been our situation for too long. We come bearing richly diverse understandings of what it truly means to be church together, demanding that the body of Christ be recognized in its rich and colorful diversity as gift to all of the people of God.

By the year 2010, the U.S. church will be almost 50 percent Hispanic. When black, Asian, and Native Catholics are added to the mix, we realize that the church of the third millennium will assuredly be one of persons of color. However, in order to truly represent the body of Christ, the church must reflect the diversity and universality that it claims in more than just numbers. The presence of persons of color must be found and encouraged at every level of the church and in every possible role. Failure to do so will result in a false face, in which whites, although no longer dominant in numbers, will still hold power and authority in a tight grasp. Sadly, the possibilities of this happening still exist, for the sin of racism persists within our church.

Sharing a Piece of or the Whole Pie

Increasingly, articles and books as well as discussions on the issue of race are emerging at every level of the church and U.S. society. For many, this issue is clearly painful and threatening, as President William J. Clinton discovered when announcing his National Dialogue on Racism. Many fear that ugly wounds will be reopened, not realizing that such wounds have never healed—nor will they heal until opened to the cleansing air of truth. Others encourage the dialogue, but only as a way of promoting division rather than healing, seeking to further subdivide persons of color into manageable blocs that can be manipulated one against the other when necessary. Still others search for new definitions of what it means to be Latino/a, black, Asian, Native American in order to further muddy the waters of a stream that is already about to overflow. Who is black? Asian? Indian? Hispanic? What is the significance of these terms? There is power in naming, empowerment in the naming of oneself and loss of power in being named by others, as all persons of color have experienced throughout their lives.[26] While the power to name can be used to label and thereby control a people, it can also prove liberating for those who name themselves, especially if, in so doing, they lift up a name formerly used to denigrate and dehumanize.[27] Yet others, in efforts to shift reality, set out to redefine whiteness. This, however, is not new, since immigrants from Ireland and other parts of Europe had to earn the "privilege" of whiteness. Today, by defining Hispanics as of any race,

---

[26] See the discussion of the significance of naming in Segovia, "Aliens in the Promised Land," 31.

[27] See, for example, current discussions regarding the use of the term *nigger* and *nigga* by young people in hip-hop music and among their friends, where the former term still retains the negative connotations of slavery and the latter is seen as a term of affection and friendship. Some see this as a self-defeating argument, while others, usually the younger generation, see it as a proclamation of selfhood and self-determination.

their dominance can be diluted as well. Those able to pass the "tests" can be welcomed into the "white" or dominant society, thereby enlarging its ranks over against those of darker complexion.

Another factor under study is the rise in marriage across racial lines. While for some this is a cause for concern, others see it as yet another way of bolstering the ranks of dominant society, as Asians, Indians, and Latinos/as intermarry with European Americans. Interestingly, their offspring are often accepted as white, while the offspring of similar marriages with persons of African descent are still labeled as black or African American, reinforcing thereby the presumed unassimilability of these latter groups.[28] Rather than listening to the tortured and convoluted reasoning of those frantically seeking to maintain the hegemonic dominance of persons of European descent by creating more and more artificial categories and definitions that only serve to divide rather than unite, it would be far more profitable for persons of color to recognize that they share in more ways then they differ. As long as we allow ourselves to be divided against one another, we will continue to struggle for the same small piece of America's "pie," while allowing the greater portion of it to be devoured by those who seek to keep us apart.

TO BE THE BRIDGE

José Vasconcelos, in a ground-breaking essay published in 1925,[29] looked ahead to a world vastly different from the one in which he lived and in which we still live today. Ours is a world where peoples and nations are in constant conflict over their alleged differences—whether racial, ethnic, religious, political, social, or economic. Vasconcelos conceived instead of a world that would do away with such artificial barriers to a common humanity and thus called for the recognition of a *raza cósmica* (cosmic or universal race), a *mestizo* or mixed race containing all of humanity within it. This *mestizaje* or mixture would come about through evolutionary means, the beginnings of which, he believed, were already present in the peoples of Latin America: "The various races of the earth tend to intermix at a gradually increasing pace, and eventually will give rise to a new human type, composed of selections from each of the races already in existence."[30]

Vasconcelos's understanding of race is rooted not in the "scientific" categories that have served to divide the contemporary world (the Caucasoid, Negroid,

---

[28] The entire issue of race in the United States, its formulation and application, stands much in need of further explication; such a task, however, goes beyond the boundaries of the present chapter. In the last decade hundreds of books have appeared on this topic, including those that continue to support a "scientific" basis for the division of the world's people into separate races and those that set out to show the fallacy of such efforts. On this, see Allen, *The Invention of the White Race.*

[29] J. Vasconcelos, *The Cosmic Race/La raza cósmica*, trans. with intro. D. T. Jaen (Baltimore and London: The Johns Hopkins University Press, 1979).

[30] Ibid., 3.

and Mongoloid races),[31] but rather on nationalities (ethnicity), since he speaks of Spaniards, American Indians, Germans, and others as races. However, his understanding is still limited by his assumption that there are differences great enough between these peoples to speak of them as "races" of people—some closer, others more distant—in terms of compatibility with each other. Vasconcelos's ideas were criticized by many at the time for what they felt to be a racist insistence on the superiority of Hispanic peoples, in whom he saw the fruition of this new race. However, his ideas, viewed from a religious and philosophical rather than scientific or genetic basis, have a certain credibility, especially if viewed from the Catholic vision of unity (universality), which arises, albeit regrettably at times, at the expense of individual freedoms.

Envisioning a new era of humanity, the Aesthetic Age, in which individual and material concerns would give way to an inclusive concern for the good of all, Vasconcelos saw the beginnings of this age, as already stated, in Latin America, but also as threatened by the growing individualism and consumerism of Western society. All of the races are present, he declares, in the Hispanic peoples (Indian, African, and European), an assertion reiterated today by Hispanic/Latino/a theologians, who seek to provide an opening for dialogue among the different peoples in the United States.[32] The Hispanic peoples, he argues, have taken the best qualities of each race and will emerge not as a superior race but as a race infinitely suited, as a result of evolutionary progress, to move the human race forward into the new Aesthetic Age, in which all will be in harmony.

> In the third period [of Vasconcelos's Aesthetic Age], whose approach is already announced in a thousand ways, the orientation of conduct will not be sought in pitiful reason that explains but does not discover. It will rather be sought in creative feeling and convincing beauty. Norms will be given by fantasy, the supreme faculty. That is to say, life will be without norms, in a state in which everything that is born from feeling will be right: Instead of rules, constant inspiration. The merit of an action will not be sought in the immediate and tangible results, as in the first period; nor will it be required to adapt itself to predetermined rules of pure reason. The ethical imperative itself will be surpassed. Beyond good and evil, in a world of aesthetic *pathos*, the only thing that will matter will be that the act, being beautiful, shall produce joy. To do our whim, not our duty; to follow the path of taste, not of appetite or syllogism; to live joy grounded on love—such is the third stage.[33]

---

[31] See Part 2, "Science Constructs Race," in The "Racial Economy of Science": Toward a Democratic Future, ed. S. Harding (Bloomington, Ind.: Indiana University Press, 1993), 84-193.

[32] See F. F. Segovia, "Two Places and No Place on Which to Stand: Mixture and Otherness in Hispanic American Theology," in *Mestizo Christianity: Theology from the Latino Perspective*, ed. A. Bañuelas (Maryknoll, N.Y.: Orbis Books, 1995), 28-43.

[33] Vasconcelos, *The Cosmic Race*, 29.

Without an understanding of the context in which he wrote, many of Vasconcelos's comments regarding other peoples (their history, traditions, culture, and capabilities), especially those of African descent, appear to be racially biased.[34] However, unlike many, he does recognize an evolution in human understanding and identity that is belatedly being acknowledged today. He also looks ahead in his vision to an era which, in many ways, resonates with the kingdom of God proclaimed by Jesus Christ, where all will live in peace and harmony.

The *mestizo* (whether called mixed race, multiracial, or multicultural) already exists and has, in fact, existed for centuries in the Americas. Laws against miscegenation notwithstanding, persons of allegedly singular and insurmountable "racial" differences have joined in sexual union, producing offspring who have themselves joined with others, producing thereby the diversity that exists in the United States today and is reflected in its churches.[35] It can be argued that, with the exception of the most recent immigrants, anyone who has lived in the United States for more than a few generations is *mestizo/a*.

Persons of African descent who are African Americans, although some may deny knowledge of it, are of African, European (usually Celtic, Anglo-Saxon, French, or Spanish), and Native-American ancestry. How they define themselves depends more upon the particular communities and cultures into which they are born than any specific physical attributes. It is dominant society in its zeal for categorization that requires a person to choose a particular racial group to which to belong, and that classification is often made without any input from the one so named. Native Americans as well find that they have similar mixtures within them, in company with African and Hispanic Americans. The *raza cósmica*, in a certain sense, can thus be seen to have existed in the United States unacknowledged for centuries. At various times, depending on the value in so doing, these different peoples, along with whites who also have similar unnamed and unacknowledged racial backgrounds, raise up one or another aspect of their ancestry as a means of moving forward.

Vasconcelos was correct, therefore, in predicting the emergence of a new people, a mixture of all of the nations and peoples in the world. He was, however, incorrect in locating this new people or race within only one group, Latin Americans. In reality, the cosmic race exists throughout North and South America. Today, we are all, for the most part, *mestizaje* people in the United States: a people of mixed races and, at the same time, of the same race, as the Book of Genesis has eternally proclaimed. It is time to recognize this unity within ourselves and to see it as God's gift to humanity, a part of the salvific plan since the world began. Rather than denouncing such changes, we must learn from and teach one another and ourselves in order to be about the building

---

[34] Ibid., 16-22.

[35] See R. Cloker's discussion of the laws against miscegenation and their disregard by many in dominant society in her chapter in *Hybrid: Bisexuals, Multiracials, and Other Misfits under American Law* (Bloomington, Ind.: Indiana University Press, 1996), 121-62.

of God's kingdom here on earth. This does not mean that we deny the richness of the different cultures in which we all have been formed and shaped, for that would simply replicate the errors of forced assimilation into a nonexisting melting pot. Rather, it should be recognized that the coming together of the peoples and cultures of Hispanic, African, Asian, Indian, and European ancestry serves as a model for the mosaic or tapestry that is the true future of the United States and the church.

In ways that are only now becoming clear, we have been doing this all along— learning from and teaching each other, sharing each other's pain and rejoicing in each other's successes. The Los Angeles riot/rebellion of 1992 provides an example of our struggle, both apart and together, to recover our pasts, reclaim our present, and proclaim our future to all who are in solidarity with us and with the plan of God for a new world. We do well to recall the character of this event:

> The L. A. riots took place in South Central L.A., nearly one-half of which is now Latino. Of those involved who were arrested, only 36 percent were Black; the majority were Latino, with a number of Asians and Whites thrown in for good measure. Yet the media persisted in depicting the disturbances as Blacks versus Whites, ignoring the fact that others were involved and that the businesses damaged or destroyed were not only white but also Black, Latino, and most importantly, Asian (Korean specifically). This is said not to get Blacks "off the hook" in any way but to expose today's racially driven reality.
>
> Reality: The majority of businesses destroyed were in Koreatown. The memory of media shots depicting armed Koreans patrolling the roofs of their stores, guarding them against looting Blacks and Latinos, is still with us, but little or nothing was said about why they were forced into this situation (the failure of the police to respond to their 911 calls) or that Blacks and Latinos were often patrolling (off camera, of course) with them. Once again a false duality has been set up, with Blacks as the problem and others, even their fellow people of color, allegedly finding it difficult, if not impossible, to work with them in any reasonable way.[36]

Like many persons of color in the United States whose parents were immigrants, Elaine Kim, a Korean American, learned about oppression and the struggle to survive as a non-white by observing the struggle of black Americans in the 1960s to gain civil and human rights. She notes that this is when she first began to understand her own experiences as a woman of Asian descent growing up in Los Angeles:

> It was the courageous African American women and men of the 1960's who had redefined the meaning of "American"; who had first suggested

---

[36] D. L. Hayes, "My Hope Is in the Lord: Transformation and Salvation in the African American Community," in *Embracing the Spirit: Womanist Perspectives on Hope, Salvation and Transformation*, ed. E. M. Townes (Maryknoll, N.Y.: Orbis Books, 1997), 15-16.

that a person like me could reject the false choice between being treated as a perpetual foreigner in my own birth place, on the one hand, and relinquishing my identity for someone else's ill-fitting and impossible Anglo-American one on the other. . . . My American education offered nothing about Chicanos and Latinos, and most of what was taught about African and Native Americans was distorted to justify their oppression and vindicate their oppressors.[37]

As Kim realized, just as we share in our mixed heritage and our situation of oppression, so do we share in survival against all odds in opposition to the dehumanization and marginalization imposed upon persons of color of whatever heritage by those of the dominant culture of the United States. Rather than seeking to be more like them, we need to teach them to be open to a more holistic, inclusive, and communitarian way of living and working in the world. Rather than competition and individual success at the expense of others, we should be seeking to develop avenues of communication and paths of dialogue that will enrich us all, not just a few. Such a mode of being in the world would certainly be more in keeping with the true model of church given to us by Jesus in his mission and ministry of love, compassion, and community.

We who are persons of color, historically "non-persons" in U.S. society and in our own church, are now in a position to help others learn how to become more Christlike. We who have had to fight to maintain our identities, our cultures, and our languages against those who would blot us out, washing away our very memories of self, recognize that we cannot do the same. We learned of ourselves and others in order to survive. We must now offer the hand of friendship to those who turned away from us time and again. We must do this, not simply for their sake or ours but for the sake of our community, the people of God, who are truly the body of Christ. The indigenous people of South Africa, under the charismatic leadership of Nelson Mandela, have shown us the value of turning the other cheek, not in fear or in submission but in proud recognition of our own strength, instead of demanding an eye for an eye and a tooth for a tooth, too often the cowardly bully's way. But this must be done as equals, standing before the table of the Lord with all of our gifts acknowledged and welcomed, not as recipients of charity from others.

Today, it is our responsibility to rebuild our church so that it truly reflects the many images and likenesses of God, which God created, and to rebuild our society, which the church so much reflects, in ways that are both healing and holy, attempting to bind up our nation's and our Lord's wounds caused by a blind and ignorant fear of those unlike ourselves. These wounds are caused by racism, classism, sexism, ethnocentrism, homophobia, and all of the other ills that plague our lives today. But to do so requires that those who formerly were the givers open themselves up to being receivers as well, in humility and faith.

---

[37] Elaine Kim, cited in ibid., 16.

CONCLUSION: WOMANIST HEALING

Womanist theologians have been instrumental in beginning the healing that is necessary by recognizing and challenging the absence of their voices and presence from the prophetic theologies of liberation that emerged in the aftermath of the Civil Rights Movement. We have experienced oppression as women, as women of color, as women who are poor. This triple oppression has caused us to realize that the struggle for liberation is incomplete as long as anyone is oppressed. Thus, our struggle crosses the artificial barriers that have heretofore prevented a multilayered dialogue among all people. We seek to become united with men and women across the United States in order to rebuild the shattered and dying communities that once sustained and nurtured so many of us. Recognizing that, as women, we have been instrumental in educating the children of our communities and handing down our faith, our stories, our traditions, we must now seek to teach them to love rather than to fear the neighbor, to accept rather than just to tolerate difference, and to recognize the diversity that was created and blessed by God and that makes of our lives the ongoing miracle of the unfolding of God's salvific plan for us all.

The voices of those once silenced and invisible are now breaking forth in songs of joy and sorrow, in shouts of praise of God and critique of the status quo, in prayers that uplift but that also call for the justice and righteousness of God to break forth within our midst. Today the "non-persons" are speaking out on issues that concern the lives of us all, calling for our church and our nation to live up to their self-proclaimed mission as sources of salvation and liberation in this world and the next. Women throughout the United States are recognizing that they are united by more than gender alone and that their social, economic, or political status should have no bearing on their ability to work together to bring about a new and better world for all of our children.

Like Mary, we too proclaim the dawning of a new era in which all will be made whole, but, unlike her, we need not begin our task alone. Just as she was eventually joined by Mary and Martha, Mary of Magdalene, and so many other women who saw in her son the hope for their future and the future of the world, so must we look at every child born to us or in our community, whether male or female, of any race or ethnicity, as the one who will remake this world into God's world, where we will all share in the joy of peace, justice, freedom, and God's righteousness.

We must be about the developing of a contextual theology for the United States that reflects the voices of all United Statesians. The foundation has been laid by the many liberation theologies that now exist both in the United States and around the world. These theologies are still needed, for they serve as a source of empowerment for those doing them. At the same time, however, we must be in dialogue across theological lines, recognizing that the center no longer holds. There are many centers brought into creation by those on the margins who refuse to remain there but unite with others also marginalized to share life-giving and life-changing stories, histories, and strategies.

We speak from within the contexts of our lives, which have been painful but also sources of strength, courage, anger, and therefore hope. We challenge our church not just to hear our raised voices but to listen to our actual words. For we are stepping forward to take our rightful places in a church and a world that we have helped to create, as the beloved children of God, forged in a fiery furnace, coming forth through the flames as true gold—a cosmic race that holds within itself all of the promise of the United States.

We know that our God is with all of us. That our words are inspired by the God of Abraham and Isaac and all of the heroes and sheroes of our collective peoples. That God calls us forth to serve not as barriers but as bridges that cross over racial, ethnic, and gender lines; that do away with class and religious restrictions; that allow us not only to speak to each other as equals but also to share each others' lives, entering into each others' communities, learning of them, and returning to our own bringing others along with us to learn, share, and teach in turn.

In this way, a new way of thinking about, talking about, and living out God's word shall emerge in the places where we have been broken and cast aside, forged into a renewed unity of hearts, minds, and spirits. It will foster a new theology, one that emerges from the true histories and experiences of all the people in this land, bringing us to a fuller understanding of the One who walked the earth two thousand years ago.

Jesus walked, talked, ate, and shared with everyone with whom he came into contact. He condemned no one, seeking only to heal, to encourage, and to foster hope, love, and compassion for others. He gave up his life so that we might live, but not to live lives of passive co-sufferers, because his agony and death were once and for all. We are called to condemn injustice, to care for those unable to care for themselves, to build a new and better world out of the crumbling, shattered shell of a world in which we presently dwell. To do so, we must be willing to become reconciled with past hurts and those who inflicted them, to hold out hands that welcome and offer love, to build communities that nurture rather than destroy, recognizing that we are truly one people of one God, howsoever named. We must start not just with the children but with all people, whoever and wherever they may be. In the words of the black bishops of the United States,

> We must work with all who strive to make available the fruits of creation to all of God's people everywhere. It was in chains that our parents were brought to these shores and in violence were we maintained in bondage. Let us who are the children of pain be now a bridge of reconciliation. Let us who are the offspring of violence become the channels of compassion. Let us, the sons and daughters of bondage, be the bringers of peace.[38]

It is time to be about the building of the true "kin-dom" of God Almighty.

---

[38] *What We Have Seen and Heard.*

3

Womanist Theology and Black Theology

Conversational Envisioning
of an Unfinished Dream

DWIGHT N. HOPKINS
LINDA E. THOMAS

Since 1997 we have been co-teaching regularly a three-hour course, once a week, called "Black Theology and Womanist Theology," both at the University of Chicago Divinity School and at Garrett-Evangelical Theological Seminary. To our knowledge, this is the first time that a black male theologian and a womanist theologian have undertaken such a joint project. While the course title has remained the same, the plethora of new publications by womanist and black male theologians force us to rearrange periodically the syllabus and required readings. In this manner the course remains fresh, and we are able to feed ourselves intellectually with the latest texts. The core methodology of the course centers on *conversation*.

First, the course is an interdisciplinary conversation among theology, anthropology, political economy, and African-American studies. Second, the syllabus itself is an interrogation of five dimensions common to both theological perspectives. We spend two weeks each on the notions of race, gender, class, sexual orientation, and ecology. Third, we divide each of the two-week segments into conversational format. The first week focuses on a womanist theology or black male theology stance on the particular category assigned for that week. If we begin with race and the black male theologian's voice, the readings for the first week come from the corpus of black theology. The second week on race then includes books and articles from the vantage of womanists. Thus each week is a different voice in an ongoing conversation throughout the ten-week academic quarter. Fourth, during each class session itself the womanist voice is presented and then the black male theologian's, or vice versa. Finally, the womanist and black theologian voices together are put into challenging conversations with all the students during each class session. In each meeting all students are required, at some point, to contribute their ideas to the discourse.

It might be helpful to examine a typical classroom session. If the topic is gender, then the womanist theologian starts with a lecture, not directly on the assigned womanist readings regarding gender but rather on a social-scientific definition of gender accompanied by a theological interpretation. The assumption is that all students have completed the readings and gathered their own burning questions for that day. Consequently, the lecture offers a broad contextual backdrop that puts into conversation social-science and theological points of view on gender. Next, students enter the dialogue by offering clarification queries on the lecture, agreements and disagreements, and assessments of the lecture based on their personal experiences and theoretical knowledge base. The black male theologian, after this part of the dialogue, leads the class discussion on the gender reading assignments. Here a process of critical and close reading of the texts unfolds.

For instance, we might take a paragraph or two and engage in deep and thoughtful debate over this pericope. Usually we stop for a class break; during this brief period of time, the professors converse about questions and process from the first half of the class, sizing up key points to explore as well as student participation.

After the break the professors debate each other regarding the gender topic and bring into play their personal experiences, the assigned readings, their own personal intellectual expertise, and other bodies of knowledge. Finally, students again enter the conversation and offer their conclusions on what has just been debated and other issues relevant to that day's topic.

As a result of pursuing the conversational method in this co-taught course, we have discovered some ongoing ways to bring critical questions and reflections to black theology and womanist theology for the new millennium. This dynamic leads us to the following challenging theological visions for each discipline, as we pursue "the unfinished dream."

RACE

For black male theologians and womanist theologians, race continues to persist as a defining reality in the struggle of African-American people for full humanity.[1] The daily challenge of living out their lives fully as children of God, enjoying the gifts God has granted them, is the primary dynamic that glues black folk together on several levels. Regardless of denomination, gender, class, sexual orientation, occupation, professional level, and political orientation, race

[1] On race and theology, see J. H. Cone, *Black Theology and Black Power* (Maryknoll, N.Y.: Orbis Books, 1997; reprint of the 1969 original); D. N. Hopkins, *Shoes That Fit Our Feet: Sources for a Constructive Black Theology* (Maryknoll, N.Y.: Orbis Books, 1993), chap. 1; K. Brown Douglass, *The Black Christ* (Maryknoll, N.Y.: Orbis Books, 1994); and J. M. Terrell, *Power in the Blood: The Cross in the African American Experience* (Maryknoll, N.Y.: Orbis Books, 1998).

matters in America. The "mattering" of race entails a dimension of difference and a dimension of theology.[2]

Race concerns a biological and a sociological viewpoint. We are all born with certain characteristics that facilitate classification in one (and sometimes more than one) group. Phenotype, hair texture, lip size, nose shape, eye pigmentation, skin color—all imply, prima facie, certain racial locations. At the same time, especially in the U.S. context of a highly charged but often unspoken color hierarchy, race is a social construction. For instance, it is assumed in the United States that black or African blood automatically makes one a black American. Similarly, though the black race probably has the most variegated rainbow colors of any group, still all those colors indicate what it means to be black in America. There are many African-American individuals who, in other global contexts, could pass as southern European or Latin American or Middle Eastern or certain dark Asian peoples. Yet, the system of racial hierarchy in the United States locks in its citizens based on color gradation. Whites occupy the apex, with light-skin Asians, light-skin Latinos/Hispanics, dark-skin Asians, and brown and black communities following suit. Even within African-American groupings, the five or six different color shades situate the near-white skin to black-skin members at opposite extremes on a value scale.

Prejudice exists when one race (determined biologically and/or sociologically) feels that it is superior to another race simply because of perceived racial difference. Prejudice can be benign, a sort of racial nationalism of self-affirmation and self-preference of one's own kind. Or it can facilitate negative energy over against racial difference; that is, one can have an attitude that reclassifies another race into a lower or subhuman racial status. In its negative manifestation prejudice can lead to verbal assaults or harmful physical acts. Prejudice in this regard is associated more with individual behavior. For instance, lighter-skin blacks can express prejudice toward darker-skin African Americans.

Racism is the ability and the power of one race to implement negative prejudice against another race. In the American context racism is seen in the maiming and killing of Jews, blacks, and other people of color. It reveals itself when people in power use their power against black folk, because those with power do not want African-American lifestyles, cultural differences, and potential power holders to have access to resources that God has given all people for communal ownership, distribution, and use. Racism is prejudice plus power to implement.

White supremacy is the most concentrated form of racism in the United States. It is the systematic strategy—conscious and unconscious, intentional or by force of habit—that institutionalizes power in the hands of white people as a group. It is no accident that every major institution in American society is either headed

---

[2] On race beyond an explicit theological focus, see L. Liebermann, "The Debate over Race: A Study in the Sociology of Knowledge," *Phylon* 29 (1968): 127-41; F. Boas, *Race, Language, and Culture* (New York: Free Press, 1966); C. West, M. Omni, and A. Hacker, *Two Nations: Black and White, Separate, Hostile, Unequal* (New York: Scribner, 1992); and R. Frankenberg, *White Women, Race Matters: The Social Construction of Whiteness* (Minneapolis, Minn.: University of Minnesota Press, 1993).

by whites (mostly white men) or backed by whites with decisive resources. The culture of white supremacy is quite sinister, because it points to the human kindness of individual whites while perpetuating a way of being in America where there is an absolute glass ceiling for people of African descent in every major institution in society. For the majority of black folk, it seems that the founding documents of the republic speak in glowing and encouraging terms about salutary human interaction. But, like the emperor-without-any-clothes story, black people are not blind to the systemic and institutional reality that deploys the fullest expression of race, prejudice, and racism in a national dynamic of negative affirmative action for whites simply because they are white.

Moreover, white supremacy often portrays itself as fair play for individual initiative. With this logic, each individual black, like each individual white, has a level playing field and a similar starting point. Yet, in reality, the playing field and the starting points are rigged in favor of white supremacy. The system defines qualifications, criteria, and norms from a white, European-American perspective. The system defines itself as true success. Those who are already part of that system are, by definition, exemplars of success and civilization.

Furthermore, white supremacy is a system that, through historical amnesia or a revisionist hand, denies the reality of history. The system was intentionally constructed so that some would monopolize resources based on skin color while others would be pushed aside or occupy servant or manual labor roles. Native Americans lived with the land prior to European colonization. Subsequently, through force and then immigration laws—laws that allowed Europeans relocation privileges over Africans, Asians, and Latin Americans—a white supremacy system solidified itself. Again, we are reminded that U.S. history is not absent of humane white citizens whose intentions flowed from the highest ideals of human civility or Christianity. However, individuals and progressive communities for justice have never altered radically the entire system. The history and current force of habit of white supremacy represent a confluence of interlocking institutions that tend to give white people the benefit of the doubt.

Again, one only has to ask why every major institution of power, influence, decision-making, and force (within the mainstream of America) is owned, controlled, defined, and determined by individual or groups of white citizens. Is it because God ordained it that way? Is it by means of nature's survival-of-the-fittest natural selection? Is it because of intelligence, that is, because some have more reasoning faculties than others? Is it by fate, that is, the fate of time and random selection responsible for racial configurations? Is it due to some objective aesthetic trait that some have over others? Is it an inherent creative genius pertinent to one race and not others? Indeed, one can only conclude that the emperor has no clothes. White supremacy is power institutionalized categorically.

The theological good news is that human beings, not God, created and participate in the system of white supremacy. God did not originate this evil, nor does God intend for this evil to exist. If humans are the authors of such a satanic expression, then humans, answering the divine calling for liberation and freedom, can dismantle white supremacy, remove the force of habit privileges for one race, and establish social relations where all races own, control, and distribute God's resources communally. Restated, the hope for civilized race relations in America surfaces from the depths of a belief that institutions and social relations in the United States are human-made and, consequently, can be altered fundamentally by human effort. Hence, the power of God to surpass all human-created realities inspires oppressed black folk, other people of color, and all progressive people to struggle to overthrow white-skin privileges. Then, for the first time in U.S. history, we would experience a racial democracy.

Coupled with the realization that there is nothing divine about the racial hierarchy in the United States, we have to grasp the initial point of creation. God created all of humanity to live in harmony. The end goal, the *telos*, likewise draws all humanity toward harmonious living. Yet, the evil of white supremacy has subverted both sacred creation and holy goals. Whites with power redefined black as evil. Hoarding communal resources as monopolized private property, powerful white families defied divine creation and its *telos* and crafted one of the most sinister racial asymmetries in human history. Thus, white supremacy constitutes a large part of the fall of humankind.

Nevertheless, the fall did not eliminate absolutely the sacred original purpose and long-term goal. The mark or internal implantation of God's created racial harmony based on justice within each person, race, and among races holds true even today. The sin of white supremacy did not and does not eradicate what God has created—the African origins of black Americans. Consequently, the fall has not erased the spark of racial harmony inclusive of African lineage. The vision of authentic racial sisterhood and brotherhood persists within the breast and make-up of all peoples, regardless of color. Moreover, white-skin privileges lack the ability to subvert the *telos* of the Creator. In spite of all apparent material and spiritual manifestations to the effect that the racial hierarchy of America seems permanent, God's future consummation of an equalized racial harmony grounded in all races communally owning divine resources will prevail. Nothing is static. Systems can be changed radically. What seems everlasting in human eyes is fluid for God. Transformation is inevitable.

In addition, the incarnation of Jesus Christ among visible, material, flesh-and-blood humanity indicates that God has not left the "little ones" on earth by themselves. Jesus Christ is black with the black poor. Indeed, the historical Jesus would be classified as an African American phenotypically. Many black scholars, especially in the biblical field, have substantiated this argument.[3] The more the black poor and other freedom-loving people perceive the implications of this historical reality, the more clear will God's intent for racial harmony be. The false portrayal of Jesus as white has been a major racial stumbling block to racial harmony today. The predominant notion conceives of and paints pictures

---

[3] W. A. McCray, *The Black Presence in the Bible, Volumes One and Two* (Chicago: Black Light Fellowship, 1990); J. V. Crockett, *Teaching Scripture from an African-American Perspective* (Nashville, Tenn.: Disciples Resources, 1990); S. B. Reid, *Experience and Tradition: A Primer in Black Biblical Hermeneutics* (Nashville, Tenn.: Abingdon Press, 1990); C. H. Felder, *Troubling Biblical Waters: Race, Class, and Family* (Maryknoll, N.Y.: Orbis Books, 1989); and C. H. Felder, ed., *Stony the Road We Trod* (Minneapolis, Minn.: Fortress Press, 1991).

of Jesus as white. Until this theological aesthetic heresy is rooted out of American Christianity and its civil religious culture, white supremacy will remain a wall separating the beautiful rainbow colors of U.S. citizenry. In the Christian scriptures of the Bible, the only whites present are the Roman colonizers and exploiters from Europe. The historical Jesus was a dark-skin human being with hair like wool and skin like bronze. Today's ongoing depiction of a white Jesus in Christian churches and homes perpetuates the falsehood of the historical Jesus and substantiates the false ideology and structure that the system of white supremacy receives from a mythological white Jesus. Despite claims that race does not matter, it does play a profound role in religion. If this were not the case, there would not be such virulent and visceral reactions to the truth of portraying Jesus with an Afro hairstyle and dark skin.

Like the historical Jesus, the Christ of faith carries profound theological resolution for the sin of white supremacy and the future of racial harmony. Christ's Spirit today manifests itself among those poor African Americans, and others, who are struggling to make a way out of no way to practice their God-given full humanity. Because God chose to empty the divine self in the poverty of a manger, in the form of a black historical Jesus, and among the poor and outcast of Palestine, the Spirit of the same Jesus reveals itself as the Christ of faith among the African-American poor today. The contemporary Spirit pursues the clear original sacred revelation. Jesus, God's incarnation, chose with intention, consciousness, and specificity to dwell with the poor of his day, not the rich and powerful. So too Jesus's Spirit as the Christ of faith undertakes, with direct purpose, to be with the black poor and others. The revelation of the Spirit portends universal liberation for all colors of people. By empowering and laboring with the black poor and others, Christ seeks to transform the asymmetry of the institutions and systems of white supremacy, so that all will be equal and own God's resources communally. The more the poor pursue liberation as the norm, the closer will all of humankind approach the divine *telos* on earth as it is in heaven. Affirmation of African heritage, black folk's right of self-determination and self-identity, and communal stewardship complement one another.

GENDER

When we engage the notion of *gender*,[4] we do so with the following in mind: gender is a socially constructed category. By this we mean that it is not

---

[4] On gender, see E. Townes, ed., *Embracing the Spirit: Womanist Perspectives on Hope, Salvation, and Transformation* (Maryknoll, N.Y.: Orbis Books, 1997); D. N. Hopkins, "Black Women's Spirituality of Funk," in Hopkins, *Shoes That Fit Our Feet*; G. Baker-Fletcher, "New Males? Same Ole Same Ole" and "Taking Sisters Seriously," in G. Baker-Fletcher, *Xodus: An African American Male Journey* (Minneapolis, Minn.: Fortress Press, 1996); J. H. Cone, "Black Theology, Black Churches, and Black Women," in J. H. Cone, *For My People: Black Theology and the Black Church, Where Have We Been and Where Are We Going?* (Maryknoll, N.Y.: Orbis Books, 1984); and J. H. Evans, "Black Theology and Black Feminism," *Journal of Religious Thought* 38/1 (Spring-Summer 1981): 43-53.

a biological category; different societies define what it is and proceed to social-
ize females and males into accepted gender roles. Gender is not formed overnight,
nor is it ever a finished product; it is dynamic and subject to the ongoing formation of human culture. It is dynamic in the sense that the cultures of diverse
groups of people are not static; cultures continually modify themselves. In the
process of such modification, cultures adjust the definition of gender. Since
socialization takes place in myriad human cultures, this means that there is no
absolute denotation of gender. In effect, there is no right or wrong definition of
gender, because gender results from how each society enculturates people into
gender roles. Thus, all human cultures provide the content of what is considered
female or male. Society uses a variety of sources or means of socializing genders. Economic systems, family roles, school curricula, sports activities, visual
and audio entertainment, jobs and professions, church and religious institutions,
news media, language, myths, rituals, laws—all these contribute to the process
of what it means to be female or male in any given society.

By *sex* we signify the biological designation that human beings receive at
birth. Thus, sex is a biological construction based on genitalia. In other words, a
man and a woman are distinguished in the area of sex by their distinctive biological births.

The normal usage of the gender rubric *he* to refer to God is derived from
patriarchal notions of the male gender as automatically including the female
gender. However, this attempt at inclusivity is really false; it is exclusive. For
example, *man* or *mankind* in most English-speaking cultures incorrectly denotes universal humankind and thus includes both genders, even though women's
gender construction and biology differ from those of men. We must ask for the
reason why one gender has come to designate two different expressions of gender, when such demarcation is really false and exclusive. Clearly, the answer
has to do with the underlying meaning structures behind a given culture's social
construction of man or maleness.

We believe that a logical and theological solution to moving beyond a male
construction of God—or, in other words, moving beyond a delimitation of the
Deity as male—is to include female and other expressions to reference God.
Hence, true inclusivity instructs us to expand our language about God to embrace male and female in order to name God's meaning in the lives of all human
beings. If we are free to use the gender of *he* to describe our experiences with
God, we are also at liberty to designate God as *she*. Both *he* and *she*, as applied
to gender categories, are socially constructed. In other words, there is nothing
sacred in using the male gender when referring to the divine. The gender of our
ultimate concern is both female and male. The way we presently signify God
underscores the propensity we have toward generalizing maleness as a classification of God for both male and female; in contrast, expansive language requires
the deployment of all genders when depicting God.

The link of gender construction to sex also requires us to portray God as *she* as
well as *he*, because God's unfathomable nature does not have a biology. Human
beings—that is, those who are created in God's image as female and male—are
concrete manifestations of God and consequently reveal God's presence.

Given this set of definitions and our concern about the relation of theology to the black church, we pose the following questions: What would the African-American church look like if it took gender as seriously as it does race? To take gender seriously mandates a close examination of our naming of God. Why is it still so difficult for the black church to use expansive language about God?

Part of the reason is that women, who comprise the overwhelming majority of the black church, continue to use exclusive language. Many black church women (65 percent to 80 percent of the church) continue to call God "he" both during worship and in the course of their everyday affairs. If we believe that black women are made in the image of God, then why do we not also call God "she"? This is a profound theological question bordering on heresy—that is, the curtailing of God's power of self-revelation only to *he*. Such an incomplete grasp of God's being and doing provides a favorable condition for black male clergy and laymen to maintain male privilege. Likewise, we discover similar contradictions among some womanist scholars. All womanist theologians have moved beyond the sexist sin of calling God only "he" in their writings, but some fall back on the negative dimensions of black culture—a patriarchal comfort zone—and use only "he" for God in their preaching.

One might ask why there is such a debate about language in the black church, when there are so many other pressing material issues. Expansive language has to do with the construction of the black self and, hence, is a foundational issue of *imago dei*. We dare not ignore language, or else we will find both black men and black women slaves to a white male patriarchal system rather than experiencing the male and female creation standing equally before God. Until this authenticity is the case, the whole black race suffers. Moreover, while it is true that male and female are different and that God made us to complement one another, this must be done from the strongest position possible. Equality is that position.

Gender is not simply a woman's issue. It denotes both male and female. As a result, a theological task for black men is to reconfigure what it means to be a healthy, Christian, black man in patriarchal and racist American society. In the socialization of the black male gender in the United States, black men undergo at least two processes. First, white society defines the black male as subordinate to white males. Consequently, the black male is socialized as a man, but one subject to the white supremacy of another male gender. Second, within the black community black men are socialized to adopt the normative definition of the male gender established by patriarchal white culture. In a word, the force-of-habit arrogance of sexist white culture, when adopted by black men, translates into black male patriarchy. So sexist black men within the black community routinely expect and actually enjoy male privileges over black women and children.

A negative byproduct of adopting and implementing the patriarchy of distorted white culture is that too often black men redirect their frustration with white men with power away from the system of white patriarchy and onto women, children, and other black men in their community. What cannot be carried out creatively against the white system is too often acted out within the African-American community. To re-vision a new black male requires several approaches.

First, black men (and women) have to realize that gender does apply to and speaks about the male gender. Gender also includes men. Therefore, when the notion of gender surfaces, black men should not think or feel that now it is time for black women to ventilate the problems confronting them. Usually, when gender topics arise, black men remain silent and black women begin to talk. However, both are wrong. Both genders need to be involved actively in reconceptualizing what healthy female and male genders are.

Second, black men need to experience and have faith in a black God. Part of the rage burning within the African-American male psyche is the conscious or unconscious worship of a white divinity. One cannot be anything but angry at or overly accommodating to white patriarchal culture, if the God whom black men worship on their knees looks just like some of the people oppressing them. Hence, a black God enhances the psychological self-empowerment of African-American men. And since more and more literature indicates that the historical Jesus would be considered a black man today, from both a healthy psychology and historical fact, black men are compelled to worship a black God.

Third, African-American men need to experience and have faith in a black God who is both mother and father. All black men should use the simultaneous salutations of "Our mother and father, who art in heaven" and "Dear mother God and father God." If God is a spirit and is not defined by a male biology, then God can be envisioned as a woman and a man. When African-American men take the lead in praying to mother God, not only is this the correct faith and theological position to hold, but also a liberating experience for each individual African-American male who chooses to serve a female (and male) divinity. It is freeing to surrender one's all not only to a father God but also to a mother God.

Fourth, African-American men are made in God's image. God loves them. And, because of divine love, they should love themselves and those in the black community with whom they are the most intimate and the most familiar. When black men feel and know that God loves them, they can feel good about themselves and love themselves. It is usually when black men feel bad about themselves—especially when they react to the system of white supremacy—that they are aggressive against women and children and other black men.

Fifth, in addition to dealing with internal demons within their souls, spirits, and psyches, African-American men are called by God to construct relationships and a new society on earth based on communal ownership over and communal distribution of God's resources. God has called them to a vocation of liberation, which suggests the practice of living as if they were free and equal. Liberation entails ongoing struggle against the structures of racism, sexism, monopoly capitalism, heterosexism, and the thirst for power and control over others. To be free, consequently, is to live one's life as if one were really liberated from these demonic systems. To be equal is to live out the beauty of one's own black and African identity as a gift from a black God. Moreover, to be equal is to claim one's space and the resources around oneself as a divinely ordained steward of sacred resources. To be equal is to share the wealth in one's country, community, and family. Simultaneously, one struggles for communal ownership and distribution of God's resources while embodying certain humane values toward one's wife and children—respect, trust, support, honesty and accountability, responsible parenting, shared responsibility, negotiation and fairness, and non-threatening behavior.

Finally, redefining the black male gender includes learning how to identify emotions and how to be vulnerable emotionally with wives, girlfriends, children, and other black men. In summation, to redefine the black male gender is to have a positive, active posture, or way of life, marked by one's ultimate allegiance to one's creation in God's image, the love of God, and the vocation of treating oneself as a child of God. Black men need to continue to develop healthy everyday practices spiritually, physically, intellectually, sexually, and emotionally.

SEXUAL ORIENTATION

In addition, black people's vision of and struggle for full humanity would have us appreciate one's sexual orientation.[5] How can African-American Christians have constructive reflection about human sexuality? For many African-American men and women, any conversation about sexuality is taboo. As we approach even more complex ways of being in the world, we will find that, as people of African descent, we have no choice but to engage topics such as human sexuality and sexual orientation. To be indifferent toward, to avoid, to deny, or to ignore such a central issue of human life would be similar to bypassing the black color of our skin or forgetting that we are female and male. Each characteristic of who we are (for example, race, gender, sexual orientation) makes a difference about who we are in the world and how others interact with us and we with them.

Furthermore, Christianity moves us to contemplate what it means to be fashioned in the image of the divine. If we believe that each person is made in God's image, then it follows that every person has sacred worth and is to be loved and affirmed as embodying the Holy Spirit. Also, if we profess that whosoever believes in Jesus Christ will have salvation, then how can we summarily dismiss, as we often do, lesbians and gays as unworthy of this grace? More specifically, what are the dynamics of the gap between our beliefs and our actions? For instance, why is it that many black lesbians and gays find that they are not welcomed in many African-American churches and are referred to as deviant, sick, immoral, and sinful? Why is it easier for heterosexual black Christians to

---

[5] On sexual orientation, see R. Hill, "Who Are We for Each Other?: Sexism, Sexuality, and Womanist Thought," in *Black Theology: A Documentary History, Volume 2: 1980-1992,* ed. J. H. Cone and G. S. Wilmore (Maryknoll, N.Y.: Orbis Books, 1993), 345-51; K. Brown Douglass, *Sexuality and the Black Church: A Womanist Perspective* (Maryknoll, N.Y.: Orbis Books, 1999); C. J. Sanders, "Christian Ethics and Theology in Womanist Perspective," in Cone and Wilmore, *Black Theology: A Documentary History, Volume 2: 1980-1992,* 336-44; B. Smith, "Liberation As Risky Business," in *Changing Conversations: Religious Reflection and Cultural Analysis,* ed. D. N. Hopkins and S. Greeve Davaney (New York: Routledge, 1996), 207-33; P. J. Gomes, *The Good Book: Reading the Bible with Mind and Heart* (New York: W. Morrow, 1996); E. Farajaje-Jones, "Breaking Silence: Toward an In-the-Life Theology," in Cone and Wilmore, *Black Theology: A Documentary History, Volume 2: 1980-1992,* 139-59.

focus on the so-called profane behavior of homosexuals than it is to examine the base ways of heterosexuals? Indeed, heterosexists would rather cling to the idea that homosexuality is wrong than to consider the problem as the "phobic reaction of heterosexual people."[6]

African-American Christians must talk about sexual orientation and appreciate the fact that there are varieties of sexuality. Just as God created texture when it comes to race and gender, so the Creator chose to differentiate sexual orientations. What is sexual orientation? By sexual orientation we denote the gender to which we are attracted naturally. It is that deep sense of knowing toward whom we have deep and earnest feelings; it is the gender with whom we desire to be involved emotionally, erotically, and sexually. Typically, human beings do not choose their sexual orientation but rather become aware of it over time. It is important for black Christians to learn about and understand the diversity of human sexual orientations. Black Christian heterosexuals must come to value and understand sisters and brothers who are of other sexual orientations. Moreover, it is extremely important to recognize that, while the issue of race/racism has been a basis for discrimination against African Americans in general, African Americans who are lesbian and gay find themselves further marginalized. Barbara Smith traces the conundrum of life for black lesbians and gays:

> So I think that one of the challenges we face in trying to raise the issue of lesbian and gay identity with the Black community is to try to get our people to understand that they can indeed oppress someone after having spent a life of being oppressed. That's a very hard transition to make, but it's one we have to make if we want our whole community to be liberated.[7]

It is a heavy burden to experience loathing from white culture because one's skin happens to be black. Similarly, the burden is excruciating for lesbians and gays who encounter discrimination in the black community because of homosexuality. It is harder to realize that the same sisters and brothers who experience the pain of racism now proceed to label, in the name of Jesus, lesbians and gays with derogatory terms.

Black heterosexuals can be theologically progressive on the issue of race and regressive on the issue of "in the life" lifestyles of black lesbians and gays, many of whom were raised in the black church and are still members. Sometimes aloud and sometimes in their own minds, black church congregants declare: "I don't care if they come to church, but they don't have to flaunt their stuff in our faces." Basically, this position sets up a climate in which lesbians and gays can participate in worship only on the terms set by heterosexuals. Not only does such a position establish a dangerous dichotomy, but it also forces gays and lesbians to live inauthentically. In other words, it forces gays and lesbians in the

---

    [6] H. Wishik and C. Pierce, *Sexual Orientation and Identity: Heterosexual, Lesbian, Gay, and Bisexual Journeys* (Laconia, N.H.: New Dynamics Publications, 1991), 48.

    [7] J. L. Gomez and B. Smith, "Taking the Home out of Homophobia: Black Lesbian Health," in *My Heart: A Lesbian of Color Anthology*, ed. M. Silvera (Toronto: Sister Vision Press, 1991), 41.

black community to live as heterosexual persons in order to avoid rejection as well as physical and emotional harm. If they were to "become" heterosexual and to accept being forced into something which they are not, homosexuals would be committing a sin—the denial of God's presence in them. How can Christian heterosexuals label homosexuals as unacceptable to God when God has already accepted them?

We live in a heterosexually dominated society, and too many of us participate in black churches that perpetuate bias and discrimination against African-American gays and lesbians.[8] When black Christians behave in this fashion, we accept hetero-patriarchal notions of sexual orientation and, as a result, participate in a destructive system of devaluing human beings who are made in God's image. No black person can attain his or her fully ordained humanity while oppressing or remaining silent on the marginalized status of another. Our vocation is a calling of justice and love as God extends compassion and liberation to all.

ECOLOGY

Why should the black church have an active vision about ecology and the environmental movement?[9] Is not that topic an idle and frivolous pastime of spoiled, white, middle-class activists? Unfortunately, too many African Americans hold this view, and too many are not even aware of the ecological threats to the black community. In a word, those who speak on the issue tend to associate it with activists outside of the life-and-death challenges of African Americans. Besides, most black folk lack knowledge of the complexity of the ecology's well-being in relation to black humanity. However, the earth is the Lord's and the fullness thereof. We are to be stewards of God's creation. The call to be caretakers of creation is a holy calling, something we unfortunately let monopoly capitalism determine.

Accordingly, black people find themselves dealing with another whole level of atrocities that pollute our neighborhoods with toxic fumes and waste heaps. Capitalism has determined that the neighborhoods of poor black people can be the dumping grounds for deadly chemicals and other lethal toxins that shorten our lives. We have to be concerned about water, air, animals, plants, and land in order for black humanity to have a future, a viable future. Environmental racism is alive and well, particularly in the poorest communities. What will it mean to speak of black pride, economics, politics, culture, sexual orientation, and coalescing with other progressive people of color if we sit idly by as Mother

---

[8] Two positive counter-examples among black churches are the Allen Temple Baptist Church (Oakland, California; J. Alfred Smith Sr., senior pastor) and Trinity United Church of Christ (Chicago). Since 1979 Jeremiah A. Wright Jr. (Trinity's senior pastor) has been preaching about the humanity of black homosexuals.

[9] The only sustained black theology or womanist treatment of ecology is that of Karen Baker-Fletcher, *Sisters of the Dust, Sisters of the Spirit: Womanist Wordings on God and Creation* (Minneapolis, Minn.: Augsburg/Fortress Press, 1998).

Earth dies? The *telos* of full humanity for all, especially the poor, includes a healthy earth, wind, fire, and water.

God created all of the visible and invisible world to be in relation, balance, and harmony. As profit-oriented enterprises begin to pursue wealth over an integrated approach to the ecology, the natural interdependency of humans on nature and nature on humans weakens and, in some instances, dies. American Indians have consistently attempted to remind us and teach us about living with Mother Earth.[10] For them, the land is part of the Spirit, and we are part of the land. To destroy the *ecos*, therefore, is to destroy oneself. No one can hide from the damning effects of human hubris against the land. Nuclear tests on dark-skin Pacific Islander peoples affect the ozone levels, fish, ocean floor, and wind currents of the globe. No one can hide, not even the small group of families controlling the world's wealth.[11]

CLASS

The question of economically poor blacks living in the primary monopoly finance capitalist country in human history is the decisive question for both womanist and black male theologians.[12] All else in God-talk and God-walk stands or falls on how Jesus Christ calls us to measure our everyday living by whether

---

[10] See G. E. Tinker, *Missionary Conquest: The Gospel of Native American Cultural Genocide* (Minneapolis, Minn.: Fortress Press, 1993).

[11] For instance, the richest 20 percent of the world's people takes in 82.7 percent of the total world income, while the poorest 20 percent receives only 1.4 percent. The richest 225 individuals in the world constitute a combined wealth over $1 trillion. This is equal to the annual income of the poorest 47 percent of the world's population. The three richest people on earth own assets surpassing the combined gross domestic product of the 48 least developed countries. See *Forbes* (October 12, 1998): 4; and *As the South Goes* 6/1 (Spring 1999), a publication of the Institute for the Elimination of Poverty and Genocide, 9 Gammon Ave. S.W., Atlanta, GA 30315.

[12] On class, see L. E. Thomas, *Under the Canopy: Ritual Process and Spiritual Resilience in South Africa* (Columbia, S.C.: University of South Carolina Press, 1999); L. E. Thomas, "Womanist Theology, Epistemology, and a New Anthropological Paradigm," *Cross Currents* 48/4 (Winter-Spring 1998-99): 492; M. Riggs, *Awake, Arise and Act: A Womanist Call for Black Liberation* (Cleveland, Ohio: The Pilgrim Press, 1994); K. Canon, "Racism and Economics: The Perspective of Oliver C. Cox," in *Katie's Canon: Womanism and the Soul of the Black Community* (New York: Continuum, 1995); P. Hill Collins, *Black Feminist Thought: Knowledge, Consciousness, and the Politics of Empowerment* (London: HarperCollins, 1990), chap. 3; D. N. Hopkins, "Malcolm and Martin: To Change the World," in Hopkins, *Shoes That Fit Our Feet*; C. West, "Black Theology and Marxist Thought," in *Black Theology: A Documentary History, Volume 1: 1966-1979*, ed. J. H. Cone and G. S. Wilmore (Maryknoll, N.Y.: Orbis Books, 1993), 409-24; and C. West, "Black Theology of Liberation as Critique of Capitalist Civilization," in Cone and Wilmore, *Black Theology: A Documentary History, Volume 2: 1980-1992*, 410-26.

or not poor black people are getting better or worse. If black and womanist theologians are concerned with liberation and not only with band-aid reforms, then class, poverty, ownership of wealth, finance, and the means of production in the United States—indeed, in the world—need to be top priorities. As Jesus is calling us and determining our vocations, is the plight of the black poor and working people key to our faith vocations?

The notion of class connotes various dimensions of human interaction—stratification, prestige, power, and status. However, we highlight the centrality of the category of wealth to lend texture to class arguments. A wealth perspective facilitates the demythologizing of the American myth of individual citizens working as hard as they can and of each generation becoming better off than the previous generation. The Horatio Alger dimension accompanies this folklore. Somehow, if we allow the invisible hand of the market to play out its natural tendency of providing an equal playing field for all citizens and if we all labor as hard as we can and play by the economic rules of good American citizenship, then each person has the equal opportunity of moving from "rags to riches."

A wealth-class hermeneutic, furthermore, makes plain the prevailing misconception of the overrated importance of income in social analysis. American culture prides itself on lacking strict class differentiations. Hence, income, not class, becomes the operative nomenclature. Somehow, continuing the rationale of this misconception, Americans forged a new way of being in the New World, where issues of class from the old countries (in Europe) have been supplanted by more fluid rubrics of economic income and social status. The porousness of the social economic divide becomes evident when a poor janitor wins the lottery for over $100 million. Or perhaps, resuming this misconceived logic, a couple of people have an innovative idea, obtain start-up capital from Silicon Valley, and eventually revolutionize the information industry.

The reality of wealth monopoly ownership and distribution, however, debunks all myths and misconceptions. One receives income from working for someone else. In contrast, owners of wealth own land and the natural minerals in the land, the commercial real estate on the land, the air over the land, communication networks, industries, technologies, companies, and corporations. Wealth denotes exactly the undemocratic minority of American families who monopolize, through private ownership, the vast majority of the means of production and the distribution of production.

Black and womanist theologians re-envision class from the perspective of communal responsibility of God's resources. The air, land, sea, the rest of creation, and all that human kind has created—all are gifts from God for collective stewardship. Ultimately, though, everything belongs to God. Hence, the notion of a monopolized, private ownership of wealth is anathema to divine intent, divine possession, and divine proclamation. The Bible is replete with prohibitions against exploitation of the weak by the mighty. For example, Jesus calls on the rich man to sell all that he has and, furthermore, laments the seeming impossibility of a rich man entering the kingdom of heaven; Mary's Magnificat sings praises to God's overthrow of the system of the rich and powerful; Jesus explicitly offers the norm for entering the kingdom in the story of the sheep and the goats; Jesus initiates his public career as God incarnate by naming his mission as the liberation of the poor, because the Spirit of the Lord is upon him.

CONCLUDING DREAM

Class—the liberation of the poor for the practice of their full humanity—is the normative thread of all vocations in womanist and black theologies. Whether the issue is race, gender, sexual orientation, or ecology, the defining theological moment centers on the location of the poor in these categories of faith and witness. Jesus calls the church and all of good will to stand with, advocate for, and lift up the least of the earth, so that all of humanity and the earth might have life and have it abundantly. Contextualized by this vision, we struggle toward the finishing of the dream.

4

"What Happens to a Dream Deferred?"

Reflections and Hopes of a Member of a Transitional Generation

MARCIA Y. RIGGS

> *What happens to a dream deferred?*
> *Does it dry up*
> *Like a raisin in the sun?*
> *Or fester like a sore—*
> *And then run?*
> *Does it stink like rotten meat?*
> *Or crust and sugar over—*
> *Like a syrupy sweet?*
>
> *Maybe it just sags*
> *Like a heavy load.*
>
> *Or does it explode?*
>
> —LANGSTON HUGHES
> *The Panther and the Lash*

I was eleven years old in 1969 when Langston Hughes penned the poem that opens this chapter. I am a member of a generation shaped significantly by a quest for an answer to the poet's question. In fact, I contend that such a quest is a necessity for those of us who are members of a transitional generation. Our lives signify a transition in the African-American community from those who had the African-American community as their primary reference group to those who have struggled to hold onto our roots while making the transition into the dream of an integrated society, seeking to make real the dream of a beloved community where we would be judged by the content of our character rather than the color of our skin.

As members of a transitional generation, many of us do not readily identify our lives as reflective of a dream deferred. Unlike African-American adults in

1969, who experienced firsthand the disquiet of riots at the decade's end as well as the backlash of conservative politics that ushered in the decade of the seventies, many of us lack a critical awareness of just how contingent gains for African Americans can be. Many of us are members of a larger and more stable middle class; some of us are even wealthy. The exposure and (sometimes) influence of prominent black public intellectuals, politicians, entrepreneurs, and entertainers in the public sphere have convinced many of us that life is better for African Americans in this society, and on many objective scales it is better.

However, as a religious ethicist, it is not the objective progress of African Americans but our subjective struggles to fulfill the hopes of the Civil Rights Movement and the theological meaning we give those struggles that I seek to address in this chapter. I am concerned with bringing to consciousness the necessity to ask and answer Hughes's question, "What happens to a dream deferred?" From my point of view, this question serves as a barometer of moral awareness and responsibility insofar as those who ignore it will inflict harm upon themselves and generations to come. This is the case because this question pushes those of my transitional generation to consider both how we understand social reality and what vision we have for the future. In this essay I use my own race-gender-class autobiographical reflections as a means to disclose subjective struggles of my generation that I think are pertinent. With the struggles outlined, I then consider what moral vision will allow us to transform our struggles and search for meaning into moral agency for liberation.

BORN TO FULFILL THE HOPES OF A MOVEMENT

I was born in 1958 into a black middle-class family in an all-black suburb. We were middle class by virtue not only of my parents' education (college degrees), occupation (public school teachers), and income (not wealth) but also the values to which we held (respectability, self-reliance, fear of God, personal dignity, integrity, importance of service to the African-American community and any others less fortunate than ourselves).

From my story it becomes evident that the transitional generation to whom my remarks are directed are those who were considered middle class at birth and who consider themselves middle class now. I am addressing this social group because I think that we are the group that is most conflicted about what strategies for social change are needed now. We seem to be torn between strategies for integration (inclusion in this society with reformation of its basic structures for equal access by everyone) and liberation (democratic participation in this society with transformation of its basic structures so as to ensure justice for everyone). One reason that we feel torn is our sense that the values we have inherited are inadequate for challenges we now face. It is not that being God-fearing and respectability, self-reliance, dignity, integrity, service, and community are not good values; the problem is that these values have been interpreted through the lens of the dream of integration.

Orlando Patterson describes the dream of integration as "the ordeal of integration" in terms of the paradoxical conditions by which it is earmarked.

According to Patterson, the core "paradox of integration" is this: While there is genuine progress for a majority of African Americans, there is a minority of African Americans for whom this is among the worst of times. This paradox leads to perceptual paradoxes such as the "radically divergent perceptions" of racial progress held by African Americans and European Americans and ideological paradoxes such as "antiracist racism." Patterson concludes his analysis by asserting that there is overall greater integration of African Americans and that "as a nation, [we must affirm that] there can be no turning back."[1] I think that Patterson's analysis is helpful, but he is still wedded to the dream of integration. I contend here that it is this very dream of integration that must be replaced by a dream of liberation.

Given the values that we, the transitional generation, have inherited and the paradoxical nature of integration as a social, political, and economic goal, I think that our first subjective struggle must be a quest to reinterpret the aforementioned values of integration and/or replace them with others more conducive to liberation. The struggle of this transitional generation is how to live into the tensions of these moral dilemmas:

- hope *vs.* meaninglessness;[2]
- rage[3] *vs.* repressed anger;
- intragroup responsibility and liberation *vs.* inclusion on terms of denial and forgetfulness.

My family (on both my mother's and father's sides) have been leaders (bishops and preachers) and lay members of the African Methodist Episcopal Zion Church (founded in 1796) for about five generations. Thus, my faith was nurtured in the womb of one of the historic independent black denominations whose origins derive from rejecting the racism experienced in the Methodist Church that formed in the United States as branches of the movement begun by John Wesley in England. The story of African-American worshipers jerked from their knees in prayer and denied communion until all Euro-American worshipers had been served is a historical memory that every child of African Methodism knows. Yet, we were never taught to hate white people; indeed, we were taught to pray for them, to forgive them, and even to welcome them into our church. We were taught that we are all God's children, created in the image of God, for God is no respecter of persons.

Nurtured in the womb of the historic African-American denominational churches, some of this transitional generation are now seeking alternative places

---

[1] O. Patterson, *The Ordeal of Integration: Progress and Resentment in America's "Racial" Crisis* (Washington, D.C.: Civitas/Counterpoint, 1997), chap. 1.

[2] C. West, *Race Matters* (Boston: Beacon Press, 1993), 14. West describes this meaninglessness as nihilism, "the lived experience of coping with a life of horrifying meaninglessness, hopelessness, and (most important) lovelessness."

[3] bell hooks, *Killing Rage: Ending Racism* (New York: Henry Holt and Company, 1995), 12-13, 16-17, 21-30. hooks suggests that rage is the appropriate anger that expresses the subjectivity of black persons under the conditions of white supremacy and institutionalized racism.

and/or styles of worship because we no longer have a church home.[4] The church of our birth seems captive to theological interpretations that undergird reformist strategies at best and retrogressive ones at worst with respect to social change. Our former church home seems to have reached the height of institutionalization, such that tradition is reified and institutional maintenance has become the focus of ministry. The profound sadness and deep alienation that some of us feel with respect to the historic African-American churches has us caught between a desire to remain in communion with that church and a need to find places of spiritual renewal that continue the nurturant aspects of the churches' tradition but are housed and practiced in radically different ways. Ours is a struggle to hold on to and retrieve from our history that which has sustained a people ("We come this far by faith"), while creating new forms of worship and practices of spirituality that will heal wounded psyches and spirits as well as undergird further social movement for liberation.

KEEPING OUR EYES ON THE PRIZE

In spite of my transitional generation's present struggles (struggles for values, purposeful strategies of liberative change, and a spiritual home), we know that our foreparents did not get us to this point in history by sheer luck. We affirm that they had faith in God on their side and a moral vision that acted as lure and judge for them as to the way that they should be church and seek change in society. Peter Paris describes this moral vision as "the parenthood of God and the kinship of all people," a moral vision earmarked by its principle of nonracism.[5] Martin Luther King Jr. and all the people who participated in nonviolent resistance for racial justice would come to embody and enact this moral vision throughout the Civil Rights Movement. King spoke of this moral vision as the quest for the "Beloved Community."[6] At the risk of sounding arrogant in the face of the historic evidence that this moral vision has the power to empower,

---

[4] See B. Hall Lawrence, *Reviving the Spirit: A Generation of African Americans Goes Home to Church* (New York: Grove Press, 1996). Lawrence documents the return of African-American thirty and forty year olds to traditional African-American denominational churches after becoming professionally and financially successful but finding themselves spiritually empty. However, my point is that a significant number of that same group are seeking alternative religious homes in other religious traditions (such as Buddhism) or in newly forming Christian groups that are based on nontraditional interpretations of scripture and new rituals.

[5] P. J. Paris, *The Social Teaching of the Black Churches* (Philadelphia: Fortress Press, 1985), 10.

[6] See M. L. King Jr., "The Ethical Demands of Integration," in *A Testament of Hope: The Essential Writings of Martin Luther King, Jr.*, ed. J. M. Washington (San Francisco: Harper & Row, 1986), 117-25; K. L. Smith and I. G. Zepp Jr., *The Search for the Beloved Community: The Thinking of Martin Luther King, Jr.* (Lanham, Md.: University Press of America, 1986), chap. 6.

the question to be addressed here is this: Is the moral vision of Beloved Community an adequate moral vision for the multiracial, cross-cultural church and society of the twenty-first century?

My basic working assumption for me is that moral visions are formed by and in community; thus, they operate as givens for those who stand within the community. I also think that moral visions must be reinterpreted and sometimes reimagined, as the community evolves in response to socio-contextual realities. For those of the African-American church community, as well as for those from a larger religious community, who have embraced the vision of the Beloved Community, the time has come to reinterpret and reimagine that vision. A first step in such reinterpretation and reimagining is to take a critical look at how the vision has functioned in the past and how it functions now.

How the Vision Functioned in the Past

When Martin Luther King Jr. espoused the vision of the Beloved Community, he did so in the midst of social justice work that was intended to eradicate legally sanctioned structures of segregation, the effects of which were apparent. Also, pronouncements of racial hatred were heard in public, even voiced by public officials. In other words, the socio-moral context of the sixties was one of explicit and overt racial discrimination defined by the binary terms of white people (white power) *vs.* black people (black subordination).

According to Anthony Cook, King's vision of Beloved Community was a catalyst for change in such a context for the following reasons:

> King . . . empowered his community through a practical effort to bridge the gap between theory and lived experience. First, he used theoretical deconstruction to free the mind to envision alternative conceptions of community. Second, he employed experiential deconstruction to understand the liberating dimensions of legitimating ideologies such as liberalism and Christianity, dimensions easily ignored by the abstract, ahistorical, and potentially misleading critiques that rely exclusively on theoretical deconstruction. Third, he used the insights gleaned from the first two activities to postulate an alternative social vision intended to transform the conditions of oppression under which people struggle. Drawing from the best of liberalism and Christianity, King forged a vision of community that transcended the limitations of each and built upon the accomplishments of both. Finally, he created and implemented strategies to mobilize people to secure that alternative vision. I refer to this multidimensional critical activity as "philosophical praxis."[7]

---

[7] A. E. Cook, "Beyond Critical Legal Studies: The Reconstructive Theology of Dr. Martin Luther King, Jr.," in *Critical Race Theory: The Key Writings That Formed the Movement*, ed. K. Crenshaw, N. Gotanda, G. Peller, and K. Thomas (New York: The New Press, 1995), 91.

The important point to be drawn from this understanding of how the moral vision of Beloved Community functioned in the past is that it was an embodied and enacted vision, that is, people struggling in a movement for civil rights made it a reality; the theoretical was not bifurcated from the practical. With the realities of blatant racist words and acts ever present and in public view, it was difficult to think of Beloved Community solely as an unattainable ideal; the brutalities of the sixties era—such as the bombing deaths of four little girls on a Sunday morning—helped to keep the vision grounded in flesh and bone. The Beloved Community was hoped and prayed for daily in the midst of struggle.

How the Vision Functions Today

Today any acts of segregation and pronouncements of racial hatred are considered residuals of a bygone era and the actions of separatist fanatics. For many, remedial action to redress wrongs (for example, affirmative action policy) has gone on long enough. In other words, in today's socio-moral context it is presumed that the errors of the past are just that—past—and/or that the redress of wrongs has occurred, so that in fact there may be a need to be active on the side of nondiscrimination against white people. Even those persons who might admit that the past errors do continue to have negative affects or outcomes for black people as a social group (and the growing numbers of racial-ethnic groups such as Hispanic Americans and Asian Americans) are unsure how to compensate in the present and redistribute power so as to ensure a liberated future. There seems to be an overriding assumption that there is a level playing field *now*.

In the face of this overriding assumption, the following assertion by bell hooks helps us to understand why the Civil Rights Movement and its guiding moral vision of Beloved Community seem unable to empower people to do justice work aimed at eradicating racism *now*. hooks asserts:

> Some days it is just hard to accept that racism can still be such a powerful dominating force in all our lives. When I remember all that black and white folks together have sacrificed to challenge and change white supremacy, when I remember the individuals who gave their lives to the cause of racial justice, my heart is deeply saddened that we have not fulfilled their shared dream of ending racism, of creating a new culture, a place for the *beloved community*. Early on in his work for civil rights, long before his consciousness had been deeply radicalized by resistance to militarism and global Western imperialism, Martin Luther King imagined a *beloved community* where race would be transcended, forgotten, where no one would see skin color. This dream has not been realized. From its inception it was a flawed vision. The flaw, however, was not the imagining of a *beloved community*; it was the insistence that such a community could exist only if we erased and forgot racial difference.[8]

---

[8] b. hooks, "Beloved Community: A World Without Racism," in *Killing Rage: Ending Racism*, 263.

Using hooks's comments as a point of departure, the limitations of the moral vision of Beloved Community as espoused by King are exposed. It is a moral vision that remains grounded in the heat of struggle. However, under current conditions of implicit and covert racist practices, this moral vision fails to hold the theoretical and experiential together. In fact, as the church today resurrects the dialogue about race within its walls, we are particularly guilty of affirming the moral vision of Beloved Community that seeks to transcend, to forget, not to see skin color. The church affirms this version of the moral vision because of a theological orthodoxy that purports that we share a common humanity and that racism is a result of human sin and pride.[9] Although I would certainly agree that racism is a manifestation of human sin, I contend with the idea that our common humanity is disembodied humanity. In other words, I want us in the church to ground our understanding of common humanity in incarnational terms rather than transcendent theological perspective, such that our racial differences are signs that we are created in the image of God in flesh and bone, in our differences. In sum, the moral vision of Beloved Community functions today less as a lure to become the ideal it represents and more as a barrier to accepting who we are.

BELOVED COMMUNITY—
VISION FOR THE TWENTY-FIRST CENTURY?

Does the vision of Beloved Community have to function as a barrier to accepting who we are? As I stated earlier, moral visions are givens for those who stand within a community, and they must be reinterpreted or reimagined in response to socio-contextual realities. The moral vision of Beloved Community is a given for those of us standing within this transitional generation; thus, it is inevitable that we will begin our search for a vision for the twenty-first century by reinterpreting and reimagining this vision.

For me, the first step in reinterpreting and reimagining the vision of Beloved Community is to think about its strengths and weaknesses. This is a vision that affirms foremost the potential of human beings to love one another. It calls upon us to be mutually empowering and to establish structures of equality. This vision engenders values such as mutual respect, the dignity and worth of each person, justice, and peace. The weakness of this vision is our tendency to interpret it through a color-blind lens, thus leading us to fail to see and accept one another.

Given this vision's strengths and its embeddedness in our collective consciousness, the task for us into the twenty-first century is to shift our lens. We

---

[9] See G. D. Kelsey, *Racism and the Christian Understanding of Man* (New York: Charles Scribner's Sons, 1965) and S. E. Davies and Sr. P. T. Hennessee, S.A., eds., *Ending Racism in the Church* (Cleveland, Ohio: United Church Press, 1998) for two representative texts in which the discussion of racism from theological perspectives seems to end with the assertion of our common humanity—a common humanity that seems to be an "essential" nature that transcends our race or gender or ethnicity.

must look at who we are through a cross-racial, cross-cultural kaleidoscope that will enable us to accept both the racial and ethnic diversity of who we are and to acknowledge the ever-shifting configuration of who we are as the promise of a future that will be richer because of our multiracial, multicultural selves-in-communities.

What are the assumptions that we must hold in order to shift from a color-blind lens to the lens of a cross-racial, cross-cultural kaleidoscope? First, we must understand the type of socio-moral context in which we live. The United States is "a racial polity." This means that

> instead of counterposing an abstract liberalism to a deviant racism, we should conceptualize them as interpenetrating and transforming each other, generating a racial liberalism. The result is a universe of white right, white *Recht*, a white moral and legal equality reciprocally linked to a nonwhite inequality. At the heart of the system from its inception, this relationship between persons and racial subpersons has produced the "Herrenvolk democracy" in which whites are the ruling race. Thus as Herbert Blumer argues, racism should be understood not as "a set of feelings" but as "a sense of group position" in which the dominant race is convinced of its superiority, sees the subordinate race as "intrinsically different and alien," has proprietary feelings about its "privilege and advantage," and fears encroachment on these prerogatives. ("Race Prejudice as a Sense of Group Position," 3-4). . . . The individualist ontology is displaced or at least supplemented by a social ontology in which races are significant sociopolitical actors. The ontology here is not "deep" in the traditional metaphysical sense of being necessary and transhistorical. It is a created, contingent ontology—the "white race" is *invented* (Theodore W. Allen, *The Invention of the White Race*, vol. I, *Racial Oppression and Social Control*)—and in another, parallel universe, it might not have existed at all. But it *is* deep in the sense that it shapes one's being, one's cognition, one's experience in the world: it generates a *racial* self. Biologically fictitious, race becomes socially real so that people are "made" and make themselves black and white, learn to see themselves as black and white, are treated as black and white, and are motivated by considerations arising out of these two group identities (Ian F. Haney Lopez, "The Social Construction of Race," 191-203). Perceived "racial" group interests (not self-interests)—"racial" interests—become the prime determinants of socio-political attitudes and behavior.[10]

Races are social actors and racial interests are critical to the way of life we have in this country. Thus, we must acknowledge that our social group identities are foundational to the way that we must think of who we are in this society.

---

[10] C. W. Mills, "The Racial Polity," in *Racism and Philosophy*, ed. S. E. Babbitt and S. Campbell (Ithaca, N.Y.: Cornell University Press, 1999), 28.

Acknowledging our social group identity will then aid us in recognizing the importance of the next assumption: we must nurture historical consciousness.

Historical consciousness is having an awareness of and an overarching perspective regarding the way social groups in a context have interacted over time. It derives from knowing the stories of these groups and acknowledging the relevance of these stories for understanding the present as well as for projecting a vision of our relationships as groups into the future. Historical consciousness must be nurtured, because it signifies a willingness to reclaim and rethink history in order to grapple with the ways the past lives on in the present. Without historical consciousness, we deny the dynamic of historical transformation and inhibit our ability to be subjects rather than pawns of history. We disable our ability to move along (what I term) a moral agency axis from complicity to accountability to responsibility with regard to social processes of oppression— processes that account for our alienation from one another as social groups who claim to want to live together in both micro contexts, such as schools and churches, and the macro contexts of society and the world. Historical consciousness is fundamental to making real the tridimensional bonds of justice, the corrective-compensatory-distributive claims, that are part and parcel of living among a diverse citizenry who have different stories to tell of their social groups' experiences in the history of this country and therefore bring forth different justice claims. Historical consciousness is key to civic responsibility as justice-making.

Alongside the nurture of historical consciousness is a third assumption, the need to develop a cross-cultural conscience. Cross-cultural conscience refers to settled dispositions of character that signify the capacity to recognize and embrace particularity and difference. The primary virtues of cross-cultural conscience are renunciation and inclusivity. Renunciation means that we renounce privileges that promote exclusion and divisiveness because of socially constructed meanings of human worth and historically transmitted, transgenerational social, political, and/or economic advantage for social groups who represent the dominant race, gender, and class in society. Inclusivity connotes striving for interrelationships between the different "we's" that we are rather than seeking homogenization to create an "us" or domination or coercion to maintain unity as conformity. Inclusivity further signifies the ability to respect and embrace differences across permeable boundaries of distinctive social groups in such a way that distinct group identities are maintained and that difference and particularity are not sacrificed to some higher *telos* such as integration.

Persons who have cross-cultural conscience respect difference as the necessary point of departure for understanding and actualizing authentic unity. Such persons will even acknowledge the need for functional separatism between groups for the purpose of pursuing genuine wholeness (healing and reconciliation) and holism (interdependency and interaction). In other words, before being intercommunally (across social groups) engaged, we have to clarify intracommunally (within our social groups) who we are as members of distinct social groups; this is a precondition of liberation (the practice of just relationships between social groups). Also, functional separatism does not preclude functional partnerships (coalition-building) for specific aims on behalf of shared interests. Cross-cultural conscience is key to civic responsibility as community-building.

With the understanding that the society is a racial polity and the assumptions of historical consciousness and cross-cultural conscience, the final assumption is the need for moral imagination. William F. Lynch describes imagination as "the gift that envisions what cannot yet be seen, the gift that constantly proposes to itself that the boundaries of the possible are wider than they seem."[11] Moral imagination, Sharon Parks suggests, is that capacity of heart and mind whereby we make moral meaning through the images of self, world, and cosmos that we hold, and moral meaning-making ("the truth we hold by means of images") requires moral courage, an act of faith.[12] Indeed, it is through the practice of moral imagination that both historical consciousness and cross-cultural conscience bear fruit.

Using their moral imagination, historically conscious citizens are not afraid to draw upon the broad range of stories of the diverse social groups for images of how to be society. Likewise, with developed cross-cultural consciences, citizens use their moral imagination to discern how to enact renunciation and inclusivity in untried and perhaps unconventional ways. With the practice of moral imagination, we are no longer determined by our pasts or bound in the present; instead, we become *informed* by our past (recovering forgotten, lost, or heretofore dismissed traditions of moral wisdom) and *awakened* in the present (reengaging normative traditions both critically and appreciatively) for the purposes of discerning new ethical insights, methodologies, and models. Significantly, practicing moral imagination is about cultivating the ability to make moral meaning and life (relationships and structures) through images and narratives that we will hold as central to our identity as a society. Practicing moral imagination as a key to civic responsibility is about restoring hopefulness and creativity to our practices of what it means to be part of a sociopolitical community.

A CONCLUDING COMMENT

Finally, given the assumptions outlined above, is Beloved Community the vision for the twenty-first century? Yes, if. If we can ground the moral vision of Beloved Community in the ethical claims of diversity (claims of historicity, particularity, social group identity, and tridimensional justice), then it is the

---

[11] W. F. Lynch, *Images of Hope: Imagination as Healer of the Hopeless* (Notre Dame, Ind.: University of Notre Dame Press, 1974), 35.

[12] S. Daloz Parks, "Professional Ethics, Moral Courage, and the Limits of Personal Virtue," in *Can Virtue Be Taught?*, ed. B. Darling-Smith (Notre Dame, Ind.: University of Notre Dame Press, 1993), 181-83.

vision for the twenty-first century. We in the church and society must learn to reinterpret constructively the vision of Beloved Community that has been bequeathed us. The vision that we have inherited is grounded in the ethical claims of egalitarianism (claims of inalienable rights to life, liberty, and the pursuit of happiness as individuals without color or gender). The vision that we need must arise from mediating the ethical claims of diversity and the ethical claims of egalitarianism.

As we imagine our way into the twenty-first century, we in the church might consider that the image of God as an image of diversity may even require us to reimagine that great gathering at the banquet table as a gathering at diverse tables beheld by a God who sees us in our particularities, in our differences, as many, yet loves us as one creation.

5

Growing Like Topsy

Womanist Reflections on Dreams and Nightmares

EMILIE TOWNES

She was one of the blackest of her race; and her round shining eyes, glittering as glass beads, moved with quick and restless glances over everything in the room. Her mouth, half open with astonishment at the wonders of the new Mas'r's parlor, displayed a white and brilliant set of teeth. Her woolly hair was braided in sundry little tails, which stuck out in every direction. The expression of her face was an odd mixture of shrewdness and cunning, over which was oddly drawn, like a kind of veil, an expression of the most doleful gravity and solemnity. She was dressed in a single filthy, ragged garment, made of bagging; and stood with her hands demurely folded before her. Altogether, there was something odd and goblin-like about her appearance,—something, as Miss Ophelia afterwards said, "so heathenish," as to inspire that good lady with utter dismay; and turning to St. Clare, she said, "Augustine, what in the world have you brought that thing here for?"

—Harriet Beecher Stowe
Uncle Tom's Cabin

The question of identity is one avenue womanists use to articulate the concerns of black women who are feminists and committed to rigorous theological reflection. Stowe's introduction of the character Topsy in her abolitionist novel, *Uncle Tom's Cabin*, is a case in point. In this vivid, yet troubling introduction we have to Topsy, Stowe exposes us to the traditional stereotypes of black women slaves (regardless of age). Topsy is black, her eyes are round and they shine—they actually glitter. Her eyes, not her body, move quickly and restlessly over the contents and the people in the room. Her blackness is contrasted with the brilliant whiteness of her teeth. Her hair is woolly and braided in such a way

98

that her plaits stick out in every direction. Her face is a mixture of shrewdness and cunning, gravity and solemnity. She has a single, ragged dress made of bagging. She appears odd and goblin-like, heathenish.

This description of Topsy, which goes on to note her "black, glassy eyes [that] glittered with a kind of wicked drollery," puts in print a character who is lazy, mischievous, wild-looking, and prone to thievery. She needs constant guidance and beatings to keep her working and out of trouble. However, Stowe's point is that Topsy is all these things because of the dehumanizing system of slavery, not because of her blackness. Yet, Stowe's description of Topsy remains troubling. It is a swill pot of caricature—Topsy is a slave girl who perfectly fits the black stereotype of the time. Stowe's description of Topsy contains imagery of a barely human young girl. In all that Stowe attempts to do in speaking out against the institution of slavery, she clings to imagery that never allows Topsy to be seen as fully human or humane. The reader never comes to know Topsy (or any of the black females in the novel) as a person, for her character (both in print and as a person) is never developed. Stowe, regrettably, repeats the very dehumanizing process she seeks to critique.

This all too cursory look at Topsy and *Uncle Tom's Cabin* is meant to underscore a major challenge that womanist thought offers to the academic study of religion—What happens when Topsy speaks? What happens when Topsy moves from a literary character functioning as metaphor to the material history and lives of African-American women? What does it mean when the one (now One and containing multiplicities) who has been described and categorized by others starts to carve out and speak out of an identity in which she is an active agent? What does it mean that womanist thought signals a commitment to *conscious* reflection on the interplay among culture, identity, community, theory, practice, life, and death?

This set of questions assumes and points to the silences found in traditional theological discourses as well as in black theology and feminist theology about black women's lives and religious experiences. Womanist ethical and theological discourses prompt a more complex, nuanced, and radical look at the nature of life in the United States, as womanist discourses push the methodological orthodoxies found in established theological and ethical reflection. As such, womanist theo-ethic discourses are not univocal. African-American women have a variety of perspectives, methodologies, and analyses when engaging in ethical discourse. The common thread, however, is a rigorous critique of hegemonic discourses and actions. Womanist ethical reflections are rooted in the movement of history for African-American women, children, and men.

The focus on culture, identity, and community through the praxeological framework of class, gender, and race analysis marks the methodological boundaries for many forms of womanist thought in the United States. This multilayered analysis is necessary to prevent easy or lazy or sentimentalized or stereotyped formulations to continue to, or enter into, theoretical and practical examinations of the nature and form of black religiosity in the fullness of the African-American community. This analysis is also absolutely necessary to add to the mix of understanding of the nature and scope of the unfinished dream in the United

States, for it is to give Topsy (in all her many sizes, shapes, voices, and perspectives) a voice in the public theological and ethical discourses in this country.

CULTURE AND IDEOLOGY

our postmodern culture suffers from the enormous impact of market
　　　　forces on everyday life
we live in a time where the united states has now replaced europe as
　　　　global hegemonist
we also see an increase of political polarizations along the lines of
　　nation
　　race
　　gender (which for me means sex, sexuality, sex roles, sexual
　　　　orientation, sexism)
　　class
　　denomination
　　faith traditions
in our world, culture is sanitized and then commodified
　　this process of changing aesthetic tastes
　　domestication of the once exotic or feared other
　　uncontrolled appropriation
　　market-driven refiners' fires
　　mass production
　　and marketing
are for our enjoyment at the expense of people's lives and shrinking
　　　　pay checks
　　and often the solution is placed in the hands of lottery games
　　　games of chance
rather than challenge and debunk master narratives such as the u.s. as
　　　　the city on the hill
　　the lone heroic self-made man or woman
　　or inevitable and unalterable progress as good and civilized
our fashionable narratives are
　　nationalist and xenophobic
　　　with strong religious, racial, patriarchal, homophobic,
　　　　　heterosexist, ageist, and classist overtones and bell tones
in our postmodern culture, the structural inequalities that form the
　　　　superstructure of u.s. society
　　are alive and well
despite various warnings of postmodern thought with
　　its critique of modernity's excessive focus on individualism
　　　universals
　　　ahistorical reason
　　　universal knowledge
　　　the elevation of science as sheer objectivity

the social contract and morality organized around civil rights
and the liberties of the free individual
our postmodern culture has
thus far
only made a creative and sociocultural space
in which racial
gender
and so-called subclasses
now have theoretical entree into the emerging global
marketplace of
power
privilege
and pleasure
this entree may be imperative for these groups that have been
until recently
among the dispossessed
too many of our postmodern conversations
do not move us beyond reform to transformation of social systems
and practices
that model justice for all peoples and a respect for creation
beyond human skin
and the violence that circumscribes our lives
this turn has been taken, in part i believe
because postmodernisms have omitted
until recently, with the development of social postmodernism,
a concern for institutions, social classes, political organization,
political economic processes and social movements
and it is here where my work as a christian ethicist seeks to
understand the absurd metaphors encircling our lives
for me, womanist ethics helps us remember and explore the fact that
inclusion does not guarantee justice
and access to an inequitable and grossly maldistributed social
order does not mean the transformation of fragmented
communities or whole ones

Historically, our understanding of culture has moved from seeing it as closely related to human perfection, to the general state of intellectual development in a society, to the arts, to a way of life that includes the material, intellectual, and spiritual.[1] We continue to live in this last understanding of culture, which, Raymond Williams notes, often provokes hostility or embarrassment. There are three categories within it.[2] There is culture as ideal—a state or process of human perfection where certain absolute or universal values hold sway. Here, the

---

[1] Raymond Williams, *Culture and Society: 1730-1950* (New York: Columbia University Press, 1983), xvi.
[2] Ibid., 41-49.

analysis of culture involves discovering and describing values that compose a timeless order or have permanent reference to the universal human condition. There is culture as documentary—the body of intellectual and imaginative work in which human thought and experience are recorded in some detail. The analysis of culture, in this case, involves a critique of the nature of thought and experience, as well as the details of language, form, and convention in which thought and experience are described and valued. Finally, there is culture as social—a description of a particular way of life that expresses certain meanings and values in art and learning, institutions, and ordinary behavior. Analysis, in this case, is clarifying the means and values that are implicit and explicit in the way of life in a particular culture.

In light of these three categories of culture, womanist ethical reflection moves more in the direction of a theory of culture that studies the relationships among the various elements that make up a society, that form its whole way of life. In doing so, the ethical analysis found in womanist thought considers the nature of the organization of a society through its complex relationships to uncover and highlight the patterns that shape us into who we are and how we are as individuals, as a society, and as a church. The relationships among these patterns can reveal, as Williams suggests, unexpected identities and correspondences among activities that we may have previously thought to be autonomous.[3] For example, the rise of conservatism that was ushered in with the election of Ronald Reagan and the policies of that administration has now turned into a moralizing conservatism that focuses on infidelity and honesty, abortion, family cohesion, and homosexual illegitimacy; it has spawned hate crimes ranging from bombing women's clinics to the brutal slaying of Matthew Shepard, a white, gay twenty-two-year-old University of Wyoming college student in Laramie by two chronically unemployed young white men who had histories of violence and criminality.

Reagan's conservatism focused on economic freedom, smaller government, and personal choice. His popularization of conservatism and demonization of liberalism and progressivism enabled a creative space for the rise of this new conservatism that is pessimistic (something that Reagan could never be accused of when it came to his view of the United States ethos) and returns to pre-Reagan conservative themes of cultural decline, moralism, and the need for greater social control. These new conservative themes, espoused by folks like William Kristol and Linda Bowles, are intolerant of any sexual diversity beyond the bounds of the nuclear family. Homosexuality, for the neo-conservatives, is a disease and not a way of life. For some, like Matthew Shepard's killers, it fed into a robbery that became a lynching in which Shepard was left to die after having his skull gashed in four places, his nose broken, the skin on his head and face cut in eighteen places (some to the bone); he was pistol-whipped and left hanging, like a scarecrow, for eighteen hours.

To look at culture, then, is to explore the ethical, political, theological, and aesthetic dimensions in the texts and practices of everyday life. It is to note the

---

[3] Ibid., 47.

ways, for instance, in which dominant groups within the United States have attempted to impose a set of values and norms on subordinate groups. In this case, the actions of the dominant group move beyond culture into the domain of ideology. Ideology, here, is an ahistorical conception of culture that imposes the culture of the dominant group on a subordinate group or groups. This is done through the media, religious communities, schools, and the workplace. This set of dynamic relationships held slavocracy in place for fourteen generations of black folks in the United States. It enables the kind of mean-spirited and racist rhetoric found in a Linda Bowles column entitled "Our First Black Woman President?,"[4] in which Bowles skews Toni Morrison's observation that President Clinton is our first black president.

Morrison noted the ways in which Clinton's family history mirrors that of many (but not all) African Americans, who grow up in single-parent homes, are poor, working class; play a musical instrument like the saxophone that is not considered "cultured"; and eat at McDonalds. Her point was that, for the first time in decades, the American public elected and then reelected a man who was not from the white, elitist establishment. Morrison's use of blackness was metaphorical, pointing to the commonness of his roots and their more intimate link with everyday citizens of the United States. However, Bowles launched into a vitriolic piece in which she noted that Morrison "left out watermelons, jig-dancing and womanizing" and stated that Morrison's point is that "Clinton is a rascally lovable black man, being persecuted and tormented by a lynch mob of white bigots." The article actually degenerated from there by using rhetoric, innuendo, and stereotype as fact and objectivity. Bowles's ideology runs roughshod over truth and humanity.

When this form of ideology is successful, members of subordinate groups eschew their allegiance to their group for an ahistorical dream that is held out by those who hold power and control as the true culture of a society. This permeates all levels of life. Martin Carnoy notes that in a democracy subordinate group members can resist accepting the dominant group ideology, but usually at considerable material and social costs.[5] Also, members of subordinate groups can choose to develop their subordinate group cultures *within* the context of the hegemony of dominant group ideology. The dominant ideology *can* change to be more inclusive and even include *some* of the values and norms of subordinate group cultures. But, as Carnoy notes, the dominant group is more willing and able to accept a call to change from subordinate groups that have accepted the ideology of the dominant group.

One example of this dynamic in ideology is hip-hop culture. Hip-hop arose out of the African-American urban experience located in poor and working-class

---

[4] Linda Bowles, "Our First Black Woman President?," *The Kansas City Star* (October 28, 1998): D-5. The protest from African Americans and other racial ethnic groups in the metropolitan Kansas City area was such that the editor of the editorial and opinion pages canceled the paper's contract with Bowles within two days of publication.

[5] Martin Carnoy, "Education, State, and Culture in American Society," in *Critical Pedagogy, the State, and Cultural Struggle*, ed. Henry A. Giroux and Peter L. McLaren (Albany, N.Y.: State University of New York Press, 1989), 13.

communities. In recent years this culture has been usurped by white-dominated media that now control and direct the consumption of hip-hop culture. The drive to "make it," which usually translates into financial success, causes many hip-hop artists to tailor their music and lyrics to "fit" into the ideological positions of record industry moguls. Rather than remain a form of expression that functions to teach the history of the black experience in the United States—a history that also includes protest and resistance, analysis and critique within the larger cultural landscape of African-American life—hip-hop has become a commodity that is directed, packaged, and consumed. The bitter irony is that this is now resold in black communities across the land as an authentic remnant of the real thing.

IDENTITY AND COMMUNITY

This cartel of ideologies by the dominant group reifies a social order in which a particular way of life and thought transcends all others to such a degree that it permeates all of culture. This hegemonic process shapes our understanding of customs, morality, religiosity, politics, and taste. All of our social relations, intellectual and moral, are shaped, then, by the ideologies of the dominant group. In the United States, increasingly, this dynamic is found in the rising power of the conservative–neo-conservative coalition. Politically and religiously, the increasing saturation of this ideology affects all of our lives, but the power of this coalition is not manifest destiny.

As Antonio Gramsci has pointed out, those who seek to dominate must demonstrate their claims of intellectual and moral leadership to the larger social and cultural order. Hence, the art of persuasion becomes crucial. This is no more powerfully evident than in the way in which a form of moral obsessiveness has taken hold in the public discourses of the United States. The conservative–neo-conservative movement has lost sight of the principle of government restraint, the boundary between the public and the private, and economic and religious freedom.

Rather than focus on these traditional conservative values, the new conservatism focuses on issues of morality, a rigid and deontological morality, that is a full frontal assault on the real and imagined beliefs and practices of the cultural revolutions of the 1960s. This has enormous implications for African-American life in the United States. Affirmative action (for all underrepresented groups), voting rights, fair-housing legislation, and other political and social reforms opened up a closed society for many, but not most, African Americans. Although the 1960s failed to produce lasting shifts toward genuine equality and democracy for black Americans, these years did provide a base from which to advocate and organize for the continuation of the democratizing process.

When the new conservatism advocates family values, it is not the traditional black extended family or the biblical notion of family it has in mind. It is a narrowly defined nuclear family that does not represent any knowledge of the complexity of family relationships found in the biblical record (for example,

"Who is my mother, who are my brothers?" [Mt 12:48-50]) or the great variety of family constructions that produce vital and healthy individuals who seek to bring their lives into the larger culture to enhance and grow the dynamics of justice and mercy for us all. To the extent that many black Christians eschew or are ignorant of the powerful historical legacy of a *variety* of understandings of family that have maintained African Americans on this continent, they are assenters and victims of the hegemonic forces of conservative ideologies that do not welcome any diversity that is not crafted by the hands of the ideologues.

This process is not inevitable. Hegemony is not invincible, because in a democratic social order, such as we are to have in the United States, even hegemony is subject to change and negotiation, since the process of domination and subordination is one of continuous tension in our society. The hope that is found in this is that, thus far, the political and theological dynamics found in the United States continue to provide opportunities for contesting the legitimacy of the system. Therefore, hegemony has to "be won, secured, constantly defended."[6]

To paraphrase Miss Ophelia, what in the world have we been brought here for? It is small wonder that Topsy becomes lost in this. Even in the communities of resistance that seek genuine diversity and equality, the worldviews of Topsy are often muted, if not negated. Rather than avoiding the reinscription of conventional oppressive hierarchies of class, gender, and race, early black and feminist ethics and theologies fell victim to hegemonic forces, with Topsy and her sisters and brothers as the casualties. The hope was that theo-ethical reflection would not further erase and exclude women of color in racial analysis, the multiplicity of sexualities for men and women, and the stratification of socioeconomics within and without black culture. This early methodological failure was due to the fact that black men and white women failed to question and cross-examine the locations from which they spoke.

The concern for identity politics was a narrow one that did not, at first, include all of the members of the marginalized groups from which black and feminist ethics and theology emerged. However, as African-American women (and male allies), gays, lesbians, bisexual and transgendered persons, working-class folks, the elderly, and others who were and remain members of these communities found their voice, the narrow formulations of identity within the African-American and feminist communities were challenged and expanded.

New formulations of identity politics in theo-ethical discourses must avoid the earlier patterns of essentialism and avoid new forms of essentialism to be true to the struggles of exploited and oppressed groups in their attempts to critique the dominant structures from positions that give meaning and purpose for this struggle. This intracommunal analysis is crucial for womanist reflection. For it is in this in-house conversation and challenge to the forms of essentialism within the African-American church, theological academy, and larger black

---

[6] Geoff Eley, "Nations, Publics, and Political Cultures: Placing Habermas in the Nineteenth Century," in *Culture/Power/History: A Reader in Contemporary Social Theory*, ed. Nicholas B. Dirks, Geoff Eley, and Sherry B. Ortner (Princeton, N.J.: Princeton University Press, 1994), 322.

culture, as these locations seek to produce and practice liberatory ethics, that womanist ethical reflections address their first audiences. Womanist ethical thought does not deny the importance and power of identity-making and shaping but explores the magnitude and scope of the diversity of black identities so that *we* do not commit the gross errors of stereotyping and sentimentalization that are often forced on our communities. In the process, we may well neglect accountability and responsibility within our own communities and fall into a warped and inarticulate rhetoric of victimization that does little to craft justice.

The interplay between identity and essentialism is not only intracommunal, it is intercommunal as well. The challenge here is to maintain the rigorous pursuit of identity as a form of resistance to hegemony. This pursuit of the authentic and varied identities in black lives in the United States combines the experiential with the analytical (often in this order) to question many of the epistemological and ideological assumptions found in the larger culture and its social institutions. There may be times when the assertion of an exclusive essentialism is a strategy to undercut and destabilize hegemonic forces. Yet, great care must be taken to avoid creating a monolithic identity that fails to represent the true heterogeneity of black life in the United States.

The task that is taken on by womanist ethics is to value identity as it seeks to analyze and critique the formation and practice of identity. Therefore, womanist thought questions the label of essentialism when it is always the marginal "other" who is essentialist.[7] As bell hooks notes so well,

> A critique of essentialism that challenges only marginalized groups to interrogate their use of identity politics or an essentialist standpoint as a means of exerting coercive power leaves unquestioned the critical practice of other groups who employ the same strategies in different ways and whose exclusionary behavior may be firmly buttressed by institutionalized structures of domination that do not critique or check it.[8]

The struggle has always been for womanist theo-ethical reflections to name, analyze, and critique the simultaneous subordinations of class, gender, and race as *lived experiences* as well as theoretical constructs. Further, it is to name the ways in which these forms of subordination and oppression are carried out within the African-American community as well as by men and women in other racial ethnic groups. Within this struggle is the recognition that accountability is paramount. This accountability functions on both the individual and the communal level. Womanist ethicists are held accountable by the African-American community for the ethical, theological, social, and political choices we make as we straddle academy, church, and community. In this vein, womanist religionists can never forget that we stand within a community as active members and participants. The

---

[7] bell hooks, *Teaching to Transgress: Education as the Practice of Freedom* (New York: Routledge, 1994), 81.

[8] Ibid., 82-83.

community functions to remind us that we may have lapses within our analysis and critique that demand we reassess our perspectives.

On the communal level, accountability means being open to the width and breadth of the community. It also means remaining vigilant to the forces of hegemony that can and do coopt authentic black life and replace it with stereotypes and innuendoes that pathologize African-American resistance struggles against a dehumanizing hegemony concocted from ideologies of elitism and repression. The question becomes how to implement accountability without reinscribing hierarchies endemic to African-American culture and its social institutions. Answering this question is one of the enduring challenges of womanist ethics to all forms of ethical and theological reflection that focus on black religiosity and an African-American liberation that is spiritual and social.

In the final analysis the articulation of identity must lead to alliances built on justice, hope, and equality. This requires a rigorous and ongoing commitment to explore the multiplicities within black identity and culture in order to rupture the bonds of hegemony that restrict the growth of black lives *and* the lives of all members of the U.S. cultural landscape.

WE DIDN'T "JUST GROW'D"

When arrayed at last in a suit of decent and whole clothing, her hair cropped short to her head, Miss Ophelia, with some satisfaction, said she looked more Christian-like than she did, and in her own mind began to mature some plans for her instruction.

Sitting down before her, she began to question her.

"How old are you, Topsy?"

"Dun no, Missis," said the image, with a grin that showed all her teeth.

"Don't know how old you are? Didn't anybody ever tell you? Who was your mother?"

"Never had none!" said the child, with another grin.

"Never had any mother? What do you mean? Where were you born?"

"Never was born!" persisted Topsy, with another grin, that looked so goblin-like, that, if Miss Ophelia had been at all nervous, she might have fancied that she had got hold of some sooty gnome from the land of Diablerie; but Miss Ophelia was not nervous, but plain and business-like, and she said, with some sternness,

"You mustn't answer me in that way, child; I'm not playing with you. Tell me where you were born, and who your father and mother were."

"Never was born," reiterated the creature, more emphatically; "never had no father nor mother, nor nothin'. I was raised by a speculator, with lots of others. Old Aunt Sue used to take care on us. . . . "

"How long have you lived with your master and mistress?"

"Dun no, Missis."

"Is it a year, or more, or less?"

"Dun no, Missis. . . . "

"Have you ever heard anything about God, Topsy?"

The child looked bewildered, but grinned as usual.

"Do you know who made you?"

"Nobody, as I knows on," said the child, with a short laugh.

The idea appeared to amuse her considerably; for her eyes twinkled, and she added,

"I spect I grow'd. Don't think nobody never made me."

"Do you know how to sew?" said Miss Ophelia, who thought she would turn her inquiries to something more tangible.

"No, Missis."

This conversation between the Yankee Miss Ophelia and the young black girl slave Topsy is instructive and subversive. Throughout the novel Stowe's gross stereotyping of Topsy also contains a liberatory note. The reader is shown the ways in which Topsy is more than capable of doing her work and learning her lessons. She is revealed as smart and capable—but she is unwilling to do the tasks assigned to her, because that is what is expected of her. Topsy chooses to wear the mask the white owners (and Stowe) had given to her.

Is the mask present in the conversation above? It is difficult to know, and it is possible to build a case for yes or no. Perhaps this is not the most pressing point, however. In this conversation, Topsy, wittingly or not, subverts Miss Ophelia's ideological assumptions and outright ignorance of the fate of most slaves. It was not unusual for slaves not to know their actual birth date, their parents, or their place of birth. It was also not a matter of rote that a slave would receive Christian religious instruction. Topsy's response speaks to the power of hegemony when it operates with such pervasiveness that it erases memories (historicity) and/or never allows the subjects to know or learn their history. This is a more profound process than historical or social amnesia, because the person or the community cannot remember what it never knew.[9]

Memory and remembrance, identity-shaping and identity-making, tradition and traditioning are pivotal functions in an ethical framework that emerges from an oppressed community. The struggle to move beyond double- and

---

[9] Katie Geneva Cannon discusses this in greater detail in her lecture "Remembering What We Never Knew: The Epistemology of Womanist Ethics," paper presented at the Soul to Soul: Women and Religion in the Twenty-First Century conference sponsored by the Center for Women and Religion, Graduate Theological Union, Berkeley, California, February 27, 1998. James Melvin Washington discusses social amnesia in the Introduction to his edited volume *Conversations with God: Two Centuries of Prayers by African Americans* (New York: Harperperennial Library, 1995), xxvii-xlii. Washington goes on to note that "there are grave consequences when we cannot locate and integrate the memories of our forebears," for this can lead to soul murder (xxxvii). For Washington, we must look at the public and collective rage at injustice through an analytical procedure he calls historical demonology. This methodology assumes that demons are intelligent but thrive best when not exposed. Hence, historical demonology unmasks the demons in our midst and names them with precision and clarity.

triple-consciousness is a confrontation with a history that is systematically and methodologically ignored. To recover the record of black women, children, and men as *communities* rather than as autonomous experiences is a part of the work of womanist ethics.

These crucial functions of community are held in tension in womanist theo-ethical reflections. The task of religiously based womanism is to move within the tradition descriptively and to jump for the sun in order to climb beyond the tradition prescriptively. As such, womanist reflections *must* be based on the communities from which they emerge, for womanist religious reflections can degenerate into flaccid ideologies if they do not espouse a future vision that calls the community beyond itself into a wider and more inclusive circle. This circle is neither tight nor fixed.

All too often black women must answer the questions, some well-intentioned, some not: Isn't this just another form of separating us? How are the lives of black women relevant to my world? Why am I blamed for something that I am not responsible for?

Womanist theo-ethical reflections respond from their own well of history and sociopolitical methodology: We cannot bring together that which we do not know. A unity forged on imperfection, romance, poor vision, limited knowledge, and tissured reconciliation will always benefit those who have the power and leisure to enforce and ignore differences. Unity as a teleological goal can be dangerous and life-defeating, for it can overwhelm and neglect equality. Unity is only vigorous in an atmosphere that is unafraid of difference and diversity, an atmosphere that does not view difference as a barrier but, like the proverbial stew, makes the aroma richer and provides greater sustenance for the work of justice and forging communities of resistance and hope.

The collective experience of black women, like the experience of any subjugated group, can inform and challenge the dominant worldview. African-American women must seriously consider a womanist analysis of society, culture, and history. For a black woman to forget her blackness is to deny a rich heritage that crosses the continent of Africa, moves in the waters of the Caribbean, touches the shores of South America, and is vibrant in the rhythms of Alice Coltrane, Miriam Makeba, Marian Anderson, and Sweet Honey in the Rock. She loses part of her very soul if she turns away from Zora Neale Hurston, Alice Walker, or Phyllis Wheatly. African-American women must continue to draw from the deep well of the lives of Fannie Lou Hamer, Cora Lee Johnson, and Septima Clark.

However, because we live in a living community, care must be taken neither to idealize nor to romanticize African-American women. An even greater danger is to confuse collective with monolithic. The crux of the matter is to increase our knowledge of our history and the myriad ways folk have done analysis, responded to circumstance, visioned a future, and also failed to do so. Relevance to our worldviews is more of a challenge than we admit or accept. True relevance implies a willingness for each of us to open our life for uncompromising and meticulous introspection, but this introspection takes place within the context of a community of communities within a larger cultural landscape and its society.

Womanist ethics does not seek to assign blame; rather, it calls us into a radical accountability with one another within community and to other communities in the U.S. cultural landscape, as well as globally. It is hard work to listen to a history and a tradition that have not been a part of dominant discourse. There are those (within and without the African-American community) who respond to such revelations with guilt, shame, and anger. Rather than explore the emotion of the response, too often the rational impulse takes over, and the result is a denial of the invitation to justice and liberatory resistance. And the response is one of feeling blamed or held responsible for the sins of the forebears and/or to deny contemporary complicity with practices of injustice. Womanist ethics makes the appeal to history and tradition and asks the question: How can an authentic ethic of justice be separated from where we have been and who we have been to one another? The contemporary scene did not emerge from a vacuum; it evolved from and in history and is immanently contextual. That context has its moments of brilliance and its seasons of mourning. We cannot divorce us from the totality of our history and expect even a glimmer of efficacious justice or a vital community that crafts wholeness for its members.

Therefore, womanist theo-ethical reflections must be as relentless in analysis as they are inclusive in their recovery of history and sociopolitical analysis. Womanist ethical reflections cannot be content with a justice that addresses only a particular person or group's wholeness. A womanist social ethic must embrace all segments of society, if it is to be thorough and rigorous and continue to push ourselves into a critical dialogue that presses the boundaries of our humanness. Class, gender, and race analyses are crucial. But we need to challenge the ageism (of both the young and the seasoned), the homophobia and the heterosexism, the myriad issues around accessibility, our own color caste system, and the Pandora's box around issues of beauty. The work of womanist ethics is not only to eradicate an unjust white cultural hegemony that names us "less than" but also to expose, examine, and eradicate the ways that black folks help that system find *new* ways to deem us children of a lesser God.

Topsy's ignorance of her history, whether feigned or real, points again to this power of community and that peculiar task of community to help maintain and shape identity, memories, legacies, and traditions for past, present, and future generations. Ultimately, this process happens in community through the grace and power and potency of the Spirit.

> there is a spirit that is within and without us
> it calls us to itself, to ourselves, to one another
> it is a spirit that moves and shapes
>> figures and reconfigures
>> it is swift, it is slow
>> it is time-less, it is time-filled
> it is a spirit that leads us beyond what we can touch
>> or see
>> or feel
>> it leads us into what we know

this knowing is not discursive and discrete
    it is not rimmed with ontological categories that serve
    to keep us from one another
        although intending to bring us two or three-together
there is a spirit within us and without us
    it is wisdom
    it is home
    it is the cosmos
    it is the amen
    it is healing
    it is knowing
it is the very heart and soul of who we are and how we are and how
        we can be and how far we have yet to go
it is the spirit of promise and hope
it is the spirit of refusing to accept the realities in which we all dwell
    in which we try to survive—and do survive
    in which we try to live and sometimes, through amazing feats of
        moving through
        we not only live, but thrive
        actually shimmer with life and hope and justice and righteous,
        righteous
        o so holy and righteous anger
respecting, building, and nurturing genuine community within
        communities in black life
    reminds us that we cannot accept the death-dealing and life-
        denying ways in which we have often structured our
        existences
    we must, through a faith that is grounded in what the wise old
        folks tell us about living and hoping and refusing and
        cussing and praying and doing
        doing, doing the work of justice and mercy
    we must reconfigure and re-form, and recast our ways of being
for many of our ways of being are killing us
    none too softly and with a song that assaults our very souls and
        spirits

but, there are alternatives to doing bad business as usual business or
        normal business

there is understanding the very dust in our souls connects us with a
        world we can scarce imagine or a world we can fully
        imagine
    it is a world that welcomes us into wholeness by pulling us beyond
        our meandering finitude and helps us discover the
        boundaries of the cosmos
there is welcoming and challenging the traditions so many of us grew
        up with

even new traditions that are meant to free us and redeem us
    when in fact, they may well keep us from that liberatory praxis
            that feeds hope and nurtures its life within us
there is listening to each other
    and taking the time to hear one another as we seek to understand
            the blighting of life and the ecstasy of salvation
there is re-membering, as we once knew, that our essence is spiritual
    that we actually do know what is right with the spirit
        but we have been taught to ignore this knowledge and turn to all
            manner of spirit-numbing behaviors that keep us locked
            in a circle of disaster and ruin
there is seeking healing and wholeness
    through turning to the divine within and without
    and listening, listening always to a cosmos that does not rend body
            from soul or soul from body
        but welcomes us all into a wholeness that transforms and sanctifies
            living and struggling and hoping and keeping on
yes, there is a spirit within us and without us
    it is the spirit of knowing the deeply known *and* the unknowable—
            in our very bones
this spirit leads us into refusing to accept the smallnesses of life
    the amazing acts of violence and hatred
    the awful indignities we inflict on others and others inflict on us
we are, in essence, engaging in communal lament
    in speaking complaint, sorrow, and grief over impending doom
            that could be and often is physical and cultural
    we recognize that we live our lives in tragedy or a series of
            calamities
    and we need divine help for deliverance[10]
but with lament also comes oracles of salvation
communal lament can help us best get at these complexities of living
            black and large in the United States as we turn into the
            twenty-first century
    lament enables us and even requires of us to acknowledge and to
            experience our suffering
womanist reflections must put words to our suffering
    so that we are moved to a pain or pains that can be named and then
            addressed
we are to be formful[11]
    for their willingness to move both in the individual and the
            communal realms

---

    [10] Paul Wayne Ferris Jr., *The Genre of the Communal Lament in the Bible and the Ancient Near East* (Atlanta, Ga.: Scholars Press, 1992), 10.
    [11] Walter Brueggemann, "The Formfulness of Grief," *Interpretation: A Journal of Bible and Theology* 31:3 (July 1977): 265.

they help us grasp the deep moral character of the spirit at work
in our lives
and it is through the communal lament that happens *in community*

in the corporate experience of calling for the healing spirit to
come by here
that makes it bearable and manageable *in* the community
there is grieving in our lament as we acknowledge and live the
experience rather than try to hold it away from us out of
some misguided notion of being objective or strong
there is hurt, some things are fractured, if not broken
there are foul spirits living in us and among us
we are living in structures of evil and wickedness that make us ill
but womanist reflections remind us
this is not the final word
there is celebrating the spirit that lives and breathes life into us
beyond the seeing and knowing and believing we can do
it is a spirit that refuses destruction and is impolite when it says a
bodacious "no" to praxeological frameworks that serve
the masters' and mistresses' houses of hegemony

THE WOMANIST DANCING MIND

With the images and reality of dreams and nightmares as a natural part of living, I close with personal if not confessional speculations on the visions found in womanist thought, as we review the past, examine and understand the present, and look to a future that does not carry all the scars of the past, which are like the folds of old wounds. The words of Toni Morrison are a helpful guide into this process of visioning. I believe that her essay "The Dancing Mind" is instructive to exploring the dynamics of the unfinished dream of womanist ethics and all womanist religious thought in the United States.

There is a certain kind of peace that is not merely the absence of war. It is larger than that. The peace I am thinking of is not at the mercy of history's rule, nor is it a passive surrender to the status quo. The peace I am thinking of is the dance of an open mind when it engages another equally open one—an activity that occurs most naturally, most often in the reading/ writing world we live in. Accessible as it is, this particular kind of peace warrants vigilance. The peril it faces comes not from the computers and information highways that raise alarm among book readers, but from unrecognized, more sinister quarters.

Morrison's essay is based on her acceptance speech for the National Book Foundation's Medal for Distinguished Contribution to American Letters in 1996. Morrison focuses on the dangers, the necessities, and the pleasures of the reading/

writing life in the late-twentieth century. For her, the dangers are captured in two anecdotes she tells. In one, it is the danger that, in her words, "our busied-up, education-as-horse-race, trophy-driven culture poses even to the entitled." In the second, she teases out "the physical danger to writing suffered by persons with enviable educations who live in countries where the practice of modern art is illegal and subject to official vigilantism and murder."

It is in the dancing mind that we meet each other more often than not. It is in our books and essays and lectures and papers that those who are not womanists most often meet us for the first if not the only time and way. It is in this dancing mind—where we tease through the possibilities and the realities, the hopes, the dreams, the nightmares, the terrors, the critique, the analysis, the plea, the witness—that womanist work is done in the academy, in the classroom, in the religious gatherings of our various communities, in those quiet and not so quiet times in which we try to reflect on the ways in which we know and see and feel and do.

This womanist dancing mind—is more than our attempt to make sense of the worlds surrounding us—sometimes enveloping us, sometimes smothering us, sometimes holding us, sometimes birthing us. It is more than our desire to reconfigure the world and then invite others to come and inspect the textures, the colors, the patterns, the shapes, the sizes of this new order, this new set of promises.

No, the womanist dancing mind is one that comes from a particular community of communities yearning for a common fire banked by the billows of justice and hope. As such, our particularity marks us with indelible ink. Our task is to explore the twists and turns of the communities from which we spring and have our very life and breath. It is to be very particular about the particular—and explore the vastness of it.

The womanist dancing mind—the one that weaves in and out of Africa, the Caribbean, the U.S. South, North, East, and West, the Christian, the Jewish, the Muslim, the Santeria, the Vodun, the Native American, the caste of color, the sexuality, the sexual orientation, the socioeconomic class, the age, the body image, the environment, the pedagogies, the academy—has before it an enormous intracommunal task. One in which we are trying to understand the assortments of African-American life. If we do this task well, we will realize the ways in which black life is not our life alone but a compendium of conscious and unconscious coalitions with others whose lives are not lived solely in the black face of United States life.

In this womanist dancing mind the expansiveness of womanist ethics must be the absolutely last thing we think about in doing our work. What I am interested in is exploring the depths of African-American life—female and male. For it is in exploring these depths, in taking seriously my particularity—not as a form of essentialism, but as epistemology—that I can meet and greet others. For we are intricately and intimately interwoven in our postmodern culture.

In this particularity I must stand toe-to-toe with the damaging and destroying effects of the African-American color caste hierarchy even as I—a relatively light-skinned black woman—am a natural inheritor of its toxic benefits. I must explore gender—sexuality, sexual orientation, sexism—not only to get at my hope for wholeness, but also to understand the ways in which age and body image, and a history that contains the castrating matriarch, the ultimate mammy, and the lascivious whore continue to ooze from the pores of videos and magazines and television and radio and music and the pulpit. Because I sit in the academy, the church, the classroom, and the community, I must explore socioeconomic class as it moves in and out of black life with blazing speed—taking the poor *and* the wealthy out of sight. Because we all have to live somewhere, the environment is something I cannot forget to call continually back into my consciousness and work—to broaden the black community's understanding of what is at stake in the atmosphere we breathe beyond the pristine and irrelevant images of Sierra Club calendars that rarely, if ever, put people in nature—the fact that postmodern culture and the air it spawns will kill us if we do not start paying attention to and then strategize for a more healthy environment for all of us to live in.

It is this focus on particularity that then invites a more expansive awareness and vision for womanist ethical reflection. I am now challenged to de-romanticize the African continent by coming to know its peoples on their terms, not from my own. I am compelled to search out and recover my Caribbean streams of consciousness and memory to understand the different ways in which black folk have survived and not survived our own diaspora and the different manifestations of the latent Middle Passage in our historic and contemporary lives. I must listen to the different rhythms of blackness that come from the different geographies that shape people's bodies and health. I am drawn, sometimes with enormous reservation and circumspection, to understand the different ways in which the religious, beyond my own Christian identity, has shaped me and my communities. And to understand what is at stake when we have lost, forgotten, or been stolen away from the rich medleys of the religious in black life. As I reach further into my particularity, I am brought face-to-face with the tremendous loss of touch with Native-American peoples.

It is through the particularity of the womanist dancing mind that I can meet and greet those parts of myself that have been lost through neglect, ignorance, well-practiced amnesia, or malicious separation. I am challenged to look at those places that the "isms" that I impose on others are turned back at me, and I am asked to see myself through the eyes of those whom I would and do reject. It does not matter that this rejection is not intentional or malevolent. What does matter is that if I say, as a womanist, that I am engaged in race, gender, class, and environmental interstructured analysis, then I must face those places within myself and within my work that ignore the ways in which that interstructuring takes place.

This womanist dancing mind, says Morrison, requires "an intimate, sustained surrender to the company of my own mind as it touches another." For Morrison, this is done in reading. For me it is in reading and listening. It is my own need, which Morrison names so well, "to offer the fruits of my own imaginative intelligence to another without fear of anything more deadly than disdain." For Morrison, this is writing. For me this is writing and speaking and working to bring justice. As I engage my work within communities of communities, I find both celebration and anguish. But mostly what I hope to find is that peace of which Morrison speaks. The peace of my mind as it dances, and dances, and dances into a new future that I have had some small part in helping craft. A future (and a mitigating hope-filled present) that is more vibrant, more life-bringing and life-giving, more welcoming, more humane. What is at stake in womanist discourses is deadly serious—it is challenging the ways we know (epistemology) and the ways we think (orthodoxy) and the ways we act (ortho-praxy). And we make judgments on these.

I suspect such a task is appealing to many who seek to reconfigure our worlds, to be about the task of transformation. I welcome allies in this enterprise. But my work cannot be their work and vice versa. Where we meet and touch and spark and burn, this is good. But we each have our own communities as well, that we must be responsive and responsible to as we challenge old paradigms of hegemony within them. As we learn from each other's struggles, so we better engage in more rigorous and thoughtful scholarship and action. But our work must have its own integrity. This peace of the dancing mind, this peace of the womanist dancing mind, is not a panacea nor is it arcane intellectual camou-flage. It is a peace that is only found in hard work, in close and respectful listening, in an openness to learn and grow, in a willingness to admit—if not confess—one's limitations and awfulnesses, to grow our lives, our scholarship, our teaching large.

For as we move into the twenty-first century, there isn't anybody else who will do this for us.

PART II

ASIAN-AMERICAN VOICES

6

Reformation of Identities and Values within Asian North American Communities

FUMITAKA MATSUOKA

Images and symbols reflecting certain distinct values are emerging as cohering forces for Asian North American communities. These images and symbols are not emerging by accident. They are born of events in history that have left a deep impact upon the lives of people, both collectively and individually. These events give rise to common narratives that are told and retold in these communities. The keystone of identity, communal as well as personal, is participation in these shared narratives. As told in these stories, the past, present, and future of Asian North Americans are bound together by the memories and hopes of the community to which they belong.

For Asian North Americans, their experiences in the North American continent have produced memories of events and incidents that now serve as the seed bed of common shared narratives, the stuff that makes their communities "home." Memory is a function of maintaining current values. History is a tale told to illustrate a presently operative philosophy of life. In exploring the way memory preserves and creates the past, the central question the individual as well as the community asks is, How did we come to be as we presently are? Several related categories yield fruitful results in response to this central question: What wounds or hurts do we resent having suffered? What gifts were we given for which we are grateful? Who were our important figures and models? What were the crucial decisions for which we were responsible? Such questions focus attention not only on the remembered facts that constitute the raw material of autobiography but also on the way in which memory functions to justify present attitudes, such as resentment or gratitude.

For this essay I have chosen the writings of two authors and one collection of essays which together reveal complex, tantalizing, and intriguing glimpses into the cultural, religious, and ethical symbols and values they name as the forces bringing Asian North American communities together. Once the integral relationship among awareness, memory, and anticipation is grasped, the unity of lifestyle begins to emerge and the story a person tells through his or her life unfolds. Identity is discovered communally as well as individually. Although born within particular Asian North American communities, my hope is that the images, symbols, and values embedded within them and named here—truth-telling, re-rooting of personal and communal identity, and reformulated community-building—will serve as proleptic signs of how U.S. society as a whole is being reformed into a yet unknown future.

SYMBOLS AND VALUES
OF ASIAN NORTH AMERICAN COMMUNITIES

The first author is Joy Kogawa, a Canadian novelist of Japanese ancestry. The second, Maxine Hong Kingston, is a Chinese-American writer. The authors in the collection deal with Cambodian culture and diaspora.[1] Each in her own way frames her writings and reflections in terms of key historical settings common to her respective ethnic groups: for Kogawa, it is the internment of Japanese Canadians during World War II; for Kingston, the experiences of Chinese immigration in the United States; for the authors of the collection, the "killing fields" of Cambodia. Such decisive historical events—each with its own poignancy involving both the painful memories that haunt people even today and a tenacious and resilient sense of joy even in the midst of such pain—have made it possible for commonly shared stories to emerge from each Asian ethnic group. Each writer is able to say a prayer and tell a story that places life within an ultimate context. Through the easing of pain, the practice of prayer, or the use of some other means of transcendence, the will of God or the gods was determined. In this way, each person, each Asian North American person, was able to live in harmony with the powers of the overworld, which exert a mysterious influence on each one's experience.

Moreover, each group of people has its own cycle of stories locating the individual within the community, the community within the cosmos, the cosmos within the overworld. The stories told by these writers are becoming commonly shared stories for each group. At least, these authors are contributing to the shaping of a thread that brings people together into a community. Each story, in turn, serves as a piece in a larger mosaic of the whole life of North America, a mosaic that is still being crafted without a clearly discernible contour for us to see.

The cultural, religious, and ethical symbols and values named by these authors in their stories are gradually contributing to the shaping of cherished common symbols and values in Asian North American communities. The values that are authentic to this new land exist with strong affinity to the cherished values of their "old countries." Amid the dynamic, fluid, and sometimes confusing identity of Asian North Americans, a contour of that identity or group of identities is emerging, though dimly at present. The act of telling stories is a

---

[1] May M. Ebihara, Carol A. Mortland, and Judy Ledgerwood, eds., *Cambodian Culture since 1975: Homeland and Exile* (Ithaca, N.Y.: Cornell University Press, 1994).

way of justifying and sanctioning those values and symbols, which are essential to the shaping and preserving of their communities and eventually of a whole society.

Joy Kogawa

> There is a silence that cannot speak. There is a silence that will not speak. Beneath the grass the speaking dreams and beneath the dreams is a sensate sea. The speech that frees comes forth from the amniotic deep. To attend its voice, I can hear it say, is to embrace its silence. But I fail the task. The word is stone.[2]

For Kogawa, it is when we are willing to remember and to admit the past, terrible as it may have been, that a truly viable present or future is possible. Admitting the past, however, is not a simple act. Given the socially created conventional myth of an event—in her case, the internment of Canadian Japanese during World War II—what Kogawa strives for is truth-telling, the corrective to "official" accounts that rationalize the mistreatment of Canadian Japanese. The importance of truth-telling becomes more apparent when one takes into account official resistance to any facing up to what really happened. It took both the Canadian and U.S. governments almost fifty years to acknowledge the nature of wartime actions against Japanese-Canadian and Japanese-American citizens. Only after considerable pressure had been brought to bear by the truth-tellers was such acknowledgment brought about.

The internment experiences of Japanese Canadians and Japanese Americans have thus become the focal event in their histories, around which a variety of stories have begun to appear in their communities. Kogawa employs the image of "speaking dreams" with the biblical passage "You shall know the truth and the truth shall make you free" (Jn 8:8) to conflate truth. Freeing speech emerges from a "sensate sea," from the subconscious, associated with the period of communion between child and mother, the fetal sleep of the child in the mother's womb. Through the story of the main character in *Obasan*, the disappearance of Naomi's mother, Kogawa unfolds a story about both the truth of what really happened to the mother and the political fate of Japanese Canadians, dispersed from and forbidden to return to their original West Coast homes and exiled to the wintry hardships of the Canadian wilderness.

Through many layers of memories intersecting one another in Naomi's discovery of the mother-daughter bond, Kogawa gradually comes to acknowledge the bond of self and race through the painful event of the internment. The "speaking silence" bears testimony and recreates the event that was the cause for the silenced voice. She declares, "I am thinking that for a child there is no presence without flesh. But perhaps it is because I am no longer a child I can know your presence though you are not here."[3] The memory of the internment of Japanese

---

[2] Joy Kogawa, *Obasan* (Boston: Godine, 1981), epilogue.
[3] Ibid., 63.

Canadians corresponds to the memory of the relationship between a silent mother and a fearful, silent child; only to an adult, in memory, can the racial mother's presence be admitted.

Kogawa's truth-telling is not merely set within the framework of recouping silenced voices. She does not place speech and silence in simply binary opposition. Kogawa departs from the conventional notion that speech is inherently superior to all forms of silence. Instead, the story offers a complex interpretation of both, loosening the strict demarcation between the two and illustrating how both can be forms of communication. The value of silence as a powerful form of communication, a distinctly Asian posture toward life, is transmuted into the racial identity of Asian North Americans in Kogawa's work.

Maxine Hong Kingston

If, in the presence of an erased maternal figure, Kogawa asks, "What are the different ways of being?" and responds in both speech and silence for the sake of truth-telling, Maxine Hong Kingston rewrites the Asian maternal figure through her articulation of a Cantonese mother's talk-stories. She asks, "Who am I?," and responds by tracing her mother's heritage. *The Woman Warrior* is an attempt to sort out what being a Chinese American means, while *China Men* deals with Chinese Americans who claim America as their home, both for the American-born and the immigrant.[4]

"I learned to make my mind large, as the universe is large, so that there is room for paradoxes,"[5] declares Kingston. The paradoxes about which she speaks concern the relationship between her perceptions of her Chinese heritage and American realities. Making her mind "large" is Kingston's way of claiming her place in American society as a person of Chinese ancestry. In her works she attempts to assert an identity that is neither Chinese nor white American but distinctly Chinese American. *The Woman Warrior*, in particular, is about her attempt to come to terms with the paradoxes that shape and often enrich her life. She uncovers a uniquely Chinese-American voice that serves as a tool to combat both the cultural parochialism existing in this society and the deep-seated sexism embedded in her ancestral culture. Both narratives are Kingston's way of re-rooting her Chinese-American identity and community in America.

The symbolic value of her identity is the vengeance expressed by reporting the injustices suffered by her Chinese women ancestors and by herself as a Chinese-American woman. It is the language of contradiction and the language of sexism and racism—a language that speaks of painful, ugly, and demeaning experiences of people of Chinese ancestry in America. Kingston, as a warrior, uses this language in her attempts to purge, to decapitate, with the vengeance of words, records, and witnesses. The image of wilderness, inherited from her own

---

[4] Maxine Hong Kingston, *The Woman Warrior: Memoirs of a Girlhood among Ghosts* (New York: Vintage, 1975); idem, *China Men* (New York: Random House, 1980).

[5] Kingston, *The Woman Warrior*, 35.

mother's stories and life, is reclaimed and adapted by the daughter with her own "witch amazons." Kingston uses the image to describe the "wilderness" of her Chinese-American experience as a woman in the territories of patriarchal culture. Her works are a journey of survival, finally coming to know what it means to be a Chinese woman in America. The result is a reconciliation of the immigrant and the American-born Chinese, expressed in terms of self-assertion amid the irreconcilable forces of culture.

"Seeing double" is the world in which, according to Kingston, Chinese Americans, particularly Chinese-American women, live. It is a world confronted with dualities, contradictions, and paradoxes. In such a world the task of explaining what they do not completely understand is formidable. Often they feel that only they understand completely how ignorant their Chinese parents and the Americans are of one another. As a result, the Chinese-American go-between is reduced to hopeless inarticulateness, which really results from the absence of a language that speaks of such an interstitial space. The person is reduced to silence.

However, silence does not remain for long. In *The Woman Warrior* Kingston shifts from physical prowess to verbal injuries and narrative power. She fights the invisible hurts of prejudice, sexism, and racism inflicted upon her and her community. She fights the suffocating experiences not only of American mainstream ideals of beauty and behavior but also of Chinese traditional views of subservient women. The new identity Kingston asserts for Chinese Americans is that of a "swordswoman," at once a fighter and a beauty. She states, "The swordswoman and I are not so dissimilar. . . . What we have in common are the words at our backs. The reporting is the vengeance—not the beheading, not the gutting, but the words. And I have so many words—'chink' words and 'gook' words too—that they do not fit on my skin."[6]

From Chinese mothers and other persons, the daughter in *The Woman Warrior* brings to her writing talk-story language—secrets, dreams, myths, folk wisdom, gossip, singing, jokes, and parables. Through the process there comes about a matriarchal bonding with slave women and with heroic, rebellious women who step outside the circle of the conventional and familiar within patriarchal society.

In *China Men* the focus shifts to "claiming America." In this work Kingston attempts to recover, from their own vantage point, the history of deceit and lies connected with the lives of Chinese men in America. The title itself points to the difference between the way Chinese immigrant men viewed themselves and the way they were perceived in a racist society: They called themselves *tang jen*, or China men, while the racist society called them Chinamen. The work consists of stories, such as the attempts on the part of missionary women to force Christianity upon them with their "grisly Jesus pictures" and to make them say "thank God." From the point of view of the Chinese immigrants, the missionaries were thought to have "asses as tight as their mouths." These immigrants also marveled at their own experiences of coming across the Pacific Ocean to the new land: They regard the Angel Island experience as "not angelic."

[6] Ibid., 63.

They conclude, "It's not true about the gold." They hide and feed one another when harassed by white vandals. When one dies in a railroad accident, the others pray over his grave that his ghost will ride the train home. Once, when Ah Goong watches the death of a worker, he is overwhelmed by a twofold desire: first, to have an arm long enough to reach out and catch him; then, to let him go, so that the conscious man may fall faster and his agony come to a quicker end. By giving voice to these and other silenced people, Kingston transforms them into the identity of Chinese Americans today—a people who refuse to remain victimized and who gradually establish their mutual claim on America by telling their stories as part and parcel of the whole nation and their history as caring and decent human beings.

The "twosomeness" that W. E. B. Du Bois pointed out as the distinct worldview and experience of African Americans at the turn of the century is thus reexpressed through the experiences of Chinese-American women and men in Kingston's works. The authenticity of their lives emerges in part out of their refusal to be redescribed by a stereotyped image of Chinese Americans. To a large part, it is expressed through Kingston's own effort to tell it "like it is," forcefully and with vengeance. Her effort discovers and reclaims cultural heritage between the Old and the New World, between the individual and the variety of communities in which she lives, between mother and daughter, between women and men. As Kingston frees her own voice, she also liberates and reroots Chinese Americans from their imposed images to their own expressed identity: "About the black mountains reddening and how mighty was the sun that shone on him in this enchanted forest and on his family in China . . . he sang to his fellow workers. 'If that demon whips me, I'll catch the whip and yank him off his horse, crack his head like a coconut.' In an emergency a human being can do miracles—fly, swim, lift mountains, throw them. Oh, a man is capable of great feats of speed and strength."[7]

Literature of the Cambodian Diaspora

Literary works emerging out of the Cambodian diaspora in North America are few and far between. "The tragedy of Cambodia has not yet run its course, nor will it for generations. Millions have died, a culture has been vanished," says Yathay Pin.[8] In addition to the land as such, knowledge, history, culture, and even the commonly held core values of Cambodian society were almost totally destroyed. A reformulation of their own identity in the new land is still a matter of speculation at this time. Furthermore, their experiences in the "killing fields" often defy any conventional language, to the point where the emergence of a new language is perhaps needed in order to discern the symbols and values that are distinct to Cambodian Americans. A period of silence

---

[7] Kingston, *China Men*, 100-101.

[8] As cited in "Introduction," in Ebihara, Mortland, and Ledgerwood, *Cambodian Culture Since 1975*, 1.

often lasts a considerable time, judging from the experiences of the Holocaust victims during World War II.

The civil war and revolution of the 1970s left almost two million Khmer dead and a half-million more scattered in foreign countries. Given this painful situation, some voices are gradually beginning to emerge. At this time in history, the voices of the exiles are likely to be "screened voices," not necessarily the voices of individuals who speak for themselves. The essays in the collection represent such "screened voices." This work attempts "to combine two perspectives: to provide some of the larger context by viewing the Khmer as people affected by national and international events, and at the same time to focus on the level of individuals and the process whereby they make decisions."[9] It is a truism to say that Khmer culture is changing, deeply affected by the traumatic events of recent years. The impact of these events is truly immeasurable. At the same time Khmer culture is among the most resilient, resisting any intrusion from the outside. Other forces are also at work. Because of the trauma of the "killing fields," the Khmer's conception of their culture "has an inherent contradiction: on the one hand, they view Khmer culture as dying or as having died; on the other hand, their fear of losing their culture leads them to the conviction that nothing should be changed."[10] In such a complex setting we see the emergence of Cambodian-American voices.

For the 150,000 Khmer who have come to the United States since the late 1970s, the era of Pol Pot and the experience of concentration-camp life, flight, refugee camps, and resettlement in a new land are virtually inexplicable. Traditional religious beliefs and worldviews, particularly Buddhism, are no longer sufficient for Cambodians in America to understand the question of the brutality of the Khmer Rouge. How could three million people have had bad karma at the same time? The central core of Buddhist teachings is thus being repudiated as a result of their experience. "As refugees, Khmer in the United States face a new world; the realignment of all that has been, is, should be, and will be . . . lead Khmer to the conclusion that their past is unique and that explanation for their past is virtually impossible."[11] This is the context in which Khmer literature is beginning to be formed: "Constant themes in modern novels both inside Cambodia and abroad are the misfortunes and tenor of the Pol Pot regime and the tragedy of life."[12]

While literature among the Khmer in the United States is still in its infancy stage, some Khmer are beginning to use traditional Cambodian stories to cope with the inexplicable. Although written in France and not in the United States,

---

Ibid., 7.

[10] Ibid.

[11] Carol A. Mortland, "Khmer Buddhists in the United States: Ultimate Questions," in Ebihara, Mortland, and Ledgerwood, *Cambodian Culture since 1975*, 87.

[12] Khing Hoc Dy, "Khmer Literature since 1975," in Ebihara, Mortland, and Ledgerwood, *Cambodian Culture since 1975*, 32.

Ing Kien's *Phka Chhouk Kampuchea* (*Lotus Flower of Cambodia*) gives us a glimpse of the possible themes and issues that are only now beginning to emerge in U.S. Khmer communities.[13] This is a story about a young woman, Kolap, whose life is full of deception, ordeal, grief, and the loss of her family members at the hands of the Khmer Rouge. She arrives in France alone, with the aid of Catholic Relief. There she meets her former fiance, Vidya, who is now married to a woman named Ma Yan. Vidya offers Kolap a room in his home with the consent of Ma Yan. The relationship between Vidya and Kolap is a complicated one. Vidya treats their previous relationship as a thing of the past, whereas Kolap still struggles with her past relationship with Vidya. Sensing the complications, Ma Yan leaves Vidya and takes refuge in a Catholic church, where Kolap meets Ma Yan by accident. Ma Yan consents to return home to the seriously ill Vidya. Eventually, Kolap accepts the reality of Vidya's marriage to Ma Yan and remains a friend to both.

The story revolves around several key themes: the destruction of past life; the emergence of a new sense of community, which is nevertheless affected by the events of the past; the role of Christianity and questions about Buddhist teachings and values; the shape of a new identity as Cambodians in a new land. Particularly persistent in the story is the formation of a new Cambodian community in exile with its accompanying transformation of values and identity for the Khmer. Religious values and practices play a prominent role. Cynthia Coleman observes, "Some Cambodians . . . had turned away from Buddhism in anger and despair, saying that Buddhism was to blame for what had happened to their beloved Cambodia. Perhaps the Christian God, working through the church groups trying to help them, was a better choice."[14] Community-building efforts in a new land are interwoven with an alternate belief system, Christianity. This newfound faith is appropriate for some Khmer, who hold it in affection because it is associated with those who have provided them with a new chance for life. Having coincided with the erosion of the credibility of Buddhism in the aftermath of the civil war, Christianity—by way of those Christians who assisted the Khmer in rebuilding their life—has become a force powerful enough to mediate their efforts toward community-building.

At the same time, other forces are also at work in the emergence of Khmer communities in diaspora. In the United States, Khmer refugees need to cope with social, economic, and cultural adjustments. Consequently, religious and traditional ceremonies, attended predominantly by the older generations of Khmer, are held in various Khmer communities. These ritual practices provide a certain measure of emotional, psychological, and cultural relief from depression, isolation, and homesickness. These ritual practices may eventually find

---

[13] Ing Kien, *Phka Chhouk Kampuchea* (Paris: Edition Anakota, 1977). There are a few emerging literary pieces out of the "killing fields" experiences of Khmer. See, for instance, Usha Welartna, *Beyond the Killing Fields: Voices of Nine Cambodian Survivors in America* (Palo Alto, Calif.: Stanford University Press, 1993).

[14] Cynthia M. Coleman, as quoted in Mortland, "Khmer Buddhists in the United States," 74.

their way into Khmer literature, just as they play a prominent role in the work of Ing Kien.

The tragedy of life brought about by the Pol Pot regime is a constant theme in Khmer literature. However, the development of alternate explanations for a framing of their lives in the post–Pol Pot era is not adequate. Khmer in the diaspora within U.S. society continue to ask a range of challenging questions in their new land, faced as they are with a set of new relationships with the people around them. These are questions they would never have thought to ask before their lives took such a radical turn. The future of Khmer literature in the United States will likely pursue these new and yet old questions.

CONCLUSION

In real life there are no beginnings or endings, no moments of intrinsic significance that form a framework of meaning around experience. There are only days "tacked on to days without rhyme or reason, an interminable, monotonous addition," as Sartre would put it.[15] Anything can really happen in real life. No universal reason sets limits to the possible and gives meaning to human history. In the face of pain, riddle, and perhaps the absurdity of existence, the only option for the lucid individual is to create a reason or perhaps just questions for existing by writing a narrative, a journal, poetry, or just plain telling a story. Only by choosing some project, however arbitrary, can the individual fill the present moment and avoid the absolute contingency and absurdity of existence.

Joy Kogawa, Maxine Hong Kingston, and the Cambodian storytellers have done just that. Each in her own way affirms the unity of reality, yet sometimes questions about radical disruptions persist. The individual, ethnicity, culture, and the cosmos present themselves in concentric circles of possible integrated meaning called life. Past, present, and future are bound together in thematic continuation. These writers, each in her own way, take courage from the knowledge that they have roots in what has been and that their memories and deeds will be preserved in what is to come. In effect, their works affirm that the reality of the individual is not reducible to the present moment of experience but belongs rather to a continuity of meaning that the flow of time cannot erode, even with its unspeakable pain and trauma. With such faith, they act with a sense of continuity and perspective, their spontaneity tempered by memory and hope.

For Kogawa, the focus is on truth-telling in the face of the society-wide deception that attempts to erase the existence of her people. The works of Kingston, spanning many decades and bringing together stories out of China and the reflective narratives of Chinese experiences in the United States, are efforts to come to terms with painful events as a prerequisite to "re-rooting." For her, what is needed is a reorientation to the paradoxical nature of life. For Cambodian Americans, the telling of their unspeakable pain is a way of justifying and

---

[15] Jean-Paul Sartre, *Nausea* (New York: New Directions Books, 1959), 56.

sanctioning the values that are essential to building a new community amid the devastation of their total humanity.

In each case the act of telling stories serves a variety of functions: philosophy, theology, history, ethics, healing, even entertainment. It serves to locate the individual within the concentric circles of the cosmos, nature, community, and the family. It provides a concrete account of what is expected of a person and of what one may expect in that darkness which lies beyond the trauma of painful historical injuries—internment, unjust immigration policies, the "killing fields." Each writer seems to have an article of faith in the very act of writing and telling her work, or at least a yearning for it. It is a yearning that would have the scale of Being be such that human beings could possibly grasp the meaning of the whole, even in their often confusing, bewildering, ambiguous, and contradictory lives. Personality is not an epiphenomenon in an alien world of matter ruled by chance but rather the key to the whole cosmos. Truth-telling, re-rooting of one's identity, and community-building anew are not just individual concerns but point to what their people are all about, and eventually to what the future of a society will become. Each individual is a microcosm. In telling their own stories, individuals have confidence that their concrete, dramatic, tear-filled images are not unrelated to the forces that shape the macrocosm. While their images and stories may reduce the proportions of reality to a scale that is manageable by the human spirit, their distortion serves the cause of truth.

Kogawa, Kingston, and Cambodian Americans are confident that their images, symbols, myths, and stories are the most appropriate means with which to grasp reality, not merely illusions projected out of their isolated, subjective perspectives. If a wider America is willing to incline attentive ears to these and other accounts told by often-neglected people—even if America remains ignorant of the names of their God or gods and the form of their religion—it may just be sufficient, at least for the moment, for the enrichment of life together.

7

A Common Journey, Different Paths, the Same Destination

Method in Liberation Theologies

PETER C. PHAN

Future historians of Christian theology will no doubt judge liberation theology to be the most influential movement of the twentieth century, possibly even since the Reformation.[1] They certainly will painstakingly document its emergence as an independent theological movement in the late 1960s and will marvel at its spectacular expansion throughout the entire ecumene in a matter of just a couple of decades.[2] The profound influence of liberation theology will be evident not only from the way it has penetrated far-flung countries and continents and permeated all the branches of Christian theology, from biblical studies through systematics to ethics,[3] but also from the critique by the magisterium as well as from vigorous attacks by political authorities, who have regarded it as the most pernicious threat to democracy and the capitalist system.[4]

---

[1] For helpful general introductions to liberation theology, which are legion, the following may be consulted: Ignacio Ellacuría and Jon Sobrino, eds., *Mysterium Liberationis: Fundamental Concepts of Liberation Theology* (Maryknoll, N.Y.: Orbis Books, 1993); Marc H. Ellis and Otto Maduro, eds., *The Future of Liberation Theology* (Maryknoll, N.Y.: Orbis Books, 1989); Curt Cadorette et al., eds., *Liberation Theology* (Maryknoll, N.Y.: Orbis Books, 1992); and Peter C. Phan, "The Future of Liberation Theology," *The Living Light* 28/3 (1992): 259-71.

[2] For an excellent documentation of liberation theology, see Alfred T. Hennelly, ed., *Liberation Theology: A Documentary History* (Maryknoll, N.Y.: Orbis Books, 1990).

[3] The series Theology and Liberation, which may include some sixty volumes, attempts to reformulate all the basic theological themes in light of the theology of liberation.

[4] For the critique by the Vatican, see the documents by the Congregation for the Doctrine of the Faith, "Instruction on Certain Aspects of the 'Theology of Liberation,'"

CONTINUED

Even though it is customary to refer to liberation theology in the singular, it is obvious, even from a cursory study of its history, that it is by no means a homogeneous and uniform system. It has been practiced in different contexts and continents—North America, Central and South America, Africa, and Asia, just to mention areas where it has attracted a sizable number of adherents.[5] It has targeted various arenas of oppression—gender (white feminist, womanist, and *mujerista* theology); sexual orientation (gay and lesbian theology); race (black theology); class (Latin American theology); culture (African theology); and religion (Asian theology), again just to cite a representative few. Of course, these forms of oppression are not restricted to a particular region; rather, they are *each* widespread in *all* parts of the globe and are often intimately inter-locked with each other and mutually reinforcing, so that any genuine liberation theology *anywhere* must fight against *all* forms of oppression, whether sexism, heterosexism, homophobia, racism, classism, cultural and religious discrimina-tion, all at once, siding in effective solidarity with victims of all forms of oppression. In this sense, it is appropriate to refer to liberation theologies in the plural. It is important to take account of this diversity of liberation theologies, since it is a common mistake to lump all liberation theologies together as an undifferentiated theological movement. This diversity has been well expressed by Mary Potter Engel and Susan Brooks Thistlethwaite:

There are distinctive emphases in liberation theologies; they are not clones. None of them—North American feminist liberation theologies, womanist,

---

Origins 14/13 (1984): 193-204 and "Instruction on Christian Freedom and Liberation," *Origins* 15/44 (1986): 713-28. It is well known that the second document takes a much more positive attitude toward liberation theology. For an evaluation of the Vatican's documents, see Juan Luis Segundo, *Theology and the Church: A Response to Cardinal Ratzinger and a Warning to the Whole Church*, trans. John W. Diercksmeier (Minne-apolis, Minn.: Winston Press, 1985) and Anselm Kyongsuk Min, *Dialectic of Salvation: Issues in Theology of Liberation* (Albany, N.Y.: State University of New York Press, 1989). For a balanced assessment of the critique of liberation theology, see Arhur F. McGovern, *Liberation and Its Critics: Toward an Assessment* (Maryknoll, N.Y.: Orbis Books, 1989). Opposition to liberation theology did not limit itself to silencing some of its more vocal exponents (e.g., Leonardo Boff); it did not hesitate to use extreme mea-sures to eliminate it, as the murder of six Jesuits and two women in El Salvador in 1989 and many other Christians engaged in the struggle for justice bear eloquent witness. Their deaths illustrate the nature of liberation theology. As Jon Sobrino has pointed out: "The corpses of the Jesuits show that this theology is not elitist but of the people, be-cause it has risen in defense of the people and shared the people's destiny" (see Jon Sobrino, Ignacio Ellacuría, et al., *Companions of Jesus: The Jesuit Martyrs of El Salva-dor* [Maryknoll, N.Y.: Orbis Books, 1990], 51).

   [5] For presentations of liberation from the global perspective, see Alfred T. Hennelly, *Liberation Theologies: The Global Pursuit of Justice* (Mystic, Conn.: Twenty-Third Publications, 1995); Susan Brooks Thistlethwaite and Mary Potter Engel, eds., *Lift Ev-ery Voice: Constructing Christian Theologies from the Underside*, rev. and exp. ed. (Maryknoll, N.Y.: Orbis Books, 1998); and Priscilla Pope-Levison and John R. Levison, *Jesus in Global Contexts* (Louisville, Ky.: Westminster/John Knox Press, 1992).

mujerista, gay and lesbian liberation theologies, African American liberation theologies, Native American liberation theologies, Latin American liberation theologies, *minjung* theologies, or others, including those who as yet have not found a way to name their theological situation for themselves—is interchangeable with any of the others. Each has its own peculiar interests, emphases, viewpoints, analyses, and aims, dependent upon the requirements of its own particular social context.[6]

While acknowledging these important diversities, this essay will focus on what binds liberation theologies together, namely, the essential elements of their method. It will examine the resources liberation theologians make use of, their hermeneutical approaches, and their criteria of truth. In other words, the essay will study the three elements of the epistemology of liberation theology, that is, the analytical, hermeneutical, and practical mediations.[7] It will illustrate these methodological considerations with a wide-ranging appeal to the writings of a variety of liberation theologians themselves. It intends to show that liberation theologians, whatever their national and cultural provenance, are fellow travelers on a common journey, albeit through different routes, to the same destination.

A VARIETY OF GRIST TO THE THEOLOGICAL MILL:
THE SOCIO-ANALYTIC MEDIATION

It has been asserted that liberation theologies are not simply a "theology of genitives," in which liberation would be no more than one subject among many, a conventional theology about some hitherto undiscovered reality or dealing with a new theme. Rather, the claim is that liberation theologies are a new way of doing theology in which liberation is a kind of horizon against which the whole Christian faith is interpreted.[8] In other words, liberation theologies are essentially theology with a new method.

---

[6] Brooks Thistlethwaite and Potter Engel, *Lift Every Voice*, 5.

[7] See Clodovis Boff, *Theology and Praxis: Epistemological Foundations*, trans. Robert Barr (Maryknoll, N.Y.: Orbis Books, 1987), xxv. These three components correspond to the three acts of see-judge-act of the method of Catholic Action founded by Joseph Cardijn. On the connection between the method of liberation theology and that of Catholic Action, see Agenor Brighenti, "Raízes da epistemologia e do método da Teologia da Libertação. O método ver-julgar-agir da Ação Católica e as mediações da teologia latino-americana," diss., Catholic University of Louvain, 1993. See also Clodovis Boff, "Epistemology and Method of Liberation Theology," in Ellacuría and Sobrino, *Mysterium Liberationis*, 57-85; and Leonardo Boff and Clodovis Boff, *Introducing Liberation Theology*, trans. Paul Burns (Maryknoll, N.Y.: Orbis Books, 1987), 22-42.

[8] See Gustavo Gutiérrez, *A Theology of Liberation*, rev. ed., trans. Sister Caridad and John Eagleson (Maryknoll, N.Y.: Orbis Books, 1988), 12: "The theology of liberation offers us not so much a new theme for reflection as a *new way* to do theology. Theology as critical reflection on historical praxis is a liberating theology, a theology of

CONTINUED

Part of the methodological novelty lies in the partners-in-dialogue that liberation theologies converse with, or, put differently, in the kinds of grist they bring to their theological mills. Gustavo Gutiérrez has argued that in contrast to theology as wisdom and theology as rational knowledge, which dialogue almost exclusively with neo-Platonic and Aristotelian philosophies respectively, liberation theology is a "critical reflection on praxis."[9] As reflection on historical praxis, liberation theologies highlight certain Christian themes that might have been obscured in the past, such as charity as the center of Christian life, the intrinsic connection between spirituality and activism, the anthropological aspects of revelation, the very life of the church as a *locus theologicus*, the task of reflecting on the signs of the times, action as the starting point for theological reflection, the (Marxist) emphasis on the necessity of transforming the world, and the necessity of orthopraxis in addition to orthodoxy.[10]

Conversation with the Social Sciences

To carry out this critical reflection on historical praxis effectively as part of their methodology, liberation theologies must enter into dialogue with the social sciences.[11] To help transform the structures that oppress the poor, liberation theologians must have an accurate knowledge of the concrete sociopolitical and

---

the liberating transformation of the history of humankind—gathered into *ecclesia*—which openly confesses Christ." In *Lift Every Voice*, Brooks Thistlethwaite and Potter Engel use the building metaphor to express the radical challenge of liberation theology: "Liberation theologies are not about rearranging the furniture in the house of theology, or even about redecorating or remodeling the house. Rather, they are about rebuilding the foundation (method) and redesigning the floor plan (categories)" (14). Juan Luis Segundo explains this new way of doing theology in detail in his *The Liberation of Theology*, trans. John Drury (Maryknoll, N.Y.: Orbis Books, 1976).

[9] Gutiérrez, *A Theology of Liberation*, 5. In an earlier lecture (July 1968; see Hennelly, *Liberation Theology: A Documentary History*, 63) given at Chimbote, Peru, Gutiérrez gave a definition of theology in relation to praxis: "Theology is a reflection—that is, it is a second act, a turning back, a re-flecting, that comes after action. Theology is not first; the commitment is first. Theology is the understanding of the commitment, and the commitment is action. The central element is charity, which involves commitment, while theology arrives later on."

[10] See Gutiérrez, *A Theology of Liberation*, 5-11.

[11] Among liberation theologians the one most insistent upon the need for theology to dialogue with the social sciences is Juan Luis Segundo, whose theological project is to dialogue with the social sciences in order to "deideologize" the customary interpretation of the Christian faith and its language, which hide and legitimate oppression or social injustice. For a helpful collection of Segundo's writings, see his *Signs of the Times: Theological Reflections*, ed. Alfred Hennelly, trans. Robert Barr (Maryknoll, N.Y.: Orbis Books, 1993), especially his two essays, "Theology and the Social Sciences" (7-17) and "The Shift within Latin American Theology" (67-80). It is important to note that in the last-mentioned essay Segundo is critical of his colleagues for having made the poor rather than the ideologizing of Christian tradition the primary locus or source of theology.

economic conditions of the people to whom they convey the Christian message. The expression "(preferential) option for the poor" describes well the fundamental commitment or the "first act," to use Gutiérrez's memorable phrase, out of which liberation theologians are supposed to do their "second step" of reflection.[12] However, to know who are the poor in our society and the causes of their poverty requires more than expertise in the Bible and philosophy; what is needed is what Clodovis Boff calls the "socio-analytic mediation."

With regard to the relationship between theology and the social sciences, Clodovis Boff rejects five ways of conceiving and practicing this relationship in the past. These he terms "empiricism" (absence of socio-analytic mediation), "methodological purism" (exclusion of socio-analytic mediation), "theologism" (substitution for socio-analytic mediation), "semantic mix" (faulty articulation of socio-analytic mediation), and "bilingualism" (unarticulated socio-analytic mediation).[13] Instead of these inadequate ways, Boff recommends that we understand the relationship between the sciences of the social and the theology of the political as "constitutive" insofar as the social theories become the data for theology: "The sciences of the social enter into the theology of the political as a *constitutive part*. But they do so precisely at the level of the raw material of this theology, at the level of its *material object*—not at that of its proper pertinency, or formal object."[14]

It is well known that many Latin-American theologians, at least in their early writings, adopted the theory of dependence to explain the economic underdevelopment and exploitation in Latin America as the historical byproduct of the development of other, mostly capitalist countries, and hence called for the abandonment of the developmental model in favor of liberation or "social revolution."[15] In his more recent writings Gutiérrez has shown himself much

---

[12] See Gutiérrez, *A Theology of Liberation*, 9: "The Christian community professes a 'faith which works through charity.' It is—at least ought to be—real charity, action, and commitment to the service of others. Theology is reflection, a critical attitude. Theology *follows*; it is the second step." For a critical evaluation of Gutiérrez's understanding of the preferential option for the poor in the light of Thomas Aquinas's notion of charity, see Stephen Pope, "Christian Love for the Poor: Almsgiving and the 'Preferential Option,'" *Horizons* 21/2 (1994): 288-312. See also Patrick H. Byrne, "*Ressentiment* and the Preferential Option for the Poor," *Theological Studies* 54 (1993): 213-41; and Stephen Pope, "Proper and Improper Partiality and the Preferential Option for the Poor," *Theological Studies* 54 (1993): 242-71. For a critical examination of the relationship between orthopraxis and doing theology, especially as proposed by Juan Luis Segundo, see Bernard J. Verkamp, "On Doing the Truth: Orthopraxis and the Theologian," *Theological Studies* 49 (1988): 3-24.

[13] See C. Boff, *Theology and Praxis*, 20-29.

[14] Ibid., 31. Using Louis Althusser's epistemology, Boff suggests that the "third generality" of the social sciences, i.e., their theories, become the "first generality" of liberation theology, i.e., its raw data. This point will be elaborated in greater detail in the second part of this chapter on the hermeneutical mediation.

[15] See Gutiérrez, *A Theology of Liberation*, 49-57. Gutiérrez cites the works of sociologists such as Fernando Henrique Cardoso, Theotonio Dos Santos, and André Gunder Frank, among many others.

more aware of the limitations of the theory of dependence.[16] Nevertheless, the tendency to seek the root causes of all forms of oppression and to consider them in their historical development remains influential on the methodology of all types of liberation theology. For example, black theology has traced the roots of African-American sociopolitical and economic oppression back to racism and the ideology of white supremacy.[17] Similarly, Asian feminist theologians have highlighted how "capitalism, patriarchy, militarism, and religio-cultural ideologies work together to escalate the degree of women's oppression."[18] Some U.S. Hispanic theologians perceive the origin of the marginalization of Hispanic Americans in the inability of Anglos to accept the reality of *mestizaje* and *mulataje*.[19]

The use of the social sciences, especially the theory of dependence and the concept of class struggle, has brought accusations of Marxist ideology against liberation theologies. Liberation theologians, from Gutiérrez to his younger colleagues, have defended themselves successfully against such a charge. They

---

[16] See Gutiérrez's essay entitled "Theology and the Social Sciences," first published in 1984 and later incorporated in his *The Truth Shall Make You Free: Confrontations*, trans. Matthew O'Connell (Maryknoll, N.Y.: Orbis Books, 1990), 53-84. Here Gutiérrez insists on the necessity of a critical use of social theories in general: "We need discernment, then, in dealing with the social sciences, not only because of their inchoative character . . . but also because to say that these disciplines are scientific does not mean that their findings are apodictic and beyond discussion" (58).

[17] See the works of James H. Cone, Gayraud S. Wilmore, and J. Deotis Roberts. See, in particular, G. S. Wilmore, *Black Religion and Black Radicalism: An Interpretation of the Religious History of African Americans*, 3d ed. (Maryknoll, N.Y.: Orbis Books, 1998); *Black Theology: A Documentary History, Volume 1, 1966-1979*, ed. James H. Cone and Gayraud S. Wilmore (Maryknoll, N.Y.: Orbis Books, 1993), and *Black Theology: A Documentary History, Volume 2, 1980-1992*, ed. James H. Cone and Gayraud S. Wilmore (Maryknoll, N.Y.: Orbis Books, 1993). George C. L. Cummings has argued that black theology is rooted in six factors: the African slave trade and American slavery; segregation in post-emancipation America; Martin Luther King Jr. and the Civil Rights Movement; Malcolm X and the Black Muslim Movement; Black Power and the black rebellions in the 1960s; and the struggle of black Christians to define their identity and mission. See George C. L. Cummings, *A Common Journey: Black Theology (USA) and Latin American Liberation Theology* (Maryknoll, N.Y.: Orbis Books, 1993), 2. For black Catholic theology, see Diana L. Hayes and Cyprian Davis, eds., *Taking Down Our Harps: Black Catholics in the United States* (Maryknoll, N.Y.: Orbis Books, 1998), in particular M. Shawn Copeland's essay "Method in Emerging Catholic Theology" (120-44).

[18] Chung Hyun Kyung, *Struggle to Be the Sun Again: Introducing Asian Women's Theology* (Maryknoll, N.Y.: Orbis Books, 1990), 106. See also Virginia Fabella and Sun Ai Lee Park, eds., *We Dare to Dream: Doing Theology as Asian Women* (Hong Kong: Asian Women's Resource Centre for Culture and Theology, 1989).

[19] See the works of Virgilio Elizondo, especially *Mestizaje: The Dialectic of Cultural Birth and the Gospel* (San Antonio, Tex.: Mexican American Cultural Center, 1978) and *The Future Is Mestizo: Life Where Cultures Meet* (Oak Park, Ill.: Meyer-Stone, 1988). See also Roberto Goizueta, *Caminemos con Jesús: Toward a Hispanic/ Latino Theology of Accompaniment* (Maryknoll, N.Y.: Orbis Books, 1995).

distinguish between Marxism as an atheistic and totalitarian ideology (which they vigorously reject) and as a tool of social analysis; they also point out the difference between class struggle as a fact (the existence of which cannot be denied in Latin America) and the Marxist interpretation of class struggle as a law of history.[20]

The Psychological Tools of Introspection and Interreligious Dialogue

Whatever success liberation theologians may have had in their self-defense against accusations of Marxism and however fruitful is the dialogue between theology and the social sciences, Aloysius Pieris, a Sri Lankan liberation theologian, while recognizing the indebtedness of Asian theologians to their Latin American colleagues, has pointed out that a "'liberation-theopraxis' in Asia that uses only the Marxist tools of social analysis will remain un-Asian and ineffective. It must integrate the psychological tools of introspection that our sages have discovered."[21] The reason for the necessity of this additional tool is that, as Pieris has argued, in Asia there is "voluntary poverty" as well as "imposed poverty"; voluntary poverty has been freely assumed, mainly by monks, to liberate others from imposed poverty, and Marxist social analysis has nothing to say about it. This "introspection" not only serves as a bracing corrective to Karl Marx's thesis that religions are opium for the people but also highlights the potential that religions have for social transformation.

Furthermore, this methodology has forged a new link between sociopolitical and economic liberation and interreligious dialogue. Since Latin America is predominantly Christian, interreligious dialogue has not been an urgent issue for most of its theologians, nor has it served as a method for theological reflection.[22] This is also true of black, Hispanic, and feminist theologies in the United

---

[20] See Gutiérrez, *The Truth Shall Make You Free*, 61-63, 69-75; Enrique D. Dussel, "Theology of Liberation and Marxism," in Ellacuría and Sobrino, *Mysterium Liberationis*, 85-102; and Arthur McGovern, "Dependency Theory, Marxist Analysis, and Liberation Theology," in Ellis and Maduro, *The Future of Liberation Theology*, 272-86. With regard to socialism in liberation theology, Peter Burns has carefully evaluated the critique of opponents of liberation theology, in particular Michael Novak, and has convincingly shown that such a critique is not well grounded. Burns also points out the danger that liberation theology may lose its distinctive thrust if it mutes its option for socialism as the result of the collapse of communism. See Peter Burns, "The Problem of Socialism in Liberation Theology," *Theological Studies* 53 (1992): 493-516.

[21] Aloysius Pieris, *An Asian Theology of Liberation* (Maryknoll, N.Y.: Orbis Books, 1988), 80-81.

[22] Instead of interreligious dialogue, Latin American liberation theologians have recently paid attention to *religiosidad popular* as a source for liberation. See Cristián Parker, *Popular Religion and Modernization in Latin America*, trans. Robert Barr (Maryknoll, N.Y.: Orbis Books, 1996), with a copious bibliography (265-84) and Michael R. Candelaria, *Popular Religion and Liberation: The Dilemma of Liberation Theology* (Albany, N.Y.: State University of New York Press, 1990). Among theologians, Pablo Richard, Diego Irarrázaval, Juan Luis Segundo, and Juan Carlos Scannone have produced significant works on this theme.

States. This is not, however, the case with Asia, which is the birthplace of most world religions and where Christians are but a tiny minority and therefore must collaborate with adherents of other religions in order to achieve their agenda for social transformation. By interreligious dialogue as a theological method is meant not only theological discussions among church representatives and academics, but also "dialogue of life," "dialogue of action," and "dialogue of religious experience."[23] It is from these four forms of interreligious dialogue that a theology of liberation must be constructed whose genuine wellspring must be spirituality and not secular ideologies. Hence, it is of great significance that of late liberation theologians have increasingly turned to Christian spirituality as the quarry of their reflections.[24]

On the other hand, thanks to its new link with liberation, the very nature of interreligious dialogue has been transformed. It can no longer be carried out as a leisurely form of inculturation in which various elements are borrowed from other religions and grafted onto one's own—a kind of "theological vandalism," to use Pieris's expression.[25] Rather, it should be practiced as part of the task of liberation, since inculturation, as Pieris puts it, is nothing but announcing "the good news *in our own tongues* to our people (that is, the content of inculturation)— namely, that Jesus is the new covenant or the defense pact that God and the poor have made against mammon, their common enemy (that is, the content of liberation). For liberation and inculturation are not two things anymore in Asia."[26]

Interreligious dialogue as part of the method of liberation theologies also valorizes sacred texts and practices of Asian religions that have nourished the spiritual life of Asian people for thousands of years before the coming of Christianity into their lands and since then.[27] Intimately connected with these religious

---

[23] See Pontifical Council for Interreligious Dialogue and Congregation for the Evangelization of Peoples, *Dialogue and Proclamation*, June 20, 1991, no. 42 (Rome: Vatican Polyglot Press, 1991). See also the rich collection of John Paul II's statements on interreligious dialogue and the reactions from Buddhists, Jews, and Muslims in *John Paul II and Interreligious Dialogue*, ed. Byron L. Sherwin and Harold Kosimov (Maryknoll, N.Y.: Orbis Books, 1999).

[24] See, for instance, Gustavo Gutiérrez, *We Drink from Our Own Well*, trans. Matthew O'Connell (Maryknoll, N.Y.: Orbis Books, 1984); Jon Sobrino, *A Spirituality of Liberation: Toward a Political Holiness*, trans. Robert Barr (Maryknoll, N.Y.: Orbis Books, 1988); Leonardo Boff, *Passion of Christ, Passion of the World,* trans. Robert Barr (Maryknoll, N.Y.: Orbis Books, 1987); Segundo Galilea, *Following Jesus* (Maryknoll, N.Y.: Orbis Books, 1981); Nestor Jaén, *Toward a Liberation Spirituality*, trans. Philip Berryman (Chicago: Loyola University Press, 1991); Virginia Fabella, Peter K. H. Lee, and David Kwang-sun Suh, eds., *Asian Christian Spirituality: Reclaiming Tradition* (Maryknoll, N.Y.: Orbis Books, 1992). On the spirituality of liberation theology, see Peter C. Phan, "Peacemaking in Latin American Liberation Theology," *Église et Théologie* 24 (1993): 25-41.

[25] Pieris, *An Asian Theology of Liberation*, 53, 85.

[26] Ibid., 58.

[27] In this respect, see Aloysius Pieris, *Love Meets Wisdom: A Christian Experience of Buddhism* (Maryknoll, N.Y.: Orbis Books, 1988) and *Fire and Water: Basic Issues in Asian Buddhism and Christianity* (Maryknoll, N.Y.: Orbis Books, 1996).

classics is what is commonly referred to as Asian philosophies.[28] Lastly, inter-religious dialogue also highlights the importance of Asian monastic traditions with their rituals, ascetic practices, and social commitment for constructing liberation theologies.[29]

Stories from the "Underside of History"

Besides social analysis and psychological introspection accompanied by interreligious dialogue as part of their methodology, liberation theologians dig deep into the humus of people's lives to find resources for their reflection. The stories of these lives are often not recorded in history books written by victors but must be retrieved from the forgotten and oppressed past to form the "dangerous memory" (Johann Baptist Metz) by which the stimulus for social transformation may be nourished and sustained. Among Asian liberation theologians, Choan-Seng Song stands out as the preeminent "story theologian." Again and again he urges his fellow Asian theologians to make use of the stories not only of the Bible but also of poor and oppressed people, the "underside of history" (Gustavo Gutiérrez), and their folktales, old and new, as food for their theological thought. Song believes that the most important skill for Asian theologians is the ability to listen theologically to the whispers, cries, groanings, and shouts from the depths of Asian suffering humanity. What is needed, says Song, is the imagination, the "third eye," that is, the power of perception and insight *(satori)* that enables theologians to grasp the meaning beneath the surface of things and phenomena. It is precisely this listening to and reflection upon the stories of suffering people that makes a theology a liberation theology.[30]

---

[28] Highly significant in this regard are the prolific writings of Jung Young Lee, especially his *Embracing Change: Postmodern Interpretations of the* I Ching *from a Christian Perspective* (Scranton, Pa.: University of Scranton Press, 1994) and *The Trinity in Asian Perspective* (Nashville, Tenn.: Abingdon Press, 1996).

[29] Even though the following authors cannot be regarded as liberation theologians, Thomas Merton, Bede Griffith, and Raimondo Panikkar have made important contributions to the dialogue on Western and Eastern monasticism.

[30] Song himself is a highly skillful practitioner of story theology. For his reflections on stories as part of the theological method, see his ten theses in *Tell Us Our Names: Story Theology from an Asian Perspective* (Maryknoll, N.Y.: Orbis Books, 1984), 3-24; and "Five Stages toward Christian Theology in the Multicultural World," in *Journeys at the Margin: Toward an Autobiographical Theology in American-Asian Perspective*, ed. Peter C. Phan and Jung Young Lee (Collegeville, Minn.: Liturgical Press, 1999), 1-21. For Song's own theological works, see in particular his *Third-Eye Theology: Theology in Formation in Asian Settings* (Maryknoll, N.Y.: Orbis Books, 1979; rev. ed. 1990); *The Compassionate God* (Maryknoll, N.Y.: Orbis Books, 1982); *Theology from the Womb of Asia* (Maryknoll, N.Y.: Orbis Books, 1986); and his christological trilogy *The Cross in the Lotus World*, vol. 1, *Jesus, the Crucified People* (New York: Crossroad, 1990); vol. 2, *Jesus and the Reign of God* (Minneapolis, Minn.: Fortress Press, 1994); and vol. 3, *Jesus in the Power of the Holy Spirit* (Minneapolis, Minn.: Fortress Press, 1994).

Telling stories of the underside of history is also practiced by Korean *minjung* theology as its fundamental method.[31] As Young-Chan Ro has argued, the reality of *han*, which is "the cumulative unresolved feeling that arises out of people's experience of injustice," and which is the source of *minjung* theology, "reveals itself in the *telling* of tragic stories."[32] This storytelling method is also widely adopted by black theology, Native-American theology, and feminist theology of various stripes. The telling, of course, often takes the verbal form, in prose or poetry, but is not limited to it. It can be done in songs, drama, dance, ritual, symbolization, visual art, and folklore.

One of the results of storytelling as a theological method is contextualization. Storytelling makes liberation theologies concrete, rooted in real-life experiences, and historical. Through stories the narrator acknowledges an inescapable social, political, and economic location and implicitly affirms the validity of his or her experience. By the same token, in recognizing the contextuality of their own theologies, liberation theologians also carry out, at least indirectly, an ideology critique, insofar as they reject the claims to universality of the dominant or official theology and show that it too is inescapably located in a particular social, political, and economic context. On the other hand, storytelling helps liberation theologians bridge the gap inhibiting communication among people of diverse cultures because stories create a communal fund from which liberation theologians can draw inspiration for their reflection. In this way storytelling contributes to building up a kind of concrete universality out of particular stories and histories, from below as it were, rather than the kind of abstract universality and normativity that the dominant theology attempts to impose on others from above.

"DO YOU UNDERSTAND WHAT YOU ARE READING?" (ACTS 8:30): THE HERMENEUTICAL MEDIATION

Out of this abundance and variety of grist, how can one bake a single loaf of bread? Or, to vary the metaphor, out of so many notes, how can liberation theologies avoid being a cacophony and instead produce a harmonious symphony? More fundamentally, how should these sources be used to construct a *Christian* theology of liberation? Like the eunuch who was asked by Philip, "Do you understand what you are reading?," readers of these sources may be forced to

---

[31] On *minjung* theology, see Jung Yung Lee, *An Emerging Theology in World Perspective: Commentary on Korean Minjung Theology* (Mystic, Conn.: Twenty-Third Publications, 1988); Andrew Sung Park, *The Wounded Heart of God* (Nashville, Tenn.: Abingdon Press, 1993); and Young-Chan Ro, "Revisioning *Minjung* Theology: The Method of the *Minjung*," in Brooks Thistlethwaite and Potter Engel, *Lift Every Voice*, 40-52.

[32] Ro, "Revisioning *Minjung*," 49. According to Ro, *minjung* theology is "*mythos*-not *logos*-oriented theology. For [the] narrative element is understood to be essential to *minjung* theology, because *han* must be told, heard, touched, felt, and resolved. *A tragedy is not a tragedy until it is told*" (50).

reply, "How can I, unless someone guides me?" (Acts 8:31). In other words, the next issue to be considered is the hermeneutical mediation of liberation theologies: How should one interpret these various sources in such a way that they acquire what Clodovis Boff calls "theological pertinency"?[33] More specifically, how should liberation theologians correlate them with the Christian sources, namely, the Bible and tradition? After all, liberation theology is, as Gutiérrez has said, "a critical reflection on Christian praxis *in the light of the Word*."[34]

The Hermeneutical Circle and Ideology Critique

One of the key elements of liberation theologians' interpretation of the Bible and tradition is the "hermeneutical circle." Juan Luis Segundo, a Uruguayan Jesuit who has written extensively on hermeneutics, describes it as "the continuing change in our interpretation of the Bible which is dictated by the continuing changes in our present-day reality, both individual and societal. . . . Each new reality obliges us to interpret the word of God afresh, to change reality accordingly, and then to go back and reinterpret the word of God again, and so on."[35] Segundo specifies further that the hermeneutical circle contains four steps:

Firstly there is our way of experiencing reality, which leads us to ideological suspicion. *Secondly* there is application of our ideological suspicion to the whole ideological superstructure in general and to theology in particular. *Thirdly* there comes a new way of experiencing theological reality that leads us to exegetical suspicion, that is, to the suspicion that the prevailing interpretation of the Bible has not taken important pieces of data into account. *Fourthly* we have our new hermeneutic, that is, our new way of interpreting the fountainhead of our faith (i.e., Scripture) with the new elements at our disposal.[36]

Most liberation theologians adopt the hermeneutical circle, especially its ideology critique, in their interpretation of the Bible.[37] Thus, feminist theologians

---

[33] C. Boff, *Theology and Praxis*, 67.

[34] Gutiérrez, *A Theology of Liberation*, 11, italics added.

[35] Segundo, *The Liberation of Theology*, 8.

[36] Ibid., 9.

[37] For general expositions of biblical exegesis in liberation theology, see Norman K. Gottwald, *The Tribes of Yahweh: A Sociology of the Religion of Liberated Israel, 1250-1050 B.C.E.* (Maryknoll, N.Y.: Orbis Books, 1979); Norman K. Gottwald, ed., *The Bible and Liberation: Political and Social Hermeneutics* (Maryknoll, N.Y.: Orbis Books, 1983); Fernando Belo, *A Materialist Reading of the Gospel of Mark*, trans. Matthew O'Connell (Maryknoll, N.Y.: Orbis Books, 1981); Michel Clévenot, *Materialist Approaches to the Bible*, trans. William J. Nottingham (Maryknoll, N.Y.: Orbis Books, 1985); J. Severino Croatto, *Biblical Hermeneutics: Toward a Theory of Reading as the Production of Meaning*, trans. Robert Barr (Maryknoll, N.Y.: Orbis Books, 1987); R. S. Sugirtharajah, ed., *Voices from the Margin: Interpreting the Bible in the Third World* (Maryknoll, N.Y.: Orbis Books, 1991).

have unmasked patriarchy and androcentrism hidden in Christianity;[38] Asian liberation theologians insist on reading the Bible in the postcolonialist context;[39] and black theology reveals racial motifs in the Bible.[40] Furthermore, liberation theologians often promote the interpretation of the Bible by the poor themselves, who learn how to question the teachings of the Bible from the perspective of their oppression.[41]

There is, however, another question that still needs clarification; namely, how to bring the various sources we have enumerated above into dialogue with the Bible so that what results from this correlation of the two sources—social theories, the teachings and practices of non-Christian religions, and stories of the underside of history on the one hand, and the Christian scriptures on the other—becomes Christian liberation *theology*, and not just religious discourse, philosophy of religion, or the human sciences of religion?

The Hermeneutical Mediation

In answering this question Clodovis Boff's reflections on the second mediation of liberation theologies—the hermeneutic mediation—are helpful. Drawing on Louis Althusser's explanation of the process of theoretical practice, Boff suggests that the production of knowledge is composed of three moments.[42]

---

[38] For white feminists, see the works of Elisabeth Schüssler Fiorenza, Rosemary Radford Ruether, and Elizabeth Johnson. For Latina feminists, see the works of Elsa Tamez, Ada María Isasi-Díaz, and María Pilar Aquino. For Asian feminists, see the works of Chung Hyun Kyung and Kwok Pui-lan. For black feminists, see the works of Diana L. Hayes, M. Shawn Copeland, Toinette M. Eugene, and Jamie Phelps. For a general evaluation of feminist hermeneutics in relation to liberation theology, see Sharon H. Ringe, "Reading from Context to Context: Contributions of a Feminist Hermeneutic to Theologies of Liberation," in Brooks Thistlethwaite and Potter Engel, *Lift Every Voice*, 289-97.

[39] See R. S. Sugirtharajah, *Asian Biblical Hermeneutics and Postcolonialism: Contesting the Interpretations* (Maryknoll, N.Y.: Orbis Books, 1998).

[40] See Cain Hope Felder, *Troubling Biblical Waters: Race, Class, and Family* (Maryknoll, N.Y.: Orbis Books, 1980). Brooks Thistlethwaite and Potter Engel (*Lift Every Voice*, 11) summarize ideology critique by liberation theologians: "All liberation theologians agree on one basic principle for the use of any source: suspicion. All sources, whether Marxist analyses, ancient Christian texts, the scriptures, or 'classic' literature, must be used critically and approached with the suspicion that they further the dominant mode of oppression."

[41] The most famous collection of these interpretations is Ernesto Cardenal, *The Gospel in Solentiname*, 4 vols. (Maryknoll, N.Y.: Orbis Books, 1982).

[42] Louis Althusser's works available in English include *Essays in Self-Criticism* (Atlantic Highlands, N.J.: Humanities Press International, 1976); *Lenin and Philosophy and Other Essays* (New York-London: Monthly Review Press, 1971); *Politics and History: Montesquieu, Rousseau, Hegel, Marx* (New York: Schocken, 1978); *Reading Capital* (New York: Schocken, 1979); and *For Marx* (New York: Schocken, 1979). For Althusser's presentation of the process of theoretical practice, see in particular *For Marx*, chap. 4, no. 3; *Reading Capital*, 40-43; and *Lenin and Philosophy*, 60-63.

First, a science as a production of knowledge begins not with real or concrete things, but with general, abstract, and ideological notions that it encounters in a given culture and that it uses as its raw material (its first generality). The second moment of the theoretical practice, called the second generality, is the "working" on these data to produce a body or determinate system of concepts that determines a specific type of science. Out of this "working" on the first generality emerges a thought-product, a specific, concrete, scientific theory, which can be called the third generality. To put it concisely, *"theoretical practice produces third generalities by the operation of a second generality upon a first generality."*[43]

Theology, insofar as it is a science or theoretical practice, follows this three-step production: "Theological practice comprises a first generality—its 'subject,' or material object—a second generality, which is the body of its asymptotic or analogical concepts, and finally a third generality, the theological theory produced."[44] Anything whatsoever can be theology's first generality; there is nothing, including every source that has been mentioned in the first part of this essay, that cannot be the raw material or subject matter of theology. But it becomes theology only if it is "worked on" in the second generality "in the light of revelation," what St. Thomas calls the "formal object" (the *objectum quo*, the *ratio secundum quam*, the *ratio qua*) of theology, that is, faith, to produce a body of theological knowledge or science.

As far as liberation theologies are concerned, according to Clodovis Boff, their first generality is constituted by social theories (the third generality of the social sciences) as well as, it may be added, by other religious and cultural data such as those mentioned above. In its second generality liberation theologies "work" on this first generality by means of theological concepts derived from the Bible and tradition through an adequate hermeneutics (the third generality of classical theologies, which Boff calls "first theology"). What results from this operation on the first generality constitutes liberation theology.

To give an example: In order to arrive at an understanding of what *liberation* means, liberation theologians must start not from the Bible or tradition but from the data of oppression/liberation as the social sciences understand them. This sociological concept forms the first generality of their theological science. The theologian does not work *with* but *upon* the concept of "liberation" derived from sociological studies. In this way the social sciences as well as other human sciences form an intrinsic and constitutive and not an adventitious part of theology. The theologian's task is to transform, with the help of the properly theological concept of "salvation" (the third generality of "first theology," now functioning as the second generality of liberation theologies), the sociological concept of "liberation" (the third generality of sociology, now functioning as the first generality of liberation theologies) in such a way as to produce a theological theory that "liberation is salvation" (the third generality of liberation theologies).[45]

---

[43] C. Boff, *Theology and Praxis*, 72.
[44] Ibid., 73.
[45] Ibid., 87-88.

Central to this theoretical practice to produce a liberation theology is clearly the second generality, that is, the "working" on the first generality of liberation theologies that is constituted by the third generality of the social and other human sciences. In other words, it is the hermeneutical mediation between the social sciences and other sciences on the one hand, and the Bible and the Christian tradition on the other hand, between our present social location and the past Christian writings. Here we come back to the hermeneutical circle spoken of above. Clodovis Boff draws our attention to the dialectical circularity between scripture as written text and word of God as scripture read in the church, between the creation of meaning and the acceptance of meaning, between structure as vehicle of communication and meaning as needing structure for support, and between hermeneutics as employment of technical apparatus of interpretation and hermeneutics as a creative *Sinngebung*.[46]

As to the process of correlating the scripture to our social location, Clodovis Boff warns us against two unacceptable common practices, which he terms the "gospel/politics model" and the "correspondence of terms model." The former sees the gospel as a code of norms to be directly applied to the present situation. Such application is carried out in a mechanical, automatic, and non-dialectical manner; it completely ignores the differences in the historical contexts of each of the two terms of the relationship. The latter sets up two ratios it regards as mutually equivalent and transfers the sense of the first ratio to the second by a sort of hermeneutical switch. For instance, an attempt is made to establish an equivalency between the ratio of the first pair of terms and that of the second pair of terms:

scripture: its political context	=	theology of the political: our political context
exodus: enslavement of the Hebrews	=	liberation: oppression of the poor
Babylon: Israel	=	captivity: people of Latin America
Jesus: his political context	=	Christian community: current political context

Although better than the "gospel/politics model," insofar as it takes into account the historical context of each situation, the "correspondence of terms model" is still unacceptable, because it assumes a perfect parallel between the first ratio and the second.

---

[46] Ibid., 135-39.

The "Correspondence of Relationships Model"

In contrast to these two models, Clodovis Boff proposes what he calls the "correspondence of relationships model," which he claims is in conformity with the practice of the early church and the Christian communities in general. In schematic form this model looks as follows:

$$\frac{\text{Jesus of Nazareth:}}{\text{his context}} = \frac{\text{Christ+the church:}}{\text{context of church}} = \frac{\text{church tradition:}}{\text{historical context}} = \frac{\text{ourselves:}}{\text{our context}}$$

Or, in reduced form:

$$\frac{\text{scripture:}}{\text{its context}} = \frac{\text{ourselves:}}{\text{our context}}$$

In this model the Christian communities (represented by the church, church tradition, and ourselves) seek to apply the gospel to their particular situations. But contrary to the other two models, this model takes both the Bible and the situation to which the Bible is applied in their respective autonomy. It does not identify Jesus with the church, church tradition, and ourselves on the one hand, nor does it identify Jesus' context with the context of the church, the historical context of church tradition, and our context on the other. The equal sign (=) does not refer to the equivalency among the terms of the hermeneutical equation but to the equality among the respective relationships between pairs of terms. As Boff puts it,

> The equal sign refers neither to the oral, nor the textual, nor to the transmitted words of the message, nor even to the situations that correspond to them. It refers to the relationship between them. We are dealing with a *relationship of relationships.* An identity of senses, then, is not to be sought on the level of context, nor, consequently, on the level of the message as such—but rather on the level of the *relationship* between context and message on each side [scripture and ourselves in the reduced schema] respectively.[47]

This focus on the relationship between the terms of each pair and the equivalency among these relationships rather than on a particular text of the scripture to be applied allows both creative freedom in biblical interpretation (not

---

[47] Ibid., 149. This by no means implies that liberation theologians will not appeal to specific texts or books of the Bible. On the contrary, as the Boff brothers have pointed out, certain biblical books are favored by liberation theologians, such as Exodus, the Prophets, the Gospels, the Acts of the Apostles, and Revelation. See L. Boff and C. Boff, *Introducing Liberation Theology*, 34-35.

"hermeneutic positivism") and basic continuity with the meaning of the Bible (not "improvisation *ad libitum*"): "The Christian writings offer us not a *what*, but a *how*—a manner, a style, a spirit."[48]

One of the merits of Clodovis Boff's correspondence of relationships model of the hermeneutical mediation is that it safeguards the exegesis of liberation theologians from the dangers of biblicism, fundamentalism, and eisegesis to which some of their early works were prone. In this respect his hermeneutics would command wholehearted agreement from most liberation theologians. On the other hand, some recent liberation theologians would contest his granting primacy to the scripture as the norm according to which later interpretations is to be measured. Though he maintains that any genuine hermeneutical relation-ship ("dialectical hermeneutic") involves circularity, Boff believes that "this circularity functions within an *articulation with a dominant term*. The thrust of the dialectic-hermeneutic movement comes from *scripture* and is measured, in the last instance, upon scripture as *norma normans*."[49]

In contrast to Boff, liberation theologians from a multireligious context in which classics of other religions are widely read tend to deny the normativeness of the Christian scriptures. For example, Kwok Pui-lan explicitly rejects the sacrality of the Bible, its status as canonical writing, and its normativeness and proposes what she calls a "dialogical model of interpretation" in which the Bible is seen as a "talking book" inviting dialogue and conversation.[50] R. S. Sugirtharajah calls for a "multi-faith hermeneutics" in which the sacred books of all religions are allowed to be unique and speak on their own terms; in which Christians do not claim that their story is superior to and more valid than other stories; and in which the universal Wisdom tradition is retrieved.[51] Furthermore, whereas Juan Luis Segundo and Clodovis Boff do not turn the hermeneutics of suspicion on to the Bible itself, many liberation theologians, especially femi-nists, have exposed the patriarchal and androcentric bias of the Hebrew-Christian sacred text.

Despite these important differences in their hermeneutical practice, all lib-eration theologians concur that the task of the interpreter is not only to uncover the objective meaning of the text and to solve the riddles of scholarship. Rather, for them the main goal of hermeneutics is to transform the unjust world, to take an "advocacy stance" (Elisabeth Schüssler Fiorenza) in favor of the poor and the oppressed, to enact the word of God in their context. In other words, essen-tial to their theological method is what has been called *praxis*, which is the third mediation of the method of liberation theology.

---

[48] C. Boff, *Theology and Praxis,* 149.

[49] Ibid., 149-50.

[50] Kwok Pui-lan, *Discovering the Bible in the Non-Biblical World* (Maryknoll, N.Y.: Orbis Books, 1995).

[51] R. S. Sugirtharajah, "Inter-Faith Hermeneutics: An Example and Some Implica-tions," in *Voices from the Margins*, 352-63.

"DOING THE TRUTH" (JN 3:21): THE PRACTICAL MEDIATION

All liberation theologians insist that prior to doing liberation theology one must do liberation:

> The first step for liberation theology is pre-theological. It is a matter of trying to live the commitment of faith: in our case, to participate in some way in the process of liberation, to be committed to the oppressed. . . . The essential point is this: links with specific practice are *at the root* of liberation theology. It operates within the great dialectic of theory (faith) and practice (love).[52]

The Theologian's Social Commitment

The Boff brothers suggest that there are three levels in which theologians can commit themselves to the poor and oppressed. The first, rather restricted, is sporadic or more or less regular participation in base communities and their activities; the second is alternating periods of scholarly work with periods of practical work; and the third is living and working permanently in solidarity with and among the people.[53] Which of these forms of social commitment is proper for an individual liberation theologian cannot be determined in advance. A choice of one or the other at a particular historical moment depends, as Clodovis Boff has shown, on the dialectical interplay among three factors or circles, namely, the relation between the social situation (society) and the personal position of the theologian (individual), the relation between analysis (sociology) and ethics (gospel), and the relation between the theologian as theoretician and the theologian as social agent.[54]

Of course, such a practical commitment does not of itself guarantee the truth of the liberation theologian's theoretical practice, since there is a difference between the epistemic locus and the social locus; in the former, the theologian acts as the epistemic agent and is related internally to the theological discipline through objective cognition, whereas in the latter, the theologian acts as the social agent and is related externally to the society through power. Nevertheless, through social commitment the theologian acquires a "sensibility" or a

---

[52] L. Boff and C. Boff., *Introducing Liberation Theology*, 22. For a very balanced reflection on the relationship between orthopraxis and theological work, see Verkamp, "On Doing the Truth."

[53] L. Boff and C. Boff, *Introducing Liberation Theology*, 23. These three models of the liberation theologian's social commitment—whereby a synthesis of theology and politics, theoretical practice and political practice, science and justice is achieved—are termed by Leonardo Boff the "specific contribution," "alternating moments," and "incarnation" models respectively (see C. Boff, *Theology and Praxis*, 168-71).

[54] See C. Boff, *Theology and Praxis*, 171-73.

heightened capacity to discern the relevance of the imperatives of the historical situation and is enabled to decide which thematic problem is of objective relevance or significance with respect to a given sociohistorical conjuncture. In addition to this sensibility the capacity for critical analysis to examine and establish in a rigorous manner the relevance of the theological problematic to a particular historical situation is required.

Objections have been raised against the liberation theologian's social commitment in the name of the disinterested nature of science and knowledge ("knowledge for knowledge's sake"). It is argued that science *qua* science is no more revolutionary or reactionary than it is religious or atheistic. To obviate these objections, liberation theologians have pointed out that, insofar as it is a science, that is, from an epistemological point of view, theology is a disinterested cognition. However, insofar as it is a social positivity, that is, in virtue of its factual insertion into the fabric of social interests, theology is not an innocent, neutral, apolitical function but a partisan and interested social instrument. Like practitioners of any science, theologians have to pass judgment on how it is to be employed, who is to employ it and for what purposes, who are to be its addressees, and so on, questions that cannot be answered in the epistemological order but only in the practical order. As Clodovis Boff has put it,

All knowledge, including theological knowledge, is interested. It objectively intends precise finalities. It is finalized, mediately or immediately, by something external to itself. The true problem, consequently, does not reside in the alternative: interested or disinterested theology. The true problem lies in questions of this kind: What are the objective interests of a given theology? For what concrete causes is it being developed? In a word, *where* are its interests?[55]

Finally, it must be recognized that there is no straight, logical path from theory to praxis, or from praxis to theory. Since theory is constituted through a breach with praxis, and since praxis is performed through a breach with theory, the passage from one pole to the other is not a necessary consequence but is always a human decision. It follows then, as Clodovis Boff argues, "that no theory, be it ever so rigorous or profound, will ever of itself engender praxis. The same holds for the inverse calculation: no praxis, be it as radical as you please, will ever, just on that account, issue in a theory. . . . Thus theory and praxis represent irreducible orders."[56]

Praxis as Criterion of Truth

In addition to the requirement of social commitment or praxis as part of their theological method, liberation theologians also maintain that there is an indissoluble link between orthodoxy and orthopraxis. Of this, priority is given to

---

[55] Ibid., 191.
[56] Ibid., 193.

orthopraxis. Sometimes this primacy of praxis over theory is expressed by saying that "praxis is the criterion of truth." Many liberation theologians are aware of the ambiguity of this statement. Gustavo Gutiérrez explicitly distances himself from the position that "praxis . . . gives rise to truth or becomes the fundamental criterion of truth."[57] For him, theology being "critical reflection on praxis in the light of the Word," the ultimate criteria of truth "come from revealed truth which we accept in faith and not from praxis itself."[58]

To prevent misunderstandings of this principle, Clodovis Boff makes a careful distinction between "theological criteriology" and "pistic criteriology." By the former he means criteria of truth for theology as a theoretical practice ("truth of theory"), and by the latter he means those of faith and love ("truth of praxis"). The former criteria are of an epistemological order and concern the theoretical practice of the theologian, whereas the latter are of an existential order and concern the concrete practice of the believer. In light of this distinction, Clodovis Boff argues that "from the viewpoint of theological practice, (political) praxis neither is nor can be the criterion of (theological) truth. . . . The thesis that praxis is the criterion of truth is theologically nonpertinent. It seeks to compare the incomparable."[59] For theology as a theoretical practice there are only two criteria of truth, one of the logical order and the other of the positive order. The former controls the internal coherence of the theological production, and the latter its external agreement with the positivity of faith (what the Christian community believes). With regard to pistic criteriology, Boff notes that liberation theologies often refer to the "capacity of faith for social transformation." While acknowledging such a capacity, Boff warns against the acritical criterion of pragmatism with the primacy given to practical effectiveness and stresses the necessity of critically evaluating the ethical quality of a course of political action through the socio-analytic and hermeneutical mediations: "We may not embrace the ideology of orthopraxy, or praxiology, dispensing ourselves from a thorough reflection on the ethical content of a given practice and from a critique of the idea of efficacity and the 'theoretical short-circuit' that it tends to provoke."[60]

While maintaining the difference between theological criteriology and pistic criteriology, Boff reminds us that theology is dependent upon the practice of justice and love, as demonstrated by the social position of theology, its thematic relevance, and its political interests (which we have discussed above). Accordingly, says Boff, "pistic truth—a truth of praxis—and theological truth—a truth of theory—call for each other, and interact upon each other. And they do so in a rhythm that is not purely linear, but is ultimately measured by the basic 'scansion'

---

[57] Gutiérrez, *The Truth Shall Make You Free*, 181 n.45.

[58] Ibid., 101.

[59] C. Boff, *Theology and Praxis*, 198.

[60] Ibid., 203. Boff further reminds us that the final and definitive verification of the truth of faith and the practice of justice does not occur until the eschaton and is the exclusive prerogative of God.

or yardstick of the reality of faith. For the dialectical balance always leans toward the practical dimension."[61]

The Dialectic between Theory and Praxis

The final issue in the practical mediation of the method of liberation theologies is the nature of the relationship between theory and praxis and its implications for the character of liberation theologies itself. This relationship has been described as dialectical. By this is meant that the relationship is not a static but a dynamic one, so that theory and praxis are related to each other in perpetual motion. Because theory and praxis are bound up with each other in mutual inclusion *(perichoresis)* and because they are distinguished from each other in difference *(chorismos)* at the same time, there is between them a ceaseless oscillation, a "dialectical movement," so that a total theological synthesis based on this kind of relationship between theory and praxis is never possible but always *in via*, under construction.[62] Consequently, liberation theologies are by necessity anti-dogmatic and "open and continually renewing."[63]

With respect to liberation theologies in particular, this dialectical drive in perpetual motion occurs first of all, as we have seen, between the two mediations— socio-analytic and hermeneutical—in the theoretical practice of theology in such a way that the pendulum of cognition never comes to a dead stop. But it occurs also at the more general level of the history in which theory and praxis are practiced. At this second level, praxis holds an analytical primacy over theory, even though theory holds the key to the identity of praxis. This relationship, notes Clodovis Boff, "must be represented as a current receiving its first thrust from the side of praxis, ricocheting off theory, and returning to praxis and dislocating it—and so on, over and over again."[64] In other words, praxis exerts pressure on theory to examine itself critically; theory, in turn, reacting, modifies praxis; then theory and praxis are transcended; and the spiraling, never-ending movement goes on and on.

"NEW WINE INTO NEW WINESKINS" (MT 9:17): A NEW THEOLOGY IN A NEW METHOD?

Liberation theologies, as has been said at the beginning of this essay, seek to be a new way of doing theology. Of course, the contents of liberation theologies

---

[61] Ibid., 205.

[62] For a description of *perichoresis* and *chorismos* between theory and praxis, see ibid., 210-13.

[63] Susan Brooks Thistlethwaite and Mary Potter Engel, "Making the Connections among Liberation Theologies around the World," in *Lift Every Voice*, 11: "Theologies that are contextual, *praxis*-based, communal, and prophetic are theologies that are bound to remain open to change and ongoing revision."

[64] C. Boff, *Theology and Praxis,* 216.

are new, at least if one goes by some of the names under which they are advocated: womanist, *mujerista, minjung*, and even queer (gay and lesbian) theologies. A couple of decades ago these appellations were not even mentioned in theological encyclopedias! But what makes liberation theologies new and for some a threat is ultimately their method. As Juan Luis Segundo stated in 1974 in his lectures at Harvard, "It is the fact that the one and only thing that can maintain the liberative character of any theology is not its content but its methodology. It is the latter that guarantees the continuing bite of theology."[65]

Of course, it is not possible to describe with historical precision what came first in liberation theologies, method or content. The question resembles the proverbial query about the chicken and the egg. Most likely, content and method occur simultaneously, though it often happens that reflections on method are undertaken only after a long practice at the craft or when the discipline is undergoing a crisis or a paradigmatic shift. At any rate, the mutual dependence between content and method is picturesquely affirmed by Jesus when he says that "people do not pour new wine into old wineskins. If they do, the skins burst, the wines spill out, and the skins are ruined. No, they pour new wine into new wineskins, and in that way both are preserved" (Mt 9:17, NAB).

This is not the place to offer an extensive evaluation of the method of liberation theologies with its three mediations—socio-analytic, hermeneutical, and practical. To do so would bring the essay to unacceptable lengths. Its principal intent has been to discern in the rich and even bewildering tapestry of liberation theologies the thread that binds them together into a common pattern. That unifying thread is methodological. In the concluding paragraphs it would be useful to enumerate in thesis form the ways in which the method as it has been described above can obviate some of the oft-repeated charges against liberation theologies.

1. It is not accurate to say that various kinds of liberation theology that have been formulated after the emergence of Latin-American liberation theology in the early seventies are nothing but clones of it. Methodologically, for example, Asian liberation theologies, though indebted to their Latin-American older sibling, have introduced new methods of theologizing (for example, "psychological tools of introspection," interreligious dialogue, inculturation, and storytelling) that make them quite distinctive.[66] Furthermore, more recent liberation theologies have brought to the theological mill a variety of materials from their own specific social, cultural, and religious backgrounds.[67]

2. It is not accurate to say that liberation theologies are fundamentally inspired by Marxism or are simply theological versions of the Marxist theory of class struggle. It is true that liberation theologies have made use of the socio-

---

[65] Segundo, *The Liberation of Theology*, 39-40.

[66] For an excellent presentation of Asian liberation theologies, see Michael Amaladoss, *Life in Freedom: Liberation Theologies from Asia* (Maryknoll, N.Y.: Orbis Books, 1997).

[67] For a description of these resources, see Peter C. Phan, "Jesus the Christ with an Asian Face," *Theological Studies* 57 (1996): 403-5.

logical theory of dependence and Marxist tools of social analysis, but these concepts and theories (the "third generality" of the social sciences) are adopted as the "first generality" of liberation theologies and are "worked" on in its "second generality" in the hermeneutical mediation by means of the theological concepts of "first theology" to produce a body of genuinely theological science (the "third generality" of liberation theologies).

3. It is not accurate to say that liberation theologies are biblically naive or are susceptible to biblical fundamentalism. The "correspondence of relationships model" is far more sophisticated than the gospel/politics and correspondence of terms models that are often thought to be the hermeneutical approaches of liberation theologies. This model avoids the Scylla of hermeneutic positivism of biblical fundamentalism and the Charybdis of *ad libitum* improvisation of postmodernism. On the contrary, it enables both creative freedom in biblical interpretation and basic fidelity to the meanings of the scripture and tradition.

4. It is not accurate to say that liberation theologians, with their requisite social commitment, abandon or at least jeopardize the objectivity and disinterestedness of theology as a pursuit of knowledge. Liberation theologians do recognize that theology, insofar as it is a theoretical practice, is a disinterested cognition and is no more revolutionary or reactionary than any other science. On the other hand, because theology is a social fact and because the theologian is not only a theoretician but also a social agent, theology is never neutral and the theologian is never socially uncommitted. The question is not whether theology is neutral or the theologian is uncommitted but to *which* cause theology is partisan and the theologian is engaged. Such a social commitment gives the theologian the "sensibility" needed to determine which theological problematic is required by a particular historical situation to which theology must be "relevant."

5. Finally, it is not accurate to say that liberation theologies lapse into epistemological empiricism and ethical pragmatism when they grant priority to orthopraxis over orthodoxy and make praxis into the criterion of truth. With a careful distinction between "theological criteriology" and "pistic criteriology," liberation theologies recognize the difference between criteria of truth for theology as a theoretical practice (that is, logical consistency and conformity to the contents of the faith) and the criterion of truth for faith as a political practice (that is, the capacity of faith for social transformation). On the other hand, while maintaining this necessary distinction, liberation theologies are able to affirm the dialectical relationship between theory and praxis, both in the theoretical practice of theology (between the socio-analytic and hermeneutical mediations) and in their actual unfolding in history, so that the character of liberation theologies as a fundamentally open, ever-developing science can also be affirmed.

While the foregoing five remarks, and of course the entire essay, may be construed as an apologia for liberation theologies and their method, the main intention is to show that liberation theologians, despite their diversity of gender and economic background, national and ethnic origin, cultural and religious membership, are, by virtue of their shared method and tasks, fellow travelers in a common journey to the same destination. The temptation must then be re-sisted to dismiss liberation theologies as passé, especially in view of the moribund condition of socialism and the near-universal domination of the free-market system. On the contrary, thanks to the virtualities of their own method, libera-tion theologies will be able to contribute to the emergence of a new kind of catholicity that is not a pretension to a false universalism but appreciates and promotes the particularity of each voice, especially the voices of those who have not been allowed to speak, and in and through these particular voices, constructs a new harmony for the coming reign of God.

8

A Theology of Transmutation

ANDREW SUNG PARK

The church is the body of Christ. However, the differences of race, gender, sexual orientation, and social class have broken the body. The mission of the church in the coming century is not just to convert people to Christianity but to convert Christians to be authentic people of God, rising above various kinds of prejudice and discrimination against others. The task of bringing racial healing is one of the most pressing issues faced by the church in the United States today. In this chapter I focus on racial relations and Asian Americans: where we have been, where we are now, and where we should be going. In the past, Asian Americans suffered institutional racism; at present, they are experiencing various other types of racism—structural, symbolic, silent, and split racism. To resolve such problems, I argue for a theology of transmutation—a theology that goes beyond the available social models of assimilationism, amalgamationism, and cultural pluralism and highlights instead the mutual enhancement of all ethnic groups.[1] This vision of transmutation emerges from both our heritage as Asian Americans and our heritage as Christians.

RACIAL RELATIONS AND ASIAN AMERICANS

Where Have We Been?

Any number of ethnic groups have experienced institutional racism in the United States. Asian Americans have suffered from it as well. Institutional racism may be defined as legally sanctioned racism, such as the enslavement of African Americans, the forced removal of Native-American children from their homes for generations, and the internment of Japanese Americans. This type of racism legally produces racial inequalities in society and drives people to discriminate against the ethnic group(s) in question even in the absence of personal

---

[1] In this article I use the term *ethnic group* to mean both the dominant ethnic group and all other such groups in the society.

prejudice. The following legal actions are good examples of the institutional racism directed against Asian Americans during the latter part of the nineteenth century and the early part of the twentieth century: the exclusion of Chinese students from public schools in San Francisco in 1859; the Naturalization Act of 1870, excluding Chinese people from citizenship; the Chinese Exclusion Act of 1882, suspending the immigration of Chinese laborers for ten years and banning the entry of Chinese laborers' wives into the country; the Congressional prohibition against Chinese immigration and denial of naturalization in 1902; the formation of the Asiatic Exclusion League in San Francisco in 1905; the segregation of the city's Japanese school children from white students in 1906; California's anti-miscegenation law, amended in 1906 to bar marriages between whites and "Mongolians"; the U.S. Supreme Court's decision of 1910, extending the Naturalization Act of 1870 to other Asians; the California Alien Land Act, preventing Asians from acquiring land in 1913 and 1920; and the Immigration Act of 1924, known as the Asian Exclusion Act and the National Origins Act.

Such measures served to halt the immigration of all Asians into the country, making it very clear that Asians were in effect undesirable. While Asians bore such institutional racism during this first period of immigration, the Statue of Liberty was dedicated, in 1886, with its inscribed poem by Emma Lazarus welcoming "the tired, the poor and the huddled masses." Such an event can only be described as a hollow mockery to Asians in general and to the Chinese in particular, whose immigration into the country had been prohibited by then.

Where Are We Now?

While the period of institutional racism is over for Asian Americans, structural, symbolic, silent, and split racism remain entrenched in U.S. culture. Since these types of racism cannot attain legal sanction, they operate in stealth, but in so doing they continue to engender racial bigotry or discrimination in a variety of ways.

Structural racism refers to customs, traditions, and practices that informally produce racial discrimination and inequalities. When legal racial discrimination is blocked, prejudice appears in this form. Such discrimination is informal, precisely because of the formal prohibition against any type of discrimination or inequality within institutions. Structural racism has no legal support, but it does have social and cultural sanction. Two examples of this type of racism are redlining and the so-called glass ceiling. *Redlining* refers to that arbitrary practice by which banks or mortgage companies limit or reject the granting of mortgage loans for houses in highlighted ethnic areas; nowadays, insurance companies also refuse to sell their premium in such areas. Because such institutions outlined these ethnic areas in their maps with red, this practice has come to be known as redlining. Thus, Korean Americans in Los Angeles's Koreatown have suffered from redlining, particularly as a result of the L.A. social eruptions of 1992: before the riots, they operated their businesses without insurance policies; afterward, they were unable to purchase such insurance. *Glass ceiling* refers to that phenomenon whereby ethnic minorities and women move up the career ladder slowly and in limited numbers. For example, according to the U.S. Commission on Civil Rights, Asian-American men born in this country are 7 to 11 percent less likely to attain managerial jobs than their white counterparts.[2]

Symbolic racism may be defined as racial prejudice and residual resentment expressed through the use of subtle symbolic language and code words. Because of public pressure, when members of the dominant group feel uneasy about expressing their prejudices overtly, they have recourse to symbolic messages. Symbolic racism represents not only concealed bigotry but also an indirect attack on constructive attempts to overcome various kinds of racism in our institutions. Those who use symbolic racism reveal their anger and resentment against ethnic minorities, arguing that such individuals are aggressive and unqualified for their present positions. This type of racism blocks, in indirect fashion, all opportunities for fairness regarding ethnic minorities, while denying the fact that it is racism. Examples abound. Public debates on crime and welfare issues can often function as subtle ways of expressing such racial bigotry and resentment. Similarly, in a political campaign one can easily spot such racism in the argument that the election of an African-American or an ethnic-minority candidate will derail the stability of social values and the American work ethic.

Silent racism refers to the racism that overlooks unjust racial discrimination. It is present in people who do not support racism in principle but also are not involved in any anti-racism activities. When they hear racial slurs, they say nothing. While some are indifferent, others lack the courage to speak out for racial justice. Saying nothing or doing nothing against injustice is saying or doing something for it. As long as enough people remain silent about racism, it can thrive, expand, and live long. Within the church silent racism appears in the form of indifference, by way of the claim that racism was already dealt with in the 1960s. This type of racism inadvertently breeds even more racism, although individuals may be opposed to it in their own mind.

Split racism makes one ethnic group compete against others by splitting their awareness of solidarity as the oppressed in the society. Putting one group above others, this elusive type of racism undermines ethnic togetherness. A good example is the myth of the "model minority." Its proponents praise Asian Americans as a model minority. To be sure, many Asian immigrants did come from the middle or upper classes and were highly educated. Even they, however, in the end run against the reality of the glass ceiling and receive unfair compensation compared with their white counterparts. According to the U.S. Census Bureau, the median income for Asian Americans with four years of college education is $34,470 a year, compared with $36,130 for whites.[3] At the same time, many Asian Americans suffer high poverty rates. In 1994, for example, the individual Asian-American poverty rate was 15.3 percent, compared to a national rate of

---

[2] Carolyn Jung, "Asian-Americans Say They Run into Glass Ceiling," *San Jose Mercury News* (September 10, 1993): 1B.

[3] Ibid.

14.5 percent and a white rate of 12.2 percent.[4] The reality of Asian Americans is, therefore, fragmented, but the myth remains quite strong and quite useful. On the one hand, its proponents use Asian Americans as a weapon against other ethnic minorities, such as African Americans, who have suffered strong prejudice, poverty, and legal discrimination for years. In so doing, they exploit the partial successes of Asian Americans as proof of a racism-free society. On the other hand, they cash in on the myth to attack affirmative action or to exclude Asian Americans from it. This type of racism saps the synergy of ethnic groups that are trying to break through the thickness of racial prejudice and discrimination.

Where Are We Going?

To deal with our interracial and interethnic conflicts and problems, sociologists have so far advanced three major models: assimilation, amalgamation, and cultural pluralism. The assimilationist model underscores the unilateral integration of all diverse ethnic groups into Anglo-American culture. William Newman expresses it as a formula, "A + B + C = A, where A, B, and C represent different social groups and A represents the dominant group."[5] This is clearly a hierarchical view, driving our society toward uniformity.

The amalgamationist or "melting pot" model stresses the oneness of the society by way of a new identity through intermixing, with the different groups losing their ethnic identities in this new world. This model is conveyed by the formula, A + B + C = D (a new identity).[6] At the turn of the century, the concept of the melting pot was widely discussed, since most immigrants came from Europe.[7]

At present, it is the cultural-pluralist model that prevails in the society, alongside that of assimilation. Newman describes it in terms of the following formula, "A + B + C = A + B + C, where A, B, and C represent different social groups that, over time, maintain their own unique identities."[8] In theory, this model espouses a society of diversity in unity and unity in diversity; in practice, however, it fosters the separation and isolation of ethnic groups, hiding as it does the reality of structural, symbolic, silent, and split racism.

Our present social atmosphere, therefore, disparages authentic diversity while deepening ethnic isolation and divisions. This is due to the lack of interethnic unity in our society. The cultural-pluralist model suggests an acceptance of all

---

[4] U.S. Bureau of the Census, *Current Population Reports*, Asian-American rate: P20-459 and unpublished data; U.S. rate: P-60 series; white American rate: P20-480 and unpublished data.

[5] William M. Newman, *American Pluralism: A Study of Minority Groups and Social Theory* (New York: Harper & Row, 1973), 53.

[6] Ibid., 63.

[7] To be sure, this model ignored the distinctive and "unmeltable" nature of non-European groups.

[8] Newman, *American Pluralism*, 67.

ethnic cultures as they are in the name of diversity but not an encounter with each ethnic culture in order to rectify injustice and improve the quality of its culture. In other words, the model is far from the theme of cultural compunction. What are we going to do with racism, sexism, classism, and hierarchies of racial and ethnic groups? Is it possible to appreciate diversity while also improving the quality of diverse cultures without sacrificing our true identity and societal unity? To meet such a challenge, I should like to propose a new model—transmutation.

Proposal: Transformation and Transmutation

To describe the reality of change, I call upon the terms *transformation* and *transmutation*. The term *transformation* is quite useful, signifying the alteration of appearance, function, and form. The term, however, can be dangerous, if it implies imposing one's own idea upon others. *Tao Teh King* recommends no interference with the lives of others: "Behave indifferently—without trying to impose your own ideas upon the lives of others."[9] From a historical point of view, oppressors have used coercive power to change others. Yet, compelled transformation is not transformation but the deformation of existence. In the name of transformation, the powerful have suppressed the spontaneity of others and deprived them of their various rights. Authentic transformation is *natural* transmutation—a transformation that comes from within through seeing rather than from without through force. We cannot compel change in others; we can only serve as an instrument for their own spontaneous change. We can cause true change in others by preparing them to realize all of their potential. People convert themselves by divine beckoning. Our goal is not to work for transformation in others but to usher a fuller divine flow into them so that they can then change by themselves. It is this process as a whole that I call transmutation.

For me the term *transmutation* expresses a change in nature, substance, and content. Although both terms, *transmutation* and *transformation*, refer to internal as well as external change, *transmutation* stresses its internal, biological, and natural aspect, whereas *transformation* underscores its external and structural aspect. Both terms are necessary. To avoid the notion of compelled change, I employ the word *transmutation*. Transmutation does not signal, however, a passive and weak work of change; rather, it signifies an active and assertive move, yet in a cordial spirit. The way of transmutation is the way of Tao, changing an object not by force but by gentle strength. One should think of a huge rock in flowing water. Water carves and rounds the rock tenderly and slowly but surely. Like water, the way of transmutation changes a human being by its soft strength without violent coercion. Such transmutation never means passivity toward the power of evil. We face oppressors by the strength of truth, not by violent force. That strength includes genuine consideration for the persons we challenge, because we believe that the care we show toward them changes them.

---

[9] Lao Tzu, *Tao Teh King*, interpreted by Archie J. Bahm (New York: E. Ungar, 1958), 56.

A THEOLOGY OF TRANSMUTATION

This concept of transmutation does not seek unity in diversity and diversity in unity. From this perspective, unity is not a goal but an outcome of moving toward the community of God and collaborating toward the reformation of unjust social systems, as well as of unfair customs and traditions of each culture. It asks that each culture care for other cultures by encouraging their strengths and challenging their shortcomings. In other words, this model respects other cultures enough to celebrate their strengths and cares for them enough to challenge their weak points. In this model, diversity takes place when each culture tries to pursue its own identity and change its own shortcomings. Diversity means not only to confirm what each culture is but also to affirm what each culture can be.

Transformity, Diversity, and Unity

This transmutation model underpins unity in transformity and diversity in transformity.[10] Diversity and unity are not automatically connected to each other. Transformity dialectically interweaves them. Without transformity, diversity turns into separation and unity into uniformity. Actual unity derives from mutual challenge. We can find such unity in two ways. One is when diverse groups work together for the transformation of social *han*, the deeply accumulated pain of a victim that has festered for a long time,[11] and social sin. The other is when diverse groups pursue their visions together. Diversity occurs through mutual enrichment. We can find such diversity in two ways as well. One is when diverse groups work on the transmutation of their own internal sin and *han*. The other is when these groups deepen their own identities through their heritages.

Mutual Enhancement: A Christic Community

In this mode of thinking, neither unity nor diversity is the goal, but rather the creation of a Christic community through transformity. A Christic community in this country is neither an Anglo-Saxonized society, nor a "melting pot" society, nor a culturally pluralistic society, but a community committed to the mutual enhancement of all ethnic groups and cultures and moving toward the full presence of Christ. Mutual enhancement means elevating one another's culture and tradition to higher levels by way of mutual enrichment and mutual challenge.[12] Mutual enrichment concerns the promulgation of each ethnic culture

---

[10] I developed the term *transformity* to express the reality of transmutation.

[11] Concerning the term *han*, see "Appendix: What Is *Han*?," the last section of this chapter.

[12] The term "mutual enrichment" is the expression that John Cobb (*Beyond Dialogue: Toward a Mutual Transformation of Christianity and Buddhism* [Philadelphia: Fortress Press, 1982], 47-53) uses for describing the aims of interreligious dialogue and life-experience. I use it in a different context.

and tradition. Diverse ethnic groups accept, encourage, and appreciate one another's culture, tradition, and custom. Mutual challenge involves three movements: respect, care, and confrontation. Respect flows from understanding one another. When we understand, we can mutually show honor, esteem, and admiration. Without respect, we should not challenge one another, for this will only serve to shut off the ears of the challenged. Care means to consider the other's situation and to listen. Through care, we heal one another's *han* by showing our genuine concerns; care leads us to face up to the cultural sins of one another. Rather than avoid conflicts among groups, we confront one another's sins with honesty and care. The goal of confrontation is not to destroy relationships but to solidify them on truthful and just grounds.

Mutual Enrichment

Mutual enrichment signifies that each group contributes to other groups, drawing upon its own unique cultural and traditional heritage. It affirms and promulgates one's own culture and seeks the same for other cultures. I will illustrate this notion of mutual enrichment by way of Korean-American life. Since Korean-American culture derives from Korean culture, I like to highlight its culture of intuition. Such a culture aims for holistic understanding rather than rationalization. The core of this intuitive culture is *seeing*. The term *noonchi* sums up this sense of intuition. Its literal translation is "awareness of the eye," pointing to the ability of intuitive seeing. In most cases Koreans communicate with one another through *noonchi*. We understand the depth of meaning beyond words through *noonchi*. In this culture of intuition, seeing becomes the primary way of knowing: Koreans see tasting, see smelling, see hearing, see knowing, see doing, see going, and see coming. Although these expressions may sound awkward, the point is that Koreans see everything!

A Comprehensive Vision

Seeing is also a key to determining the reality of the images of other groups. Seeing can be a way of solving the problem of ethnic tension. Not all sorts of seeing, however, are good. A certain kind of seeing is negative. Thus, I define *watching* as looking with suspicion. Whereas *seeing* implies a warm intention, yielding constructive transformation, watching involves a biased look, engendering harmful consequences. Seeing stands for visual dialogue and understanding, arousing sympathy; watching for a visual monologue, yielding an unpleasant staring, a cold look.

African Americans, for example, have complained about Korean immigrant shopkeepers, pointing out that shopkeepers watch their every move while they are shopping and fail to look at their faces at the check-out counter. Such tension is partially due to cultural differences as well as the antagonistic nature of the relationship between store owners and shoppers, but it can also be attributed to the suspicious watching of the shopkeepers. In interethnic relations we need to make room for seeing one another. Helen Kim, a young second-generation Korean American, has written on how to relax racial tension in Los Angeles.

She grew up in a cruel, discriminatory environment, where other kids hurled racial epithets, such as "chink," at her. She resented popular indifference toward the distinction between Chinese and Korean. Ignorance, she believes, escalates racial tensions. Consequently, she argues, understanding other cultures and heritages will bring about appreciation for such others:

> When Soon Ja Du, who shot Latasha Harlins, was given a light sentence, blacks in the community were outraged. I do not condone Du's action but I wonder if blacks know the extent to which Korean merchants are robbed and threatened by thieves. I can empathize with those who would make judgments about blacks and Hispanics after witnessing thefts firsthand at my mother's store. Mothers steal in front of their children and teenagers grab what they can and run. We have caught people red-handed yet they have the audacity to yell foul names and threats at us as they leave. A person becomes hardened and cynical after seeing this over and over again. I am tempted to make stereotypes but there are always other customers who are honest and sincere. They far outnumber those who denigrate themselves and their people.[13]

Helen had the eyes to see beyond what she saw in her mother's store. She courageously refused to stereotype her customers. She saw the goodness, honesty, and sincerity of her customers in spite of particular circumstances. It is easy for us to fall into the prison of our particular experiences. She had a comprehensive vision that perceived reality beyond the particular incidents. Her type of observation at her mother's store was one of watching the customers, but her understanding was able to turn such watching into seeing. Her comprehensive vision made her rise above her circumstantial experience. To alleviate interethnic tension, therefore, we need to convert watching into seeing. Seeing is comprehensive understanding; we understand others as much as we desire to see and we see as much as we aspire to understand.

Constructive Vision
Everyone wants to make a good impression on others. In interpersonal relationships, seeing others clearly and constructively makes a great difference with regard to the deepening of such relationships. In a racial or ethnic relationship, seeing other groups constructively engenders a warm society. The reality of people is not fixed but moldable, depending on how we see them. Thus, reality is perspectival. Is it possible to see others in constructive and creative images? I face this issue every day, particularly with regard to my children. Sometimes they make mistakes and do wrong, yet I refuse to see them in pejorative images. Eventually they see what I see in them, and we build mutual respect together toward a warm and creative future. This courage to have constructive images of others constitutes the strength of seeing.

---

[13] Helen Kim, *Korea Times: Monthly English Edition* (September 7, 1994): 7.

Young Ok Joo, a Korean-American woman, shares her story of seeing others in constructive images.[14] Since 1986 she has worked in a U.S. post office. In the beginning she enjoyed working with colleagues. Gradually, however, her supervisor and other fellow workers began to show their prejudice and discrimination against her and other Asian Americans. They assigned her to hard work and, whenever they made mistakes, they blamed them on her. They looked down upon most Asian Americans, who tend not to confront mistreatment. When she confronted them, they persecuted her more severely. Out of anger and resentment, she spent many a sleepless night. To her, the images of her supervisor and colleagues were ugly and appalling. She felt tense and frozen before her supervisor. She even thought about quitting her job. Instead, she secured a Walkman and began to listen to uplifting hymns and empowering sermons whenever she could. Slowly, she recovered self-confidence and developed a deep, merciful heart toward her tormentors. Subsequently, she began to deal calmly with her supervisor and colleagues. When they mistreated her, she corrected them gently, with genuine concern. She changed her image of them into a positive one. They eventually changed their attitude toward her and other Asian Americans. She and her colleagues were able to restore their warm friendships. Since then, her situation at work has been delightful.

The ability not to lose good images of our adversaries is critical. Our racial relationships hinge on mutual positive images, which are, in turn, expressions of mutual respect and mutual trust in our ability to change. Racial tension and conflict will only give way through such a building up of warm and cordial images. Indeed, Jesus' basic attitude toward the marginalized was affirmative and constructive. The parable of the Good Samaritan (Lk 10) shows how he refused to conjure up any pejorative image of the Samaritans and proceeded to praise them instead. Similarly, he treated Gentiles and so-called sinners as people of God who would partake in God's banquet, all part of God's intimate family. Thus, the good news or gospel is that God refuses to depict us as wretched or useless but sees us rather as friends. In the parable of the Prodigal Son (Lk 15), the father rejected a negative image of his son. Likewise, God creates and sees God's own image in us, no matter what. Is it possible to make the good news of Jesus Christ good news in our racial and ethnic relations? Can we see other races and ethnic groups with positive and constructive images (the image of God) in our daily life? This is the urgent task of the church in the United States.

An Internal Vision

Sung-Kye Yi was the first king of the Yi dynasty (1392-1910) in Korea. Monk Moohahk served as one of the king's advisors. What follows is a dialogue recorded between King Sung-Kye Yi and the Buddhist monk: "One day Sung-Kye Yi put down Moohahk: 'To me, you look like a pig.' The monk gently replied: 'To me, you look like Buddha.' 'Why are you saying that?' asked the

---

[14] Young Ok Joo, "Ill-Tur Esuh" ("At Working Place"), in *Life of Dreams, Life of Love: Stories of Korean-American Immigrant Women of Faith*, in Korean, ed. Hea Ran Lee (New York: General Board of Global Ministries, 1997), 270-74.

king. 'If you have a pig inside, you will see pigs in others, and if you have Buddha inside, you will see Buddha in others,' modestly explained the monk."[15] In effect, what we see outside of us corresponds with what we have inside. "Seeing" is pivotal in our self-understanding as well as in our understanding of the world. It cannot be just an act of reception from the outside; what we see is what we are.

The interrelatedness of internal and external seeing can be applied to both intrapersonal and interpersonal relationships. People with no self-respect do not know how to respect others. People who have little self-love cannot love others. Self-love, I should point out, is different from selfishness; selfishness is greedy egoism, while self-love means self-care and self-esteem. If we know little about how to care for ourselves, we cannot care for others. This is why Jesus asked us to love others as ourselves. If we do not love but hate ourselves, we cannot love but only hate others. This dynamic holds for group interaction as well. If a group has little self-respect, it cannot respect other groups. If a group suffers from self-hatred, it cannot appreciate other groups. What we see inside circumscribes what we see outside. A major reason why we have social and racial conflict has to do with the many broken collective images of racial and ethnic groups. Healthy intergroup dynamics start with sound group self-images. The question is how we can develop wholesome group images. The answer lies, I believe, in addressing the issue of how to resolve the *han* of ethnic America. I argue that "seeing" is the way to dissolve such *han* and to attain a healthy self-image.

Mutual Challenge

It is often true that offenders do not apologize for or repent of their sins or offenses. In such a case, what can the offended do to the unrepenting offenders? Even doing nothing is doing something. To deal with those who refuse to repent, it is sometimes necessary to confront their violation and oppression. Before we challenge our offenders, however, we need to *love* them. In fact, if we love them, we come to *confront* their injustice. It is not confrontation that changes people, but love. Indeed, to love our offenders represents the most effective challenge, "But I say to you, love your enemies and pray for those who persecute you" (Mt 5:44, NRSV).

What does it mean to love those who discriminate against us and harm us? New Testament scholar Luise Schottroff warns us not to interpret such love out of context. Any woman of that time, she argues, who would have taken such a command literally would have invited rape by sending a wrong message to her enemies.[16] To love our enemies does not mean allowing them to take advantage

---

[15] "Pigs in the Eyes of a Pig: Moohahk," *Modern Buddhism* 67, in Korean (December 1995), 47.

[16] Luise Schottroff, "The Pacifist Impulse in Historical Perspective," a paper read at the conference held in honor of Peter Brock, May 9-12, 1991, cited in William Klassen, "'Love Your Enemies': Some Reflections on the Current Status of Research," in *The Love of Enemy and Nonretaliation in the New Testament*, ed. Willard Swartley (Louisville, Ky.: Westminster/John Knox Press, 1992), 22.

of us or to harm us on a regular basis. According to Albert Camus, this world is absurd. If we are sane, we rebel against this absurd world. Rebellion, therefore, "cannot exist without a strange form of love."[17] Similarly, if we truly care for others, it is better to rectify their wrongs than to disregard them altogether. To love them is to help them change their lives of injustice and violence. In so doing, we call them to be what God created them to be. If we truly love those who injure us in God, we will not remain silent about their behavior. One way or another, we will let them know their wrongs. We love them as persons, but we renounce their injustice and evil. The Hebrew scriptures provide sound grounding for this teaching, "You shall reprove your neighbor, or you will incur guilt yourself" (Lv 19:17b, NRSV). If our son intentionally steals someone's jacket, we do not let him wear it but have him return it to the owner, and we make sure that such stealing does not happen again. Jesus teaches accountable love, even for our enemies.

Likewise, when we challenge our offenders or enemies, we need to *respect* them as well. We need to treat them as honorably as possible, although they may not deserve our respect. It is in dignity, not degradation, that people experience change. As offenders break the principle of justice, they undergo low self-esteem and poor self-respect. Before they violate the dignity of others, they violate their own. By showing respect for offenders, we confront them and, in so doing, challenge them to recollect their own image of God. In this sense, to love our enemies is to restore their dignity through respect for their own image of God. Even when the archangel Michael contended with the devil regarding the body of Moses, he did not condemn or curse him, but just said to him, "God rebuke you" (Jude 9). Michael avoided judging the devil with blasphemy. If even the devil deserves respect, how much more so our offenders or enemies!

Jesus asks victims to carry out such tenacious love toward their oppressors or enemies if they want to be his disciples. The love of Christ is that love, enduring and caring, that returns evil not with evil but with good. This mode of love, resisting evil with good, constitutes the vital message of Jesus and is not an option for us but rather part of our accountability as Christians. By avoiding our responsibility to challenge evil, we may end up returning evil with evil. For instance, by not challenging slavery or apartheid, we could prolong evil. It is our sacred call to challenge evil with the love of God. Our love in mutual challenge confronts the unjust work of our offenders, while our respect in mutual challenge allows room for them to be changed by God's grace. Like water, we slowly transmute the sharp edges of a rock through the divine Spirit, not destroying our opponents but building them up in God's plan.

Mutual Challenge for Korean-American Christians

What does such mutual challenge mean in interracial relations? As a concrete example, let me address the situation of Korean-American Christians. For Korean-American Christians, mutual challenge signifies three things:

---

[17] Albert Camus, *The Rebel* (New York: Vintage Books, 1957), 302-6, cited in William Klassen, "Love Your Enemies," 23.

First, Korean-American Christians need to challenge U.S. society. It is a society that suffers from sexism, racism, economic injustice, intolerance, media monopoly, the drug culture, and various other types of abuse and violence. These are the causes of *han* in our world. The more we care for this society, the more we must confront its wrongs. Making use of effective Christian resources and Asian-American traditions, we need to confront these problems and to unravel the *han* of the society. As we try to change the causes of social *han*, we seek the cultural, economic, social, and political reformation of the society. These problems affect all racial and ethnic groups. Diverse ethnic groups need to work together in changing our common culture by removing the collective sins of our culture and by making the victims of *han* whole. No group can escape from the collective sins responsible for social *han* or from the task of healing this deep-seated *han* of the society. In the process of diagnosing the problems of our society, devising effective ways to deal with them, and working together in eradicating them, we will find the true unity of all ethnic groups. Our goal is to create a community of God, in which each ethnic group can maximize all the gifts it has received from God, while encouraging other groups to do the same.

Second, Korean-American Christians must challenge other racial and ethnic groups when they show bias and discriminate against us. Whether it is racial or sexual discrimination, we need to stand up to the customs and cultures responsible for such prejudice. If an Anglo-Saxon group discriminates against us, we must confront its deep-seated culture of racism with the spirit of care. If an African-American group puts us or others down on the basis of ethnic bias, we have to show our opposition as well. Not out of contempt or resentment but out of care and respect for its culture and tradition, we would challenge the African-American group to change its prejudice and discrimination. Indeed, without a caring spirit and respect for any group, our challenge will only cause unnecessary or excessive conflict. In turn, the African-American group should challenge the Korean-American group to change its racism, too. This pursuit of transmutation through mutual challenge will serve to elicit the unity of diverse groups.

I believe that both love and justice are required at the social level of relationships, despite Emil Brunner's argument that love is a moral principle at the level of personal relationships and justice at the level of social relations.[18] Justice with love produces social change and inner conversion in people. Without genuine care, justice can only provoke hostility and frozenness. Young Ok Joo's case speaks to the point. When she tried to ignore her supervisor's abuse of power and her colleagues' unfair accusations, they increased their unjust violations. When she tried to confront them without the spirit of care, they escalated their behavior. It was only when she proceeded to challenge them gently, with care and respect, that they began to listen to her and to change their attitude and behavior. Love and respect, rather than confrontation alone, strike the string of a changing heart.

Third, Korean-American Christians need to change their own community. In fact, we must acknowledge that our community is guilty of patriarchalism, exploitation, and racial bias. First, the persistence of traditional patriarchy among

---

[18] Emil Brunner, *Justice and the Social Order* (New York: Harper, 1945).

us leads to domestic violence and lowers the status of women in the community. In addition, Korean-American businesses engage in exploitation by demanding long hours of labor for low wages from fellow Korean immigrants or other immigrant workers. Struggling workers need to be compensated fairly and to have shorter working hours. Finally, racial bias among Korean Americans toward other racial and ethnic groups cannot be denied. We often mirror the racist values of the society. The discriminated against also discriminate against others. Understanding the *han* of Korean Americans and other groups, Korean-American Christians should confront the racism of their fellow Korean Americans. Since we love our own people, we must challenge them to change their prejudice and injustice instead of covering them up. I have personally challenged several Korean Americans, from taxi drivers to professionals, when they showed racial prejudice in my presence. Most times the individuals in question understood my point and humbly retracted their views, as I explained the evil of racism using our own *han* of racism as a frame of reference. Such a mixture of truth and genuine concern proves quite persuasive.

CONCLUSION

In order to create an amicable and harmonious society, we need to improve our racial and ethnic relations. The present sociological models of racial relations prove insufficient for the construction of such a society. Our society requires a more qualitative unity of people, a unity based on genuine respect among diverse peoples and cultures. To meet this challenge of our time, I have advanced a new model for racial relations from a Christian perspective—the ideal of transmutation. Its fundamental points are unity, diversity, and transformity. To bring forth unity, ethnic groups must cooperate in overcoming social sins and social *han*, while moving toward mutual challenge—comprehensive, constructive, and internal "seeing." To celebrate the gifts of diversity, diverse groups need to work on the internal sins and *hans* of their own groups, while deepening and heightening their cultural identities through their own heritages.

In this process the key to interracial relations becomes the transmutation of mutual enhancement, which consists of mutual enrichment and mutual challenge. To describe the idea of mutual enrichment, I introduced the theology of "seeing," with its concepts of comprehensive, constructive, and internal seeing. This theology of seeing encourages the diversity of each group. To bring out the concept of mutual challenge, I stressed the values of confrontation, respect, and love. These I exemplified by way of the threefold task incumbent upon Korean-American Christians. This mutual challenge leads to the unity of diverse groups. It is my hope that this theological model will evoke, in the power of the Spirit, a spirit of mutual listening, understanding, appreciation, and celebration on the part of all racial and ethnic groups in the United States, thus making it possible for us to transmute our collective sins and social *han* into the community of God.

APPENDIX: WHAT IS *HAN*?

Eddy Wu, a twenty-three-year-old Chinese American, was carrying grocer-
ies to his car, when he was attacked on the afternoon of November 8, 1995, in
the parking lot of a supermarket in Novato, California. His attacker, Robert
Page, stabbed him twice. Chasing Wu into the supermarket, Page stabbed him
two more times. Wu suffered several serious injuries, including a punctured
lung. In his confession, Page, an unemployed musician, declared, "I didn't have
anything to do when I woke up. No friends were around. It seemed that no one
wanted to be around me. So I figured, 'What the f---, I'm going to kill me a
Chinaman." He added that he wanted to kill an Asian because they "got all the
good jobs." Page pleaded guilty to attempted murder and a hate crime and was
sentenced to eleven years. The experience of Eddy Wu was a nightmare. Nothing he had done deserved such suffering. He had been attacked solely on the
basis of his Asian looks.[19] Upon hearing of this heinous crime of madness, all
Asian Americans, not just Eddy Wu and his family, experience anger, frustration, and helplessness. This combination of feelings can be described as *han*.

Collapsed Core of Suffering
Han can be compared to the black hole phenomenon. When a massive star
expands and grows to be a red giant, it reaches its maximum point of expansion.
Then its inner core implodes (a supernova), and the star collapses into its center
(singularity). This collapsed center is a black hole. Its gravity is so strong that it
swallows whatever it comes upon. Similarly, when victims go beyond the maximum point of endurance, they collapse into the deep, dark abyss of pain. This
collapsed inner core governs their life agenda. Such an abysmal core is called
han in Korea and other Asian countries.

Critical Wound
Han can be defined as the critical wound of the heart generated by unjust
psychosomatic repression as well as by social, political, economic, and cultural
oppression. It becomes entrenched in the hearts of victims of sin and violence
and is expressed through such different reactions as sadness, helplessness, hopelessness, resentment, hatred, and the will to revenge. *Han* reverberates in the
souls of such groups as survivors of the Holocaust; Palestinians in the occupied
territories; victims of racial prejudice and discrimination; battered wives; children of divorce; victims of child molestation; laid-off workers; the unemployed;
exploited workers. As long as it remains unhealed, *han* continues to accumulate
with time and is ultimately transmitted to posterity as well.

---

[19] Kenneth B. Noble, "Attacks against Asian-Americans Are Rising," *Los Angeles
Times* (December 12, 1995).

Frustrated Hope

Hope lies at the very foundation of our existence. The meaning of the term *existence* is "standing out." Only when we stand out do we exist. The essence of human existence is hope. Hope is the window of the soul. When we look out and look forward, we can exist. When frustrated, hope turns into *han*, a psychosomatic pain.

9

Exodus-toward-Egypt

Filipino-Americans' Struggle to Realize the Promised Land in America

ELEAZAR S. FERNANDEZ

In recent years a host of material has been written questioning the biblical exodus-from-Egypt narrative as the paradigmatic narrative for oppressed and marginalized communities. When viewed from the perspective of those who identify with the plight of the Canaanites, this liberating narrative becomes an exodus-conquest narrative and hence a narrative of terror, for the acquisition of the promised land, Canaan, comes by way of conquest of a people, the Canaanites, with the help of Yahweh, the liberator-God turned conqueror-God.

Palestinians in particular, as pointed out by Naim Ateek and Mitri Raheb, find the exodus narrative extremely disturbing.[1] When they read it, they do not identify with the conquering Israelites but with the resident Canaanites. Exodus, for them, becomes a mirror of their oppression as well as of God's identification with the oppressors. For the Palestinians, exodus signifies conquest, not liberation. As such, the exodus narrative becomes a narrative of terror. In resonance with the Palestinians, Robert Allen Warrior argues that American Indians identify with the Canaanites on the land, not with the conquering Israelites, in the exodus narrative.[2] Like the biblical Canaanites, American Indians have also suffered conquest and genocide at the hands of those who escaped from the "Old World" and laid claim to the promised land of the "New World."

---

[1] Naim S. Ateek, *Justice and Only Justice: Towards a Palestinian Theology of Liberation* (Maryknoll, N.Y.: Orbis Books, 1989); Mitri Raheb, *I Am a Palestinian Christian* (Minneapolis, Minn.: Fortress Press, 1995). See Marc H. Ellis, *Toward a Jewish Theology of Liberation* (Maryknoll, N.Y.: Orbis Books, 1987).

[2] Robert Allen Warrior, "A Native American Perspective: Canaanites, Cowboys, and Indians," in *Voices from the Margin: Interpreting the Bible in the Third World*, ed. R. S. Sugirtharajah (Maryknoll, N.Y.: Orbis Books, 1991), 287-95.

For American Indians, therefore, the exodus narrative proves a narrative of terror as well, an exodus-conquest narrative.

For a long time I used the exodus-conquest narrative in my Sunday school classes in the land of my birth, the Philippines, without any awareness of or sensitivity to the plight of either the Palestinians or the American Indians. My most crucial ideological blinder in this regard was, I believe, my understanding that the Israelites were justified in what they had done to the Canaanites, since they were Yahweh's "chosen people" and had been charged by Yahweh to reclaim the promised land. I am not alone in this regard. Even when a biblical narrative of terror is as blatant and as nauseating as that of Yahweh's command to annihilate the inhabitants of Canaan, most readers simply push aside this dimension of the text, as I did, for it is always the well-being of God's elect (the Israelites) that matters, not that of the non-elect (the Canaanites).

Emphasizing the power of narratives, Warrior argues that no amount of critical biblical scholarship, as in the case of Norman Gottwald's *The Tribes of Yahweh*, can change the narrative of "the elect," for "people who read the narratives read them as they are, not as scholars and experts would like them to be read and interpreted. History is no longer with us. The narrative remains."[3] Yes, I agree with Warrior, the narrative remains. Indeed, the impact of the narrative seems more powerful than that of any scholarly account, aside from the fact that only a select few are able to read sophisticated historical, sociological, and theological discourses. Still, critical subaltern scholarship has, at the very least, helped us to hear the muted voices in the text. Nevertheless, what we need far more than scholarly critiques is the articulation of other narratives of liberation, for the God of liberation is not just the liberator of one "elect" people.

That is precisely my aim in this study. I seek to advance a narrative of liberation that, I believe, is more in keeping with the experience of the people to whom I am trying to give a voice—Filipino Americans. I proceed as follows: I begin with an overview of the proposed narrative, which I characterize as one of exodus-toward-Egypt; continue with a critical analysis of the present project of Filipino Americans in the light of their experience in the United States; and conclude with a call for a different project in the light of such experience and the alternative liberation narrative of exodus-toward-Egypt—a historical project for the realization of the promised land in the United States.

EXODUS-TOWARD-EGYPT: A NARRATIVE FRAMEWORK
FOR INTERPRETING THE FILIPINO-AMERICAN EXPERIENCE

Filipino Americans find resonance with the views articulated by Palestinian and American Indian theologians. Although many find themselves not just surviving in the country but actually thriving, Filipino Americans have by no means

---

[3] Ibid., 290. See Norman K. Gottwald, *The Tribes of Yahweh: A Sociology of the Religion of Liberated Israel, 1250-1050 B.C.E.* (Maryknoll, N.Y.: Orbis Books, 1979).

entered the promised land, the United States or America,[4] as jubilant conquerors; to the contrary, they have landed on these shores as a colonial people and have gone on to experience life as second-class citizens. Consequently, instead of the traditional exodus-from-Egypt narrative, with its accompanying themes of conquest and election, I suggest that the narrative that best articulates the Filipino-American experience is that of exodus-toward-Egypt.

Such a narrative framework I see as quite rich, able to conjure up variant messages and thus jar our familiar knowledge of the biblical exodus account. It is a narrative that conveys not a singular notion of liberation and the euphoria that goes with it but an ambiguous nexus of captivity and liberation, of closure and promise, of blessings and alienation. Within such a framework, the term *exodus* carries not only its ordinary meaning of "flight" or "migration" but also its positive biblical connotations of "release" and "liberation." For Filipino Americans, exodus from their homeland has meant release from poverty and fatalism—an exodus toward a land of wealth and opportunity. The irony, however, is that this exodus has as its destination the homeland of their colonial masters, where they are able to share in the cornucopia of their masters' blessings but also remain colonized in brazen as well as subtle ways every day of their lives.

Unlike the exodus-from-Egypt narrative, which begins in Egypt and then moves outside of Egypt, the exodus-toward-Egypt narrative begins in Canaan and moves toward Egypt. In this framework the exodus starts not with the exploits of Moses in the accounts of the book of Exodus but with the migration of Jacob and his descendants in the book of Genesis, especially with the story revolving around Joseph and the events that led him to Egypt. Consequently, instead of taking the flight out of Egypt as its paradigmatic lens, this narrative casts the exodus in a much broader light, so that the Moses-led exodus constitutes but a moment, though a significant one, in the overall struggle of the people. In this framework, then, Moses does not lead the people out of Egypt but leads them instead in the task of transformation within the geographic confines of Egypt.

Unlike the biblical Israelites, Filipino Americans have no intention of leaving Egypt (the United States); they have made the decision to cast their lot in this new country and have resolved to realize the promised land in Egypt. Yes, realize the promised land in Egypt, not outside of Egypt, not outside of the United States. In this new land they have started to dream dreams, yet this is also a land of unfinished dreams and, at times, of nightmares. In order to avoid any understanding of this exodus-toward-Egypt narrative as involving only movement from one country to another, the experience of emigration from the Philippines to the United States, I want to emphasize that the narrative also takes into account the process of settlement in the new country, the experience of immigration in the United States. Emigration (exodus) and immigration (settlement) should be seen, therefore, as two facets of the one exodus-toward-Egypt

---

[4] I should note that when Filipinos say "America," they basically mean the United States, not the rest of North America (Canada or Mexico) or Central America or South America; it is in that sense that I use "America" in this chapter.

narrative. Such a view of the exodus is consistent with that standing interpretation of it not as a one-time event led by the breakthrough figure of Moses but as a continuing struggle for liberation.

My purpose in advancing this alternative narrative of liberation is not to establish a correspondence between the biblical narrative and the Filipino-American experience but to engage in an inter(con)textual reading of the biblical narrative and the Filipino-American experience so that they may enrich each other, opening the way in the process for new horizons of thinking, dwelling, and acting to come. I turn first to the present project of Filipino Americans in the United States.

THE EMIGRATION AND IMMIGRATION OF "MR. PINOY" AND "MS. PINAY" TO THE NEW EGYPT: AN INTER(CON)TEXTUAL READING

In any migratory phenomenon there are always factors that "push" people to migrate; consequently, it is necessary to look at the situation in Canaan that precipitated the migration. According to the biblical narrative, there was famine in the land of Canaan and the sons of Jacob had to look for food. Famine, therefore, was the triggering factor for the move of Jacob's family from Canaan to Egypt. Given the lack of basic commodities, the members of Joseph's family, in order to survive, had to find food and jobs in other lands. If there was a "push," there was also a "pull"—another set of factors that must not be overlooked when analyzing the phenomenon of migration. Jacob and his family had heard from the caravans that the land of pharaoh had an abundant supply of food. It was thus a question of either going to Egypt or perishing from the famine.

The Filipino exodus to "the land of the free and the home of the brave" resonates with some features of the exodus of Jacob and his family to the biblical Egypt, but it is also different, more complex, textured as it is by a confluence of economic, political, and cultural factors. In fact, the Filipino exodus to the United States can be understood adequately only when seen against the wider framework of global politics and shifting world powers, from Spain to the United States. Since colonization entails political and economic control as well as mental control, the coming of Filipinos to the shores of America has been driven not only by the search for "greener pastures," the primary factor, but also by their image of America. For them, America represents the land of endless opportunities and coming to America the fulfillment of that to which they aspire in life. White America represents what is good and beautiful, noble and laudable, while the brown Philippines represents what they despise in themselves.

Except for those with economic means and those in military service, coming to the United States entails enormous sacrifices for Filipinos. Out of dire need and in the firm belief that plenty of opportunities exist in the States, Filipinos muster every available means at their disposal to come to America. Those who do not have the necessary cash on hand proceed to sell their carabao or water buffalo and, if need be, their small piece of land. Such risks are taken because of the prospect of future rewards; for example, over against the undervalued Filipino peso, a son or daughter in America can send the almighty U.S. dollar—the "God we trust"—to the family "back home." In some instances, again with the exception of families of wealthy professionals, Filipino families, echoing what Joseph's brothers did to him in the biblical narrative, not only sell their carabao and land but also "sell" their family members to U.S. citizens in the hope that they will be taken to the States. An obvious example in this regard, and a booming business in recent times, is the mail-order bride. All such sacrifices finally pay off when the first almighty dollar or box of "goodies" arrives. In the light of our contemporary situation, Filipino Americans can readily envision Joseph's orders to fill his brothers' bags with grain and to put money in their sacks (Gn 42:25), much as they themselves send money through bank-to-bank transfers or assorted "goodies" by door-to-door delivery.

When the contemporary Filipino-American Joseph goes home to his province, perhaps in time for the barrio fiesta, he brings with him *balikbayan* (literally, "returning to one's country of origin") boxes filled with *pasalubong* (gifts). If he has not been able to save much money, he must make use of his high-interest-rate credit card to pay for travel expenses as well as for entertainment for his long time–no see *barkadas* (peer group), since he has to live up to the expectations on the part of his *kababayan* (country folks) as a "dollar boy." The green-card holder or citizen Joseph is a VIP back home because of his dollar. In fact, the Philippine government regards him, like all Filipino contract workers, as the "new hero." He serves as the *alkansiya* (piggy bank) for both his parents and all other family members. Whenever there is a financial problem back home, the "dollar boy" gets a collect call. Because Joseph's parents, brothers, and sisters usually lack health insurance, he also functions as their health-insurance provider whenever folks back home get sick.

Sending money back home is but a first step in helping the immediate family. The ultimate goal is to bring the remaining family members to the States. Joseph's family cannot come at will into the new Egypt; they have to be "petitioned" by Joseph through the Immigration and Naturalization Service (INS). In this regard, the pivotal figures in making it possible for the rest of the family to follow suit are Joseph's parents—Jacob and his wife. Thus, elderly parents, who would be less lonely in their homeland, are forced to come, because it is only through them that other members of the family can be petitioned, though they also prove useful in taking care of the grandchildren (Joseph's children). *Itay* and *Inay* (father and mother) must come to the United States, no matter how frail, since their acquisition of citizenship proves crucial for the immigration of the other family members.

In resonance with the gradual immigration of Jacob and his family, Filipinos have also come to the United States in waves. The earliest group consisted of crewmen aboard the Philippine-made galleon *San Pablo* in the latter half of the eighteenth century and thus at the height of the Manila-Mexico galleon trade (1565-1815). Having suffered maltreatment at the hands of the Spanish on board, they jumped ship in Acapulco, Mexico, and went on to settle in Louisiana in 1763. Since the arrival of this first contingent, four major periods of Filipino immigration into the country can be readily identified: 1763-1906; 1906-34; 1945-65; and 1965 to the present.[5]

Struggling to "Make It" in America: Outsiders-Insiders of the American Dream

Managing to land on the shores of America is only the beginning of a long journey. Newcomers have to deal quickly with the demands of living in a new country, especially in terms of employment. The struggle to "make it" in America cannot wait. After all, this is the main reason why they have come to America: they want to "make it." Again, there is clear resonance here between the plight of Jacob's family and the plight of the Filipino "old timers."

When Jacob and family arrived in Egypt, they were given jobs that, from the masters' point of view, "fit" their occupational background and training. Because of their training as shepherds, Jacob and his family were sent to Goshen to tend sheep (Gn 47:6). Likewise, Filipino "old timers" were given jobs that, from the perspective of their employers, "fit" not only their occupational background and training but also their physical features. Being small in physical stature, their Euro-American employers thought that they would not suffer from back pain, even if they had to stoop from morning till sunset; they seemed naturally suited, therefore, for the planting and harvesting of such crops as asparagus, iceberg lettuce, spinach, strawberries, and sugar beets.[6] Others found jobs in the sugarcane plantations of Hawaii, the fish canneries of Alaska, and railroad construction on the mainland. Later immigrants were able to find jobs more in keeping with their educational and technical training in the Philippines, although many well-trained and well-educated Filipinos continued to land jobs far below their levels of competence.

Still, "making it" in America remains the goal, no matter what. To be sure, many Filipino Americans have done well and have made a mark in their chosen fields of employment. For example, Filipino-American medical doctors and nurses can be found in hospitals and clinics all over the country; indeed, Filipino Americans represent the largest racial minority group in the health-care industry.[7] Filipino Americans are steadily rising and breaking through the "glass

---

[5] Aurora Tompar-Tiu and Juliana Sustento-Seneriches, *Depression and Other Mental Health Issues: The Filipino American Experience* (San Francisco: Jossey-Bass Publishers, 1995), 8. With the last major wave of Filipino newcomers, the Filipino-American population has increased tremendously. The 1990 census counted 1.4 million Filipino Americans. Most are first-generation immigrants. If this growth rate continues, it is estimated that in the next ten years the Filipino-American population will reach over 2 million, becoming the largest Asian immigrant group.

[6] Brandy Tuzon, "The War in Salinas," *Filipinas* (October 1996): 66.

[7] David Bacon, "Living the Legacy of Unionism," *Filipinas* (January 1997): 18-21.

ceiling" in other fields as well, finding their niche in various walks of life.[8] Many, however, are just barely "making it" in America, and this is a story that needs to be told as well. Before coming to "the land of the free and the home of the brave," I had not heard this other side of the Filipino-American experience. In fact, it was not until I came across such Filipino Americans in California and Hawaii that the scales fell from my eyes. Immediately, I felt a fire in my gut.

One group whose plight represents a betrayal of the American Dream is that of World War II veterans, especially the recent arrivals. In 1990, after a long wait and struggle, Filipinos who fought under the banner of the USAFFE (United States Armed Forces in the Far East) were granted U.S. citizenship. For many of these veterans, the granting of citizenship was the fulfillment of their dream, a reward for fighting on the side of the United States against Japan. This dream, however, has become a nightmare for some and an unfinished mission for others. For Ciriaco Punla, time ran out: he died of tuberculosis, having endured the cold, damp weather of San Francisco while waiting for the promised veterans' benefits. Macario Nicdao, another veteran, could only raise these poignant questions: "We offered our blood and lives. What have they done to us? Where is America's heart?"[9]

Another group whose plight portrays the ambiguity of the American Dream includes Filipino Americans who come to the United States by way of marriage to U.S. citizens. Aside from the pursuit of higher education, marrying a U.S. citizen constitutes a ready passport to a better life for many Filipinos. The resultant stories are a mixture of "success" and dreams turning into nightmares. Although many of these Filipinos have found admirable spouses, even willing to help with their families back home, a relationship of subordination is also common. At times they end up in more abusive relationships, which they simply endure and refuse to report to the proper authorities for fear that their bid for a "green card" or U.S. citizenship may be jeopardized.[10] In extreme cases, the dreams have turned into nightmares. This was the case for Emelita Reeves, who came to America with a suitcase full of dreams, thinking that the husband she had found through a pen-pal service was her ticket to the moon. She landed in the hands of a man who murdered her.[11]

---

[8] The following are salient examples: military (Major General Edward Soriano and Brigadier General Antonio Taguba of the Army); business (Diosdado Banatao and other Silicon Valley success stories); sports (Tiffany Roberts); journalism (Carlos Bulosan, Jessica Hagedorn, Byron Acohido, Alex Tizon); show business/entertainment (Paulo Montalban, Tia Carrere, Jocelyn Enriquez, Enrico Labayen); politics (Gov. Benjamin Cayetano of Hawaii and Mayor Peter Fajardo of Carson City, California). See Ely Barros, "The U.S. Army's First Filipino Generals," *Filipinas* (October 1997): 27-28; Emil Guillermo, "Tiffany Roberts: Gold Mettle," *Filipinas* (March 1997): 38-39, 41; "Jocelyn Enriquez: Dance Music Diva," *Filipinas* (June 1998): 40; Laura Schiff, "She's Just Drawn That Way," *Filipinas* (August 1997): 38-42.

[9] Rick Rocamora, "Unfinished Mission: The American Journey of Filipino World War II Veterans," *Filipinas* (June 1998): 22-25.

[10] Tompar-Tiu and Sustento-Seneriches, *Depression and Other Mental Health Issues,* 47.

[11] Jocelyn Alvarez Allgood, "A Death in Texas: The Emelita Reeves Murder Case," *Filipinas* (March 1997): 21-22.

Filipinos have thus come to America filled with the hope of participating in the American Dream, and some have "made it" in America. Filipinos have also learned, to their shock, the other side of America: its xenophobia and oppression of racial others. As a Filipino riddle puts it, *Isang magandang señora, libot na libot ng espada* (There is a beautiful lady surrounded with swords).[12] The early Filipino immigrants had to face outright racist violence against them, such as massacres, house-burnings, and beatings.[13] Such violence, moreover, is by no means a thing of the past, certainly not for Filipino-American Derrick Lizardo, a student at Syracuse University, who, along with other Asian-American colleagues, was refused service at a Denny's Restaurant and was subsequently beaten by a group of twenty whites on the evening of April 11, 1997.[14] Carlos Bulosan captures this outsider-insider experience when he writes to a friend, "I know deep down in my heart that I am an *exile* in America."[15]

Trying Hard to Be an American: The Politics of Identity

At present, Filipino Americans rank as the second largest Asian-American ethnic group in the United States and yet we do not hear of Filipinotowns. I do not imagine that there will be Filipinotowns in the near future either, not for Filipino Americans, who have been trained to believe that they are white America's "little brown brothers," even after years of being called "brown monkeys." There will be no Filipinotowns, because Filipino Americans are proud of their effort to blend, not with other people of color in America but with dominant white America, though another factor may be at work here as well, namely, the strong regionalism among Filipino Americans. Filipino Americans have, in general, no aversion to "Americanization," because that is precisely what many aim for. What is the purpose of coming to America if not to be Americanized?

Yet, even as they try hard to be Americanized, many have come to see, as Euro-Americans keep reminding them, the futility of such efforts. "I have been four years in America," a Filipino immigrant in California said sadly, "and I am a stranger. It is not because I want to be. I have tried to be as 'American' as possible. I live like an American, eat like American, and dress the same, and yet everywhere I find Americans who remind me of the fact that I am a stranger."[16] Trying hard to be an American but falling short of the norm—the American as Euro-American—is the plight of Filipino Americans. No matter how hard they try to be Americans, such a task proves impossible, given the identification of the normative American as the Euro-American; Filipino Americans will always fall short of this norm and remain aberrations, forever "missing the mark," like sinners. Indeed, falling short of the norm is rather like falling from grace: outside the

---

[12] Ronald Takaki, *Strangers from a Different Shore: A History of Asian Americans* (New York: Penguin, 1989), 316.

[13] Dean Alegado, "Blood in the Fields," *Filipinas* (October 1997): 62-64, 76, 90.

[14] Rachelle Ayuyang, "Violence on the Menu," *Filipinas* (October 1997): 31-32.

[15] Cited in Takaki, *Strangers from a Different Shore*, 344.

[16] Cited in Takaki, *Strangers from a Different Shore*, 316.

norm is hell, a place where an encounter with God is perceived as impossible. Many Filipino-American youth, in an effort to be as American as possible, to be "cool," deny their cultural and ethnic identity and, at times, even blame their parents for their physical features. They want to be just like any white youth, since that is the key to getting out of the hell of non-acceptance. Whites, in turn, often with the best of intentions, respond: "We consider you to be just like us. You don't seem [Filipino]."[17]

"AMERICA IS A PRESENCE AS HUGE AS GOD": IN THE IMAGE OF GOD, IN THE IMAGE OF AMERICA

In the story of the garden of Eden, the serpent tempts the first couple with these words: "You will be like God" (Gn 3:5). The first couple succumb to the temptation because they wanted to be "like God." Filipinos and Filipino Americans, like the first couple in the primeval garden, have also succumbed to this temptation. They, too, desire to be "like God," but this time, more specifically, to be like the "white gods"—their colonial and neocolonial masters. The "fall" of Filipino Americans is brought about by their desire to be "white," to be an image of the white gods. "Dealing with Filipino-ness," writes Luis Francia, "is to deal with this condition, with a fall from grace, when the twin-headed snake of Spain and America seduced us with the promise of boundless knowledge—we too could be white gods!—even as we reposed in an unimaginably beautiful garden."[18]

Even before coming to "the land of the free and the home of the brave," Filipino Americans know, in the words of Eric Gamalinda, that "America is a presence as huge as God."[19] During my boyhood years on the island of Leyte, I encountered this association of hugeness with Americanness in the literal physical sense through objects, plants, and animals. For example, the largest frog was what the barrio inhabitants called the American frog, and the largest bread I dreamed of eating someday, *hanggang sawa* (eating until I drop), was the American bread, the rectangular loaf of bread. In other words, when something was huge, it had to be American. The hugeness of America, I later realized, was more than what was embodied in that frog or that loaf of bread. "America is a presence as huge as God" insofar as all Filipinos are expected to acquire an exhaustive understanding of America the beautiful and to love America with all their hearts, while denouncing whatever smells Filipino with all their might. Filipinos and Filipino Americans have a term for this, "colonial mentality," which punsters have turned into the more derogatory "mental colony."

---

[17] Grace Sangkok Kim, "Asian North American Youth: A Ministry of Self-Identity and Pastoral Care," in *People on the Way: Asian North Americans Discovering Christ, Culture, and Community*, ed. David Ng (Valley Forge, Pa.: Judson Press, 1996), 203.

[18] Luis Francia, "The Other Side of the American Coin," in *Flippin': Filipinos on America*, ed. Luis Francia and Eric Gamalinda (New York: The Asian American Writers' Workshop, 1996), 6.

[19] Eric Gamalinda, "Myth, Memory, Myopia: Or, I May Be Brown But I Hear America Singin'," in Francia and Gamalinda, *Flippin'*, 3.

The States and stateside (American products) so preoccupy the Filipino mind that they often find their way into common chitchat. Many times, such chitchat is raised to a volume that others can hear:

-*May tia ako sa California* ("I have an aunt in California").
-*Ako? may sister ako*, CPA *sa Nuyork* ("I have a CPA sister in New York").
-My son—*abogado sa Ha-why* ("My son is a lawyer in Hawaii").
-Look at my shoes. PX goods. Stateside *'yan* ("indeed").
-*Kumusta* ("Greetings") to your father, huh? Tell him not to forget us here, huh? Say hello for me. But tell me how's Woodside, Nuyork?
-When is he going to send me my Samsonite? Groovie promised me you know? When is he going to send Yardley and Ivory? They're not too expensive in the States I hear?
-Here in Manila. Here in Manila. Everything, everything too much.[20]

Since "America is a presence as huge as God," without liberation from this God any theological task about the creation of Filipino Americans in the image of God can only mean in the image of the white gods. Without decolonization from their colonial mentality or liberation from their mental colony, Filipino Americans will continue to be an image of white America. Sin for African Americans, declares James Cone, is the desire to be white; the same, I would argue, applies to Filipino Americans.[21] But with a fatal twist. The desire to be white on the part of Filipino Americans often turns against blacks. Deceived into thinking that their lighter skin complexion puts them closer to whites, Filipino Americans often behave as if they were white in relation to blacks. Filipino Americans will find a liberating image of God only when they experience liberation from the mental colony; otherwise, being an image of God will remain being an image of Uncle Sam.

"But the Moon Was Rising and It Was Bigger than in America": *Bursting from the Old Wineskin*

Simeon Dumdum's poem "America" provides a glimpse of a new consciousness that is beginning to seep through the old wineskin, struggling to burst from its encasement:

> I listened to him speak
> of West Virginia
> (he was born in Leyte
> but was living in West Virginia).
> ....
> And on that warm evening

[20] Bino Realuyo, "States of Being," in Francia and Gamalinda, *Flippin'*, 160.
[21] James Cone, *A Black Theology of Liberation*, twentieth anniversary ed. (Maryknoll, N.Y.: Orbis Books, 1986), 108.

I told myself,
That's where I want to be,
in West Virginia, or New York,
or San Francisco,
because cousin says
everything there is big
and cheap—big chickens,
big eggs, big buildings,
and big flowers.
Cousin looked at me
and said, Yes, big roses,
tea roses, and he was
about to name other roses
but the moon was rising
and it was bigger than in
America.[22]

I have traveled long and far from my boyhood home to the heartland of America. There I have come to realize that the big "American" frog I had seen and the big "American" bread I had dreamed of were but glimpses of the hugeness of America's presence in the lives of Filipinos. I have also come to realize that the American Dream itself is a quest for bigness—big houses, big bucks, big appliances, and so on. But the big must also be cheap. "Big and cheap," says the cousin from West Virginia in Dumdum's poem. How can something be big and cheap at the same time? It happens in America, of course, and somebody has to pay for it. Not the corporate welfare mamas, to be sure. Rather, cheap labor must be extracted from both inside the United States and outside in the Two-Thirds World in order to make it possible for Americans to buy "big and cheap." Bigness and cheapness rest, therefore, on the backs of others, both human and ecological.

How can the moon be "bigger than in America" if "America is a presence as huge as God"? How can the moon be "bigger than in America" for someone who aspires to be in America "because cousin says [who lives in West Virginia] everything there is big and cheap—big chickens, big eggs, big buildings, and big flowers"? Such questions defy easy answers, not simply because they are hard to understand but also because they require Filipino Americans to take account of themselves and of their aspirations. The moon is not only small but actually unnoticeable when one is surrounded by floodlights, streetlights, and neon lights or by the skyscrapers of New York, Los Angeles, and Chicago. When one's days are busy in pursuit of the American Dream, the moon proves small indeed, if not altogether invisible. For those who are busy moonlighting, noticing the moon is an oxymoron, since they have no time even to look at the moon. Nonetheless, the moon is bigger, whether in the Philippines or in the heartland of America, for those who have come to realize that the God that is

---

[22] Simeon Dumdum, "America," in Francia and Gamalinda, *Flippin'*, 238-39.

America is an idol and that the American Dream itself feeds on the blood of many. Filipino Americans, like the characters of Dumdum's poem, need to come to the realization that the moon is bigger than the big chickens, big eggs, big houses, and all the other "bigs" in America. Such consciousness requires, however, a reorientation of their sociopolitical and moral compass.

Encountering God in the Adopted Land:
A God Who Would Be "Pissed Off" if We Pass by the Color Purple and Not Notice It

The experience of exodus involves uprootedness from one's place of origins as well as from one's religious roots. While in exile in Babylon, the Israelites raised the profound issue of God's presence in a foreign land. With voices raised to the heavens, they asked, "How can we sing the Lord's song in a foreign land?" (Ps 137:4). This is a question that all Filipino Americans, whether of the first generation or of later generations, must ask again and again. It is a profound question, insofar as it calls Filipino Americans to reflect on their deep faith in God in the light of their new context and challenges. Not because God has been left behind in the Philippines, for Filipino immigrants know that God travels with them on their journey, but rather because they must learn how to discern God's presence in a new context and in a way that truly speaks to their plight and longings.

In a context where Filipino identity is despised, the God who travels with them must affirm their identity and encounter them in their ethnicity. Elizabeth Tay's confession, "I encounter God in my ethnicity," is one that all Filipino Americans should take to heart.[23] We encounter God in the context of who we are, not outside of who we are. A God who is encountered outside of who we are and who thus calls us to betray our ethnic identity is a God who works for foreign masters.

This twofold experience on the part of Filipino Americans of suffering because of their color and yet encountering a God who affirms their ethnicity can serve as grounds for an analogous construal of a God who is neither colorless nor colorblind; indeed, it is only in a white dominant society that God can be looked upon as colorless and colorblind (read: white). A God who is not cognizant of color is a God who is not cognizant of the pain of those who suffer because of color. One often hears from the pulpit such rhetoric as the following, "In the eyes of God color does not matter." I consider such a statement—no matter how good the intentions behind it may be—to be counterproductive. To speak as if color were of no concern to God is to perpetuate the denigration of color. To be sure, God transcends color, but not because God is colorless (white) but rather because God is colorful and cognizant of the beauty of each color. Such a colorful and color-loving God would be "pissed off," to use the expression of

---

[23] Elizabeth Tay, as cited in Fumitaka Matsuoka, *Out of Silence: Emerging Themes in Asian American Churches* (Cleveland, Ohio: United Church Press, 1995), 134.

Alice Walker, "if [we] pass by the color purple in the field somewhere and don't notice it."[24]

The God who affirms Filipino-American identity is the same God who raises a prophetic no to any uncritical allegiance to the American Dream. For many Filipino Americans, the American Dream has become an obsession, so much so that their relationships with others both within the Filipino-American community and in the wider society are often measured in terms of success or failure relative to the American Dream. As a result, Filipino-American communities continue to be pestered not only by traditional Philippine regionalism but also by the classism to be found under the canopy of the American Dream. Filipino Americans, like the Israelites of old, need to reflect upon both the blessings and the perils of their new life.

Vomiting One's Dream:
Breaking Silence, Breaking the Glass Ceiling

The descendants of Israel labored hard in the land of the pharaohs. As the years passed, they grew in number and the Egyptians were threatened. The Egyptians, therefore, devised a variety of schemes intended to make the lives of the Israelites in Egypt much more difficult. At first, the Israelites accepted what was demanded of them without complaint, but the situation gradually became unbearable. Finally, they broke their silence.

It is difficult to raise critical comments about America in general and the American Dream in particular in Filipino-American communities. For many, it is simply unthinkable to engage in any type of criticism of America, given their belief in America as the fulfillment of their dreams. Criticism is regarded as tantamount to ungratefulness, rather like vomiting out one's dream and then proceeding to eat back one's vomit. For many Filipino Americans, such an attitude is to be without *utang na loob* (debt of gratitude). Warts and all, one must take America or leave it. This is how many of them think they can repay America—acceptance without question. The challenge, therefore, is to raise the social awareness of Filipino Americans, so that they can come to understand that social criticism is not a betrayal of their dream but a necessary move to realize the America of their dreams. Filipino Americans must move beyond *tinikling* (native bamboo dance) solidarity during ethnic cultural events to a solidarity that deals with the sociopolitical issues faced by society as a whole.

Again, there are Filipino Americans who have broken through the glass ceiling, but one must remember that this was possible only because other Filipino Americans had broken their silence before them. This is what contemporary Filipino Americans need to realize. Whatever success stories there may be in our communities at present have come out of the struggles of the past. Breaking silence is thus a part of the Filipino-American legacy that needs to be reclaimed. Filipino Americans must realize that it does not pay to remain silent and that

---

[24] Alice Walker, *The Color Purple* (New York: Washington Square Press, 1978), 178.

silence, to paraphrase José Comblin, is a lie when the truth needs to be spoken.[25] From the early days of their settlement in America, a number of Filipino Americans have broken their silence. The Filipino *sacadas* in Hawaii, for example, organized a union and broke their silence against unfair treatment. At first, they raised their voices as an ethnic group, but later on they realized that they had to establish common cause with other minorities and form an interracial union.[26] It is very encouraging to see that new generations of Filipino Americans have reclaimed this legacy of breaking silence.

Going Public and Acting on the Vision: Taking Account of One's Location in a Globalized Context

I have focused throughout on the Israelite narrative as if the Israelites had been the only ethnic group in Egypt besides the dominant group, the Egyptians. There is no empire, however, that does not gather a variety of marginalized groups within its shadow, and each of these groups has its own narrative to tell. It is important, therefore, that, even as one such narrative is foregrounded, others also be taken into account. Filipino Americans need to realize that their presence and plight in America represents a microcosm of the plight of the Two-Thirds World in general. Here I quite agree with Robert Blauner to the effect that "the economic, social, and political subordination of third world groups in America is a microcosm of the position of all peoples of color in the world order of stratification."[27] Such subordination, Blauner continues, is not an accident but "part of a world historical drama in which the culture, economic system, and political power of the white West has spread throughout virtually the entire globe."[28] It is in the context of this global drama, then, that Filipino Americans must take account of their presence in the United States and, in so doing, contribute to the birthing of a better tomorrow, not only for the United States but also for their country of origin as well as for the world in general.

They must not only give words to their pain but also go public with their vision. Beyond sending the almighty dollar to the folks back home, Filipino Americans need to understand the interweaving of the global and the local. Once they do, they will cease to be unequivocally happy about their relative advantage over Filipinos back home, because they will come to see that this advantage of theirs is predicated on the disadvantage of others. Filipino Americans embody in their lives this interweaving of the global and the local, between a home "over here" and a home "back there." However, they must also learn to articulate what they embody, if they are to be of help in making the larger U.S.

---

[25] José Comblin, *The Church and the National Security State* (Maryknoll, N.Y.: Orbis Books, 1979), 15.

[26] Algado, "Blood in the Fields," 63-64, 76, 90.

[27] Robert Blauner, "Colonized and Immigrant Minorities," in *From Different Shores: Perspectives on Race and Ethnicity in America,* ed. Ronald Takaki (New York and Oxford: Oxford University Press, 1987), 159.

[28] Ibid.

society understand the interconnecting dynamics between the plight of the Two-Thirds World and the plight of marginalized people in the United States. They must break their silence, if they want to avert the easy scapegoating of the weakest members of American society in times of crisis.

When Filipino Americans see themselves in this interweaving of the global and the local, they will also see their ethnic identity in a broader light. Their struggle to understand who they are as well as their plight will lead them to issues that transcend specific ethnic concerns. As people who have experienced marginalization and who have known what it means to cross geographical and cultural divides, Filipino Americans can help to build bridges of connections. As people who have known what it means to suffer as a result of one's color, they can also help to articulate a vision of a just, colorful, and sustainable tomorrow. Filipino Americans must not remain passive bystanders in America, busying themselves in pursuit of all the "bigs" of the American Dream; they must live up instead to the calling of responsible citizenship.

REALIZING THE PROMISED LAND IN EGYPT: A HISTORICAL PROJECT

While the exiled Israelites longed for an eventual return to their homeland, Filipino Americans, except for some first-generation immigrants who long to spend their retirement years in the Philippines, have resolved to stay in America. They have resolved to realize the promised land in Egypt.[29] The "success" stories of Filipino Americans who break through the glass ceiling certainly call for a *fiesta*—a celebration with dances and *lechon* (roasted young pig). At the same time, we should always remember that such stories are possible only because others before us have broken their silence or have had their bodies broken by the forces of death. If the new generations are to express their *utang na loob* to those who broke their silence, they must do so by turning these monuments of past accomplishments into movements of today—movements of transformation, movements to forge a colorful tomorrow. America is in the hearts of Filipino Americans, and they have not given up the America of their dreams. The task is not only to understand America, as Carlos Bulosan put it, but also to make America a just society. This is to realize the America of one's heart.[30] The America that Filipino Americans desire in their hearts can only become a reality through a historical project—a project of breaking silence, of naming the pains, of articulating a colorful society, of acting on dreams so that the promised land may be realized in Egypt.

---

[29] Therese Hermosisima Finnegan, "An Endless Search for Home," *Filipinas* (July 1996): 70.

[30] Carlos Bulosan, *America Is in the Heart: A Personal History* (Seattle, Wash.: University of Washington Press, 1973; orig. publ.,1946).

PART III

HISPANIC-LATINO/A VOICES

10

Constructing Our Cuban Ethnic Identity While in Babylon

MIGUEL A. DE LA TORRE

Hispanics in this country are a people in exile—some by conquest (Mexico and Puerto Rico), others as a result of "gunboat diplomacy" (Central America and the Caribbean). While Mexicans and Puerto Ricans, whose presence is a direct consequence of this country's territorial expansion, are exiles in their own lands, we Cubans had our independence from Spain abrogated due to the avarice of the United States. Territorial invasions and the exploitation of our natural resources by U.S. corporations led to the conditions that fostered the revolution of 1959. We find ourselves as refugees in the same country responsible for our being here. We have lost the land of our birth and have come to the realization that, when our bodies are finally laid to rest, it will be as foreigners interred in an alien soil. We are a people without a land, not only marginally welcomed in this country but also despised because we refuse to assimilate totally. Like other Hispanic groups, we Cubans face hostile Congressional laws and proposals. However, unlike other Latino/a groups, our socioeconomic location as exilic Cubans radically differs. We face repression from the dominant culture until we move to Miami, Florida.

El exilio,[1] besides a geographic reality, is a culturally constructed artifact imagined as a landless nation complete with its own history and values. As

---

[1] *El exilio* is a term mainly used by exilic Cubans to name our collective identity. The term connotes the involuntary nature of displacement and constructs us as sojourners in a foreign land. *El exilio* is an in-between place, a place to wait and hope for a return to our homeland. It is more than geographic separation; it encompasses disconnection, displacement, disembodiment. *El exilio* is existence in a reality apart from what one loves. *Exilio* exists for the exilic Cubans who were forced to wave goodbye to their homeland and loved ones, as well for the resident Cubans who watched us leave. In Miami, longing for Cuba, or the "rhetoric of return," becomes the unifying substance of our existential being, yet this hope is being replaced with a stronger desire to adapt and capitalize on our presence in this country. Taking our cue from José Martí, *el exilio* becomes a sacred space making morality synonymous with nationality. Living in exile is a sacrifice constituting a civic duty representing a grander moral basis.

travel writer David Rieff observes, "The country of which Miami is the capital is an imaginary one, that of *el exilio*."[2] Dis-membered Miami becomes re-membered La Habana. We construct a sociopolitical space in which we cease being victims of the Anglo dominant culture by striving to become the new oppressors.

Theologians who operate from a liberationist perspective usually focus on the exodus as a source of hope for their existential situation. The story of a God who hears the cries of an oppressed people and personally leads them toward liberation is a powerful motif. The exodus, however, is not the rubric exilic Cubans use to read the scriptures. It is the second exodus, narrating the Babylonian Captivity, that resonates within our very being. Like the Psalmist (Psalm 137), we sit by the streams of this country, singing about our inability to sing God's songs.

How does our social location as exilic Cubans contribute to the oppression of other Hispanic groups, and how have we recreated our ethnicity in order to mask that position of power? These questions will be explored by juxtaposing the biblical story of the Babylonian Captivity with the experience of exilic Cubans in order to discover possible paradigms that might lead toward reconciliation. First, I shall define the "we" that sits by the river weeping by exploring the social dynamics that lead to both the Babylonian and Cuban exilic experiences, emphasizing the deportees' demographics and how it contributes to how exilic Cubans see themselves and others. Second, I shall elucidate the power relations existing among Hispanics. If we are only the Anglo's "other," then how do we begin a discourse between a socially empowered exilic Cuban and a disempowered Latino/a? Finally, I will explore the sociopolitical ramification of a postexilic community in a post-Castro Cuba. If our goal as a Cuban community is unification instead of "dashing babies against rocks," then the course taken by exilic Jews, which is the same course currently being advocated by exilic Cubans, was and still is erroneous.

BESIDE THE MIAMI RIVER WE SAT AND WEPT AT THE MEMORY OF *LA HABANA*, LEAVING OUR CONGA DRUMS BY THE PALM TREES

If we define power as repressive, we adopt a purely juridical conception of power. Power, identified with law, says no. Michel Foucault maintains that such a view of power is wholly negative and narrow. The hold power has upon us is its ability to traverse and to produce things. Power creates pleasure, constructs knowledge, and produces discourse. Power can be positive, producing reality and creating the subject's opinion of what is truth.[3] Through power, an exilic

---

[2] D. Rieff, *Going to Miami: Exiles, Tourists, and Refugees in the New America* (Boston: Little, Brown, 1987), 149.

[3] M. Foucault, "Truth and Power," in *The Foucault Reader*, ed. Paul Rabinow (New York: Pantheon Books, 1984), 60-61.

Cuban ethnicity was created and normalized in our minds as true. This ethnicity was not imported from the island; rather, it was constructed within the context of *el exilio*. From a restaurant in Miami, we can begin to understand this construction.

In *la sagüesera* (Southwest Miami), on *Calle Ocho* (Eighth Street), is a restaurant called Versailles, dubbed *El palacio de los espejos* (the mirrored palace). Like other popular restaurants in Miami, Versailles attempts to copy the exclusive nightspots of La Habana. What makes this particular restaurant unique are the mirrored walls. Sitting at the table in the crowded salon, one constantly sees oneself reflected in one of many heavily gilded mirrors. As we look in the surrounding mirrors, we are in fact searching for our ontological origin—not so much what we are, but what we see ourselves as being.

Versailles serves as a vivid illustration of Jacques Lacan's theory of the "Mirror Stage." While I look at myself, I assume that what I see is a reflection of a self, a secondary reflection faithful (more or less) to the likeness of an existing original self. Lacan would propose the opposite: the image in the mirror is what constructs the self. My encounter with the mirror literally reverses the direction and serves the function of forming my "I." Lacan's theory describes the fact that the delusive reflection of the Cuban in the mirror constructs an exilic Cuban "self" captivated by the belief in the projected "imaginary," where both future and past are grounded within an illusion. In short, the ideal formed in the mirror situates the agency of the "ego" in fiction, while projecting the formation of the "self" into history.[4] My history, as an exilic Cuban being seen by an exilic Cuban, is the "future perfect of what I will have been for what I am in the process of becoming."[5]

My Cuban eyes see in the mirror the anticipated maturation of the power I desire to possess and read into my history, the illusion of a "golden Exile." Our striving for power creates a history where we tell ourselves that, before we Cubans came to this place, *Miami era un campo con luces* (Miami was a village with fancy lights). We who possess the power to transform a tourist town into the epicenter of U.S. trade with Latin America see within ourselves a superior distinction when compared to other ethnic groups who have not transcended the *barrio* or ghetto. But as Lacan would ask, which is the illusion, the self or the reflection? To see myself as an exilic Cuban through the mirror's "imaginary" places the subject "I" in a privileged space of observation, while imposing an oppressive gaze upon other Cubans who do not look like me, such as those who came through Mariel in 1980, or those who stayed on the island. They become my "other" (as well as Mexicans and Puerto Ricans), categorized by their class and skin pigmentation.

How I see my "other" defines my existential self. To "see" implies a position of authority, a privileged point of view. "Seeing" is not a mere innocent metaphysical phenomenon concerning the transmittance of light waves. It encompasses a mode of thought which radically transforms the "other" into an

---

[4] J. Lacan, *Écrits* (Paris: Seuil, 1966), 94-95.

[5] Ibid., 300.

object for possession. My subjective "I" exists when I tell the "I" who I am not. The subject "I" is defined by contrasting it with the seen objects, "*marielito*" or "resident Cuban." In socially constructing "I" out of the differences with the "them," there exist established power relations that give meaning to those differences. Specifically, when I look in the mirror, I do not see a "*marielito*" or "resident Cuban." By projecting my "I" into *marielitos* and resident Cubans, I am able to define myself as a white *macho* who is civilized and successful. As long as I continue to reconstruct myself in the mirror, any type of reconciliation between the two Cubas is futile. Our task is to learn how to see authentically by debunking the image in the mirror.

The image in the mirror takes form as *la lucha*, a counter-memory established as the starting point for our sacred space. *La lucha* (the struggle), also known as *la causa* (the cause), ceases to be a struggle for liberation by becoming a false religion campaigning for our roles as sub-oppressors. *La lucha* has its roots in the nineteenth-century struggle against Spain for liberation. Later it became *la lucha* against the United States as represented by Gerardo Machado and Fulgencio Batista. Today, exilic Cubans understand *la lucha* as a continued struggle against Fidel Castro and all who are or are perceived to be his allies. *La lucha* is our false religion, a sacred space representing the cosmic struggle between the "children of light" (exilic Cubans) and the "children of darkness" (resident Cubans), complete with a Christ (José Martí), an anti-Christ (Fidel Castro), a priesthood (CANF or the Cuban American National Foundation), a promised land (Cuba), and martyrs (those who gloriously suffer in the holy war against evil, Castro).

Seeing our "self" in the mirror is internalized, naturalized, and legitimized in order to mask our position of power as we shape Miami's political and economic structures along the tenets of our false religion. We initiate an active self-formation, complete with a long and complicated genealogy, so that we can blame our "other" for their deserved constructed space. The ethnicity we construct attempts to imitate the dominant culture, the same culture whose neocolonial ventures on our island caused us to be refugees now. We construct a genealogy that proves we are a white people coming from a white nation, fleeing tyranny with only the clothes on our backs and leaving behind *la Cuba de ayer* (the Cuba of yesteryear), which encompassed a seemingly idyllic way of life. Re-membering *la Cuba de ayer* becomes a strategy against oblivion, a tactic by which we can survive as a people.

Looking in the mirror, I reread my history as that of one who escaped. Fulgencio Batista's departure from Cuba on New Year's Eve, 1959, triggered panic as party goers rushed to their houses to collect their sleeping children, money, and anything of value. Those who were able to leave arrived in this country still in their tuxedos and dress uniforms, their wives in formal gowns and high heels. These first refugees arrived with "class"—not so much in the elegance of their attire but in their high economic social stratum. Unlike other contemporary examples of refugees, both the Babylonian-bound Jews and the U.S.-bound Cubans belonged to the privileged upper social class. The biblical account tells us that Nebuchadnezzar carried off "*all* Jerusalem into exile."

"All" is defined as the officers, the mighty men of valor, the craftsmen and the blacksmiths. Those left behind were the "poorest people of the land" (2 Kgs 24:14). These exilic Cubans, like their Jewish counterparts, were not necessarily numerous. Yet, they represented the top echelons of their country's government and business communities, facilitating our reestablishment in a foreign land while creating a "brain drain" that literally emptied the resident community of trained personnel indispensable for the socioeconomic development of the country. Undoubtedly, the mass exodus of Cubans from the island created regrettable consequences for both communities.

The surreal scene at the Miami airport of well-dressed refugees was caused by the same forces that brought about the Babylonian exile. In both cases, the hegemonic northern power was responsible for the circumstances that led to refugee status. Cuba's political system (especially under the Batista regime) was designed to protect the commercial interests of the United States.[6] As vassals, both Cuba and Judea were desirable prizes: Judah as a buffer zone between the powers of the north and south, and Cuba as a key to the entire hemisphere. While Judah's exile was triggered by the physical invasion of Babylon, Cuba's revolution was a backlash to the hegemony of the United States.

The economic restructuring of Cuba by the United States created presocialized refugees. An anglocized elite that formed linkage with upperclass groups in the United States and Latin America was created to protect U.S. interests. Clearly, these refugees represented the political, economic, and social structures of the neocolonial U.S. Republic of Cuba. As a form of protecting themselves economically against Cuba's political instability, they hoarded their capital and educated their children in the United States. Most of the anglocized elite managed to transfer their assets out of Cuba prior to Castro's victory, while others held the bulk of their investments abroad.[7] Protected capital eased the transition to exilic existence.

This first wave (1959-62) brought to these shores 215,000 refugees who could be considered political exiles. Demographically, these new Cuban refugees were quite homogeneous. The vast majority composed an elite of former notables who were mostly white (94 percent), middle-aged (about thirty-eight years old), educated (about fourteen years of schooling), urban (principally La Habana), and literate in English.[8] Not wanting to minimize the trauma and hardship of

---

[6] Batista's utility to the United States was best expressed by William Wieland, Cuban desk officer at the State Department, who said, "I know Batista is considered by many as a son of a bitch . . . but American interests come first. . . . At least he is *our* son of a bitch, he is not playing ball with the Communists" (Hugh Thomas, *Cuba: The Pursuit of Freedom* [New York: Harper & Row, 1971], 971).

[7] Marifeli Pérez-Stable and Miren Uriarte, "Cubans and the Changing Economy of Miami," in *Latinos in a Changing U.S. Economy: Comparative Perspectives on Growing Inequality*, ed. Rebecca Morales and Frank Bonilla (Newbury Park, Calif.: Sage Publications, 1993), 135.

[8] Richard R. Fagan, Richard A. Brody, and Thomas J. O'Leary, *Cubans in Exile: Disaffection and the Revolution* (Stanford, Calif.: Stanford University Press, 1968), 19-28.

being refugees, we who settled in Miami held an advantage denied other immi-grating groups by entering a social environment made familiar through years of prior travel and business dealings. South Florida, especially for the *habaneros/as*, was seen as a pleasant vacation hub from which to await Castro's immediate downfall. The second wave (1962-73) brought 414,000 refugees who were pre-dominately white, educated, middle-class, and willing to work below the minimum wage. While in Cuba, they mostly represented those who directly relied on economic links with the United States. On average they were semi-skilled, working-class individuals, who capitalized on the emerging economic enclave being established by the first-wave Cubans.

Our hatred toward communism facilitated our usefulness as a Cold War pro-paganda tool for the dominant culture in the United States. A "golden exile" was constructed to contrast with Castro's Cuba. The United States virtually allowed any Cuban arriving to stay and assumed a great deal of the financial responsibility for helping "those escaping the horrors of communism, yearning to breathe the airs of freedom."[9] Anyone who arrived in this country was la-beled a political refugee and within two years was able to obtain residential status. With the end of the Cold War, however, exilic Cubans lost their sym-bolic importance. Attorney General Janet Reno declared in September of 1994 that Cuban refugees were no longer welcomed and would not be admitted into the United States.

While all strata of Cuban society were represented in these first two waves, the vast majority consisted of those from the upper echelons and the middle class, who most benefited from the pre-Castro regime. Pierre Bourdieu's con-cept of the *habitus* illuminates how these exilic Cubans ascended the socioeconomic institutions of Miami. Being born into a position of privilege in Cuba, our socially constructed lifestyle facilitated our rise to the echelons of Miami's power structures. These social constructs—manifested as customs, lan-guage, traditions, values, and so forth—existed prior to our birth. From the moment of birth, these constructs were imposed on us, molding our childhood and guiding us through adulthood. We merely had to assert what we were in order to become what we are, an effort done with the unself-consciousness that marks our so-called nature.

---

[9] For the first time in U.S. history, this country became an asylum for a large group of refugees by assuming the financial burden of resettling them. Total aid of approxi-mately $2 billion was disbursed through the Cuban Refugee Program. Over a twelve-year period, aid consisted of direct cash assistance, guaranteed health care, food subsidies, retraining and retooling programs, college loans, English-language instruction, and fi-nancial assistance for establishing small businesses. Even though most assistance was contingent on resettlement to another part of the United States, Miami's economic base was greatly affected, triggering the transformation of South Florida. See Sylvia Pedraza-Bailey, "Cuba's Exile: Portrait of a Refugee Migration," *International Migration Review* 19 (1985): 4-34.

"SING," THEY SAID, "SOME MAMBO."
HOW CAN WE SING OUR RUMBA IN A PAGAN LAND?
MI HABANA, IF I FORGET YOU MAY MY RIGHT HAND WITHER

People usually define their ethnicity by the land that witnesses their birth. We call ourselves Cubans because we were born on that Caribbean island. If the island of Cuba had never existed, then there would be no such thing as Cubans. What happens when the land of your birth is no longer available to you? What if your love for La Habana remains stronger than your allegiance to Babylon? How can we continue to be Cubans without a Cuba? These questions go to the heart of understanding why we cannot "sing our rumba in a pagan land."

Those of us who arrived in Babylon from Cuba as infants or small children struggle with the realization that we do not belong to the mythical *Cuba de ayer* of our parents. In spite of our determination not to forget "*mi Habana*" lest "my right hand wither," the paradoxical space we find ourselves in loudly asks, "How can we remember that which we have never seen?" As I look at my two children, born in the early 1990s, I realize that, in spite of my efforts to raise them as Cubans (a term I struggle daily to define for myself), their skin is light enough and their socioeconomic (middle) class sufficiently well-established for them to assimilate easily to the dominant culture. Their blond hair and blue eyes allow them to "pass" for Anglos. In 2030, when my children are my age, will they define themselves as Cubans?

The pain that prevents me from "singing my rumba" is the knowledge that while my parents, my children, and myself belong to the same biological family, we live in separate cultural families. My parents will die as broken-hearted Cubans who will never again bathe at Cuba's warm tropical beaches. I will die as an unfulfilled exilic Cuban, for even if the future allows me to visit or resettle on the island, it will never compare to the mythical Cuba my parents have taught me to love. My children will die as new Americans, remotely remembering their roots. They are no more Cubans than my parents are Americans. Both exist in two different worlds, connected only by my generation.

Cuban sociologist Rubén Rumbaut has labeled this in-between space the "one-and-a-half" generation. While the first generation, consisting of our parents from the "old" world, faced the task of acculturation and managing the transition from one sociocultural environment to another, the second generation, consisting of our children from the "new" world, face the task of managing the transition from childhood to adulthood. We who are caught between these two spaces are forced to cope with both crisis-producing and identity-defining transitions.[10]

---

[10] R. G. Rumbaut, "The Agony of Exile: A Study of the Migration and Adaptation of Indochinese Refugee Adults and Children," in *Refugee Children: Theory, Research, and Services*, ed. Frederick L. Ahearn Jr. and Jean L. Athey (Baltimore: The Johns Hopkins University Press, 1991), 61.

Every exilic Cuban has heard Celia Cruz sing the popular tear-jerker "Cuando salí de Cuba" ("When I Left Cuba"). No other song better summarizes the pain of our existential location: "Never can I die, my heart is not *here*. Over *there* it is waiting for me, it is waiting for me to return *there*. When I left Cuba, I left my life, I left my love. When I left Cuba, I left my heart buried." This popular Cuban ballad, written by a Chilean and sung as a hymn of the faith, illustrates the denial of accepting the reality of being, living, and most likely dying on foreign soil. Both exilic Jews and Cubans were forced to deal with this incomprehensible pain. Judaism was constructed in Babylon through the pain of questioning the sovereignty of a God who would tear God's people from their homes and plant them in an alien land. Likewise, we exilic Cubans subconsciously reconstruct ourselves in Lacan's mirror. We internalize and naturalize our image in the mirror, so that we can begin to shape outside structures, always masking our drive toward mastering them. This reconstruction took form as *la Cuba de ayer*.

La Cuba de ayer on U.S. soil created a landless Cuban territory with distinct cultural milieu and idiosyncrasies that served to protect us from the pain of the initial economic and psychological difficulties caused by our uprooting. Cuba became more than just the old country; it was the mythological world of our origins. Cuba is an ethereal place where every conceivable item *es mejor* (is better), from the food to the skies to pests. Everything *aquí* (here) when contrasted with *allá* (there) is found lacking. Unlike the stereotypes of other immigrant groups who left painful memories of the old country behind, joyfully anticipating what they perceived was a new country where "the streets were paved with gold," Cubans did not want to come to what we perceived to be an inferior culture.

Is it any wonder that when exilic Cubans read Psalm 137 we are stirred to the core of our souls? We fully comprehend the tragic pain of sitting by the rivers of an alien land unable to sing to a God the Psalter secretly holds responsible. The hope of returning to our land becomes a foundational building block for the construction of our exilic Cuban ethnicity; yet, with the passing of each year, the cemeteries of Miami increase with headstones engraved with Cuban surnames. Rather than proclaiming "next year in Jerusalem," we tell each other, "this year Castro will fall," as though this one person is the only thing that prevents us from "going home." In reality, the hope of returning home has been replaced with a private desire to adapt and capitalize on our presence in this country.

Jeremiah writes a letter to the exilic Jews telling them to forget about their hope for a speedy return. He tells them to "build houses and live in them; plant gardens and eat what they produce. . . . But seek the welfare of the city [to which exiled] . . . and pray to the LORD on its behalf, for in its welfare you will find your welfare" (29:5-9). Like the Jews, exilic Cubans are forced to relinquish the old world and deal with the realities of the new space they occupy. Our adherence to Jeremiah's dictates was facilitated through our former contacts with elites in other Latin American countries, the possession of the necessary language skills and cultural links to deal with these contacts, our confidence to succeed due to our *habitus*, and our connections with U.S. corporations developed when we were their representatives back in the homeland.

These advantages created a space that allowed us to bring new businesses to Miami and gain positions of power within the banking industry. We established "character loans" as a way of providing entrepreneurs with the seed money required to start up businesses. This action helped create an ethnic enclave. With time, exilic Cubans with business acumen acquired in La Habana filled an economic space in Miami by offering U.S. products to Latin America. Even though exilic Cubans constitute 4.8 percent of the Latino/a population in the United States, a third of all the large Hispanic corporations are based in Miami.

The creation of an economic ethnic enclave eventually led to replacing the old Anglo political elite with rising exilic Cuban entrepreneurs. Like the exilic Jews, Cubans suffered no unusual physical hardship. On the contrary, life in exile opened up opportunities that never existed in the homeland. Like the Babylonian Jews, Cubans entered trade and grew rich, with some, like Nehemiah, ascending the political structures to hold power over those who did not go into exile. The United States became the space where exilic Cubans placed their hope.

As Jerusalem was falling, however, Jeremiah bought a plot of land (32:9-11). His message juxtaposes God's judgment with deliverance. The true hope for Jerusalem did not lay in Babylon; rather, it was rooted in the homeland. Similarly, exilic Cubans see their exilic experience as positive due to their individual economic advancement. While we look toward the United States to define the future of Cuba, we also look toward Cuba to define our present reality in this country. The historical activity of remembering *la Cuba de ayer* protects us from the apocalyptic danger of having our history come to an end. The greatest danger of landlessness is the ushering in of the end of history for a people. Separated from our land, *la Cuba de ayer* protects us from extermination and creates the hope of one day returning to the "promised land."

Self-deception and denial are manifested in the construction of our ethnic identity. Identity as an exilic Cuban is a social construction created from the pain of living in *el exilio*. A foundational tenet of this construction claims we are victims who "fled" tyranny. The image of our people constructing rickety rafts and braving shark-infested waters to escape communism for the land of opportunity has become a major motif in our story. Yet from 1960 to 1980, only sixteen thousand—2 percent of all exilic Cubans—left on small boats or rafts.[11] We minimize the heroic actions of these few by making the raft experience normative. The construction of "fleeing communism" was necessary because it produced advantages for the dominant Anglo culture. In the 1960s the United States lost Cuba to the communists (assuming Cuba had belonged to the United States and thus could be lost) and was defeated at *Playa Girón*. These were major setbacks in the ideological struggle against the Soviet Union. The image

---

[11] T. D. Allman, *Miami: City of the Future* (New York: Atlantic Monthly Press, 1987), 302.

of Cubans getting off rafts and kissing U.S. soil provided powerful propaganda showing the superiority and desirability of capitalism over communism.

"Fleeing communism" also afforded Cubans benefits that simply did not exist for other immigrating groups, specifically $2 billion in resettlement aid and immediate resident status. It hid the fact that later refugees were not so much fleeing tyranny but seeking economic prosperity. They closely resembled "classical immigrants" who were "pulled" by the glittering allure of economic opportunities found in the United States, as opposed to being "pushed" by the Castro regime.[12] The economic "pull" to the United States complicates the reductionist explanation that the sole reason for Cuban immigration is political. It ignores the natural flow of people from underdeveloped to developed countries, a trend that has existed in Cuba since Hernán Cortés left for the greater riches of Mexico. While the overall rubrics for an individual to leave a country may be expressed as a dissatisfaction with the current situation, it is impossible to discern any clear dividing lines between political, economic, and psychological reasons.

The construction of our ethnicity remembers Cuba as a white nation. This remembrance is rooted in the fact that 99 percent of exilic Cubans prior to 1980 were white. Cuban census information has always been manipulated prior to and after Castro's revolution to ensure the reputation of a predominance of whites, even though the non-white population throughout the century has ranged from 50 to 80 percent. The construction of Cuba as a white nation was challenged by the 1980 Mariel boatlift. Unlike the elite first wave, or the middle-class second wave, these Cubans best resembled the population's masses. Forty percent of these refugees were biracial. An immediate distancing between the established exilic Cuban community and these new arrivals began due to racism and classism. They came to be known as *marielitos*, in an effort to differentiate this group of Cubans from all previous exilic Cubans. *Marielitos* occupied their own constructed space, defined by both exilic and resident Cubans as "criminals, homosexuals, and scum."

The negative images of *marielitos* surfaced in the midst of the established community (both Anglo and Cuban) through the reporting done by *The Miami Herald*. While it is true that more than one-fifth of all *marielitos* had prison records, the majority of these incarcerations were as political prisoners or traders in the underground market. Less than 2 percent were hardcore, recidivist criminals, and only a few thousand suffered from mental illnesses.[13]

Marielitos' darker skin provided a scapegoat for the exilic Cuban's flawed character. They were seen by the established white exilic community as a threat to their social construction of "model immigrants." According to a 1982 poll conducted by the Roper Organization about attitudes toward U.S. ethnic groups

---

[12] N. V. Amaro and A. Portes, "Una sociología del exilio: Situación de los grupos cubanos en los Estados Unidos," *Aportes* 23 (1972): 10-14.

[13] Mark F. Peterson, "The Flotilla Entrants: Social Psychological Perspectives on Their Employment," *Cuban Studies/Estudios Cubanos* 12 (1982): 81-86.

held by the U.S. public, only 9 percent felt Cubans have been good for the country, while 59 percent saw Cubans as making the country worse. The remaining 32 percent held mixed feelings or did not know. The transition from "model citizen" to least favored ethnic group in the nation caused the established community to blame the new arrivals from Mariel.[14] Not surprisingly, three years after arriving, 26 percent of polled Mariel refugees believed they were discriminated against by Anglos, while 75 percent believed they were discriminated against by longer-established exilic Cubans.[15] *Marielitos* quickly became our "other."

Ironically, part of the white Cuba construction is the assertion that Cuba was free of racism. While discrimination may have existed in some sectors, it was presented as never as bad as in the United States. Love and respect supposedly existed between the races in Cuba. As expected, this view is mostly held by those exilic Cubans who are white. The economic and political structures of *la Cuba de ayer* and the Miami of today are designed so Cuban whites with privilege can foster an ideology that justifies and maintains white rule over black nonexistence. Paradoxically, those of us who constructed ourselves as white are only white in Miami. Once we leave Miami, we are seen by the dominant U.S. culture as non-white, non-center.

Finally, our constructed ethnicity stresses being model citizens who embraced the North American work ethic. During the early 1960s the U.S. media broadcasted numerous stories of penniless Cubans rising from adversity to success. These stories stereotyped us as "the Cuban success story." The rags-to-riches discourse benefited both the United States and the exilic Cuban community. The Cuban success story was created when the Civil Rights Movement was beginning to be established in Miami. While the city's black community began to organize and make demands for justice, Cubans began to arrive. This created a diversion for the white establishment to ignore and avoid dealing with the issues the black community raised. The Miami power structure was able to point at the Cubans and in effect say to the black community, "Stop complaining, look at these 'amazing Cubans' who came with only the clothes on their back, not speaking the language. All they brought was their desire to work. Just look at them pull themselves up by their bootstraps. What's your excuse?"

Exilic Cubans learned all too well how to perform on what Foucault calls the "strange theater." It was necessary for exilic Cubans to master the structures of oppression, not only to get the attention of the dominant culture but also to replace it. The public narrative of "those amazing Cubans" allowed the exilic Cubans to move from refugees to model immigrants and now to Miami's ruling elite. Sheila Croucher shows how the social and political construction of the exilic Cuban success story created a public narrative that reflected and reinforced

---

[14] Alejandro Portes and Alex Stepick, *City on the Edge: The Transformation of Miami* (Berkeley and Los Angeles: University of California Press, 1993), 30-33.

[15] Alejandro Portes and Juan M. Clark, "Mariel Refugees: Six Years Later," *Migration World* 15 (1987): 14-18.

the changing character of power and politics by forging the success story "truth" and linking it to power.[16]

James Scott, pondering the arts of domination, demonstrates that the successful communication of power and authority (as in the case of the success story) produces a circle of self-fulfillment. While being socialized into our constructed ethnicity, we learn how to act with the authority and self-assurance that both result from and reinforces the success story. If others can believe in our success story, then the impression will contribute to our emerging power.[17] While the "truth" of the success story may vary from the reality of the 1970s, the construction of the success story served the domestic and foreign interest of the United States, while transforming the exilic Cuban community from refugee to immigrant to center of Miami's power, a center whose political and economic force as a single-issue voting bloc and interest group is felt in Washington, D.C., as well as around the world.

YAHWEH, REMEMBER WHAT THE COMMUNISTS DID— A BLESSING ON HIM WHO DASHES THEIR BABIES AGAINST ROCKS!

The Psalmist prayed for the enemy's babies to be dashed against the rocks. The pain of exile dreams of revenge toward those perceived to be responsible for one's expatriation. Even though the Cold War against communism has ended, Miami remains the only place on the face of the earth where Cold War hatred and fervor have not abated. Mimicking the Psalmist, the exilic Cuban U.S. Congressman Lincoln Díaz-Balart, ironically a nephew of Castro, called for a post-Castro Cuba to launch a campaign of retribution against anyone who participated in "collaborationism with tyranny." Ten years in prison will not be enough for those who are guilty. The congressman even called for the abduction of foreign investors presently doing business with Cuba and having them brought to the island to be punished.[18]

Congressman Díaz-Balart assumes that the vision held by exilic Cubans is the hope of the majority of resident Cubans. Sociologist Egon F. Kunz maintains that the "majority-identified refugees are firm in their conviction that their opposition to the events (in their homeland) is shared by the majority of their compatriots."[19] Gerald Poyo develops this theme and demonstrates how each separate Cuban exilic community—whether in New Orleans in the 1850s, in

---

[16] S. L. Croucher, *Imagining Miami: Ethnic Politics in a Postmodern World* (Charlottesville, Va.: University Press of Virginia, 1997), 102-8.

[17] J. C. Scott, *Domination and the Arts of Resistance* (New Haven, Conn.: Yale University Press, 1990), 48-49.

[18] Patrick J. Kiger, *Squeeze Play: The United States, Cuba, and the Helms-Burton Act* (Washington, D.C.: The Center for Public Integrity, 1996), 57.

[19] E. F. Kunz, "Exile and Resettlement: Refugee Theory," *International Migration Review* 15 (1981): 42-51.

Tampa in the 1890s, in New York in the 1930s, or presently in Miami—assumed that how they "saw" Cuba was shared by those who remained on the island. Such a vision provided moral justification to struggle to change the island's ecopolitical reality.[20] Exilic Cubans "take actions, make decisions, and feel concerns, and develop identities within social networks" that simultaneously connect them with both Cuban and U.S. society; this phenomenon is what Nina Glick-Schiller terms "transnationalism."[21]

Because of transnationalism, violence is legitimized and elevated to the realm of reason. Covert activities include the bombing of the Mexican (1979) and Venezuelan (1983) consulates in Miami, the 1979 bombing of the TWA terminal at Kennedy Airport, the 1978 Avery Fisher Hall bombing at Lincoln Center, the multiple bombings of the Cuban Mission to the United Nations, the machine-gun assassination of Cuban attaché Félix García Rodríguez, and the attempted assassination of the Cuban U.N. ambassador Raúl Roa Kouri. These forms of violence are advocated within an atmosphere where Miami airwaves constantly call for vengeance, openly advocating the "dashing of babies." To suggest dialogue invites punishment.

Although exilic Cubans consider themselves to be free, the reality of Miami is that we are imprisoned. Miami is Foucault's Panopticon. Panopticism describes a model prison where the center is occupied by a guard tower that can gaze at the prisoners in their individual back-lighted cells; the prisoners are unable, because the tower is dark, to gaze at the guard. The gaze of the guard confers power to the observer, while becoming a trap to the ones being observed, even when the surveillance is not constant. The mere possibility of being watched forces its object to internalize the power relation.[22]

For Foucault, it would be naive to view power as being centralized in the hands of the elite. Power is everywhere, forming and passing through a multitude of institutions. It is most effective when it is exercised through a coercion that appears natural and neutral. The Panopticon serves as a model for how oppressive power works on the streets of Miami. The bomb that overtly was targeted for the one offending "heretic" was symbolically directed at all potential "sinners." The fear of punishment, in the form of bombs and machine guns, is no longer needed to maintain discipline within the exilic Cuban community. Like a punishing guard, weapons have been used effectively in the past, and the guard's ubiquitous gaze has been internalized: past punishment served as the instrument to reach the goal of preventing others from straying from the official religious doctrines of *la lucha*.

---

[20] G. E. Poyo, "The Cuban Exile Tradition in the United States: Patterns of Political Development in the Nineteenth and Twentieth Centuries," in *Cuba: cultura e identidad nacional* (La Habana: Ediciones Union, 1975), 76-98.

[21] N. Glick-Schiller, "Postscript: Haitian Transnational Practice and National Discourse," in *Caribbean Life in New York City: Sociocultural Dimensions*, ed. Constance Stutton and Elsa Chany (New York: Center for Migration Studies of New York, 1992), 185.

[22] M. Foucault, *Discipline and Punish: The Birth of the Prison,* trans. Alan Sheridan (New York: Vintage Books, 1995), 202-3.

A shift in the "technology of power," à la Foucault, has been made from yesterday's tortured public bodies spewed on Miami's sidewalks in the wake of a bombing to today's docile private bodies confined to their individual cells. As the eyes of exilic Cubans witnessed and recorded in memory the terror of swift punishment, a system of diminishing penalties took effect. Instead of brute force, public ridicule and/or ostracization from the socioeconomic spaces of Miami became sufficient to ensure obedience. A shift has occurred from the bomb-throwing "patriots" operating within the "theater of punishment" to the bureaucratic capitalist "patriots" within the Cuban American National Foundation (CANF).

La lucha develops comprehensive systems of domination. The exilic Cuban radio stations of Miami become the unblinking eye of *la lucha,* serving as the guard tower. The gaze of the radio stations produces conformity to our false religion. These stations are not the terminal points of power. Rather, they serve *el exilio* as the official pulpit whose sermons contain news, disseminate rumors, denounce heretics, and constantly call for the "dashing of babies against rocks." The airwaves of Miami normalize the "sinner's" punishment, not as vengeance in the hands of some terrorists but as a result of divine retribution. When the "instruments of God's wrath" are prosecuted by the U.S. government, they become martyrs of the faith. The guard in the tower, the power that demands obedience, is disguised in daily participation in one of the basic rights of a free society, a free press.

Bernardo Benes, considered the leading exilic Cuban in the late 1970s, lost his position of power and privilege when he met with Castro to explore the possibilities of reconciliation. He was labeled a communist by Miami's exilic Cuban radio stations. Benes described the Panopticon-type function of these radio stations when he stated:

> A million Cubans are blackmailed, totally controlled, by three radio stations. I feel sorry for the Cuban community in Miami. Because they have imposed on themselves, by way of the Right, the same condition that Castro has imposed on Cuba. Total intolerance. And ours is worse. Because it is entirely voluntary.[23]

The pain caused by our Panopticon is captured by Joan Didion when she writes, "The scars *el exilio* inflicts upon its own do not entirely heal, nor are they meant to."[24]

These scars are not caused by a centralized Cuban elite. Rather, as Foucault argues, the power to inflict scars on the docile body resides in multitude networks (like the radio stations and their listeners) interwoven with the political economy of the elite. Because power cannot be limited to the realm of the elite, replacing the elite would not suffice in eliminating these networks ingrained in every fiber of Miami life. Benes's experience proves the autonomy of a disciplinary structure designed to punish any heretic of *la lucha*, even those among the elite. The tragedy of Miami's Panopticon is that those who exercise power

---

[23] J. Didion, *Miami* (New York: Simon and Schuster, 1987), 113.

[24] Ibid., 114-15, 120.

are unaware of their complicity and self-subjugation within the oppressive system because of their blindness to the hateful tenets of *la lucha*.

Hatred is not limited to one side of the Florida Straits. While the exilic community calls a person "a Castro agent" for suggesting any deviation from the tenets of *la lucha*, the resident community calls a person a *gusano* (worm) for leaving the island in the first place. Each Cuba sees itself in the mirror as the true remnant. Resident Cubans see themselves as the true Cubans, just as King Zedekiah's nobles who remained in Judah saw themselves as true Jews (Ez 11:14, 33:24). Similarly, exilic Cubans see themselves in their mirror as God's "good basket of figs" as opposed to the "bad basket of figs" with which Jeremiah (24) represents King Zedekiah and all those who remain behind. Resident Cubans are seen as pseudo-Cubans in need of education in the ways of capitalism and democracy. *La lucha* is reduced to a struggle to promote new oppressors.

Before we exiles attempt paternalistically to educate resident Cubans, we of *el exilio* must first recover from our amnesia. Jeremiah strives to overcome the Babylonian Jews' attempt to displace blame. He explains that their condemnation is due to "no one doing justice." Our own sins, and the sins of those to whom we have become vassals, are the causes of our exile. Our reconstruction of *la Cuba de ayer* ignores the reality that La Habana was an exotic space constructed by the United States, where the repressed libidinous appetites of the Anglos could be satisfied. The commercialization of vice afforded North Americans the opportunity to experience life outside of their accustomed moral space. La Habana of 1958 was a United States brothel with Mafia-controlled casinos, holding the infamous distinction of being the sex-and-abortion capital of the Western Hemisphere. As a playground for North Americans, Cuba developed an unequal distribution of wealth and violated basic human rights. Jeremiah's condemnation of King Jehoiakim also applies to Cuba's elite who profited from this arrangement. They built their house through the oppression of people (Jer 22:13-17). No communal covenant based on justice and compassion existed between the elite and the masses. By continuing to scapegoat the communists, we deflect attention from our own responsibility. Castro is not the one responsible for our landlessness; the Cuban elite who profited from the U.S. neocolonial venture is responsible. Many of those responsible form today's exilic Cuban elite.

Maintaining *la Cuba de ayer* ensures the condemnation of our perceived enemies today, while it mythically creates the Cuba of tomorrow, a post-Castro Cuba based on horizontal oppression, where resident Cubans will be subject to exilic Cubans. The overwhelming support of the embargo by exilic Cubans denies resident Cubans basic medical supplies and causes death among the sick, the elderly, and infants. From a sanitizing distance we are dashing the "enemy's" babies against rocks when we deny insulin to those born diabetic.

The Panopticon paradigm can be expanded to explain how exilic Cubans morally justify the exercise of their power over the resident Cuban community through the support of the U.S. embargo. The embargo against Cuba, redrafted and maintained through the efforts of CANF, is an example of disciplinary technology on a global scale. The embargo is a controlled space that represents a standardized action persisting over a period of time. It normalizes the New World Order by punishing those who refuse to obey. The embargo presupposes the hierarchical power to gaze, a gaze that comes from the U.S. center allowing exilic Cubans in Miami to qualify, classify, and punish Cuba. The attempt to exercise discipline over Cuba presupposes a mechanism that coerces by means of observation. Once the United States, as the perfect eye, "sees" Cuba conforming, then the embargo would be loosened or lifted. The "babies dashed against the rocks," the victims of this institutionalized violence, are labeled by the exilic Cubans as the cause of the violence. Meanwhile, the gaze creates on the island a siege mentality and justifies their own internal actions of oppression.

While our two Cubas struggle with each other, the United States is positioning itself to reimpose its hegemony. In the same way that the Persian court created a postexilic community to secure its national interests, the United States has promised to "rebuild" Cuba, ensuring that any post-Castro government sacrifices its sovereignty. Such a future would create a hierarchical community dominated by those dedicated to the economic concerns of U.S. business. Proposed horizontal oppression among Cubans is thus masked by patriotism (patriotism at a profit).

CONCLUDING COMMENTS

From the periphery of the Jewish exilic community's epicenter of power, a prophet arose who became a subversive yet redemptive voice. While we do not know his name, his work is found in the later chapters of Isaiah. Appealing to the community's old memories, he plots a new trajectory to discern reality, a reality that conflicts with the self-deception of the exiles. Second Isaiah's vision is inclusive (49:6; 56:1-8; 66:18-21), calling the exilic community to become "a light to the nations, that [God's] salvation [reconciliation] may reach to the end of the earth" (49:6). The focus is on a God who acts on the side of the afflicted. Such a God opposes the partisan politics rampant in the postexilic Jewish community. Rejecting this prophetic voice, exilic Cubans are aggressively taking the opposite role, that of the Zadokite priestly party.[25] The

---

[25] The Zadokite priesthood was responsible for the reforms made during the reign of King Josiah in 622 B.C.E. They held exclusive responsibility for the temple cult, facilitating their leadership status within the exilic Jewish community. Their leadership expanded to civic matters with the mysterious disappearance of the Davidic prince Zerubbabel. Just as the CANF holds official sponsorship by the U.S. government and has set out to create plans for the "restoration" of Cuba, so the Zadokites were also officially sponsored by the Persian court and given the task of restoring Judea as vassal to Persia. A twenty-four-page report titled *Support for a Democratic Transition in Cuba*, submitted to the United States Congress on January 28, 1997, by President Clinton, outlines the administration's intention of providing $4 to $8 billion to establish an approved governmental and political system. The conditions for replacing the ongoing thirty-five-plus-year trade embargo with this assistance package includes the departure of the Castro brothers ("horizontally" or "vertically," as per Senator Helms), the release of all political prisoners, the dismantling of the interior ministry, and the holding of a U.S.-style public election. The report also calls for a possible renegotiation of the soon-to-expire lease of Guantanamo Bay, where a U.S. military presence still exists.

inclusiveness of Second Isaiah's community is met with accusations of being communist dupes or agents. Biblical scholar Paul Hanson points out that the Zadokites: (1) moved away from Second Isaiah's egalitarian call for a nation of priests by firmly holding power in their own hands (60:21, 61:6); (2) replaced Isaiah's mission to the nations with a pragmatic and parochial strategy of domestic consolidation (56:3-7); and (3) confused the sovereignty of God with that of the Persian emperor, even to the point of proclaiming that God elected a pagan, Cyrus, to be God's messiah.[26] The failure to pursue Isaiah's vision can be traced to the Persian court's self-serving support of the Zadokites. The construction of a postexilic Judah was possible because it contributed to Persia's international goal of creating a buffer between Persia and its enemies, the Egyptians. As such, Judah's existence depended on Persia's good will (Ezra 7:11-18). The nation was rebuilt at the price of being a vassal (583-332 B.C.E.) to its more powerful northern neighbor. The parallels to modern Cuba are striking.

Ezra (7:25-26), with legal and financial support from Persia, was sent to create this buffer zone, where the inhabitants would strictly obey the "law of your God *and the law of the [Persian] king*" (italics added). The land was controlled by the returning Jews. Like Ezra's approach, exilic Cubans are preparing to demand that resident Cubans "put away their foreign wives." Some of those "wives," however, may be worth keeping (such as high literacy rates, a 100 percent social security system, high doctor-per-patient ratio, low infant mortality rate, and long life expectancy). Ignoring Second Isaiah's egalitarian call, the postexilic community soon found itself weakened by internal economic abuses. Exilic Jews benefited from the economic misfortunes of the resident Jews, while concealing their profiteering in piety (Is 58:1-12, 59:1-8). The resident poor found themselves enslaved, losing their lands to the returning exiles (Neh 5:1-5) and cheated from wages by returning Jews who set up new business (Mal 3:5). The book of Ruth, written during this period, becomes an alternative voice to the imposition of Zadokite power. Here, God uses a "foreign wife," a Moabite, similar to the ones put away by Ezra, to represent society's most vulnerable members. Ruth is saved by the egalitarian laws that the exilic leaders aborted.

This biblical paradigm of domination will repeat itself. The planned post-Castro community will lead to the subjugation of resident Cubans by exilic Cubans, who in turn will be subjugated to U.S. hegemony. We can follow the example of Ezra, forcing resident Cubans to "put away their foreign wives," establishing a vassal political system that enriches the exilic community elite to the detriment of the resident community. Or we can follow Second Isaiah's egalitarian vision, which attempts to construct a reconciled and just community. As long as we exilic Cubans maintain our mirror-like construction of ethnic identity and participate in the false religion of *la lucha*, and as long as exilic Cuban theologians define our theological location in terms of some general

---

[26] P. Hanson, *The People Called: The Growth of Community in the Bible* (San Francisco: Harper & Row, 1986), 255.

Hispanic perspective "from the margins," reconciliation between the two Cubas remains impossible. On the contrary, I propose a biblical reading that constructs our identity based on our sociohistorical reality, unmasking the power and privilege held by exilic Cubans and debunking our ethnic construction, which prevents dialogue between us and our "other." A liberationist approach to theology liberates the oppressed as well as the oppressors. As present oppressors in Miami, and as future oppressors in a post-Castro Cuba, we exilic Cubans are in need of a biblical reading that fosters liberation and reconciliation.

11

A New *Mestizaje/Mulatez*

Reconceptualizing Difference

ADA MARÍA ISASI-DÍAZ

Difference plays a significant role in all that we are and all that we do. Without any doubt whatsoever this is the key issue we will have to deal with in the twenty-first century, for it affects all. Any worldview that wants to remain vital needs to take difference into consideration. All societal institutions, every community and every person, all without exception, have to examine what they understand by difference, what role that understanding plays in both self-conception and relationships, and what part difference plays in plans and strategies, in the everyday course of life.

Those of us who come from marginal communities are positioned in a most advantageous way to reconceptualize the meaning of difference, to deal with it in a constructive manner, to choose to embrace difference as a necessary ethical action, if our world is to move beyond the prejudices and divisions that exploit and maim, that thwart and constrain, that limit possibilities and threaten the very survival of the human race. It is not that we in marginalized communities are morally better or intellectually more capable than those of the dominant group, who consider themselves normative and decide who is "different." Rather, it is because we are the ones who are labeled different, because we suffer in our own flesh the negative understanding that such a label carries, because we have nothing to gain in this regard from the present situation. This is why marginalized people are the ones best situated to imagine another way of understanding and dealing with difference than the present one.

The importance of difference for Latinas and Latinos is made obvious by the insistence in Hispanic/Latino theology, including *mujerista* theology, on recognizing the importance of *mestizaje/mulatez*, a concept which originally referred to the mingling of Amerindian and African blood with European blood, but which now also includes the present-day mixtures of people from Latin America and the Caribbean both among ourselves and with people of other ethnic/racial and cultural backgrounds here in the United States. *Mestizaje/mulatez* also refers to the mingling of cultures, the creation of a new culture that embraces elements from the African, Amerindian, and Spanish cultures. In our theological endeavors, *mestizaje/mulatez* constitutes our *locus theologicus*—the place from which we do theology precisely because it is intrinsic to who we are. It situates us as a community in U.S. society. *Mestizaje/mulatez* is so important to us that we have suggested it as an ethical option, because it has to do with an understanding of difference that is intrinsic not only to the Latina[1] community's identity but to everyone's sense of self.[2]

In this article I want to suggest that it is precisely because of our recognition of the importance of *mestizaje/mulatez* and what it means that we must contribute to the conversation with other marginalized communities in the United States. I propose that in *mestizaje/mulatez* we find a way out of the excluding and oppositional understanding of difference so prejudicial to our own community and to all marginalized people.

EMBRACING DIFFERENCES: AN URGENT NEED

I begin with a number of salient facts about the differences that make for marginalized communities:

- We start the new millennium with barely two hundred mega-transnational corporations controlling no less than one fourth of the economic activity of the whole planet. This in many ways is why the richest fifth of the world population receives 82.7 percent of the resources of our planet, the second fifth richest 11.7 percent, the fifth in the middle 2.3 percent, the fourth fifth 1.9 percent, and the poorest fifth 1.4 percent of total world income.[3]
- One hundred and eighty million children the world over are malnourished. Fourteen million children die every year before they reach the age of five.[4]
- The richest countries, with about 25 percent of the world population, consume 70 percent of the world's energy, 75 percent of its metals, 85 percent of its wood, and 60 percent of its food.[5] All the trees of the world would disappear in two years if the whole world were to use the amount of paper

---

[1] All nouns in the Spanish language have grammatical gender and so do their modifying adjectives. *Comunidad* (community) in Spanish is feminine, and so must be the adjectives that modify it, in this case *Latina*. This gives me the opportunity of using the feminine form *Latina* as a way of breaking through the traditional use of the masculine form to refer to a group of many women and only one man. Throughout this article, then, my use of *Latina* should be read to refer to both men and women from the Latina community.

[2] Ada María Isasi-Díaz, *En La Lucha–In the Struggle: Elaborating a Mujerista Theology* (Minneapolis, Minn.: Fortress Press, 1993), chap. 6.

[3] *United Nations Development Report 1992* (New York and Oxford: Oxford University Press, 1992), 34.

[4] Ibid., 14.

[5] Ibid., 35.

that is used in the United States, where only 6 percent of the world population lives.[6]

- Women account for 67 of each 100 hours of work done in the world but control only 9.4 percent of the world's income. Of the estimated 1.3 billion people living in poverty, more than 70 percent are female. The number of rural women living in absolute poverty rose nearly 50 percent in the last 20 years. One can thus readily agree that, "increasingly, poverty has a woman's face."[7] Only 4 percent of women are in positions where decisions are made. Although women constitute half the electorate, we hold only 10 percent of the seats in the world's parliaments and 6 percent in national cabinets.[8] Women constitute 66 percent of the illiterate people of the world.[9]

This view from the underside of the world is obvious to those who are willing to hear the cries of the poor and the oppressed. The unwillingness or perhaps (perhaps?!) the incapacity to see the misery of such a large percentage of the human race is grounded, I believe, in the refusal to recognize that these vast numbers of suffering humanity are our sisters and brothers—people to whom and for whom we are responsible. There are two main reasons for not accepting the poor and the oppressed as our responsibility. First, we suspect or know that their misery is directly related to the privileges and goods that so few enjoy and will do anything to protect. At the root of such selfishness lies prejudice. Of course, those who act counter to the interests of the poor are prejudiced, so they rationalize their actions by thinking that there are valid reasons for what they do or do not do: they have worked hard for what they have; they have paid good money for it; they have sacrificed themselves so that their children can have a better life (more material goods). Prejudices are grounded in the belief, at times unstated and unexamined, that those who are different from the dominant group are inferior. This is a second reason why we do not want to recognize our responsibility for the poor and the oppressed: we believe that their inferiority absolves us from responsibility. We have convinced ourselves that it is their inferiority and not our prejudice that is the reason for oppression and poverty.

Situations of apartheid based on a prejudicial understanding of difference are being created all over the world: an ever-smaller group of people control resources and decision-making processes, effectively setting up in the process separate spheres for relating, acting, being, and living. At the same time, because of the almost instantaneous accessibility to worldwide information and the possibility of quick communication with and traveling to any part of the world, we have to deal with differences repeatedly in all areas of our lives, as a quick glance at our world shows. Religious difference is intrinsic to the conflicts in

---

[6] Pedro Casaldáliga, "El pregón del jubileo," *Presencia Ecuménica* (Caracas) 46 (January-March 1998): 23.

[7] *United Nations Development Report 1995* (New York and Oxford: Oxford University Press, 1995), 36.

[8] Ibid., 41.

[9] Casaldáliga, "Pregón del jubileo," 23.

Eastern Europe, which are supported by an ideology of genocide. Religious difference upholds the conflict between Palestinians and Jews, as well as the conflicts within countries that include Muslims of different persuasions. What is decided by and happens to people different from us on the other side of the globe affects us in many ways. This is made obvious not only by the economic world, where markets are so interrelated, but also by such phenomena as acid rain, which does not stay inside any given country's borders, global warming, and the deterioration of the ozone layer. It is also what is obviously at stake with the AIDS epidemic, which ignores all differences. Such realities affect all, regardless of differences.

The present understanding of difference "defines it as absolute otherness, mutual exclusion, categorical opposition."[10] Such an understanding leads to a conceptualization of those who are different as outsiders, with those belonging to the dominant group having the power to decide what is normative (themselves) and what is deviant (others). As long as this continues to be the prevalent understanding, there is no possibility of having just personal relationships or of creating just societal structures that will not benefit some groups at the expense of others. As long as this is the prevalent understanding of difference, we will always be oppressing those who are outside our group, threatening both them and ourselves with destruction.

A HISTORY OF THE ELABORATION OF *MESTIZAJE/MULATEZ* IN HISPANIC/LATINA THEOLOGY

In our Hispanic/Latina communities a similar understanding of difference prevails. Our marginality, however, makes us question it in ways that the dominant group does not. The reconceptualization of difference, therefore, follows a practice born of the need to survive within a dominant culture. Latinas and Latinos have learned that, when we face the dominant group, we have to think in another way about difference. Although indeed sexism, racism, and other prejudices are operative in Hispanic/Latina communities, the need to present a united front makes it imperative for us to overcome them. Yet, the way we think about difference at present makes this impossible.

The insistence in Hispanic/Latina theology, including *mujerista* theology, on seeing and using *mestizaje/mulatez* as a positive element and proposing it as an ethical choice is indicative of our preoccupation with understanding and dealing with difference. Virgilio Elizondo, whose work established *mestizaje* as a key element of Hispanic/Latina theology, speaks of it as "the birth of a new people from two preexistent peoples."[11] In the first instance, he argues, *mestizaje* "de facto . . . [came] about through military conquest, colonization, religious imposition. This certainly was the case in the Spanish-Indian *mestizaje*."[12]

---

[10] Iris Marion Young, *Justice and the Politics of Difference* (Princeton, N.J.: Princeton University Press, 1990), 169.

[11] Virgilio Elizondo, *Galilean Journey* (Maryknoll, N.Y.: Orbis Books, 1983), 10.

[12] Ibid.

Elizondo also points to a second *mestizaje*, going on at present here in the United States between Mexican people and other peoples.[13] For Elizondo, therefore, *mestizaje* generates a new people, a new ethnic group, with cultural as well as biological characteristics. He considers acculturation as an accommodation to the dominant group that makes one leave behind one's own culture. Elizondo sees "group inclusion/exclusion"—that is, the social distance among groups that set up the superior/inferior relationship as well as the need to eliminate anyone who attempts to destroy these barriers—as "anthropological law[s] of human nature." But Elizondo is not willing to accept these "laws" as immutable. His work is an attempt to show that Mexican Americans can live out a radical understanding of *mestizaje* that would relativize these laws and bring richness to all. For Elizondo, the Christian faith plays a central role in what *mestizaje* is, means, and signifies.[14]

Although Elizondo speaks about *la raza* (the race), he does not make direct reference to José de Vasconcelos, the Mexican philosopher who proposed the concept of "the cosmic race." It is in the work of Andrés Guerrero that we find *la raza* directly linked to *mestizaje*.[15] Guerrero claims that Vasconcelos's concept "stressed the inclusivity of the four races" and seems to use this concept as a way of grounding and perhaps even amplifying the idea of *mestizaje*. Guerrero proposes *la raza* as a symbol of *mestizaje*, of hope, of unity, of new creation, and of liberation. It is important to note that this way of using *la raza* is something that Guerrero develops on the basis of what leaders from the Mexican-American community whom he interviewed told him.

When others among us Latinas and Latinos who are not Mexican Americans started contributing to the elaboration of Hispanic/Latina theology, including *mujerista* theology, we appropriated this concept of *mestizaje* and proceeded to expand its meaning. In the first book I co-authored with Yolanda Tarango, published a year after Guerrero's, we start by specifying that we are talking about Hispanics, particularly about the three most numerous groups of Hispanics— Mexican Americans, Puerto Ricans, and Cubans.[16] There, using *mestizaje* as a way of explaining *la raza*, we talk about the three-pronged *mestizaje* of Hispanic women that includes race, culture, and history. In a second book I expanded

---

[13] Ibid., 13-16.

[14] Ibid., 16-18.

[15] It is not my intention here to critique or endorse the use of Vasconcelos's concept of *la raza cósmica*, which some claim has strong undertones of racism. I do think that Guerrero uses it as a springboard, not necessarily claiming to embrace all that Vasconcelos meant by it. In this regard it is important to notice that Elizondo's use of *la raza* without any mention of Vasconcelos, as well as the popular use of this word/concept, seems to indicate that it has a meaning and a relevance among the people that go far beyond Vasconcelos's elaborations. See Andrés Guerrero, *A Chicano Theology* (Maryknoll, N.Y.: Orbis Books, 1987), 118-37.

[16] Ada María Isasi-Díaz and Yolanda Tarango, *Hispanic Women: Prophetic Voice in the Church* (San Francisco: Harper & Row, 1988; reprint, Minneapolis, Minn.: Fortress Press, 1993), xi.

on the understanding of *mestizaje* from a *mujerista* perspective, working to develop what Elizondo had called the second *mestizaje*, the one occurring here and now among Hispanics. In the last chapter of this second book, I began to elaborate a non-exclusionary and non-oppositional perspective of differences and concluded by proposing the embracing of *mestizaje* as an ethical choice, as a *mujerista* truth-praxis: a denunciation of the racism and ethnic prejudice of this country that, together with the poverty it generates, constitutes a key element in the oppression of Hispanics in the United States.[17]

In *mujerista* theology we have proposed an understanding of popular religion as a form of *mestizaje* in itself, as well as a key factor of *mestizaje* at large. We also recognize that both African and Amerindian religious understandings and practices are intrinsic elements of popular religion as well as of *mestizaje*. Our intention has been to broaden *mestizaje* to include African cultural, historical, and biological elements. However, given the racism in the country and in own our societies of origin, we have come to realize that we needed to name specifically the heritage we have received from Africa. Following the lead of Fernando Segovia, we started to add *mulatez*, which refers to the mixing of the white and black races, to *mestizaje* instead of including our African heritage under this term.[18]

Roberto Goizueta's work in 1995 pushed the understanding of *mestizaje* further. Working to develop a sense of praxis that is non-instrumental, Goizueta turns to Vasconcelos to find an understanding of human action as essentially aesthetic. In Vasconcelos's thought it is the special pathos of beauty that is the unifying principle of intellectual, moral, and aesthetic forms of action. Goizueta indicates that Vasconcelos's "special pathos of beauty" means "empathic fusion," of which,

> Latin American people are the progeny . . . which occurred historically between the Spanish culture and people, on the one hand, and indigenous and African cultures and people on the other. It was precisely through its openness to these "other" races and cultures and its willingness to intermix and interrelate with them, that Spain gave birth to the Latin American mestizo people, *la raza cósmica*.[19]

For Vasconcelos the *mestizo* community goes beyond a homogeneous community. Goizueta sees this as a key to the reason why the *mestizo* community "does not impose unity, but achieves it through empathic love. In so doing, the mestizo

---

[17] Isasi-Díaz, *En La Lucha–In the Struggle*, Chapter 6.

[18] We heard Fernando Segovia use *mulatez* before he put it in writing. Orlando Espín and other Cuban as well as Puerto Rican theologians also use *mulatez*. See Fernando F. Segovia, "In the World but Not of It: A Theology of Exile," in *Hispanic/Latino Theology: Challenge and Promise,* ed. Ada María Isasi-Díaz and Fernando Segovia (Minneapolis, Minn.: Fortress Press, 1996), 196.

[19] Roberto S. Goizueta, *Caminemos con Jesús* (Maryknoll, N.Y.: Orbis Books, 1995), 97-98.

community affirms the identity of other persons as particular, unique, and different subjects (i.e., historical agents in their own right) who, as subjects, can be known only through love."[20] This calls for an understanding of difference that does not focus on opposition and exclusion but rather can make "emphatic fusion" possible without destroying the specificity of historical, moral agents. This new understanding of difference will make it possible to create a way of relating that leaves behind the prejudicial understanding of difference that we have at present.[21] I am convinced that a change in the notion of difference will yield a kind of moral subject for whom goodness is relational, for whom love and justice are inseparable, and who finds expression in effective solidarity. For *mujeristas,* this is precisely what *mestizaje/mulatez* points to and should mean; this is precisely what the moral option of justice-seeking people should be about.

DIFFERENCE: RELATIONAL RATHER THAN EXCLUSIONARY

In *mujerista* theology we have been working to reconceptualize our understanding of difference, because we believe that the way difference is thought about today is the basis for all prejudices and hate crimes. Difference is seen as what separates us from others, as what makes each of us unique. The preciousness of every human person, his or her intrinsic importance as a human being, has been linked to the person's uniqueness—to whatever he or she is, has, or does that is different from others. Following these understandings, attempts to relate to others or to be a community or to work in coalition have depended mainly on emphasizing what different peoples or groups have in common. This means that, following the logic of this schema, one has to leave behind and to ignore what makes one precious and important in order to be able to relate to others individually or communally.

The other conclusion one may draw from this way of understanding difference is that the only solution lies in doing away with differences. This understanding is the operative one in theories of assimilation, which, regardless of some claims to the opposite, are still the controlling worldview in this society. Assimilation leads to three negative consequences. First, ignoring differences means forcing those who are different into the mainstream. It means that the dominant group defines the standards used in society, and that those who are not like them have to abide by what has been set as the norm. Those of the dominant group do not recognize the norm they have set as "culturally and experientially specific" but rather hold to it as the ideal of a common humanity that poses as universal and neutral, in which all can participate without regard to race, gender, religion, or sexuality.[22] This is the second negative result of assimilation: "It allows the privileged group to ignore their own group specificity."[23] This leads

---

[20] Ibid., 98.

[21] See Audre Lorde, "Age, Race, Class, and Sex," in *Sister Outsider* (Trumansburg, N.Y.: The Crossing Press, 1984), 114-23.

[22] Young, *Justice and the Politics of Difference*, 164.

[23] Ibid., 165.

the dominant group to claim neutrality and to regard not itself but the groups that are different as having particularity, as marked with a specificity whereby they can be considered as "other." Perhaps the third consequence is the most insidious one: Assimilation often makes those who are different internalize the negative understandings the dominant group has of them. Assimilation demands of those who are different to fit, to be like the dominant group, leading to "the self-loathing and double consciousness characteristic of oppression. . . . When participation is taken to imply assimilation, the oppressed person is caught in an irresolvable dilemma: to participate means to accept and adopt an identity one is not, and to try to participate means to be reminded by oneself and others of the identity one is."[24]

In order to survive as a marginalized group within a dominant culture, Latinas and Latinos have developed, mostly unconsciously, great flexibility in shifting from "the mainstream construction of life" to our own construction of life, where we feel at home.[25] Our own construction of life is a hybrid reality, a *mestizo/ mulato* reality which we create from elements of Latina culture and elements of the dominant culture that we import as we need them.[26] This flexibility, this traveling between worlds, is a "skillful, creative, rich, enriching and, given certain circumstances . . . a loving way of being and living."[27] However, ethnic prejudice and racism turn this world-traveling into a negative experience, making it compulsory for us marginalized people but absolving the dominant group from any responsibility to engage in it. The lack of knowledge and appreciation of marginalized cultures makes world-traveling mostly a one-way affair, because Latinas and Latinos are not allowed to bring into the dominant construction of the world elements from our own culture. It is also a one-way traveling because the few people of the dominant group who travel to our world insist on changing it by acting in the Latina world the way they act in theirs.

Such lack of ability for world-traveling and such insistence on assimilation on the part of the dominant group are the result of identifying people and things by highlighting difference instead of similarity. Identifying similarity and difference seems to be part of the way people "describe and sort their perceptions of the world."[28] However, accepting that boundaries created by differences are needed "to make sense of perceptions, experiences, identities, and human obligations"[29]

---

[24] Ibid.

[25] María Lugones, "Playfulness, 'World-Traveling,' and Loving Perception," in *Making Face, Making Soul-Haciendo Caras*, ed. Gloria Anzaldúa (San Francisco: An Aunt Lute Foundation Book, 1990), 390.

[26] Of course, when imported within a mainly Latina frame of reference, the elements of the dominant culture undergo certain modifications. For example, Latinas may be on time for meetings, but our meetings still have to start with time for personal relationships instead of diving right into business.

[27] Lugones, "Playfulness, 'World-Traveling,' and Loving Perception," 390.

[28] Martha Minow, *Making All the Difference* (Ithaca, N.Y.: Cornell University, 1990), 4. The elaborations of the meaning of differences that follows is based on Minow's work and is also influenced by the work of María Lugones and Iris Marion Young.

[29] Ibid., 7.

does not necessarily have to lead to assigning consequences to difference and positioning ourselves in relation to them. In other words, most of the time the way we understand and deal with difference includes making moral judgments about it, "automatically" deciding that, because people are different, they are either better or worse, never just different. Society has insisted on capitalizing on "categories of difference that manifest social prejudice and misunderstanding,"[30] while ignoring ongoing relationships among people based on similarities. Society understands boundaries as what keeps us out of or away from each other, instead of highlighting that "the whole concept of a boundary depends on relationships: relationships between the two sides drawn by the boundary, and relationships among the people who recognize and affirm the boundary."[31] Since boundaries do not exist outside connections among people, this means that, in order to bring about a paradigm shift in our understanding of difference, we need to emphasize how difference is related to relationships rather than to distinctions.

The moral judgment that surrounds differences, especially the judgment of the dominant group, results in prejudice and discrimination. The basis for the negative moral judgment—and, therefore, for prejudice and discrimination—rests upon five unstated assumptions. First, "we often assume that 'differences' are intrinsic, rather that viewing them as expressions of comparisons between people on the basis of particular traits."[32] Since we are all different from others in many ways, what is at stake is the selection of particular traits as the ones that are vested with negative or positive importance. Second, we assume that when we consider and judge others we do not have prejudices as our point of reference. The unstated point of reference of the dominant group, prejudice, "promotes the interests of some but not others; it can remain unstated because those who do not fit have less power to select the norm than those who fit comfortably within the one that prevails."[33] A third unstated assumption is that persons doing the judging do not have a perspective, as if one could be truly free from a perspective or one could see from someone else's point of view. Fourth, the dominant group assumes the luxury of thinking that it does not have to take other points of view into consideration, that the perspectives of those being judged are irrelevant or have already been taken into consideration. Fifth, there is an assumption that the existing social and economic arrangements of society are "natural and neutral" and that, therefore, the differences in the way people are treated and the way they live are matters of their own personal choice. These unstated assumptions lead to an understanding of difference as intrinsic to human persons:

> If difference is intrinsic, then it will crop up whether noticed or ignored. If difference is knowable by reference to an unstated norm, then the norm

---

[30] Ibid., 9.
[31] Ibid., 10.
[32] Ibid., 51.
[33] Ibid.

itself remains hidden from evaluation. If an observer such as a judge can
see difference without a perspective, then those who "are different" have
no chance to challenge the assignment of difference or its consequences.
And if the status quo is natural, good, and chosen, then efforts to alter its
differential burdens on people will inevitably seem unnatural, undesirable,
and coercive. Noticing difference and ignoring it both recreate difference;
both can threaten such goals as neutrality, equality and freedom.[34]

How do we face unstated assumptions that are considered natural and that, if
noticed, are considered neutral? The only way is to turn to experience. Latinas
and Latinos often notice that there are gaps between our experience and the
prevailing presuppositions, that often we ourselves or people we know do not
fit in the slots society (the dominant group) assigns us. Our experience often
makes us realize that we deal with people we consider "different" but who matter to us differently from the way in which we treat those whom we do not know
or who do not matter to us. This leads us to understand how relationship is
essential to the way we conceptualize difference: we may see persons as not
similar to us, but in one case it matters and in the other it does not. This does not
mean that the unsimilar characteristics disappear but rather that, in the case of
the persons with whom we have a relationship, these characteristics are neither
considered determining nor looked upon as signaling exclusion and opposition.

Relationships make it possible to understand that differences are relative.
Relationships make it possible for us to share the point of view of those whom
an essentialist understanding of differences may have classified as deviant or at
least as "other." The goal here is not to replace our perspective with that of
another but rather to embrace the partiality of all human perspectives and to
admit the point of view of others as a corrective lens to our own. We see that the
present understanding of difference depends on a comparison between people
with reference to a human-made norm that need not remain the way it is. It is a
norm that must be challenged. Relationships make it possible to realize that
once differences stop being unfamiliar, they are no longer frightening. Not being afraid opens the door for understanding that our point of view and experience
of reality are as different to others as theirs are to us and that the concept we
have of difference is a conceptual simplification that serves our interests, that
reflects where we stand.[35]

As social beings we are called to relate to all those around us, and this we can
do in a nondiscriminatory way only if we emphasize what connects us, if we
understand the injuries produced by exclusion and isolation. Decentralizing
ourselves would help us to be cognizant of what connects us, and to do this we
must stop making ourselves the point of reference. We must stop having what
has been called "boomerang perception."[36] The best way to explain what this

---

[34] Ibid., 74.

[35] Ibid., 379.

[36] Elizabeth V. Spelman, *Inessential Woman: Problems of Exclusion in Feminist
Thought* (Boston: Beacon Press, 1988), 12.

concept means is by way of an example. Think of the well-meaning, committed-to-justice, Euro-American mother who sends her daughter to school on the first day of classes. When the little girl comes home and tells her that she has a Hispanic classmate, the mother, not wanting her daughter to be racist, reassures her by telling her that there is nothing to worry about, that the little Hispanic girl is just as she is. It is very difficult to imagine that such a mother in today's society would tell her daughter, "Do not worry, you are just like that Hispanic girl." The mother's comment reasserts the centrality and normativity of the dominant race and culture. Ultimately, boomerang perception indicates that those of the dominant group do not consider the difference important, something worth exploring. If it were important, the dominant group would see those of us who are different as mirrors who reveal them as no other mirror can. We, of course, are not the only mirror that they have or should use, but we do show those of the dominant group a face of the people they are.[37]

Overcoming boomerang perception is directly connected to the ability to travel between worlds. I want to insist that this is not a matter of a tourist-like visit in which we look at life but do not enter into it. Traveling between worlds means entering the world of other people in such a way that not only do we learn how they see us but also we come to understand better how they construct themselves in their own world and the role we play in that construction. It is important here to understand that we all inhabit many different worlds—worlds that are never complete but only under construction—and that therefore we are always sorting out what to include and what to exclude. Additionally, because our social context is not, most of the time, completely of our own choosing, we may not understand or accept the prevalent construction of our world or how that world constructs us.[38]

This idea of traveling to different worlds relates to the need to "unlock subjectivity, such that self functions as a fluid, internally diversifying, and temporally open-ended process rather than as a product of an autonomous essence."[39] This kind of social ontology necessitates fluidity, to which world-traveling refers at the same time that it supports mutuality, which is a key element of solidarity.[40]

---

[37] María C. Lugones, "On the Logic of Pluralistic Feminism," in *Feminist Ethics*, ed. Claudia Card (Lawrence, Kan.: University Press of Kansas), 41-42.

[38] Lugones, "Playfulness, 'World-Traveling,' and Loving Perception," 394-96.

[39] Catherine Keller, "Seeking and Sucking: On Relation and Essence in Feminist Theology," in *Horizons in Feminist Theology: Identity, Tradition, and Norms*, ed. Rebecca S. Chopp and Sheila Greene Davaney (Minneapolis, Minn.: Fortress Press, 1997), 55.

[40] This idea of world-traveling moves away from a static notion of subjectivity while still insisting on subjectivity, since we do not lose ourselves as we cross worlds. Furthermore, this idea of traveling to other worlds to change ourselves involves a kind of reciprocity between the worlds we relate to and our own agency as well as to the need to be open to those worlds and their construction of us as intrinsic to our own agency. This has ontological implications, but our emphasis here is on unlocking subjectivity through world-traveling more as a strategy to change the way we conceptualize difference. I am grateful to Darla Jean Fjeld, a PhD graduate from Drew University for her helpful analysis of Lugones's concepts ("Gender and Divine Transcendence: Preface for a Philosophy of Religion" [Ph.D. dissertation, Drew University, 1998]).

This world-traveling points to better possibilities for coalition-building, which in return opens doors for more effective world-traveling. Working in coalition with other marginalized groups once we redefine difference in a non-opposi-tional and non-exclusionary way leads to coalition-building beyond a very specific issue; it leads to understanding coalition-building as an effective way to bring about radical change in society.

World-traveling helps one to understand coalitions in more than an instru-mental fashion, because in the process of coalition-building one learns to look at the "other" from within his or her world and how the "other" understands us. If coalitions were to organize this or that strategy across interest groups, they would become much more effective, not only bringing about a limited intended goal but also possibly contributing to radical societal change. When we look at coalition-building in this fashion, we move from pragmatic action to building that strong sense of solidarity needed both within and among marginalized groups.

Solidarity among Latinas and Latinos as well as between our community and other marginalized groups and justice-seeking peoples is not a matter of agree-ing with, supporting, liking, or being inspired by a cause. Though all these might be part of solidarity, solidarity itself goes beyond all of them. Solidarity has to do with understanding the interconnections that exist among us. Solidarity is the union of kindred persons "arising from the common responsibilities and interests . . . ; community of interests, feelings, purposes, or action; social cohe-sion."[41] Solidarity, then, is grounded in "common responsibilities and interests," which necessarily arouse shared feelings and lead to joint action. This solidarity is not possible without mutuality, which is established through dialogue—world-traveling—and requires conscientization, a process that remains as important and relevant today as it was in the decades of the 1960s and 1970s. Conscientization is a process through which one becomes aware, with no more than a moment of insight, that there is something suspicious about one's condi-tion. Almost anything can create the spark that moves people "from a 'naive awareness,' which does not deal with problems, gives too much value to the past, tends to accept mythical explanations, and tends toward debate, to a 'criti-cal awareness,' which delves into problems, is open to new ideas, replaces magical explanations with real causes, and tends to dialogue."[42] Conscientization enables us to understand the real causes of oppression and the need to engage with others in changing a situation. The process of conscientization is not some-thing that happens once and for all, but rather it is a permanent personal effort to situate oneself in time and space, to exercise one's creative potential, and to assume one's responsibilities.[43] Conscientization is always a praxis, not just an intellectual understanding apart from action.[44]

---

[41] *The Random House Dictionary of the English Language*, 2d unabridged ed. (New York: Random, 1987).

[42] Gustavo Gutiérrez, *A Theology of Liberation: History, Politics, and Salvation*, rev. ed. with new intro. (Maryknoll, N.Y.: Orbis Books, 1988), 92.

[43] Ibid., 92.

[44] Paulo Freire, *Pedagogy of the Oppressed* (New York: Seabury Press, 1973), 3.

A NEW *MESTIZAJE/MULATEZ* AND THE STRUGGLE FOR JUSTICE

Unfortunately, even within marginalized groups the prevailing understanding of difference as exclusive and oppositional is operative. None of the marginalized groups in the United States has the power to impose its understanding of "other," and yet we reproduce it. It seems impossible not to fall under the spell of the preponderant characteristics and perspectives of the dominant group. Part of this problem derives from the fact that a negative understanding of differences is also the one operative in our countries of origin. *Mestizaje/mulatez* is not always seen as a positive element in our societies back home. However, it is my contention that the view the dominant culture has of us, Latinas and Latinos in the United States, has helped us to recognize the value of diversity and to embrace it as something precious.[45] I am not denying that the way the dominant culture homogenizes us under the label Hispanic is prejudicial to us. Nonetheless, such homogenization has also been instrumental in our coming to recognize ourselves as a community, at least vis-à-vis the rest of society. I am not denying or minimizing the injurious effects for us of the erasure and displacement we suffer when we are blanketed as one under the label of "Hispanics." Nevertheless, this oppressive mechanism has forced us to come together in ways that we would not have done otherwise, to deal with each other across class, sex, and race as we have not done in our countries of origin. The labeling and marginalization of Latinas and Latinos make it difficult for us to have a positive sense of self and often lead us to internalize the negative understanding of us on the part of the dominant culture.[46] However, the need to present a united front to oppressive forces and groups makes us come together, create and sustain liberative strategies, and understand ourselves as a community with certain shared characteristics and goals. This is what creating a new *mestizaje/mulatez* is all about.

This new *mestizaje/mulatez,* which in *mujerista* theology we consider not only our *locus theologicus* but also a moral choice we need to make and effectively sustain, is not "an ethnic identity that Spanish-speaking people bring with them when they arrive but something they create in response to the conditions here in this country."[47] In many ways it is a result of the need to fight against discrimination, but it is also a result of the seeds planted in our countries of origin regarding the races that have come together in those lands. Notice, for example, how politicians in countries such as Mexico and Peru refer to the Aztecs and Incas in order to support claims of identity and greatness for their countries and to identify themselves with the people. This entails a certain

---

[45] I first introduced this idea in *En La Lucha–In the Struggle*, 192-93.

[46] Suzanne Oboler, "The Politics of Labeling: Latino/a Cultural Identities of Self and Other," *Latin American Perspective* 19:4 (Fall 1992), issue 74: 18-36.

[47] Geoffrey Fox, *Hispanic Nation: Culture, Politics, and the Construction of Identity* (Tucson, Ariz.: The University of Arizona Press, 1996), 239.

ambivalent embracing of *mestizaje* even as laws and policies continue to oppress indigenous peoples.[48] The new *mestizaje/mulatez* being created here is at the base of what is called the Hispanic/Latina community, a community that needs an identity as a whole in order to create solidarity and fight injustice.

The cohesiveness that allows us to see ourselves as a community revolves around five elements: the Spanish language; popular religion; social-cultural-psychological survival; economic oppression; and our vision of the future.[49] These elements are the building blocks of *mestizaje/mulatez*. The last one—our vision of the future—is most important, because it takes note of the fact that the reason for *mestizaje/mulatez*, for mutuality and solidarity among Latinas and Latinos, is not to make us good but to allow us to struggle for justice for our community. As a matter of fact, commitment to *mestizaje/mulatez* is what makes it possible for us to maintain the revolutionary momentum of the struggle for liberation. We are convinced that the liberation of Latinas and Latinos cannot be at the expense of any other marginalized group. *Mestizaje/mulatez* allows us to hope for our own liberation, but it also makes clear that to this end we need to be in solidarity with other marginalized groups. Solidarity is made possible by mutuality and world-traveling, by intersubjectivity and an understanding of difference that is relational and determined to include rather than exclude.

Solidarity and mutuality in *mujerista* theology are key elements of the struggle for justice. An important though ignored element of justice is directly related to mutuality: justice as right relationships. "Justice" throughout the Hebrew scriptures refers to "righteousness" (*tzedeka* in Hebrew), not so much in the sense *righteousness* is used today but in the sense of right relationships.[50] Justice is not a matter of "a behavior in accordance with an ethical, legal, psychological, religious, or spiritual norm. It is not a conduct which is dictated by either human or divine nature, no matter how undefiled. It is not about actions appropriate to the attainment of a specific goal."[51] Rather, *righteousness* in the Hebrew

---

[48] Once I was watching the Republican national convention on television with a Euro-American friend, and, after about an hour of reference to the United States as the best country in the world, the most powerful country in the world, I could not take it any more and began to rage against the self-aggrandizement of this country. My friend looked confused and explained that politicians always have to extol this country and that the only way to do that was by claiming to be the best. Did not politicians everywhere do that? When I answered that was not the case, she asked how politicians in other nations extolled their countries. I explained that in most countries they did so by reference to some sort of "glorious past," including their indigenous cultures. I remember her look of astonishment as I insisted that being better than others, being unique and the most powerful, was not the only way or necessarily the best way for politicians to instill pride in the country.

[49] Isasi-Díaz, *En La Lucha–In the Struggle*, chaps. 1 and 2.

[50] *Tzedeka* is paired off with *mispath*, which is more closely related to legal rights.

[51] Elizabeth R. Achtemeier, "Righteousness in the OT," *The Interpreter's Dictionary of the Bible,* 4 vols. (Nashville, Tenn.: Abingdon Press, 1962), 4:80.

scriptures refers to the fulfillment of the demands of a relationship with others, with the divine, and—today we need to add—with the rest of creation.

The Hebrew concept of righteousness is a relational one. The person does not exist outside the community. Each of us is set within a multitude of relationships: parents; siblings; neighbors; friends; work mates; bosses; people who sell to us; people who work for us; people who govern society; priests or ministers; people whom we do not know personally but upon whom we depend, like garbage collectors, mail deliverers, migrant workers who pick the fruit and vegetables we eat, factory workers in this country and abroad; researchers, scientists, and doctors on whose work we depend for living healthy and long lives; the poor and oppressed, particularly those for whom we have to take responsibility, because their condition is caused by our high standards of living.

Righteousness also has to do with our relationship with nature, a relationship that we have ignored for so long that we need to rediscover and attend to it in a very special way. We are related to the rain forests in Brazil, which are being destroyed daily at an incredible rate, to the dwindling world oil reserves, to all the animal species that are part of the biosphere in which we exist but which we continue to extinguish, to the atmosphere that our greed damages in so many different ways every day. Righteousness has to do with a right relationship with the divine, a relationship that happens within history, a relationship that God has chosen to have in and through the way we relate to all of creation.

In the Hebrew scriptures not only are those who fulfill the demands of a relationship called righteous but also those who have had their rights taken away from them within such a relationship. Those who have been deprived of what was rightfully theirs, those who are in need, those who are oppressed or afflicted are righteous and must have their legal rights restored. Psalm 146 talks about this very clearly:

> Happy are those whose help is the God of Jacob, . . .
> who keeps faith forever;
> who executes justice for the oppressed;
> who gives food to the hungry.
>
> The LORD sets the prisoners free;
> the LORD opens the eyes of the blind;
> the LORD lifts up those who are bowed down;
> the LORD loves the righteous.
>
> The LORD watches over the strangers;
> he upholds the orphan and the widow. (Ps 146:5-9)

This is taken up and forcibly repeated in Matthew 25, where we are told specifically that we must restore our broken relationships if we want to enter the reign of God: we must feed the hungry, give drink to the thirsty, welcome the stranger, clothe the naked, visit the sick and those in prison.

THE ROLE OF THEOLOGY
IN RECONCEPTUALIZING DIFFERENCE

As we move into the twenty-first century, we are faced in this country with the fact that in about twenty years there will be no racial/ethnic majority. Therefore, unless we want to help develop and sustain a system of apartheid, unless we want to feed the present system, which makes oppression possible, we must change radically our understanding of difference. We must establish a strong solidarity among marginalized groups based on the struggle for liberation, on the restructuring of society so that justice for all can flourish. Restructuring society means not only a change of structures but also a radical change in culture. Changes in structures forced on society that are not complemented with changes in culture do not last.[52] Theology also has an important role to play in changing culture, of which it is an integral part.

In *mujerista* theology culture embraces whatever we fabricate to deal with our world: customs, understandings, practices, artifacts that have been developed by our ancestors and continue to be created by us today to contribute effectively to our own lives and to the society in which we live. Cultures share many common elements, but what establishes the distinctiveness (not uniqueness) of each is the way in which such common elements "are used, how they are handled and transformed. The distinctiveness of cultural identity is therefore not a product of isolation; it is not a matter of a culture being simply self-generated, pure and unmixed; it is not a matter of 'us' versus 'them.' Cultural identity becomes instead, a hybrid, relational affair, something that lives between as much as within cultures."[53]

Given this understanding of culture, theology is to be viewed as part of culture. It is a cultural activity, because humans produce it, because it is a human activity. Theology is particularly related to that aspect of culture that deals with the worldview of a people, with the lens through which a people view life, work with it, and find meaning in it. As Kathryn Tanner puts it,

> Theology is a particular version of this search for meaning, for a pattern of fundamental categories that will, as cultures do, orient, guide, and order human life. The adequacy of theology can therefore be judged by how well it performs these general cultural tasks. Does it, for example, help people successfully navigate their world and cope effectively with life's vicissitudes?[54]

---

[52] In no way am I opposed to structural changes such as those brought about by changes in laws. But we cannot think that because structural changes have happened they will be permanent. For radical change to happen, the structural change has to go hand in hand with cultural change, with changes in the values and priorities of society.

[53] Kathryn Tanner, *Theories of Culture: A New Agenda for Theology* (Minneapolis, Minn.: Fortress Press, 1997), 57-58.

[54] Ibid., 58.

The theologies of marginalized groups help us find our world in the many worlds we have to travel to survive. At the same time, they have to critique the dominant culture that limits our choices, that keeps us from contributing to society, that uses us instead of enabling us. Hispanic/Latina theology, including *mujerista* theology, uses *mestizaje/mulatez* as our *locus theologicus* precisely because it identifies our culture. And insofar as *mestizaje/mulatez* refers to our culture, it critiques the dominant culture against which we have to struggle to survive. *Mujerista* theology offers our relational understanding of difference as a contribution to a deeper understanding of *mestizaje/mulatez* in Hispanic/Latina theology and to the elaboration of a liberating culture, of a justice-seeking culture, of an embracing culture that allows and enables fullness of life for all.

12

La otra América—The Other America

DAISY L. MACHADO

I am a Latina, born in Cuba and raised in New York City, more specifically in "Crooklyn," as Spike Lee has called that large and interesting borough. I am not part of the first great wave of Cuban refugees, which arrived at the port of a then-small and insignificant city in southern Florida called Miami. My father and mother did not flee the Cuban Revolution of 1959 but rather fled unemployment and government repression. Like the millions of immigrants from Europe before them, they believed that in the United States life would be different and perhaps even better. My father had all of seven dollars in his pocket when he arrived at La Guardia International Airport in July of 1956. He spoke no English, knew no one in this country, but, at twenty-five years of age, he felt he could do anything.

And he did. He saved his earnings and six months later brought his wife and daughter to this new and strange land. He worked hard and learned English. He was a factory worker, one of the many immigrants who make up the statistics collected annually by the Census Bureau. But to my sister and to me he was *papi*. After telling us his wonderful bedtime stories, he would whisper in our ears that we could do anything, we could be anything, we could climb as high as the stars. He whispered how we were no different from the Jewish or the Polish or the Italian or the black children that made up our multiracial community in Brooklyn. He helped us see beyond the poverty of our inner-city neighborhood and dream of being and becoming and doing and succeeding. "This is not Cuba," my dad would say. "Here in this country," he would continue, "we do not need to fear the police or the government. We do not need to whisper our discontent. We can claim the *dignidad* that is ours to claim as human beings." He seemed so sure of himself. He seemed so sure that we would one day leave that ghetto and pass through the doors of opportunity and self-realization using the keys of education, hard work, and faith in God.

However, my dad and my mom were very peculiar about one thing: They would not let us forget that we were Cubans, and in so doing they made us aware of the duality of our existence. Spanish was the only language spoken at home, even though they made sure that we learned English and did well in school. We ate the foods of their childhood. We savored the spices of their far-away home. I was often annoyed at my mother for thinking that cold cuts or peanut butter and jelly were not really food, and I often faced the taunts of my elementary school friends who could not understand why I did not eat "normal" foods. Then, something happened that reinforced how much I did not belong to the big North American world in which I lived. In the fourth grade my teacher punished me for speaking in Spanish with a classmate. She made me stand before the class and apologize for speaking that "nasty language." Right then and there it became evident to me that I was not like everybody else. I was different. I was an outsider. I did not belong.

And the search began. I wanted to understand why in a nation that promoted itself as a haven for immigrants, why in a nation that talked about God and had reminders of God even in its currency, why in such a nation there were still so many millions of outsiders, of people who did not belong and who were systemically kept on the margins. I first worked as a social worker dealing with abused children and women, often testifying in the family courts in an effort to avoid further violence and pain. I translated for Latino/a clients in the welfare offices of the city of New York. I visited the homes of children, women, and men where poverty and racism had consumed all joy and hope. I had gone into the belly of the beast, and I knew there was no heart beating within it. Then I entered seminary. My decision to begin theological studies was not only a response to my faith commitment to become a pastor. It was also clear to me that as a pastor I would be able to work through the church community, because the church in the Latino/a community is a place that, I believed, harbored hope and helped to bring about change. I pastored inner-city congregations in communities surrounded by gang violence and a thriving drug industry, a place of abandoned buildings and empty lots littered with broken bottles and garbage. I asked myself: Was this the world my father wanted us to prepare for? Was this the world my father had brought us to with such deep aspirations for a better future? Was this *my America*?

I thought back to the many years of conversation with my father. I recalled the many heated discussions between us about politics during my years in college. I tried to recall his words and his expressions, and then I began to understand. I began to understand my father's continued effort to make me believe in myself and in who I was. I began to understand his insistence that I know who *I* was before I had to deal with the North American reality outside. That was why my father wanted me to be proud of my Spanish. Why he wanted me to understand the meaning of our migration to this country. Why he wanted me to learn that home and nation were more than a house or a neighborhood or a naturalization card. He wanted me to know that what I carried within me, my identity as a Cuban immigrant, my history as a *caribeña* (a person from the Caribbean), was not only of great worth but also necessary to sustain me in a society and a nation that did not know *how* to include me.

Yo soy cubana-americana—I am a Cuban American. This is so not because a legal document from the Department of Justice or the Bureau of Immigration and Naturalization says so, but because I truly do belong to *América*, that other

América which is much larger than the borders of the United States of America (which continues to claim to be the only America, the one with the capital "A"). The *América* that gave life to my parents and their parents is older than the first British colonies on the eastern seaboard of the North American continent. In the *América* I am talking about, English was not spoken until the late nineteenth century. In that *América* people come in all the colors of humanity—a great *mestizaje* of indigenous, black, and European blood. I had finally understood the full meaning of my father's subtle lesson about life as an immigrant: I live in the world of two Americas. José Martí had already written about these two Americas in his great work *Nuestra América*, published in 1891. It is ironic that over one hundred years later Martí continues to map out for the more than thirty million Latinas/os living in this country a very important reality, a reality that we must all face: There is *nuestra América* (our America), and there is the other America that will never be ours. It was now clear what my father had tried to do. He had tried to prepare me for my encounter with the other America. That is why he wanted us to know who we were and to be able to celebrate the life-giving connection with *nuestra América*, to have a clear sense of belonging despite the fact that we would exist in the margins of this other America.

AMERICA LEFT ALONE

In the September 1992 issue of *The Journal of American History*, David Thelen, its editor, published an article entitled "Of Audiences, Borderlands, and Comparisons: Toward the Internationalization of American History."[1] The purpose of this article was to explore the benefits of inviting foreign historians of the American past to "encourage exploration of alternatives to the narrowed academic conversations that shape our field."[2] Thelen went on to list the benefits of writing American history for foreign audiences, including the fact that such a process forces scholars to come to terms with the question, "How do people use words, and ultimately create lives, out of materials from two or more cultures in the borderlands between those cultures?"[3]

The reason I mention this article is because it provides such a clear example of precisely how the other America perceives itself. It points to the mythology that this other America has created about itself and how the academy has helped and continues to help in perpetuating this national self-understanding. The question that I would pose to all who in one way or another participate in and help create the history of both Americas is: Why is it that only those who live in countries defined as "foreign" are invited to bring "new perspectives"? I find myself suspicious of those who continue to define *global* or *borderland* in terms

---

[1] David Thelen, "Of Audiences, Borderlands, and Comparisons: Toward the Internationalization of American History," *The Journal of American History* 79:2 (September 1992): 432-62.

[2] Ibid., 432.

[3] Ibid.

of events that take place overseas rather than of events that go on right across the street in Newark or Dallas or Hartford or Los Angeles or New York City. The history of foreign missions in mainline or historic denominations has shown that there is a safety that comes with distance and that lies at the core of funding and promoting such missions. However, when that same missionary work is redirected toward racial and ethnic populations within the country, not only is funding hard to come by, but also such work is carried out mostly by way of "special ministries" projects, designed to be of short duration. Can it be that the history told and examined by *americanos* who are Mexican, Cuban, Nicaraguan, Puerto Rican, Salvadorean—who are citizens of *las Américas*—poses a threat to the accepted national historical themes? Can it be that, like the foreign missions of historic denominations, safety comes with distance and that Latinas/os living in the United States are just too close for comfort?

What is going on in the other America? Some historians use the term "American exceptionalism" to describe the process of creating a space between Americans (those with the capital "A") and all others. Joyce Appleby defines American exceptionalism as a process which "projects onto a nation . . . qualities that are envied because they represent deliverance from the common lot."[4] Appleby argues that, while this concept of exceptionalism helped to generate a national identity for the revolutionary generation of 1776, at present, more than two hundred years later, it "has closed other ways of interpreting the meaning of the United States."[5] I think we need to pause here and examine what Appleby is saying. It is very important that, in this new century, Latinas and Latinos within the academy, as well as those preparing to serve Latino/a congregations, critically and unashamedly examine the ways in which the theological education we have received (and often impart) has served as an "intellectual wrap," hiding the reality of diversity that has been a fundamental part of the formation of this nation from the beginning. I want to go even further here. I want to say that what remains hidden is the reality of an American diversity that has been and continues to be much broader than the commonly held notion of race in the United States as a black/white issue.

Why is this so crucial for the liberation and empowerment of Latinas/os, African Americans, Native Americans, Asian Americans? Because if we continue to accept uncritically the new forms that American exceptionalism has taken—as, for example, in the debates about bilingual education, affirmative action, the militarization of the Río Grande border, or "work-fare" versus welfare—we lose sight of very important realities. We lose awareness of the systemic use of racism in the courts, the corporations, and the government of this country. We forget that there was a very intentional and planned ejection and extermination of the indigenous peoples throughout the country. We accept the criteria of progress as the only way to measure the worth of a person or a group

---

[4] Joyce Appleby, "Recovering America's Historic Diversity: Beyond Exceptionalism," *The Journal of American History* 79:2 (September 1992): 419.

[5] Ibid., 421.

of people or a nation, simply dismissing those who do not measure up as useless or backward. We also suffer the grave loss of seeing with clarity how interconnected we all are. There can be no understanding of the issue of slavery without a corresponding understanding of the results of the mass killings of indigenous peoples in the Caribbean by the Spaniards years before there was a slave trade in this hemisphere. There can be no understanding of border issues and immigration from the South to the United States without an accompanying analysis of the political and military maneuvering of the U.S. government in the unstable government of the newly formed Estados Unidos Mexicanos, the United States of Mexico, in the nineteenth century. There can be no understanding of Fidel Castro's influence in the Caribbean Basin and throughout Latin America without a parallel examination of U.S. foreign policy not only in the last forty years but also at the turn of the century, and even earlier. The Spanish-American War of 1898, the warning issued to Simón Bolívar—Latin America's most famous liberator—by the Monroe government in the 1820s to stay out of the Caribbean, the making of Puerto Rico into a colony—all these historical realities had to do with a political worldview that was fed by this earlier sense of exceptionalism, a concept that has by no means gone away despite the fact that we have entered a new millennium.

The idealization of the United States by the Europeans of the Enlightenment had a strong influence on the national myths created. Today, these myths have become as well-known and as palatable as "Mother, Flag, and Apple Pie." The enthusiasts of democracy in the eighteenth century created a chauvinistic sense of importance and nationhood. The strength of this great national myth of the conquered frontier lay in its use of Divine Providence and the Bible. This use of Divine Providence and the Bible created an intricate rationalization or, to use Appleby's term, an "intellectual wrap" that carefully hid the real and intentional application of theories about race and gender. In the early years of the nation, statesmen like Benjamin Franklin and Thomas Jefferson, followed by historians like Francis Parkman, George Bancroft, and Frederick Jackson Turner in the late 1800s and early 1900s, made the connection between the westward movement of the United States across the continent and democracy itself. The result was the creation of a direct correlation between God's will for the newly emerging nation called the United States and the people who would become its citizens.

The myth thus created told of an almost primeval western frontier that could only be "conquered" by a particular or "chosen" people. As this myth was told and retold, it gave shape to both the *public* persona of the ideal American (with a capital "A") and the *individual* persona of the ideal American (also with a capital "A"). It became ever more apparent that not only had God chosen the United States to be the "ark of salvation" for the nations, but also that its citizens possessed unique and exceptional characteristics: intelligence, strength, and industriousness; the ability to overcome odds; love of freedom; rugged individualism; the ability to develop and master technology. It was also said that the crowning glory of this new man (women were not included) was his ability to establish and protect democracy. There was, however, one major problem with this mythology: The creation of a "chosen" nation to be possessed by a "chosen" people necessitated a virginal land. God needed a clean slate to produce this new nation whose light would shine as an example to an old and corrupt Europe. In order to create such a "clean slate," the value and importance of the people already there had to be eliminated. Thus, the people already inhabiting the land were deemed less human by virtue of their skin color or their religion or their way of life. Once the categories that defined the "other" were firmly set, it became much easier forcibly to move the Native Peoples from the Southeast to the Midwest in what became known as the Trail of Tears. When thousands of Native Americans died on this terrible journey toward hopelessness, the fact that they had been categorized as lacking in worth, as inferior and destined to eventual extermination, transformed their deaths into further proof of their unworthiness to possess the land.

The same scenario was played out in the takeover of the Mexican territories by the United States in the nineteenth century. The colonization of Texas constitutes a clear example of the type of thinking that takes place in the creation of the clean slate necessary for the national myths of this country. By devaluing Roman Catholicism and seeing it as mere superstition, it became much easier for Stephen Austin falsely to pledge allegiance to the Roman Catholic government of Mexico when he entered the northern borderlands of the territory then known as *Coahuila y Tejas*. Austin and the first Euro-American settlers, who in the early 1820s moved into what is today Texas, not only displayed little respect for Roman Catholicism but were just as demeaning toward the *mestizo* people they encountered. The *mestizaje* of the *Tejanos*—the mixture of indigenous, African, and Spanish blood—was believed by Austin to produce a people who were inferior, depraved, incapable of governing themselves, sexually promiscuous. Austin wrote, "To be candid the majority of the people of the whole nation as far as I have seen them want nothing but tails to be more brutes than the apes."[6]

In examining this process of the creation of national identity, the sense of nationhood, the role played by religion must be addressed as well. It is true, as Barry Kosmin and Seymour Lachman argue, that "the relationship between politics and religion has developed much differently in the United States than in the leading nations of Europe."[7] However, from the beginnings of U.S. history, the pulpit has often united with political goals and ambitions to shape public opinion and reinforce national myths. While it may be true that in this country there is no established national church as in Britain and that a historical claim exists for the separation between church and state, in actuality the United States "and its political landscape have nonetheless resonated with religious rhetoric."[8] Clear evidence of this reality can be found as recently as in the 1992

---

[6] David Weber, *Myth and the History of the Hispanic Southwest* (Albuquerque, N.Mex.: University of New Mexico Press, 1988), 157.

[7] Barry A. Kosmin and Seymour P. Lachman, *One Nation under God, Religion in Contemporary American Society* (New York: Harmony Books, 1993), 157.

[8] Ibid.

reelection campaign of President George Bush. Addressing the delegates of the National Religious Broadcasters, who represent the Christian television and radio industry, Bush stated, "I want to thank you for helping America, as Christ ordained, to be a light upon the world."[9] This statement is not historically out of character with the nationalism and nationalist mythology that have shaped U.S. self-identity. In fact, the statement shows how the language at work still has recourse to the opposition of "us *vs.* them," even after years of a changing demographic reality in which racial and ethnic groups, particularly the Latino/a population, have altered the overall hue of this country. This nation is still believed to possess a divinely ordained responsibility to lead other nations, to lead other non-Euroamerican races. It is a language that continues to use the paradigm of "insiders and outsiders," "more advanced *vs.* less advanced," "those who can *vs.* those who cannot." In effect, the country continues to be an America (with a capital "A") that still cannot see the reality of the racial, religious, and cultural diversity that exists within its borders.

CONCLUSION

Social historians have been busy for over two decades recovering the memories of communities all over the United States. Popular culture as well as political culture have kept pace. The biggest hit on public television stations in the spring of 1998 was the historical mini-series "The Irish in America." Today we celebrate Martin Luther King's birthday as a national holiday. February is Black History Month. *El Cinco de Mayo* has become a statewide holiday in Texas, even though most Texans, Anglos, and Mexicans do not know that they are celebrating an event in the history of Mexico and thus an event that has nothing to do with Texas. The media has even focused on the Chinese New Year, providing the nation with some history in this regard and a glimpse of community celebrations around the country. The United States wears the badge of multiculturalism as a means of showing that Americans (with a capital "A") have moved into a new day. But is this really so? How comfortable are Euro-Americans with the reality of diversity (racial and religious) or multiculturalism or racial inclusiveness? And an even more difficult question: How much are racial and ethnic groups willing to give up in order to be accepted by those in the majority? What is the ultimate cost of this loss for the individual and for the community he or she comes from?

I say that we still have a long journey ahead of us. The myths created in the past to forge a sense of nationhood have not gone away; they have merely been reworked and updated, as shown by the not-too-distant political rhetoric of our presidents. Further evidence can be found in the language of U.S. foreign policy today. We have heard President Bill Clinton and members of Congress describe the role of the United States today as that of protector of the world's peace and democracy. However, in this new century there is no more "virginal continent"

---

[9] Ibid., 158.

to conquer. The Native Peoples have been boxed in in the reservations; the West has been forever won by larger-than-life male pioneers, the likes of which continue to be resurrected on our television screens, along the lines of that greatest of all Hollywood western prototypes, John Wayne. Our worldview seems to have shifted. Our culture, greatly influenced by the Generation X'ers, thinks in terms of popular television programs like "Star Trek: The Next Generation," "Deep Space Nine," or "Voyager." Our television sets bring us aliens from other galaxies with funny sounding names like Changlings, Bajorans, Klingons, Ferengi, and Cardassians. While many think that these programs are about an imagined future, I argue that they may also be seen as a revisiting of our past as a nation.

In the races of the different television aliens and their particular characteristics, we find embodied the struggles, concerns, hatred, violence, greediness, untrustworthiness, as well as the hopes, dreams, aspirations, and visions we find in ourselves. Because these beings are portrayed as distinct from who we are as a nation, or as a racial group, or as humans, it is safe to become moral critics of their behavior. Much more than fictional characters, however, these strange-looking aliens serve as a reminder that this country has never been one nation made up of one people with one vision; such has been the ideal but not the reality. If knowledge is indeed power, and history, as Joyce Appleby says, "exercises that power by awakening curiosity, stretching imagination, deepening appreciation, and complicating one's sense of the possible,"[10] then we must boldly take possession of that knowledge by recovering the diversity of the history of *both* Americas. Such a move has nothing to do with political correctness or liberal politics. For Latinos and Latinas, it has to do, at its very core, with the ability to free ourselves from the restrictions imposed by the ideological imperatives of an idealized history that has been used to exclude and marginalize. What I am referring to is the role Latinas/os must play in the re-definition of what has been defined by dominant society as the norm. It is to acknowledge that Latinas/os are also normative because our foreparents, our ancestors, have been residents of this hemisphere for centuries. We are not the aliens. We are the heirs of a rich and diverse history that has been over five centuries in the making. We are the daughters and the sons born of the interactions of diverse races and cultures that, as a whole, make us who we are today. We refuse to be haunted by a national historical memory that barely includes us as a people, as a result of which we remain faint figures of an ancient past. The new millennium demands that Latinas and Latinos be seen, heard, understood, and embraced. After all, this is *nuestra América,* and we are its citizens.

---

[10] Appleby, "Recovering America's Historic Diversity," 431.

13

Melting and Dreaming in America

Visions and Re-visions

FERNANDO F. SEGOVIA

BACKGROUND

For some time now I have been engaged on a threefold front within Christian studies or the academic study of the Christian religion. Two of these have to do with my work in biblical studies and are highly interrelated. Given my option for the paradigm of cultural studies in the discipline and its ideological mode of discourse, I have been at work on the construction of a reading strategy and theoretical framework, both based in my own experience of the diaspora, as an exile from the non-Western world residing in the West. On the one hand, I have worked toward a hermeneutics of otherness and engagement—a view of texts, readings of texts, and readers of texts as others to be acknowledged and critiqued. On the other hand, I have argued for a reading strategy of interculturalism—an approach to texts, readings of texts, and readers of texts as literary, rhetorical, and ideological constructs. The third front concerns my work in theological studies and provides a grounding for the other two fronts. Given my view of religious discourse as contextual and perspectival, I have argued for analysis of and dialogue with religious perspectives, individual or corporate, in terms of their constructions of the this-world, the other-world, and the relationship between the two, while pressing toward such a construction of my own on the basis of my experience of diaspora as a non-Western minority in the West— a theology of otherness and mixture.

The present study constitutes a further step in the development of this theological vision of and from exile, forged within the experience and reality of Hispanic Americans in the United States. In effect, I should like to address, to view and re-view, the core concepts of the American melting pot and American Dream: the vision of the country as a crucible for the nations whereby a new society and a new individual come into being—a new creation where all things become possible for those who have the willingness and the determination to achieve them. Such a task is not only quite in keeping with the evolving agenda of diasporic theology but also a logical progression in that agenda. A review of the project and its path thus far is in order, therefore.

A Theology of Mixture and Otherness

In a first formulation of diasporic theology, I outlined certain major lines of development in the light of the social context of Hispanic Americans in the United States.[1] The context itself I characterized as highly complex, given the many similarities and differences exhibited by the group. The latter I identified as sociocultural, sociopolitical, and socioreligious in nature—variations in national origins, political status, and religious affiliations. The former I listed as follows: first, a highly disparaging external perception of the group as a whole— an inferior people, uncivilized and unenlightened; second, a people of profound hybridity, physiologically and/or culturally—children of Mediterranean and Catholic Europe via Spain, children of indigenous America and transplanted Africa, and now children of Nordic and Protestant Europe via the United States; third, a people marked by a tradition of the political realm at its worst and a vision of the body politic at its best; finally, a people marginalized and disadvantaged in U.S. society. In the end, I described U.S. Hispanic Americans as living in two worlds but at home in neither one—a sort of permanent "others"— and doing so in the light of many faces, many histories, and many visions of God and world.

Such a context, I argued, could only yield a theological "manifest destiny" best characterized as a "locus" with a wide variety of "vibrant currents" or a "voice" with a broad variety of "distinctive inflections." My own theology of diaspora I advanced as one such inflection or current. Grounded in a profound sense of otherness and mixture, of having two places but no place on which to stand as well as of expansive and expanding hybridity, it would be a theology of and for life, committed to a vision of a different and better world. This commitment it would pursue in two ways: with regard to the group itself, given the many barriers faced, a path of struggle, liberation, and self-determination; with regard to those outside, given its own treatment as "other," a stance of respect for and exchange with the "other," all others. A fundamental hallmark of this theology, I specified, would be an embrace of criticism in the interest of freedom and justice for all.

A Theology of "Alien-ation"

In a subsequent expansion of diasporic theology, I proceeded to analyze in greater detail the social context of U.S. Hispanic Americans as an ethnic-racial

---

[1] F. F. Segovia, "Two Places and No Place on Which to Stand: Mixture and Otherness in Hispanic American Theology," in *Hispanic Americans in Theology and the Church*, ed. F. F. Segovia, special issue of *Listening: Journal of Religion and Culture* 27:1 (Winter 1992): 26-40.

minority group. This I did in terms of both the sociopolitical matrix as such and the social status of the group within this matrix.[2] The former I developed by invoking a set of core concepts from the national mythology: the vision of the country as a "promised land" uniquely blessed by God and entrusted to a "chosen people" with a "mission" to the world—a gospel involving a mixture of religious beliefs (Protestant Christianity), political structures (republican government), and economic principles (capitalist system)—by means of which the blessings of God would be extended to all other peoples and nations. The status of the group I presented by way of conflict between external perception and internal perspective. From the outside, immigrants from Hispanic America shared a similar vision, though devoid of religious trappings: the United States as a country of unquestioned material and moral superiority—a paragon of progress and abundance as well as freedom and justice. From the inside, Hispanic Americans experienced profound cultural shock. To begin with, they found a less than ideal world in both material and moral terms—the promised land possessed a much more somber side as well. In addition, they came to realize the extent to which the policies of their new country had contributed to the present state of affairs in their own countries of origin—the mission to the world revealed a most uncivilized and unenlightened, if not downright barbarian, underside. Finally, they encountered a system of ethnic-racial stratification in which they, as hybrid children from the undeveloped South, did not fare very well—the chosen people did have its aliens, its unwelcome outsiders and strangers.

The result of such anagnorisis was twofold: on the one hand, inevitable erosion and deconstruction of any such vision of the country; on the other hand, a determined struggle for survival on the basis of persistent dreams and hopes. This, I argued, would serve as crucible for our theological "manifest destiny," including my own theology of diaspora. Renouncing all claims to national election, promise, and mission, whether at home or abroad, it would embrace its own context of "alien-ation" not by way of silent submission but rather of open defiance and thus as point of departure to speak on behalf of liberation, of freedom and dignity as well as justice and well-being. This it would do, moreover, not just on behalf of the group itself but of all, regardless of race and ethnicity. Such a theology would be one of "manifest destiny" but with a twist.

A Theology of Exile

In a further exposition of diasporic theology, I highlighted the differences to be found within the group itself—the sociocultural, sociopolitical, and socioreligious variations that accounted for the many currents and inflections of U.S. Hispanic American theology—and argued that it was imperative for each component within the group to lift its own voice and offer its own conception of the this-world and the other-world, just as I was attempting to do by way of

---

[2] F. F. Segovia, "Aliens in the Promised Land: The Manifest Destiny of U.S. Hispanic American Theology," in *Hispanic/Latino Theology: Challenge and Promise*, ed. A. M. Isasi-Díaz and F. F. Segovia (Minneapolis, Minn.: Fortress Press, 1995), 15-42.

diasporic theology.[3] This course of action I urged in the face of a twofold danger: on the one hand, as a defense against the dehumanizing universalism inherent in any agenda of the melting pot, where differences are looked down upon and dissolved; on the other hand, as a way to avoid the creation of a parallel version of the melting pot within the group itself. The theology of diaspora would thus affirm and emphasize, rather than bypass or submerge, differences, as indicated by its very own creation and formulation.

Viewing and Reviewing the American Melting Pot and Dream

The preceding trajectory readily situates the present task within the ongoing elaboration of diasporic theology. To begin with, I have described in general terms how, within the world constructed by the national mythology of the "promised land" and related concepts, U.S. Hispanic Americans stand as aliens—inferior others, uncivilized and unenlightened, hybrid and marginalized. Against this background the theology of diaspora espouses a full appropriation of such otherness in order to move beyond it, to propose a different vision of the group, the country, and the world—one of freedom and justice, dignity and well-being, for all. In addition, I have called more concretely for a rejection of any agenda of melting pot, internal or external. Against this background, the theology of diaspora advocates a full surfacing and embracing of differences. Given such a line of argumentation, it is not only proper but also expedient to turn to the related core concepts of the American melting pot and the American Dream. First, because such concepts constitute a fundamental dimension of the national mythology and thus of the social context in which we as U.S. Hispanic Americans find ourselves and do theology. Second, because they also affect in a very direct and significant way our experience and reality as an ethnic-racial minority group in the country. Third, because they also affect all other ethnic-racial minority groups in the country and can thus serve as an excellent point of departure for critical dialogue among such groups in the face of similar histories, expectations, and challenges.

In what follows, then, I shall proceed in three stages: I begin with a comparative analysis of two conflicting visions of the American melting pot and the American dream; continue with a review of current appraisals of such concepts in the light of recent patterns of immigration into the country and a consequent shift in its demographic balance; and conclude with a re-visioning of these concepts from the perspective of diasporic theology.

AMERICAN MELTING AND DREAMING: CONFLICTING VISIONS

To set the stage, I should like to bring together two visions of the American melting pot and American Dream that are at complete variance with one another.

---

[3] F. F. Segovia, "In the World But Not of It: Exile as Locus for a Theology of the Diaspora," in Isasi-Díaz and Segovia, *Hispanic/Latino Theology*, 195-217.

These are visions, moreover, that, placed side by side, span the whole of the twentieth century, the "American century."[4] The first of these represents not only an exaltation of such ideals, a panegyric of "Americanism," but also a main driving force for one of the concepts in question—a play written at the beginning of the century (1908) by Israel Zangwill entitled *The Melting Pot.*[5] The second offers a radical deconstruction of this mythology, not so much a diatribe as an exposé—an article written at the end of the century (1995) for *The Atlantic Monthly* by Benjamin Schwarz, by title "The Diversity Myth: America's Leading Export" (1995).[6] Together they offer an excellent framework for any critical discussion of identity in the United States.

Exaltation of American Melting and Dreaming

The overall context for this exercise in exaltation is that of the Zionist Movement and its deliberations regarding the future of Judaism at the turn of the twentieth century, in light of the general situation of the Jews in Europe and, above all, of the specific practice of pogroms in Russia—officially organized and encouraged persecution and massacres of the Jews in "thunderlike" fashion—first unleashed in the early 1880s in southern Russia and recurring intermittently through the early 1910s. Its author, Israel Zangwill (1824-1926), was both a well-known figure in English literary circles and a well-known activist in Jewish political circles.[7] However, Elisa Bonita Adams, a student of his work, argues that these two dimensions of Zangwill pretty much divide his extensive literary activity and output into two fairly distinct and sequential stages.[8] Thus, through the 1890s, Zangwill was widely praised for his essays, novels, and short

---

[4] Actually, they do so in two ways. First, they appear at opposite ends of the century: one in its first decade; the other, in its final decade. Second, each vision has its respective counterpart at the other end of the century. This ebullient phrase, "the American century," was coined by Henry R. Luce in 1941 in an essay published in *Life* magazine; the essay was later published with a number of responses in *The American Century* (New York: Toronto, Farrar, & Rinehart, 1941).

[5] I. Zangwill, *The Melting Pot,* new, rev. ed. (New York: Macmillan, 1914). The play was first produced at the Columbia Theater in Washington, D.C., in October 1908. A first edition was published in 1909; a second, revised edition in 1914. All references will be to this second edition, with page numbers in parentheses within the text.

[6] B. Schwarz, "The Diversity Myth: America's Leading Export," *The Atlantic Monthly* 275/5 (May 1995): 57-67.

[7] Zangwill was born of immigrant parents—father from Latvia; mother from Poland—in the Whitechapel ghetto of London. His early academic formation took place in Bristol, where the family settled not long after his birth; upon the family's return to London in 1872, he attended the Jews' Free School in Whitechapel, where he would become a pupil-teacher; in 1882 he graduated from the University of London, with an honors degree in French, English, and Mental and Moral Science; with an incipient literary career already under way, he resigned his position at the Jews' Free School in 1888 and devoted himself to writing, both fiction and journalism. His first acquaintance with the United States did not come until 1898 by way of a highly successful lecture tour.

[8] See E. B. Adams, *Israel Zangwill* (New York: Twayne Publishers, 1971), 19-24.

stories—a first phase as realist and humorist. In this period he first became known through his adherence to the New Humor Movement—a type of humor marked by a focus on the trivial and the facetious, the use of comic satire, and recourse to such techniques as puns and inverted epigrams, exaggeration, and lavish detail. In time he attracted enormous attention by his depiction of life in the ghetto, a realistic portrayal of Jewish life tempered by two distinctive traits: a strong affirmation of Jewish values (faith, family, social responsibility) and a pointed sense of humor (a type of humor with a focus on the serious side of life and a touch of satire, and thus of a "bittersweet" kind).[9]

Then, from the 1900s through the 1920s, Zangwill's mounting literary reputation witnessed a progressive decline—a second phase as social critic and Zionist. This was a period in which he devoted himself, for the most part, to writing about issues of a controversial and unpopular nature (political corruption, the failure of diplomacy, the evils of nationalism and war, women's rights, tolerance of minorities) and composing plays with a strong social message.[10] Indeed, after his death in 1926, Zangwill would be remembered only in Jewish circles, with hardly any mention of him in literary circles.

Adams accounts for the change in question, and hence for Zangwill's reversal in fortune,[11] in terms of two key events in his life: his encounter with Theodor Herzl in 1895, as a result of which he joined the Zionist movement, becoming one of its early leaders; and his "mixed" marriage of 1903 to Edith Ayrton, a novelist in her own right and an activist in the feminist movement, which led to a growing commitment on his part to a world religion of solidarity and love, with equal rights for all human beings. The paean to the United States offered by his play of 1908, *The Melting Pot*, with its vision of the country as a crucible for all peoples and all nations, reflects both of these developments in his life.

The relationship of this work to his involvement in the Zionist cause is clear. In 1903 the Zionist quest for a Jewish state led to a profound division in the movement regarding its location. By then, the need for a solution had become quite pressing, given the continuing pogroms in Russia, yet Palestine remained out of the question, under control by the Ottoman Empire. When in 1903 the British offered—through the agency of Joseph Chamberlain, the colonial secretary—part of Kenya toward the creation of a Jewish homeland, Zionist leaders brought the proposal before the Sixth Zionist Congress, meeting that year in

---

[9] Such work included *Children of the Ghetto* (1892); *Ghetto Tragedies* (1893); *The King of Schnorrers: Grotesques and Fantasies* (1894); *Dreamers of the Ghetto* (1894); *"They That Walk in Darkness": Ghetto Tragedies* (1899). Such work may be found in the second stage as well, but much less prominently: *Dreamers of the Ghetto* (1907).

[10] In addition to *The Melting Pot*, actually the first in such a series of plays, they include *The War God* (1911), on the conflict between pacifism and power politics; *The Next Religion* (1912), on religious fanaticism and the need for a religion built on the ideals of peace, love, and brotherhood; and *Plaster Saints* (1914), on the problem of perfection and hypocrisy in religion.

[11] In this she follows the position of another student of Zangwill's work, Maurice Wohlgelernter (*Israel Zangwill: A Study* [New York: Columbia University Press, 1964], 38-40).

Basel. Fierce debate between supporters of the proposal, known as the Uganda Plan, and strict Zionists, who would settle only for Palestine, led to the appointment of an investigating commission that was to visit the territory in question and report back to the Congress; at the Seventh Zionist Congress of 1905, upon submission of the report, the British offer was officially rejected. Thereupon Zangwill, an ardent supporter of the proposal, broke with the Zionists and formed the Jewish Territorial Organization (ITO), devoted to the creation of a Jewish state anywhere in the world, especially in the wake of the great Russian pogroms of 1905. As president of its Emigration Regulation Department, Zangwill campaigned for the acceptance of Jews throughout the diaspora and engaged in the settlement of thousands of Russian Jews in the western part of the United States. In the process, as he explains in the afterword to the second edition of the play,[12] he came to view the United States as not just a haven for Jews but as a beacon for all the oppressed peoples of Europe. Thus, the relationship of the work to his involvement in the cause of universal solidarity is quite clear as well.

By the time of its opening in 1908, approximately three years had elapsed since his break with the Zionist movement—years devoted, at the height of the second massive wave of immigration into the country, to the resettlement of Russian Jews in the United States and years of optimism regarding the promise of America for Jews and non-Jews alike. Such sentiments are readily palpable in the dedication of the printed edition to President Theodore Roosevelt, who had attended its opening-night performance in Washington, offering his warm congratulations to the author for a "great" play,[13] and whom Zangwill describes in the afterword as a perfect example of Aristotle's ideal spectator:[14] "In respectful

---

[12] The second, revised edition of the play of 1914 contained two major additions: the rather lengthy afterword (199-214) and a series of five appendices. The former provides valuable information about the reception, background, and interpretation of the play. The latter all have to do with the question of immigration into the United States and highlight in various ways the unique place and role of America in this regard, certainly for Jews but also in general. The appendices are as follows: (A) "The Melting Pot in Action"—a listing of all aliens admitted into the United States in the year ending June 30, 1913 (187); (B) "The Pogrom"—two published reports on the Russian atrocities (188-93); (C) "The Story of Daniel Melsa"—a note on the enormous similarity between the main character of the play, David Quixano, and an individual mentioned in another report about the Russian pogroms from 1913 (194-95); (D) "Beilis and America"—a note on the place of America in Russo-Jewish thought (196); (E) "The Alien in the Melting Plot"—the reproduction of a commentary by Frederick J. Haskin in the *Chicago Daily News* summarizing in litany-like fashion the contributions of immigrants to the United States (197-98). Both afterword and appendices underline the heavily didactic character of the play as a work with a pointed social message.

[13] Adams, *Israel Zangwill*, 110. I have not been able to establish whether the dedication was found in the first edition of 1909 or was added in the revised edition of 1914.

[14] Zangwill, *The Melting Pot*, 199. As opposed to the critical press, which he takes to task for its negative reaction to the play, portraying it as out of touch with popular experience and sentiments, President Roosevelt's positive response is accounted for precisely in terms of the possession of such experience on his part, "with his multifarious American experience as soldier and cowboy, hunter and historian, police-captain and President."

recognition of his strenuous struggle against the forces that threaten to ship-wreck the Great Republic which carried mankind and its fortunes, this play is, by his kind permission, cordially dedicated" (v).

The action of the play takes place just prior to the time of its initial representation, in either 1907 or 1908, given an internal reference to a particular pogrom that took place in Kishineff, Bessarabia, "four or five years ago" (109), specifically dated by Appendix B to 1903. This event overshadows the whole of the plot and its two main characters, David Quixano and Vera Revendal, although in different ways. David—son of the cantor at the Jewish synagogue, a descendant of *hidalgos* (nobility) from the Spanish court who in 1492 opted for exile in Poland against baptism, and a genius of the violin though entirely self-taught—was present at the massacre, which he survived when, having lost consciousness as a result of a shoulder wound, he was left for dead. Not, however, before having witnessed the barbarous death of his entire family at the hands of the Russian mob and troops, led by an officer whose figure he remembers in vivid detail. The mere recollection of such carnage and such a figure throws him into a state of near delirium. Vera—daughter of a leading loyalist and Orthodox Christian family, a descendant of Russian nobility, and a musician with professional training from the St. Petersburg Conservatory—had already left Kishineff by that time. Yet, it was her father, Baron Alexis Revendal, officer in charge of the local district, who served as leader of the Russian regiment that day and was thus the one responsible for the annihilation of David's family. His is the figure that haunts David's memory.

By the time the play begins, both characters find themselves in the United States. David is a recent arrival; after the pogrom, he has joined his uncle, Mendel Quixano, a piano teacher and halls-and-weddings performer, in New York City, where he too scratches out a living by performing and teaching.[15] Vera is an earlier arrival; wanted in Russia for her activities in radical circles, she has fled the country and settled in New York City, where she works in a Settlement for new immigrants (where no Jews are to be found), thus carrying on her commitment to activism, now with poverty rather than absolutism as target.[16] By the time the play starts, both characters have met each other as well—David has given a concert at the Settlement—but know nothing about each other's background.

---

[15] Years before, Mendel Quixano had brought over from Russia his mother, David's grandmother, Frau Quixano, who lives with the two of them. These relatives of David represent, in varying degrees, continuing attachment to the traditional ways of Judaism. They serve, therefore, as direct counterbalance to David's vision of America—opposition from the outside.

[16] Vera lives alone in the United States, with no ties whatever to her family in Russia, but she does have a romantic pretender, Quincy Davenport, the son of a business magnate and thus a representative of American "nobility"—the stock image of the spoiled playboy. This acquaintance of Vera represents not only continuing attachment to the traditional ways of Europe but also nativist opposition to the new waves of immigration into the country, with special disdain for its Jewish component. He serves, therefore, as further counterbalance to David's vision of America—opposition from the inside.

The action begins with a visit of Vera to the Quixano home in order to extend an invitation to David for a second concert at the Settlement. This visit lays the ground for a romantic relationship between the two, and with it a most problematic union between Jew and Gentile—the basic framework for the plot in the four acts to follow. Through its ups and downs, David unveils, by way of impassioned and rapturous outbursts, his vision of a raceless and creedless America. There are four such instances in all, one in each act, with any number of additional brief declarations throughout. Within the play this vision takes concrete form in two ways: first, by his unfolding love for a Gentile woman; second, by his composition of a musical piece on America in which he seeks to capture the refugee experience of Gentile and Jew alike. In what follows I trace this vision act by act in order to bring out its close connections to both relationship and composition.

The first act provides a basic introduction. Vera's visit to the Quixanos yields a number of important disclosures for both the immediate and subsequent development of the plot: (1) the Jewish origins of the Quixanos, which at first brings out Vera's anti-Semitism, almost putting an end to both visit and invitation; (2) the common Russian background of both the Quixanos and the Revendals, which leads to key personal information about Vera (opposition to absolutism) and David (pogrom survivor); and (3) the musical promise of David—not only as performer but also as composer, presently at work on a symphonic piece—vis-à-vis the harsh reality of life in America, which brings forth the prospect of possible patronage by friends of Vera. David is introduced by his uncle as "crazy about America" (23) and first appears on stage singing the words of "My Country 'Tis of Thee" (26). The invitation to play at the Settlement, "before all those happy immigrants you gather together" (30), sets off his first hymn to America (31-33). From the outside, he begins, America appeared to him while in Russia as "waiting, beckoning, shining—the place where God would wipe away tears from off all faces." Indeed, that same America, that "great touch of liberty," was also reaching "all those other weeping millions of Europe, shining wherever men hunger and are oppressed." From within, he continues, America now appears as part of a divine plan, "God's crucible, the great Melting-Pot." The plan itself is quite clear: in America the "fires of God" are "melting and re-forming" all the races of Europe, with all of their ancient animosities and disputes. Its outcome is also quite clear: the emergence of the "American" as "the fusion of all races, the coming superman." This outcome, however, is still in process, like his symphony, waiting for a finale that could capture such a vision. By the end of the act, the relationship between the two main characters is also under way: Vera, gradually overcoming her initial anti-Semitic sentiments, becomes quite interested in David, while David is overjoyed at the thought of having found in Vera a fellow-believer.

The second act introduces conflict. The action takes place a month later and revolves around another visit on the part of Vera to the Quixano home, this time accompanied by friends who come to establish David's musical talent with the possibility of sponsoring his studies in Germany—Quincy Davenport, whose sole interest lies in pleasing Vera; and Herr Pappelmeister, a stock German character who serves as conductor of Davenport's private orchestra.[17] In the intervening period David has been hard at work on a revised finale, driven by a vision of a thousand Jewish children pledging allegiance to the flag at the People's Alliance—"little Jews," he declares, whose "souls are melting in the Crucible" and who will "grow up Americans" (53).[18] At one level, the visit proves a dismal failure. Aware of Davenport's utterly trivial pursuit of pleasure and unreserved love for all things European, David launches into a bitter tirade against his "breed" (86-89), whom he accuses of "killing [his] America." This is the first part of David's second hymn to America: Europe, that Europe which Davenport reveres and would perpetuate at home, is but a "failure," a "morass of crime and misery"; America, on the other hand, is the "land of to-morrow," the "last and noblest hope of humanity."[19] At another level, the visit proves thoroughly successful. David's defense of his ideals and Vera's admiration for such a stand bring about a mutual declaration of love. Subsequently, when his uncle objects to such love as impossible, David launches into a spirited defense (94-98). This constitutes the second part of the hymn: in the "Crucible" of America, the "fires of God" shall fuse the Jews along with all other races. While unthinkable in the past, given the attachment of all other nations to a civilization and a creed, America represents a country in the making as well as a secular republic, where all "races and religions" will yield to the "Republic of Man" and the "Kingdom of God." The act ends with David's departure from home—a departure both demanded by his uncle, for having "cast off the God of our fathers" (98), and embraced by David, as he realizes his "need for a wider world" (98).

---

[17] As a stock ethnic character, Pappelmeister is both a serious and comic figure. While his stereotypical German appearance, expression, and behavior render him comic, his depiction as an expert musician brings a sense of seriousness as well. This latter aspect is ironically heightened by the task with which he has been entrusted by Davenport, the production of the comic opera repertoire. Herr Pappelmeister is not the only stock ethnic character in the play. The Quixanos, despite their evident limited means, also employ an Irish maid by the name of Kathleen O'Reilly, a comic figure, who, as the play unfolds, undergoes a transformation from an attitude of anti-Semitic intolerance, though by no means of the virulent type, to one of sympathetic identification with the Jewish way of life. Within the play both characters clearly serve as contrast to Quincy Davenport; their foreignness and openness to Jews stand opposite to the latter's nativism and anti-Semitism.

[18] The pledge itself is as exalted as David's own outbursts: "Flag of our Great Republic, guardian of our homes, whose stars and stripes stand for Bravery, Purity, Truth, and Union, we salute thee. We, the natives of distant lands, who find rest under thy folds, do pledge our hearts, our lives, our sacred honour to love and protect thee, our Country, and the liberty of the American people for ever" (53). This pledge David himself recounts in tears, "almost hysterically" at the end.

[19] The attack brings about a strongly anti-Semitic response from Quincy Davenport as well as an unreserved statement of support from Pappelmeister. The latter confirms the genius of David, declaring that Germany has nothing to teach him and thus making any need for studies abroad and patronage quite unnecessary. Before leaving the scene in a huff, Davenport summarily dismisses Pappelmeister from his employ, thereby making it possible for the latter to pursue serious music once again.

The third act brings mounting conflict. The scene takes place at the Settlement, a month later. Davenport has taken it upon himself to bring Vera's family, the baron and the new baroness (Vera's stepmother, whom she has not met), to the United States as a measure of last resort to prevent the marriage of Vera and David and thus further his own matrimonial designs. It is a context full of rabid anti-Semitism on the part of the Russian guests and outright nativism on the part of their American host. The conflict comes to a climax when, out of love for his daughter and moved by her entreaties, the baron consents to meet David, thereby bringing face to face victim and murderer from the Kishineff pogrom—the figure from the past now very much a figure of the present. The result is a scene of horrendous accusations on the part of David and horrendous invectives on the part of the baron. Rejected by his own daughter in the light of such revelations and recriminations, the baron offers his life to David, but the latter does not follow through, reaching instead for his violin and walking out of the room. The sole release from such tension comes by way of an intervening visit from Pappelmeister, strategically located between the initial meeting of Vera and her family and the climactic encounter between David and the baron. Pappelmeister brings a twofold offer for David: a position as first violin in what has now become his orchestra, thus making his marriage to Vera possible, and the production of his "American" symphony.[20] This visit triggers David's third hymn to America, set within the context of a love scene (144-48). Theirs, David proclaims, is a union that will bring suffering, for "it is live things, not dead metals, that are being melted in the Crucible." This is inevitable, for the "ideals of the fathers," such as the narrowness of Holy Russia and the narrowness of Holy Judea, cannot be "foisted on the children"; each generation "must live and die for its own dream"—and theirs, of course, is the dream of America. Only afterward will there be healing. However, by the conclusion of the act, suffering has left the vision in total disarray: Vera, turning her back on her Russian roots and invoking the example of Ruth, declares her intention to adopt David's people and god as her own; David, turning against Vera and heeding the voice of his people, declares that a "river of blood" has come between them and that he must go home.

The final act yields resolution. The action again takes place at the Settlement, about three months later, on the roof-garden, from where the whole of New York is visible, including the Statue of Liberty in the distance. It is late afternoon on the Fourth of July. It has been raining, but the sun is just beginning

---

[20] The symphony has presumably been finished by now, although this is never quite made clear. In any case, both offers are accepted. However, David refuses to have Carnegie Hall as the venue for the premiere of his symphony on the grounds that the work is meant for the new immigrants, those who have known the "pain of the old world" and "the hope of the new" and who will thus understand it "with their hearts and their souls" (141). At Vera's suggestion, the Settlement itself is chosen for the occasion—a concert in its roof-garden—to take place on the Fourth of July. David's ecstatic reply replicates his longer outbursts: "My American Symphony! Played to the People! Under God's Sky! On Independence Day!" (142).

to break through the heavy clouds. The symphony has been a total success, as the unending cheering of the audience from below makes clear, but David sits alone and despondent, refusing to return for a bow. A parade of characters—from his uncle, to his grandmother and the Irish maid, to the German maestro—find their way to the garden to offer their congratulations, culminating with an appearance by Vera herself. The result is a second love scene, within which can be found the fourth and final hymn to America. David first acknowledges that he has utterly betrayed his vision of America—that he has been false to his soul, "its own music, its own mission, its own dream"—by turning to the past, to his "heritage from the Old World" of "hate, vengeance, and blood," at a most crucial moment (179). From his point of view, he declares, the symphony is a failure. He then goes on to ask Vera's forgiveness for having cast her aside and begs for her love, against all her protestations, so that the "ghosts" of the past can be finally "exorcised," so that "love triumphs over death" (180-83). When she consents, he looks to the future once again with a ringing endorsement of his vision (184-85): America is indeed the "Crucible" and the "great Melting Pot," with New York as "the harbor where a thousand mammoth feeders come from the ends of the world to pour in their human freight." Here the "great Alchemist" is melting and fusing, through his purging fires, all the races and nations of the world, including the Jew and the Gentile, bringing them all together to build the "Republic of Man" and the "Kingdom of God." Here, as opposed to Greece and Rome, the nations and races come not "to worship and to look back," but rather "to labour and look forward." The scene comes to a close with David's benediction for God's peace on all the "unborn millions" destined to populate the continent—the "Americans." All this time the sun has been setting in glorious splendor; now, in twilight, the city lights gleam and the torch from the Statue of Liberty twinkles as a "lonely, guiding star" (185), while from below rise the words and music of "My Country 'Tis of Thee," on the lips and instruments of the assembled immigrants, as the concert comes to an end.

As a dramatic piece, it is not at all difficult to see why the play met with less than critical success, full as it is of conventional melodrama, gushing sentimentality, stock characters, and heavy-handed didacticism. In this regard the play is best understood and more easily tolerated, I believe, if approached as an example of romantic expressionism. As a cultural document, however, the play proves far more significant, especially when one realizes that such a panegyric to Americanism is not entirely without conflict. This is evident from the play itself, where one finds not only unrelieved opposition from the Jewish side, by way of the foreign-born Mendel Quixano, but also radical nativism from the American side, in the person of the native-born Quincy Davenport, who argues for an end to all alien immigration. It is also clear from both the dedication and the afterword. While the former speaks vaguely of forces "that threaten to shipwreck" the republic, the latter names such forces explicitly. Here, in addition to those already surfaced in the play (the presence of anti-Semitism in the country, resistance on the part of Jewish immigration, the drive to slam shut the doors of immigration), a fourth is added: the presence of "negrophobia." For Zangwill, therefore, this vision of a raceless and creedless America, concocted by God for the creation of a super-humanity, is not so much a vision of what-is but of what-could-be—of America's "true significance and potentiality for history and civilization" (215).[21] To think otherwise, he argues, would be "to despair of all humanity, not to mention super-humanity" (204).

Nonetheless, it is clear that this vision of America has been drawn largely with immigration from Europe in mind. To be sure, in his last hymn to America, David does include the "black" and the "yellow" in the fusion, but that is the sole mention of non-European immigration, aside from a brief but telling reference from Baron Revendal to the lynching of "niggers" in the South (111). However, when the question of the "African Negro" is raised in the afterword (204-7), separation is proposed as the best option—whether by way of transplantation to Liberia, the formation of a state of their own, or their confinement to the southern states. The rationale, in my opinion, can only be described as racist, despite a certain element of appreciation and commendation. In America, Zangwill argues, there is clear antipathy between black and white, whether as a result of racial instinct or social prejudice. The result is a negrophobia born of panic and founded on myth. In point of fact, he retorts, racial and social intercourse are both a historical fact and an ongoing phenomenon, with both "colours" having derived their own specific "virtues and graces" from the process of evolution (206). Indeed, the positive contributions of the "negro" to the fusion would be clear—"joy of life, love of colour, keen senses, beautiful voice, and ear for music" (206)—and would serve, in time, as an antidote to "an anaemic and artless America" (206). Yet, the negative aspects are just as clear—an ugly and undesirable complexion (prognathous) as well as lower intelligence and ethics—and would only serve to drag down the fusion. The two races, Zangwill notes, are simply too far apart "for profitable fusion" (206). Consequently, whites and blacks are better off separate from one another, biologically as well as physically, though "spiritual miscegenation" is both inevitable and beneficial. In sum, for Zangwill, the hoped-for "super-humanity" does have its limits, European

---

[21] It is precisely for this reason, he explains, that he has chosen as his protagonists "historic enmities at their extremes" (203-4), the persecuted Jew of Russia and the persecuting Russian. It is a way of showing how the fusion of America can bring together, by way of love and co-citizenship, "the most violent antitheses from the past" (203). The choice of a Jewish protagonist he further explains as follows. First, because the Jew represents "the toughest of all the white elements" (203) for the proposed fusion, given the history of anti-Semitism and their power of survival. Second, because there is no other "race," given its lack of a homeland, more in need of a land of liberty; in fact, Zangwill argues, in America the Jew "has come into his own again" (208). It is a way of showing, therefore, how even that group most resistant to fusion of any sort can leave behind its past for the sake of the future in America—a republic based on principles of justice and equal rights, without a state religion. For the Jew, however, such "dissolution must be necessarily slower" (209) but no less inevitable. However, Zangwill cautions, should the vision prove a mirage, then their mission would become one of "fighting for the preservation of the original Hebraic pattern" (209), and in this, he adds, they shall not be alone.

limits,[22] and these would presumably apply not only to the black but also to the yellow and the (unmentioned) brown.

Deconstruction of Melting and Dreaming

The overall context for this exercise in deconstruction is that of geopolitical reflections on the foreign-affairs policy of the country in the aftermath of the Cold War. Its author, Benjamin Schwarz, was, at the time of composition, a senior fellow at the World Policy Institute, a part of the New School for Social Research in New York City since 1991. Traditionally, the Institute, publisher of the *World Policy Journal,* had engaged in policy research and advocacy on critical world problems within the established framework of international diplomacy and world politics. Upon joining the New School, it proceeded to redefine its mission in the light of two developments: the dramatic world changes introduced by the end of the Cold War, and the increasing blurring of the line between domestic and international concerns. This new mission was set forth as follows: offering innovative policy proposals for public debate toward the goal of internationalist consensus on matters economic (world market economy), political (system of collective security), and social (transnational civil society); promoting greater public understanding of the relationship between domestic and international policy; nurturing a new generation of writers and public intellectuals committed to internationalist thinking. The piece written by Schwarz for *The Atlantic Monthly* was very much in the mold of such internationalist thinking.

Its point of departure is the geopolitical model adopted by the "foreign-policy community" toward the phenomenon of "ENS wars"—ethnic, nationalist, separatist conflicts. For the model, the outbreak of such wars around the globe points to a world that has become more dangerous than during the Cold War itself. In response, the model urges the liberal notions of pluralism and tolerance: unity through the avoidance of domination politics and the allowance of a voice for minorities in national affairs, both political and cultural. This paradigm, Schwarz charges, is thoroughly misguided, not only naive but also ahistorical. It is naive insofar as it wrongly assumes that the dominant group in a society would be willing to go against its own interests; it is ahistorical insofar as it fails to see that ENS wars have been a regular feature of history, hardly unknown during the Cold War and very much present at the heart of modern Europe itself. Such a paradigm, Schwarz further suggests, only reflects the profound anxiety present in this community as a result of its own sense of increasing fragmentation in the country.

---

[22] By way of contrast, Zangwill evaluates the potential contribution of the Jews to the fusion as follows: "And there is assuredly none which has more valuable elements to contribute to the ethnic and psychical amalgam of the people of to-morrow" (203). It is also interesting to note that, while in the play biological interaction between Jew and Gentile is a crucial element of the vision, in the afterword such interaction is described as unnecessary for Jewish Americanization (207).

Indeed, the paradigm presupposes a highly idealized view of America's history and development—"a sanctimonious tissue of myth and self-infatuation" (58). The America in question emerges as a "highly successful model of a multiethnic, multicultural, multireligious, and polyglot society" (60). This America becomes, as a result, the country's "leading export"—*the* model of tolerance and diversity urged upon all fragmented societies. Thus, in promoting the model abroad, the foreign-affairs community is ultimately trying to reassure itself of its own validity at home. However, Schwarz counters, in order to understand the present world, we must begin to understand ourselves: our own process of nation-building, like any other, was brutal. In other words, Schwarz sees the need for a radical exposé in this regard, which he promptly undertakes from a variety of different angles.

First, America engaged in swallowing up peoples and cleansing ethnics. From before the formation of the country through the 1960s, unity among the different immigrant groups was achieved not by the amalgamation of peoples into a new creation but by the imposition of Englishness on the part of the dominant élite. Cultural plurality gave way to cultural homogeneity through the creation not of a "new American" but through the formation of a "modified Englishman" (62). "Americanization" was thus not a process of openness to differences but of coercive conformity to the particular identity of Anglo-Americanism. It was this agenda of cultural predominance, of swallowing up peoples and cleansing ethnics, that the concept of the "melting pot" was meant to capture, in direct opposition to any sense of tolerance or pluralism.

Second, America subscribed to a project of imperial expansion. The process of nation-building, conceived from early on as a process of geographical aggrandizement, proved as ruthless as any other, driven by the usual factors of national security, economic development, and racial chauvinism. The process involved the vision of a continental expansion through the acquisition of land that belonged to others, including England and Spain; a war of conquest against Mexico, leading to the annexation of one-half of the Mexican territory; and three centuries of genocidal wars, involving obliteration and confinement, of Native Americans. This was an America that was put together, therefore, not by conciliation and compromise but by conquest and force.

Third, America experienced a typical example of nationalist-separatist conflict, which it resolved in typical fashion as well. The episode involved a collision between two different economic and ideological sectors of the country, based on antagonistic systems of property—a capitalist North, industrial and liberal-bourgeois, and an anti-capitalist South, agricultural and aristocratic-paternalistic—over the future vision and direction of the country as a whole, with a separatist attempt on the part of the South. The resolution was a devastating civil war, which resulted in the military occupation of the vanquished and the imposition of a new order, both political and economic, by the victors—capitalist development by way of a powerful centralized state.

Fourth, America followed, from the beginning and in systematic fashion, a policy of racial exclusion and maltreatment toward a significant component of its population—all those of African origins. On the question of black and white, therefore, the goal was never racial unity but racial domination. Here the possibility of "cleansing" or "swallowing up" was never entertained; in fact, for those opposed to domination, the only other alternative seriously contemplated was transplantation, removal from the country. At the same time, the policy of racial domination proved effective in the process of "Americanization," insofar as the specter of the "black" was used to unite the different immigrant groups as "white." Thus, racial homogeneity served to sharpen and reinforce cultural homogeneity.

Such contrary historical recollections, Schwarz argues, call into question any claims of uniqueness on behalf of the United States as a nation and hence any portrayal of the country as the very model of tolerance and pluralism for a fragmented post–Cold War world. This history of cultural aggression, imperial design, civil breakdown, and racial superiority point instead to a process of nation-formation and a model of nation-state no different than any other, past or present. Consequently, geopolitical reflection on the contemporary world would have to begin with this realistic view of America's history and development and thus deploy a very different paradigm of foreign affairs altogether. The result is a radically different approach toward the phenomenon and resolution of ENS wars. Not surprisingly, what emerges is a far more pessimistic view of world affairs, far less "reasonable," and a far more tentative, far less "reassuring" view of the country's success and future as a multiethnic society.

The basic tenets of such a model, along the lines of functionalist *Realpolitik*, are as follows. To begin with, the ideal of developing a true democracy in a multiethnic society is a well-nigh impossible task. On the one hand, the option of granting special privileges to minority groups amounts to much less than what such groups desire, resulting in deep dissatisfaction. On the other hand, the option of creating a civil state asks the majority group to settle for less than it has, causing profound dissatisfaction as well. In addition, in and of itself the ideal of democracy promotes competition for power, thereby enhancing rather than palliating tensions and conflicts among groups. Consequently, it is best to allow "historically workable solutions" to take their course (66)—some form of domination; ethnic cleansing and partition; the logic of force. Thus, the United States should intervene in ENS wars only when vital interests are at stake and, then, only in one of two ways: purely by way of peacekeeping, when the conflict has given way to mutual exhaustion or unilateral triumph, or by actually helping one side impose its will on the other. To proceed otherwise, to promote diversity and pluralism, is ultimately fruitless; we need only recall our own history and development.

Finally, to reassure ourselves by promoting such a model abroad is pointless. Our own situation should be clearly faced: the evident fragmentation of the country along ethnic and cultural lines is but the result of an elite that is increasingly unwilling or unable to impose its hegemony on society. In the absence of such traditional cultural dominance, we have but one option: face up to our own myth, our leading export, as a nation; admit that we have not found a solution

toward the creation of a democratic multiethnic society; and face the prospect
that "perhaps such a solution cannot be found" (67). What this prospect entails
Schwarz does not pursue, yet the ominous tone of the pronouncement is unmistakable—at the very least, ongoing fragmentation as a civil state, solely brought
together by the very fragile bonds of diversity and tolerance.

Melting and Dreaming: New Creation or Total Assimilation

While engaged in very different tasks with respect to the American mythology of melting and dreaming, it is fair to say that both Zangwill and Schwarz
approve of the process as such. Where they differ, and radically so, is in their
respective evaluations of its goal and outcome: Zangwill posits a new creation
altogether, a super-human American, not as a present reality but as a future and
imperative desideratum; Schwarz sees full assimilation to the dominant culture,
an Anglo-Saxon America, as an enduring reality in the past, but less and less so
in the present. Interestingly enough, both point to and comment on the opposite
position. Zangwill, in his afterword of 1913, specifically attacks the "common"
notion that the process of amalgamation is one of assimilation to the dominant
type (203).[23] To the contrary, he argues, the American fusion involves "all-
around give-and-take" in which all groups take part and affect the final type, for
better or for worse. Similarly, Schwarz specifically challenges any notion—
such as Zangwill's, whom he mentions by name—that the process of Americanization involves a "colorful blending" of ethnic and national differences (62).
Rather, he counters, the American fusion has always involved an exercise in
coercion toward a final type of "'American-looking' Americans" (62). In
Zangwill and Schwarz one finds, therefore, two very different conceptions of
melting and dreaming in America, though basic agreement on the fruitfulness
of the process.

Both positions also have important subtexts that should not be passed over.
Zangwill is sharply aware of the ideal nature of his race-less and creed-less
ideal for the country, for many are the forces that labor against it. Schwarz is
similarly aware that the ideal of cultural uniformity for the country, longstanding
and highly successful, proves increasingly fragile, for many are also the forces
that work against it. For Zangwill, therefore, it is the specter of uniformity that
threatens in the background—the possibility that America may turn out to be a

---

[23] A good representative of such a position was the Jewish-American philosopher
Horace Kallen. See "Democracy versus the Melting-Pot: A Study of American Democracy," *The Nation* (February 18, 1915): 190-94, and (February 25, 1915): 217-20; idem,
Culture and Democracy in the United States (New York: Boni and Liveright, 1924); for
this reference I am indebted to the work of Arthur M. Schlesinger Jr. Kallen argued for
"cultural pluralism": the preservation of ethnic groups and traditions against the ideal of
the melting pot on the basis of a highly essentialist conception of ethnicity—a view of
the ethnic bond as involuntary and immutable. For Kallen, the nation involved political
and administrative unity but not cultural unity, not one people but a democracy of peoples.

nation-state like any other.[24] America must hold its course. For Schwarz, it is the specter of fragmentation—the possibility that America may become but another casualty of the ENS phenomenon. Given the collapse of the old course, America must steer a new course. For both, therefore, melting and dreaming emerge as essential for the country, whether by way of a new-American identity or Anglo-American identity.

AMERICAN MELTING AND DREAMING: RECENT VISIONS

In the 1990s, as the impact of non-Western immigration on the country was becoming evident in both the short term and the long term, the issue of immigration rose steadily to the forefront of the national political discussion. In what follows I examine a number of contributions to this discussion on the part of highly respected figures from the academic world. I do so not only to avoid the shrillness and the demagoguery that mark much of this discussion but also, and above all, to gauge the mind and heart of the dominant culture at its most enlightened and benevolent level at this crucial moment in the demographics of the country.

Arthur M. Schlesinger Jr.: Pluralist Expanding, Not Multicultural Unraveling

For the first contribution I turn to the widely sold volume of Arthur M. Schlesinger Jr., University Professor of the City University of New York Emeritus, with the sharp title *The Disuniting of America: Reflections on a Multicultural Society*.[25] The subtitle reveals the immediate context for such reflections; the

---

[24] For Zangwill, it should be noted, America is neither the first nor the only "melting pot"; in fact, all nations can be properly described as "melting pots" (215). America is, however, the quintessential example of such a process, "*the* Melting Pot," given its enormous size, the unprecedented number of components involved, and the rapidity of immigration. The difference lies not in the process as such, therefore, but in the outcome envisioned—the kind of nation America stands for in its ideals and is presently becoming through its ongoing fusion. Whereas nations of the Old World revolved around unity of race and religion and nations of the New World are hardening into a similar homogeneity of race and religion, America signifies a secular republic, based on principles of justice and equality for all. Should this vision founder, America would become but another nation-in-the-making, not the Republic of Man or the Kingdom of God.

[25] A. M. Schlesinger Jr., *The Disuniting of America: Reflections on a Multicultural Society*, rev. and enl. ed. (New York and London: W. W. Norton & Company, 1998). There were two earlier editions: the original, published by Whittle Books in 1991; a slightly revised edition brought out in 1992 by W. W. Norton. Besides the addition of an epilogue on the impact of the Bill of Rights on the culture wars and a bibliographical appendix, the newest edition is described as updating the text, amplifying points of argumentation, and including new issues for discussion. All references are taken from this edition.

volume, included within the Larger Agenda Series of Whittle Books, was meant
as a contribution to the debate on multiculturalism and thus as a position piece
in the so-called culture wars of the 1980s.[26] The title proper captures Schlesinger's
own stance in this national debate: multiculturalism, radically understood and
applied, leads to the disintegration of the country.[27] The foreword summarizes
the background and rationale behind such a position. He argues that the age of
the Cold War has given way to an era of ethnic/racial animosity, exacerbated by
an unrelenting process of globalization (a rapidly shrinking world with currents
beyond people's comprehension and control) and the massive movement of
peoples across borders (a rapidly diversifying world in which people cling to
in-group loyalties). The result of this dual process is evident: a worldwide collapse of nations as a result of tribalism. Within the United States itself, the
traditional exemplar of the successful multiethnic state, a similar drift toward
fragmentation can be detected, driven by both massive immigration from non-
European sources and the rise of the "cult" of ethnicity. The result of this twofold process is also evident: the disuniting of the country as a result of tribalism.
In the face of such related developments, the volume may be seen as undertaking a twofold task: the refutation of radical multiculturalism, involving long and
repeated attacks on a recurring circle of targets in both the academic and the
educational realms, with Afrocentricity as primary; the advancement of a blueprint toward the recovery of the "unifying ideals" and the "common culture" of
the country, but now with the ideal of "a fair and just land for all our people" (24).

Both tasks are undergirded by a review of the path and consequences of
immigration into the country. Schlesinger speaks of an enduring ideal and posits a fourfold historical sequence. The ideal is that of a "new race": immigrants
would leave behind their ethnic cultures and identities and become, through intermixture with all other ethnic groups, a new people, with a new culture and a new
world. The sequence reveals a division between European and non-European
immigration. The first three stages consist of migration waves from Europe,

---

[26] For the background, contours, and implications of multiculturalism, see F.
Standley, "Multiculturalism," in *A Dictionary of Cultural and Critical Theory*, ed. F.
Payne (London and Cambridge, Mass.: Routledge, 1996), 353-55; see also the entry in
J. Childers and G. Hentzi, eds., *The Columbia Dictionary of Modern Literary and Cultural Criticism* (New York: Columbia University Press, 1995), 196. Within the United
States the primary reference has been to the study of ethnic diversity and pluralism as a
way of making both the academic establishment and the educational system more inclusive. This effort can range from a basic expansion of liberal pluralism to a form of
radical separatism. The strong political thrust involved in such efforts has called forth a
conservative backlash, generating the so-called culture wars.

[27] Schlesinger (150-51) outlines three variations of contemporary multiculturalism:
(a) mild: focusing on neglected groups, themes, and perspectives in life and history—all
with a sense of a shared culture; (b) militant: opposing any concept of a common culture—rejection of assimilation and celebration of separatism; (c) extreme: espousing
ethnocentrism—belief in the superiority of the ethnic group. The charge of national
disintegration would comprehend the last two variations, which are often brought together under the title of "radical" multiculturalism.

identified as follows: (1) Anglo immigration, through the seventeenth and eigh-teenth centuries—primarily from Great Britain; (2) a first wave of non-Anglo immigration, prior to the Civil War—from western and northern Europe; (3) a second wave of non-Anglo immigration, after the Civil War—from southern and eastern Europe. The fourth and ongoing stage, at work since the mid-1960s, involves immigration from the whole of the non-Western world. For Schlesinger, the actual unfolding of the sequence bears important consequences for the de-velopment of the ideal.

To begin with, within the new race one particular stage and one particular group prove dominant—the Anglo Americans. In the forging of the new race, the first stage emerges as foundational: the British tradition, recast through the colonial experience, becomes the matrix for assimilation and hence the model for all subsequent immigrants to follow; such recasting gives shape to what becomes known as the American Creed. This tradition—the WASP (white, Anglo-Saxon, Protestant) phenomenon—includes language and literature; laws, institutions, and political ideas; customs and precepts; religion. As Schlesinger puts it, "The smelting pot thus had, unmistakably and inescapably, an Anglocentric flavor" (34). Later waves of European migration, through the nine-teenth century and into the early twentieth century, would follow suit. Although gathering into ethnic enclaves at first, the new arrivals ultimately became mem-bers of the new race—Americans by assimilation. But not without difficulties. Both waves, Schlesinger points out, brought forth disdain for the newcomers, their looks and ways of life, giving rise to the formation of nativist movements and organizations, not only opposed to further immigration but also engaged in agitation against on-site immigrants. Nevertheless, despite such seemingly in-surmountable obstacles as discrimination by the WASP culture and the emer-gence of ethnic redoubts, most immigrants aspired and subscribed to the ideal of the new race.[28]

In addition, the new race was meant only for European whites. If non-Anglo Europeans experienced rejection and hostility, non-European groups fared much worse: on the part of Native Americans, conquest and transplantation; on the part of African Americans, slavery and segregation; on the part of Mexican Americans, peon labor and expulsion; on the part of Asian Americans, above all the Chinese, indenture and exclusion. Despite such seemingly overwhelming odds, Schlesinger claims, the ideal of the American Creed retained its attraction and force even among these groups, ultimately leading, in the wake of World War II, to a fundamental assault on the "curse" of American racism, what Schlesinger characterizes in no uncertain terms as "the great failure of the Ameri-can experiment, the glaring contradiction of American ideals and the still crip-pling disease of American life" (18-19).

---

[28] Here Schlesinger cites the vision of Israel Zangwill as conveyed by *The Melting Pot*, where the "original faith" of the new race is described as having received its "most celebrated metaphor" (38). It should be noted, however, that in Zangwill the concept of assimilation to an Anglo-American foundation is not only nonexistent but actually re-jected.

Only with the twentieth century Schlesinger claims, does one find resistance to the traditional ideal of a "new race" among the immigrants themselves or their descendants, culminating in the recent explosion of radical multiculturalism. Thus, in the early part of the century, a number of ethnic spokespersons began to raise their voices against the process of Americanization, characterizing it as a device to impose Anglocentric values upon immigrant groups. Such individuals he portrays as having, to be sure, a real interest in ethnic values, but also a "vested" interest in the preservation of ethnic constituencies (40)—in effect, a brief minority motivated by self-interest. This incipient resistance, however, did not go very far, given a number of historical developments with powerful centralizing effects: the outbreak of World War I in the 1910s; the emergence of xenophobic nationalism in the 1920s; the effects of the Great Depression in the 1930s; and the outbreak of World War II in the 1940s. Then, in the aftermath of World War II, the assertion of ethnic identity made a strong comeback, beginning among marginalized minorities in the 1950s and ultimately expanding to the old "ethnic" groups of the second migration wave by the 1970s.[29] For Schlesinger, this was a protest against the dominance and racism of WASP culture—a mild form of multiculturalism, entirely justified. Finally, in the 1980s such protest began to turn into a counterrevolution against the notion of one people, a common culture, and a single nation—the "cult" of radical multiculturalism. Yet, Schlesinger blames not the minority groups at large for such rejection of the new-race ideal but rather certain "self-appointed spokesmen" with "vested interest in ethnic identification" (48)—once again, a small minority driven by self-interest. Rhetorically, therefore, Schlesinger drives a wedge—whether at the beginning of the twentieth century or at its close—between the proponents of radical multiculturalism and the groups they claim to represent, which by and large are represented as pursuing the ideal of the new race by way of expansion.

In this regard, Schlesinger observes, the fourth stage of immigration has had a decided impact, given the dramatic numbers in question and its provenance from all corners of the non-European world (126). The new immigrant groups from Africa, from Asia and the Pacific, from Latin America and the Caribbean, have brought along with them—largely, Schlesinger stresses yet again, by way of their "self-appointed spokesmen"—a deep hostility toward the West as a result of their long experience of colonialism, racism, and exploitation at the hands of the West. Moreover, such immigrant groups are bringing about a significant change in the composition of the country. Indeed, the theoretical possibility now exists that in the twenty-first century the Eurocentric optic of the country will be displaced by the formation of a "minority majority" with a multicultural optic. For Schlesinger, the remedy lies not in the curtailment of immigration, for such a step would go against the very soul of the nation, but in

---

[29] Schlesinger highlights the work of Michael Novak (*The Rise of the Unmeltable Ethnics: Politics and Culture in the Seventies* [New York: Macmillan, 1972]) in this regard, with its affirmation of the need for a politics of identity and its view of the country as a nation of groups.

its proper control through the reexamination of its criteria and a reinvigoration of the process of assimilation. The focus by far is on the latter measure: new-comers must be led "to an acceptance of the language, the institutions, and the political ideals that hold the nation together" (127). The solution, therefore, is quite traditional but does have a strong critical edge to it.

First, the facts of history cannot be obliterated or ignored: the links between the United States and Europe are long-standing, numerous, and profound. Thus, the country is said to represent an "extension of European civilization" (128). Second, the Western tradition, like any other, brings together highly negative as well as highly positive elements: its crimes are many and undeniable, but so are its ideals, which include the power of self-criticism, protest, and reform. In fact, Europe is described as "the source—the *unique* source—of those liberating ideas . . . that constitute our most precious legacy and to which most of the world today aspires" (133). Consequently, the process of assimilation into the ideal of the "new race," with its European structure and English foundation, must continue, but with the further integration of non-European components, both old and new, into this formation. This process, moreover, is one that is favored by the masses of such minorities, both new immigrants and old residents, and opposed only by "romantic ideologues and unscrupulous hucksters" (136).

For the process to succeed, certain principles of action become imperative. First, on the part of non-European Americans, new immigrants and old residents alike, allegiance to the American Creed, with its focus on individual rights and democratic principles and its view of an open society founded on tolerance and mutual respect. Such allegiance may come about in two ways, either through the "shedding" of ethnicity or through a mutual celebration of distinctive ethnicity and common culture (137). Second, on the part of white, European Americans, coming to terms with the "great national tragedy" of racism (24)—acknowledging and eradicating the reality of ethnic and racial oppression wielded for so long at the expense of the ideal of equality, central to the American Creed itself. Such coming to terms demands the welcome and incorporation of new arrivals and old minorities on the part of "those who already think they own America" (24). Finally, on the part of all Americans—European and non-European, citizens and immigrants, majority and minorities—a commitment to the American experience as inherited. Such commitment calls, to be sure, for a sense of history with "due appreciation" for the diversity of the country, but also with "due emphasis" on its grounding and unifying European experience (147). Such are the weapons to be deployed against the specter of radical multiculturalism and the means by which the unity of the country will be not only preserved but enhanced. In this regard it should be noted that Schlesinger places the greater burden on the "complacent majority" rather than on the "beleaguered minorities" (24).

Though a salvo against multiculturalism in the context of the culture wars, Schlesinger's vision remains fundamentally optimistic, quite contrary to the title chosen for the volume. Not only are the proponents of radical multiculturalism regarded as a small coterie, out of tune with their respective constituencies, but also a number of arguments are said to militate against any success on their part: the attractive and unifying power of the American Creed; the desire for achievement and success; the superficial character of ethnic identification; the intermixture already present in the country (138-39). A further historico-moral argument is invoked as well: historically, the movement of the country has been from exclusion to inclusion. Ultimately, all groups contribute to the formation of the new race—this has been so in the past and will continue to be so in the future. This is so because the new-race ideal is always in a process of revision, as the national identity, grounded in England and nurtured by Europe, is "modified, enriched, and reconstituted by transfusions from other continents and civilizations" (142). Schlesinger's salvo, therefore, is that of a mild multiculturalist—a believer in cultural pluralism, but only by way of expansion of the traditional ideal.

Concluding Comments. Given the spectrum extrapolated from Zangwill and Schwarz, signified by the models of new creation and total assimilation respectively, Schlesinger advances a highly conflicted position, seemingly tending toward the former pole but actually veering much more toward the latter. Schlesinger clearly speaks of a "new race" as not only the traditional ideal of immigration but also an enduring and future desideratum, indeed imperative, for the country. Furthermore, this new-race formation is described as undergoing constant revision as new and different immigrant groups find their way into the country: their original cultures and identities affect the ongoing fusion of Americanism. At the same time, Schlesinger speaks of this "new race" as having an Anglocentric foundation, laid down by the first wave of migration, as well as a Eurocentric structure, added on by the second and third waves of migration. Furthermore, such foundation and structure are presented as the sine qua non of the process of Americanization, to be followed by all immigrant groups regardless of origins. Thus, what appeared at one level as a new fusion altogether, a new people, turns out in the end to be a variation of the longstanding model of Anglo-Americanism—an essential core of British tradition surrounded by a twofold layer of accidental accretions, consisting of an inner layer of European traditions and an outer layer of non-European traditions. In this proposal the stark overtones of Schwarz yield to a more beneficent vision of assimilation—a ringing endorsement of Western ideals alongside a stinging denunciation of Western practices. A number of comments are in order:

- The story of immigration emerges as one of halting though progressive success—a story of conflict as well as a story of accommodation. One finds a frank account of ethnic/racial oppression at work from the very beginning: Anglo-Americans discriminated against Europeans of non-Anglo descent to follow; Euro-Americans discriminated against all those of non-European descent—whether red or black, brown or yellow; Euro-Americans further discriminated against the new immigrants of non-European origins. One also finds an upbeat account of how all of these different minority groups struggle and succeed in the face of forbidding odds. Yet, on the whole, the story exhibits a romantic tilt toward a narrative of successful accommodation rather than to one of social conflict. While this latter narrative is highlighted, even blamed for the present state of affairs in the country, its force is subdued by the historico-moral argument of long-term success. Here, I argue, not only the opposition to immigration but also the travails of immigration must be fully and consistently foregrounded.

- With regard to the country's way of life, the story emerges as one of both permanent and changing identity—a story of an essential core, a formative structure, and a flexible superstructure. At the heart of America, one finds a static and inflexible formation—an Anglo foundation that precedes and controls all further migration waves from Europe, let alone non-European outsiders. Then, upon such a foundation, one comes across a fixed and irreplaceable structure—a European formation that precedes and guides all further migration waves from the non-Western world. Finally, around this structure, one encounters an expansive decorative superstructure—a pluralist ornamentation that is always in flux. Should this superstructure have designs on the structure or the foundations, the entire formation collapses. Consequently, this is a formation, a way of life, that is very much affected by cultural exchange, but only in its incidentals. The process of identity-formation envisioned is thus unidirectional at the depth level, Anglo as well as Euro assimilation, but multidirectional at the surface level. The process is not unconflicted: racism is identified at both the essential and the structural level.

- This tri-level concept of American identity is accompanied by an explicit statement of its superiority vis-à-vis all other national or cultural identities on two counts: the unique character of its underlying base, the British foundation and the European structure, given the power of the American Creed and the principle of self-criticism; the open nature of its new-race ideal, given its power of endless accommodation and of long-term inclusion. Such an identity must, therefore, be preserved as is, with all three layers in their proper place, but with a pointed alteration: the base must triumph over its constitutive racism and welcome all strangers and newcomers to the superstructure. Within this model, immigrants have much to contribute to the country—a contribution largely described in cultural terms, with hardly a mention of the economic dimension—but above all at the surface level.

To conclude, Schlesinger sees the country as in the midst of a fourth great migration, now from the non-Western world. With such a migration the numbers of Americans of non-European descent—present as minority groups in the country throughout its history—swell to such an extent that the very ethnic/racial composition of the country undergoes a palpable change. Yet, such a development, in and of itself, poses no problem. Regardless of origins, what such immigrants want is to become, like their earlier counterparts, a part of America. And, regardless of origins, the country offers a process of Americanization based on the vision of a new race guided and informed by the principles of the American Creed. Two obstacles do stand in the way. A lesser one is a refusal to assimilate on the part of the immigrants—an option preached by a vocal and self-serving minority. A greater one is racism on the part of the country—dominant from the beginning, but always yielding. Both can and must be surmounted: proper Americanization by the new immigrants, with the British foundation and the European structure as nonnegotiable; outright confrontation by the white majority, with commitment to cultural pluralism as nonnegotiable. Such a vision of America is, in the end, quite optimistic: denizens of Western and non-Western descent standing together—born-again pluri-Americans and born-again Euro- and Anglo-Americans, respectively—as equal subscribers to the ideal of the new race, the new American people.[30]

David Kennedy: Avoiding a Future Quebec

A second contribution comes from the pen of David M. Kennedy, the Donald J. McLachlan Professor of History at Stanford University, and appeared as an article in *The Atlantic Monthly*.[31] Its title was in the form of a pointed question: "Can We Still Afford to Be a Nation of Immigrants?" Rhetorically, as signified by the presence of the adverb "still," the question conveys the sense of an unambiguous stance in the past but of a debatable proposition for the future. The point of departure, therefore, is the history of American immigration. Kennedy distinguishes between two major migrations: the first, largely of European origins, which he sees as taking place over the course of a century (1820s-1920s); the second, mostly of non-European origins, which he traces to the mid-1960s and views as continuing indefinitely into the present century. Looking back, the answer is decidedly affirmative: the country could well afford to be a nation of immigrants and reaped huge benefits from such immigration. Looking forward, such a response is no longer automatic. Two reasons account for such a fundamental reconsideration of the national mythology (the United States as a nation of immigrants): the high population of the country and the unprecedented level of immigration into the country. The latter is sharply highlighted: since the Immigration and Nationality Act of 1965, the country has experienced the influx of about twenty million people in all, far more than during the previous

---

[30] In a later article ("Has Democracy a Future?," *Foreign Affairs* 76:5 [September/ October 1997]: 2-12) Schlesinger approaches the future from a broader, geopolitical perspective and with a similar attitude of guarded optimism. Despite the great failures of liberal democracy in the twentieth century, it managed to survive "by the skin of its teeth" (11), emerging triumphant at the very end. Still, triumphalism is out of the question, since many are the forces that work against it: the intensified revolt against the racism of the West; the exponential growth of technology, now by way of a computer-based economy, bringing about the destruction of untold jobs and the creation of ever-sharper social barriers; the rise of unbridled capitalism, with its move toward globalization and its glorification of market values. Given such a climate, Schlesinger argues, liberal democracy will survive in the twenty-first century only if it proceeds to carry out what it failed to do in the twentieth, "to construct a humane, prosperous, and peaceful world" (4).

[31] D. M. Kennedy, "Can We Still Afford to Be a Nation of Immigrants?" *The Atlantic Monthly* 278/5 (November 1996): 52-68.

period of highest immigration—the quarter-century that preceded World War I
(1890-1914). A proper response, Kennedy argues, calls for careful historical
analysis, for which he proposes a comparative analysis of the reasons for immigration in both past and present as well as the consequences of such migrations
for the nation and the groups involved.

With regard to rationale, Kennedy finds no difference whatever. The reasons
behind both migrations remain fundamentally the same: rapid population growth
alongside profound economic transformation. The same process that accounts
for the coming of thirty-five million people from Europe from the 1820s to the
1920s lies behind the arrival of those twenty million largely from outside Europe who have entered the country since the 1960s. As the twin forces of population explosion due to advances in health and hygiene and economic upheaval
due to industrialization spread through Europe and then on to the non-Western
world, excess population, displaced from its traditional contexts and occupations and unabsorbed by the local markets, seeks refuge in the United States.[32]
Thus, what took place in Europe through the nineteenth century and into the
beginning of the twentieth simply repeats itself outside the West in the later
twentieth century and into the twenty-first. With regard to consequences, however, Kennedy does posit a major difference between the two migrations.

In the past, he argues, the process of mutual accommodation between nation
and immigrants proved relatively free of social conflict, despite the undeniable
attestations of immigrant hardship and the sustained expressions of anti-immi-
grant fervor: the resettlement of the European migration was, on the whole, a
"success" story (58).[33] Three historical factors account for this: relative numbers, economic growth, cultural pluralism. First, immigrants, despite the numbers involved, never amounted to more than a small minority of the population.
Even at the height of this migration, in the period from 1890 to 1914, the Census of 1910 records the number of the foreign-born at 14.7 percent of the population. Second, immigrants were readily absorbed into an ever-expanding American economy, softening thereby the impact of their presence on the native
workers. Finally, immigrants came from a broad variety of cultural, religious,
national, and linguistic groups and settled as such across a vast expanse of the
country. As a result, it became impossible for any one group to preserve its

---

[32] With regard to Mexico, for example, the largest source of numbers in the present
migration, the following points are noted (64): since World War II the population has
tripled, surpassing in the process the rate of growth in Europe in the nineteenth century;
since World War II the economy has grown, by and large, at twice the rate of that of the
United States, but it has not been able to accommodate the excess population flowing
into cities from traditional locations and occupations. Since the 1970s, therefore, more
than five million have entered the United States.

[33] Here Kennedy goes directly against, as he himself acknowledges, the bulk of
historical inquiry, with its focus on such hardships and attacks. While such elements of
immigration history "we would forget . . . at our peril," nevertheless, he points out, the
"right" and "richer" question to be pursued in this regard, from an analytical perspective, is that of its success (58).

traditional ways for very long or to contest in any significant fashion the existing way of life in the country.

In the present, however, a very different situation looms, not so much in
terms of relative numbers or economic growth but rather in terms of cultural
pluralism. In fact, in the mid-1990s the number of foreign-born in the country
stood at 8.7 percent, half of what it was in 1910—a very sharp decline. Thus,
what had been, even at its peak, a small minority of the population had now
become even smaller. From this point of view, the impact of the present migration could only be assessed as much less problematic. Likewise, immigrants
continued to serve as an indispensable source of labor for an expanding economy.
To be sure, the situation had become more complex: the economy itself had
experienced a shift away from unskilled to skilled labor; and immigration now
included a sharp rise in dependents, as a result of the family reunification policies put into effect by the Act of 1965. Nonetheless, immigrants still functioned
as "productive participants" in the economy (67). From this point of view, the
impact of the present migration was assessed as slightly more problematic, but
not significantly so.[34] For Kennedy, therefore, it is the dimension of cultural
pluralism that now proves profoundly problematic—so much so that he refers
to its impact on the nation as that of a potential *Reconquista* (68), a reference to
the Spanish crusade to wrest control of the peninsula from the hands of Islam,
which came to a successful conclusion with the conquest of Granada in 1492,
and hence a reference not to the present migration as a whole but to a particular
contingent within it, immigration from Mexico.

With Mexico, in effect, the previous pattern of pluralism is said to collapse
in several respects: first, such immigration involves a large influx from a single
cultural, linguistic, religious, and national grouping; second, this grouping is
settling in the same region of the country, the Southwest; third, in so doing, this
grouping remains in a region contiguous to and historically part of its source.
Hence, the specter of a modern-day *reconquista*—a reclaiming, not by force of
arms but of numbers, of that area of Mexico wrested away by the United States
in the wake of the Mexican-American War (the Treaty of Guadalupe-Hidalgo

---

[34] The problematic character of this impact was more sharply assessed in an article
that appeared alongside that of Kennedy: George J. Borjas, "The New Economics of
Immigration: Affluent Americans Gain; Poor Americans Lose," *The Atlantic Monthly*
278/5 (November 1996): 70-80. From a strictly economic perspective, Borjas argued:
(a) the net gains for the country as a whole from current immigration are negligible and
may even be outweighed by the costs of increased social services; (b) such gains are
distributional—wealth is redistributed from unskilled workers to skilled workers and
company owners (since immigrants lower wages) and from taxpayers to consumers (since
the former pay for the social services used by immigrants, while the latter use the goods
and services produced by immigrants). For Borjas, therefore, the immigration question
amounts to "a tug-of-war between those who gain from immigration and those who lose
from it" (80). The danger to the national interest comes, he concludes, from the fact that
only a few groups gain much from it. What is needed, then, is the development of an
immigration policy that maximizes gains and minimizes losses, and for this a focus on
skilled workers rather than family reunification would represent a significant step.

[1848]). The consequences for the nation of such a development would be profound: the group would be able not only to preserve its traditional way of life for an indefinite period of time but also to challenge the country's way of life—from language, to institutions, to foreign affairs—bringing about thereby a thorough redefinition of its identity.[35] In fact, Kennedy suggests a close historical analogy and not at all a comforting one: the transformation of the American Southwest into a Chicano Quebec. The proposed remedy is a most traditional one: redoubled efforts at assimilation.[36] In the end, therefore, the answer to the pointed title of the article is a guarded one: yes, "we" can still afford to be a "nation of immigrants," but only if we "help our newest immigrants, those from Mexico especially, to become as well integrated into the larger American society as were those European 'new' immigrants" (68) of the first migration.

Concluding Comments. Within the spectrum constituted by Zangwill and Schwarz, this proposal for continued and enhanced assimilation falls squarely within the ambit of the latter vision. One finds in Kennedy mention not of a new American creation or of a Mexican addition to the ongoing fusion of Americanism but rather of the need for new immigrants to adopt the established "way of life" of the country in the same way as the earlier immigrants had done. That, it seems to me, is the ideal of Anglo-Americanism, though presented in a most positive vein, without the highly ironic overtones of Schwarz. A number of comments are again in order:

- Although the story of immigration is carefully described as one of relative success, the darker side of this mutual accommodation receives far too little attention. Both the travails of immigration, the poverty and exploitation, and the opposition to immigration, the prejudice and discrimination, must become integral parts of the story, in the past as well as in the present. As it is, the narrative of successful accommodation tends to overwhelm the narrative of social conflict.
- The proposed story presupposes a concept of the country's established way of life that is quite static and inflexible, a formation that precedes both great migrations and to which the present migration must, like the earlier one, conform. As such, this is a formation that emerges quite early on and that then remains curiously unaffected by the process of cultural exchange constantly

---

[35] Such a formation, Kennedy suggests, may even lead to the claim of a "special relationship" with Mexico, a clear reference of course to the often-cited "special relationship" with Great Britain claimed in the national discussion on American identity and its role in the world (68).

[36] Such assimilation can be heavy-handed or generous (68). The former approach, involving the use of "ham-handed and provocative devices" (such as the campaign, at both the federal and state levels, to make English the official language of the country for the transaction of civil business) is ultimately counterproductive—a possible point of departure for "prolonged cultural warfare." Thus, for Kennedy there is only one option: "We will have to be . . . less confrontational, more generous, and more welcoming than our current anxieties sometimes incline us to be."

at work in the country. The result of such a process emerges as always the same: unidirectional by way of assimilation.

• This concept of a long-established and long-lasting American way of life presupposes a sense of its superiority vis-à-vis all others, regardless of provenance, whether European or non-European. As such, it must be preserved at all cost. From the point of view of the model, therefore, immigrants have much to contribute to the country by way of economic growth but not by way of cultural expansion.

In sum, for Kennedy, the country is undergoing at present a second great migration from a largely unfamiliar source, the non-Western world, above all Latin America and the Caribbean as well as Asia and the Pacific. Yet, the question of origins as such does not emerge as at all problematic. In fact, only one contingent emerges as worrisome, indeed as posing an unprecedented threat to the country—the influx from Mexico. Such a threat, however, must and can be defused: not by an end to immigration, for it is necessary for the national economy; not by heavy-handed tactics, for they prove ultimately counterproductive; but by greater efforts at assimilation—the Americanization of the Mexican. In the end, then, all of the new arrivals from outside Europe would join the former arrivals from Europe as co-subscribers to the established way of life—born-again Anglo-Americans.

Samuel P. Huntington:
Collapse of National Identity and Purpose

The third contribution, a piece written for *Foreign Affairs* by Samuel P. Huntington, the Albert J. Weatherhead III University Professor at Harvard University and director of the John M. Olin Institute for Strategic Studies, is a reflection on national identity and purpose from a geopolitical perspective.[37] Its point of departure is the end of the Cold War and the emergence of a new world marked by enormous complexity at the global level and drastic changes at the national level. The result of such interrelated developments has been twofold: first, as conveyed by the title, an "erosion" of national identity in the country and of national purpose in the world; second, the rise of non-national forces, both subnational and transnational, in their stead. This shift can be readily captured by a comparative analysis of Huntington's views regarding American identity and purpose prior to and following upon the close of the Cold War.

During the Cold War, Huntington argues, both elements were clearly defined. National identity consisted of two core components: First, a set of values and institutions inherited from the original settlers (primarily British and primarily Protestant): the English language, separation of church and state, individual rights. Over time, as a result of sustained immigration from the rest of Europe, this culture was modified but "not fundamentally altered as a result" (29).

---

[37] S. P. Huntington, "The Erosion of American National Interests," *Foreign Affairs* 76/5 (September-October 1997): 28-49.

Second, a set of ideas and principles derived from the founding documents: the "American Creed" of liberty, equality, democracy, constitutionalism, liberalism, limited government, private enterprise. National purpose grew out of a world at war—a bipolar confrontation between the democratic world, with the United States as leader, and the socialist world, with the Soviet Union as leader; engaged in a representation of the "other" as undesirable and hostile—the evil empire of centralized communism; and involved a single-minded mission—combating and containing communism on a worldwide scale. For fifty years such singularity of purpose provided the country with enormous cohesion, greatly reinforcing thereby its traditional sense of identity, with its twofold set of cultural and political values.[38] After the Cold War, however, Huntington portrays both definitions in tatters, with momentous consequences for the country.

To begin with, national identity is said to be under siege from two different though related sources: a change in the pattern of immigration, and a rise in the forces of multiculturalism. Present-day immigration is described as highly problematic, not so much because of the origins of the new groups as such—their provenance from Asia and the Pacific as well as Latin America and the Caribbean, duly highlighted[39]—but rather because of a new attitude toward what Huntington calls, following the thesis of Peter Salins, "assimilation, American style" (33).[40] Such assimilation consisted of an implicit contract between nation and immigrants whereby the former would accept the latter as equal co-citizens on two conditions: acceptance of the English language, the principles of the American Creed, and the Protestant work ethic; and confinement of ethnicity to the privacy of their homes and the sphere of their local communities. The result was the preservation, with renewal, of "American culture."[41] Nowadays this

---

[38] Indeed, Huntington adds that at the heart of American cohesion from the beginning has been the identification of an undesirable and hostile "other" (30): (a) at the time of independence, Great Britain—the embodiment of aristocracy, tyranny, and oppression; (b) through the end of the nineteenth century, Europe in general—the preserve of feudalism, monarchy, and imperialism; (c) then, for the first half of the twentieth century, imperial and Nazi Germany—the main challenge to Euro-American civilization. It was this mantle that the Soviet Union inherited from the end of World War II to its dissolution in the late 1980s. Such an attitude, Huntington explains, is not only grounded on sound psychological theory but also has proven quite beneficial for the country. In fact, the country could well use such an unmistakable and undesirable "other" at this point (32).

[39] It should be noted, nonetheless, that Huntington does refer to the dramatic levels of such immigration as well as to the high birthrate of some of the groups in question, which together are bringing about a change in the racial, religious, and ethnic constitution of the country. Thus, while the question of origins is not actually presented as a problem, I believe such a view lies just below the surface.

[40] See P. D. Salins, *Assimilation, American Style* (New York: Basic Books, 1996).

[41] On the whole, Huntington argues, such assimilation worked well, even if "at times" immigrants, such as the Irish in the 1840s and 1850s, experienced discrimination and became the target of major programs of "Americanization" (33). In what can only be described as a euphemism, he further explains, "Over the course of three centuries, black people were slowly and only partially assimilated into this culture" (29).

contract no longer holds: immigrant groups—always unnamed and mostly referred to in the partitive ("some")—not only seem bent on remaining themselves but also claim discrimination if not allowed to do so by the mainstream.
This drastic change in the relationship between nation and immigrants has been
considerably sharpened by the claims of the "cult" of multiculturalism (32): the
denial of a common culture in favor of a diversity of cultures and identities; the
substitution of group rights for individual rights, along the lines of gender,
ethnicity/race, and sexual preference. In sum, the former ideal of national identity, well captured by the national motto of *e pluribus unum*, has yielded to the
relentless advance of subnational identities, at the expense of the nation as a
cohesive entity.

In addition, national purpose is characterized as rudderless, devoid of both
an unambiguous opponent and a grand strategy. Thus, since the breakup of the
Soviet Union and the socialist bloc of nations, no formation—national or
transnational—has assumed the role of the country's undesirable and hostile
"other": not China, for its dangers are not perceived as immediate; not Iraq, for
it is too insignificant; not Islamic fundamentalism, for it is much too distant and
much too diffuse. Similarly, no interest—national (a public good of concern to
all or most citizens) or vital (calling for a sacrifice in both lives and funds)—has
managed to capture the attention of the country as a whole, although several
have been advanced by the foreign-affairs community.[42] The results of this
vacuum are evident. First, given the lack of a binomial "other," the country has
witnessed a proliferation of *transnational* interests. Diasporism has become the
primary goal of ethnic groups, both recent and established: promoting the interests of their respective homelands. Such interests are characterized as
transnational insofar as such groups, turning from cultural communities within
the country to cultural diasporas across countries, advance the interests not of
the American nation as a whole but rather of other nations. Second, given the
lack of a grand strategy, the country has experienced the spread of *subnational*
interests. Commercialism has emerged as the dominant objective of the government: promoting American exports abroad. Such interests are portrayed as
subnational insofar as they further the interests not of the American public at
large but rather of particular segments thereof. In sum, the former ideal of national purpose has become steadfastly "domesticized," subject to a host of commercial and ethnic interests, at the expense of the nation as a collective entity.

Needless to say, each process of disintegration has only served to hasten and
to deepen the other: the lack of an undesirable and hostile "other" and the de-
mise of national interests have contributed as much to the collapse of a national

---

[42] Huntington (36) lists five such interests proposed by the 1996 Report of the Commission on America's National Interests: attacks with weapons of mass destruction; rise
of hostile hegemons in Europe or Asia; emergence of hostile powers on borders or in
control of the seas; collapse of global systems for trade, markets, energy supplies, or the
environment; collapse of national allies. Of these, he argues, only the first could be seen
as short-term, with the emergence of China as long-term. Thus, he concludes, "it is hard
to see any major looming challenges to the commission's vital interests."

identity as the message of diversity preached by multiculturalism and the dynamic of nonassimilation espoused by present-day immigration have to the collapse of a national purpose. In the end, national identity has been reduced to one of its traditional components—the set of political principles and ideals that make up the "American Creed"—and national purpose to a cacophony of highly specific subnational and transnational interests. For Huntington, such a dénouement does not bode well for the future. In the absence of an underlying common culture, in itself the grounds for any type of overarching common purpose, such a creed may not be able to withstand competing ideologies in the long run and thus may not be able to hold the country together indefinitely. Thus, he concludes, the country may well "join the Soviet Union on the ash heap of history" (35).[43]

The question of what is to be done in the face of such disintegration proves crucial, therefore. From the point of view of national identity, the solution is clear: a nationalizing policy by way of control and assimilation—placing limits on immigration; mounting programs of Americanization; and countering the agenda of multiculturalism. From the point of view of national purpose, the remedy is equally clear: a nationalizing policy by way of restraint—limiting American involvement abroad at this time and thus the use of American resources. Only then will the country be able to respond in the future as a country, with a renewed sense of national cohesion and national collective, in the face of a "combination of security threat and moral challenge" (49).

Concluding Comments. Given the spectrum extrapolated from Zangwill and Schwarz, Huntington belongs within the vision represented by the latter pole, but with a twist. In effect, as an advocate of limits on immigration, Huntington espouses a position that is explicitly rejected by Zangwill and not at all entertained by Schwarz. On this point he is also at complete variance with both Schlesinger, who argues against any curtailment of immigration as contrary to the American soul, and Kennedy, who sees immigration as a continuing and necessary component of an expanding economy and thus as a positive contribution to the country. However, with regard to immigrants already in the country or to come, Huntington does opt for the traditional solution: renewed and vigorous efforts at Americanization. There is no mention here of either a new American creation or of the virtues of new immigrant contributions to the ongoing fusion of Americanism. Indeed, what one finds is sharp disapproval of what the new immigrant groups are doing to the country, both in terms of identity, given their refusal to assimilate and their assertion of ethnicity, and purpose, given

---

[43] A very similar assessment, though with much greater emphasis on both racism against African Americans and discrimination against immigrants, is offered by Bruce D. Porter: "Can American Democracy Survive?," *Commentary* (November 1993), 37-40. Porter advances three scenarios: (a) worst: replacement of the present political system by anarchy and authoritarianism; (b) probable: sharpening internal strains (public alienation from political process; rising racial tensions and unrest; partisan and ideological acrimony; deepening social divisions; campus radicalism; political turmoil); (c) best: solution by way of a foreign diversion: a new enemy.

their development of diasporic communities and espousal of transnational interests. For Huntington, there is only one way of reversing the process of national disintegration already well under way, and that is through a systematic reassertion of national identity, with a particular focus on assimilation to traditional cultural identity. This, of course, is the ideal of Anglo-Americanism, presented without the ironic overtones of Schwarz but with a sense of urgency if not desperation about it. A number of comments are once again in order:

- The story of immigration receives a most irenic treatment. Throughout its long history, a contract between the nation and the newcomers is presented as both operative and accepted, leading to a highly successful process of assimilation. Deviations from this norm receive but brief mention: the process was not as successful with "black people" and, "at times," certain groups, like the Irish, did experience discrimination, but seemingly as a result of the numbers involved. Such a social-contract theory thus leaves aside, for the most part, the other and darker side of the story. It fails to address the material basis for immigration in the first place—the need for plentiful cheap labor in an expanding capitalist economy. It also considerably downplays the opposition to and the travails of immigration—the record of nativist prejudice and discrimination as well as of social exploitation and poverty. Here the narrative of successful assimilation to American culture more than overwhelms the narrative of social conflict in the nation.
- This irenic story presupposes a fairly static notion of culture: a formation forged at the beginning, highly British and highly Protestant in character, and preserved through the 1980s. In the inevitable process of cultural exchange brought about by ongoing immigration, this core formation undergoes renewal but not alteration, although what such renewal entails is not at all pursued. Clearly, however, whatever it does mean does not affect the formation in its essentials, only in its incidentals. As such, the process of cultural exchange envisioned emerges as singularly lopsided: assimilation to the core formation in keeping with an implicit social contract, extended by the nation and accepted by the immigrants. Central to this irenic story, moreover, is the strategic deployment and invocation of a varying "other" that is totally distinct, thoroughly rejected and actively opposed. The preservation of the core formation, therefore, is both driven and facilitated by a strong element of fear. Great pressure, therefore, is put on all immigrants to submit to the established "American" culture—in effect, an annihilation of their own ethnicities, save for the private and local spheres. Even here, however, the irenic character of the process shows through prominently, for immigrants are portrayed as only too willing to do so: the traditional goal has been none other than to become "Americans."
- This operative concept of a core American culture, enduring through time in the face of a changing "other," further presupposes a sense of superiority with regard to other cultures. Consequently, any deviation from the core formation deemed fundamental rather than accidental is looked upon as corrosive and severely frowned upon. Assimilation becomes the supreme

value, with immigrants having little to offer by way of cultural expansion. Indeed, present-day immigration is portrayed as just such a deviation: an undesirable and hostile "other" within the country itself—collapsing national identity into a host of subnational diasporas; forsaking the national purpose in favor of transnational interests; feeding the multicultural strains that have developed from within the country itself. Any attempt to problematize the Anglo-American identity of the country is perceived as subverting both the national identity and the national collective.

To conclude, for Huntington, the present massive migration into the country proves exceedingly worrisome, not so much because of the non-European origins of such immigrants but rather because it puts aside the traditional social contract offered by the nation and opts instead for a foregrounding of ethnicity in every realm—not just the private and the local but also the national and the geopolitical. Consequently, the country stands in near-mortal danger of disintegration—a splintered culture and a fractured purpose, fueled by the phenomenon of multiculturalism and the agenda of commercialism. Only a nationalizing trend can halt any further disintegration, but this calls for a strong program of Americanism, so that new immigrants can join the former arrivals from Europe as co-citizens in the established way of life bequeathed by the early settlers—born-again Anglo-Americans.

DIASPORIC RE-VISIONS

The time has now come for me to inscribe my own critical reflections on "melting" and "dreaming" in America from the perspective of diasporic theology, to offer a re-vision of these core concepts of the national mythology from the standpoint of a first-generation immigrant, a member of the latest migration wave from the non-Western world. As set forth in the introduction to this essay, I characterize my theology of exilic diaspora, forged in the experience and reality of the massive influx from the hispanophone Caribbean and Latin America since the 1960s and thus within the framework of the U.S. Hispanic American community,[44] as one of otherness and mixture—a theology propelled by a two-fold sense of living at once in two worlds and no world, and of expansive and expanding hybridity. I am particularly interested, therefore, in analyzing and critiquing the constructions of otherness and mixture that undergird the national

---

[44] I should point out that my own participation in this influx, which took place in mid-summer of 1961, precedes by a few years the enactment of the Immigration and Naturalization Act of 1965 and the liberalization in immigration policy that resulted from it. In effect, I entered the country with a waiver visa under a policy of admissions of refugees from communist countries (outside the annual quota system and thus in the nonquota category) variously invoked during the years of the Cold War and specifically extended to displaced persons from Cuba (and China) by way of the World Refugee Year Law of 1960.

discourse about melting and dreaming. Such a task I carry out, once again, from within the context of an alienated and marginalized community and with both a vision of a different and better world, a world of freedom and dignity as well as of justice and well-being for all, and a commitment to life in light of that vision.

As point of departure for my reflections, I turn to the overall spectrum proposed from the positions of Israel Zangwill and Benjamin Schwarz, with its opposite poles of new creation and total assimilation respectively.[45] Both positions, I find, are similar to the extent that they call for and entail a surrender of difference in the formation of national identity, though in sharply different ways. In the case of the new-creation model, which Zangwill advances as an ideal desideratum, a new identity is contemplated in which all other identities are fused and no one configuration predominates—a born-again Americanism. In the case of the full-assimilation model, which Schwarz offers as a historical given, a new identity emerges in which one configuration does prevail and to which all other identities must conform—a born-again Anglo-Americanism. At both ends of the spectrum, therefore, a preservation of former identities—with the highly ironic exception of WASP culture in the assimilationist model—is rendered, rhetorically and ideologically, undesirable and unacceptable: quite harshly so in the assimilationist model, where traits of all identities must yield to the traits of one identity in particular; more leniently in the creationist model, where some traits of all identities survive in a new identity.

Yet, I have spoken of a spectrum, and it is the middle range of this spectrum that I find most attractive: neither wholesale assimilation to Anglo-Americanism nor full-scale smelting into Americanism, but a situation of flexible, ongoing, and far-reaching cultural exchange, involving both old and new identities and worlds—a situation in which the principles of otherness and mixture remain operative throughout. I specified in the introduction that my exilic theology of the diaspora was opposed in principle to any agenda of the melting pot, whether external or internal to the group. Any such program I characterized as a dehumanizing universalism in which differences are frowned upon and actively disarticulated. Both the new-creation and the total-assimilation models I regard as variations of such an agenda and thus as objectionable. The model I propose would be along the lines of creative encounters with otherness that result in mixture, a model involving porous and profound cultural exchange among different identities. In such a model a degree of assimilation is inevitable and rewarding, and not only to Anglo-Americanism; a degree of creationism is to be expected and beneficial, as new groups interact with established groups; and a regard for one's past, one's traditional identity and world of origins, is desirable, allowable, and life-giving. Such a model would amount to the creation of a new identity in which any number of sub-identities from both past

---

[45] Such a spectrum could be logically expanded to yield two different poles: total assimilation and total separation, with a middle encompassing variations of intermixture, in itself a spectrum ranging from a position of a new creation to that of thorough biculturalism to that of plural though uneven identity. Given the rarity of the separatist option, however, I opt for this more limited spectrum.

and present cohabit and cofunction—a multifaceted Americanism, the result not of rebirth but of expansion, in which strong similarities as well as evident differences come together in critical dialogue. In such a model differences would be neither bypassed nor submerged but affirmed and emphasized.

From the standpoint of such a model, I should like to re-vision those fundamental questions arising from the review of recent visions of American melting and dreaming, all of which, as I pointed out, subscribe firmly though in varying degrees to the assimilationist model of identity: the story of immigration, the definition of national identity, and the evaluation of national identity.

Story of Immigration

In all three visions of the process, the story of immigration receives a highly favorable treatment: from the irenic reading of Huntington, with its all-too-brief asides regarding the less than successful inclusion of African Americans and the sometime discrimination of other groups; through the economic take of Kennedy, with its stress on relative success over and above undeniable hardship and rejection; to the long-term optic of Schlesinger, with its emphasis on inclusion in the long run despite the foregrounded presence of racism. The immigration story I propose would involve intertwined accommodation and conflict. In this story the elements of opposition, of prejudice and discrimination, of travail, of poverty and exploitation, must be highlighted at all times. In this story the elements of success—of struggle, survival, and integration—must be foregrounded as well. In such a story neither the narrative of social conflict nor the narrative of social accommodation must be allowed to overwhelm the other; both narratives must be kept side by side at all times.

Such re-visioning of the immigration story grows out of my experience and reality as a diasporic immigrant from Latin America and the Caribbean and a first-generation member of the U.S. Hispanic-American community. In the introduction I portrayed this community—in itself encompassing a number of long-established groups, many of whom did not come into the country but were rather taken over by the country, as well as a host of recent arrivals—in the same general terms, regardless of length of time in the country: on the one hand, with respect to external perception, as an inferior people, uncivilized and unenlightened; on the other hand, with regard to internal conditions, as a people marginalized and disadvantaged. From such a standpoint, I approach the issue of immigration as follows: on the one hand, this is a community for which social conflict constitutes very much of a present reality—a community affected by poverty and exploitation and/or subject to prejudice and discrimination; on the other hand, this is also a community that, despite such odds, struggles for social accommodation—for survival and integration in a spirit of liberation. From such a standpoint, a quasi-idyllic reading of the immigration process à la Huntington seems unreal if not ludicrous; an economic reading à la Kennedy comes across as on target, while its judgment of relative success proves hardly comforting if not too benign; and a long-range reading of inclusion à la Schlesinger appears as less than reassuring if not utopian, though its pointed acknowledgment of dominant racism and concomitant call for conversion are most welcome. For me, therefore, the story of immigration, whether in the present or in the past, emerges as a twisted story, a story of ever-interweaving accommodation and conflict, of great hopes and great frustrations, of depression and determination.

National Identity

In all three visions the definition of national identity reveals a definite essentialism, static as well as narrow, not surprisingly in light of the pronounced tilt toward a narrative of accommodation in the story of immigration. This essentialism ranges from the unnuanced in Kennedy and Huntington, where "American" identity is taken as set before the migration waves of the nineteenth century and where immigrants integrate themselves into such identity in ready if not eager fashion, at least in the public sphere, to the subtle in Schlesinger, where "American" identity exhibits a three-tiered formation, with an essential core in place prior to the great migrations and with accidental layers forming around this core as a result of these migrations. For all three visions, therefore, at the heart of national identity lies "Anglo-Americanism." The concept of national identity I propose would be more pragmatic. In this vision "American" identity would possess no essential ethnic core as such but would be the result of flexible and ongoing cultural exchange among the various groups, yielding a broad range of variations involving old and new identities. In this scenario the impact of Anglo-Americanism would not be denied or rejected, but it would not be claimed as either the center or the sine qua non of national identity for all.

This re-visioning of national identity again emerges from my own standing as a first-generation member of the U.S. Hispanic-American community and a diasporic immigrant from Latin America and the Caribbean. In the introduction I depicted this community—in itself comprising a wealth of sociocultural, sociopolitical, and socioreligious variations—as a community with many faces, many histories, and many stories of God and world. From such a standpoint, I approach the issue of identity as follows: First of all, this is a community for which such differences prove neither debilitating nor threatening but a fact of life to be acknowledged and appropriated and in which the different groups engage in cultural exchange with one another and, in so doing, give birth to an ongoing and flexible sense of identity. Thus, the earlier groups in the country, such as Mexican Americans in the Southwest or Puerto Ricans in the Northeast, do not insist on assimilation to their own social formations by newcomers from the Americas. Second, this is a community that is quite aware of the fact that its own ancestors formed part of what would eventually become the United States long before the English settlements in Virginia and New England and yet remain out-of-sight in the construction of national identity. Finally, this is a community for which further cultural exchange with other groups within the context of the United States presents no fundamental problem but rather the continuation of a longstanding process of hybridity. From such a standpoint, the affirmation of an indispensable core à la Kennedy or Huntington despite the reality of cultural exchange becomes a flight of imagination, if not a denial of everyday life, while the proposal of an essential core with surrounding accidental layers à la Schlesinger appears as quite fragile in the end, if indeed not a measure of last resort, despite the admiration for the sense of mixture introduced into the discussion. For me, therefore, the question of national identity emerges, whether in the present or in the past, as a construction ever in the making, yielding a range of variations from the first.

National Evaluation

In all three visions the evaluation of national identity is thoroughly chauvinistic, not surprising given the insistence on a particular ethnic dimension, Anglo-Americanism, as the heart of "American" identity. This sense of superiority can be readily traced from Huntington, with his view of any deviation from the original formation as subverting the national collective and of unassimilated immigrants as "others" dangerous to national cohesiveness; through Kennedy, with his view of immigrants as necessary for the national economy but only by way of integration into the original formation; to Schlesinger, with his view of the unique character of the essential core and his argument for the preservation of the three-tiered structure of identity as is. Clearly, for all three visions the Anglo-American heart of "American" identity must be preserved at all cost, qua superior. The attitude toward national identity I propose would be more self-critical. In such a vision all formations of "American" identity would be subject to critique in terms of inclusion and exclusion, including any proposal for a particular formation as heart or core of such identity. In this scenario the purportedly unique value of Anglo-Americanism could not be simply presupposed but would have to be closely examined.

Such re-visioning of national evaluation is once again framed from within the context of my own status as a diasporic immigrant from Latin America and the Caribbean and a first-generation member of the U.S. Hispanic-American community. In the introduction I referred to this community—in itself embodying profound hybridity, given its roots in Europe, both Mediterranean and Catholic as well as Nordic and Protestant, as well as in indigenous America and transplanted Africa, with additional and important touches from Asia—as in cultural shock, a community for which the expectations of a "promised land" brought a number of unexpected surprises: a somber side in both material and moral terms; a realization of the uncivilized and unenlightened policies followed with regard to their countries of origins; and a system of ethnic-racial stratification with a set of unwelcome outsiders and strangers. From such a standpoint I approach the question of national evaluation as follows: this is a community for which "American" identity must make room—at every step of the way—not only for its own presence in the country but also for that of Native Americans, African Americans, and Asian Americans; a community for which the heritage of Anglo-Americanism must be weighed as a whole, not only in the light of the American Creed but also of the genocide and displacement of Native Americans, the slavery and segregation of African Americans, and the rejection and discrimination of

Hispanic Americans and Asian Americans; and a community for which the opposition of willing integration into national life and purpose on the part of earlier non-Anglo Euro-American arrivals vis-à-vis resistant turning to subnational
and transnational interests on the part of recent non-Western immigrants needs
to be thoroughly challenged. From such a standpoint, Huntington's evaluation
of present-day immigrants as a hostile and subversive "other," a dagger at the
heart of the country, comes across as patrician disdain, if not unwitting racism—why should the concerns and interests of the new groups be classified as
transnational rather than national, and, for that matter, who decides what is in
the national interest?; Kennedy's view of a developing Mexican-American Quebec in the American Southwest as a fundamental threat to national life and
culture appears as ethnic blindness, if not unintentional baiting—why should
residents of Mexican descent not develop the same attitude toward their country
of origin as those of English descent did?; and Schlesinger's view of an ever-
expanding new race by way of the outer layers stands, despite its laudable openness, as indefensible, if not contradictory—why should a "center" with such
acknowledged fundamental racism be preserved rather than radically redefined
or decentered? For me, therefore, the issue of evaluation emerges, from beginning to finish, as a mangled project—a project of lofty claims and infamous
practices: global superiority alongside vicious racism; unmatched uniqueness
alongside barbarous commonality; universal inclusion alongside pointed exclusion.

Diasporic Visions

Given the preceding re-visions of immigration story, national identity, and
national evaluation, I should like to conclude with a re-vision of the national
future. All three recent visions of American melting and dreaming coincide on
the need for heightened Americanization, not surprising given their assessments
of the present state of affairs in the country in the light of the most recent influx
of immigrants from the non-Western world. Such Americanization calls for thorough assimilation to the way, the life and culture, of the nation—whether conceived along the lines of an Anglo-American essential core and a Euro-American inner layer, as in the case of Schlesinger; an Anglo-American original
formation involving both cultural and political dimensions, as with Huntington;
or an Anglo-American original way of life, as in the case of Kennedy. Without
such a revived program of Americanization, the country is said to stand in peril—
if not of disintegration, certainly of polarization across its many tectonic faults.
Here Schlesinger proves the most optimistic of the three, but only because he
sees the new immigrants as only too ready to be Americanized, to be reborn as
Anglo- and Euro-Americans.

I offer a less restrictive and more optimistic view of the national future. To
begin with, the process of Americanization is not at all in question; it is, rather,
inevitable. From the point of view of cultural exchange, newcomers will, regardless of intention and praxis, follow and appropriate, sooner or later, many
features and traits of those already in the country. Regardless of origins, the

new immigrants will never remain what they were. In addition, the process of Americanization stands in need of a broader conceptualization and formulation. From the point of view of cultural exchange, the presence of Anglo- and Euro-Americans cannot be denied, but neither can that of any other grouping, whether indigenous, long-established, or recently settled. Regardless of origins, the new arrivals will interact with all such formations of American identity. Finally, the process of Americanization is by no means unidirectional; it goes both ways. From the point of cultural exchange, the new immigrants will affect those already in the country as much as they themselves will be affected. Regardless of origins, the new immigrants will have enormous impact upon all existing formations of "America." What this vision offers by way of national future is openness to otherness and dynamic mixture—an ever-evolving America.

In the introduction I described the U.S. Hispanic-American community as having a memory of the political realm at its worst and a hope for the body politic at its best. I further explained that my exilic theology of the diaspora involved a renunciation of any and all claims to national election (a "chosen people"), national promise (a "promised land"), and national mission (a "light to the nations"). The re-vision of the national future advanced above is in keeping with such guiding principles. The model of an ever-evolving America is not dependent on an idyllic or unproblematic story of immigration, a strictly tiered concept of identity, or a glorification of such identity. It is rooted rather in a twisted story of accommodation and conflict, ever-present and ever-expanding hybridity, and a mangled project of exalted principles and despicable behavior. Such a model of "America" is a construction-in-the-making, where the principles of freedom and dignity as well as justice and well-being—the traditional values of the American Creed and the aspirations of most human beings—must prevail *for the benefit of all*. Such an "America" requires a manifest destiny with a twist: not a narrative of melting and dreaming of all things but a narrative of mixing and a dream of liberation.

Conclusion

On Unfinished Dreams, Defiant Hopes, and Historical Projects

ELEAZAR S. FERNANDEZ

It took longer than I expected for our project to be given birth. There were times when I thought that it had lived up to its title, "A Dream Unfinished." At last, a testament of our collaborative effort has come to its final shape. Our book project is no longer an unfinished dream but a completed volume. Book projects such as ours, although they take time to unfold, usually come to completion. As a project, it is finished, and I, as a co-editor, am proud to have it released to the world of readers.

UNFINISHED DREAMS AND THE RISE
OF THE FORCES OF CLOSURE

Yes, our collaborative book project is finished, but I do not have the slightest illusion that the dreams of racial minorities in "the land of the free and the home of the brave" are finally finished. Our collaborative project is finished, but the dreams of people of color in the United States remain unfinished. To say otherwise is to betray their actual plight and aspirations. The essays in this volume, in fact, testify to the unfinished dreams as well as to the turning of dreams into nightmares. Many Americans can say with Malcolm X: "The American dream looks like a nightmare to me."[1]

When we look at events from a certain angle, we can say that significant breakthroughs have been made in society at large. Ethnic and racial minorities are not only surviving, many of them are also thriving, even in the face of major obstacles. Significant legislation has been passed to improve their status and situation. Some racial minorities have broken the glass ceiling, and their "success" stories have been told. These "success" stories have been given media attention

---

[1] Malcolm X, *The Autobiography of Malcolm X as Told by Alex Haley* (New York: Ballantine Books, 1964), 281.

as a way of saying that the system really works for all, regardless of color, religion, gender, sexual orientation, and so forth.

On the other hand, the gains that we can lift up are not unambiguous. For every inch of progress made, new forms of forces of closure appear that are more sophisticated or new realizations happen that offset such progress, so that progress, it seems to me, has only occurred against the measure of older forms. While every inch of victory needs to be celebrated to sustain us in the long and arduous journey, self-satisfaction can be self-delusion. Gloria Yamato's comment about racism can be applied to other forms of systemic evils as well: "Like a virus, it's hard to beat racism, because by the time you come up with a cure, it's mutated to a 'new cure-resistant' form. One shot just won't get it."[2] Francis Garchitonera's words can also be appropriate here: "If you build a better mousetrap today, it doesn't mean you'll have fewer [mice] tomorrow. What you will have [are] smarter mice."[3]

The virus has not only become cure-resistant and smarter, but it is fighting back with renewed strength and greater ferocity, both subtle and brazen. It does not require much careful scrutiny to observe that there has been an increasing momentum toward what has been called a "postmodernism of reaction."[4] I am referring in particular to those who are determined to turn the clock back in order to stay in the comfort of their old beliefs. Postmodernists of reaction are determined to frustrate the dreams of racial minorities as well as the dreams of all who care for a just and democratic society.

We see the rise of postmodernism of reaction not only in the realm of public rhetoric but also in a variety of legislative projects as well as in the rise of hate crimes and police brutality against minorities. *Filipinas* magazine calls the year 1999 "a bloody year for Asian Americans." Within the span of twelve months, five were brutally murdered by white supremacists.[5] One of these five victims was Joseph Ileto, a Filipino American, into whom white supremacist Buford Furrow pumped nine bullets on August 10, 1999. In his essay on Ileto, Emil Guillermo painfully reminds us that "hate and ignorance die hard in the land of the free."[6]

The pervasiveness of the forces of closure and their power to fight back prevent me from thinking about history in a linear fashion as a history of progress. I continue to long and struggle for a better tomorrow, not because I stick to the comfortable notion of linear progress or because of assurances of eventual victory, but rather as a wager of hope.[7] There is more to learn from Michel

---

[2] G. Yamato, "Something about the Subject Makes It Hard to Name," in *Experiencing Race, Class, and Gender in the United States*, ed. V. Cyrus (California, London, and Toronto: Mayfield Publishing Company, 1993), 207.

[3] F. Garchitonera, presiding justice of the Sandigan Bayan of the Philippines (antigraft court), on curbing corruption within the government, in *Filipinas* (August 1998): 37.

[4] See H. Foster, ed., *The Anti-Aesthetic: Essays on Postmodern Culture* (Port Townsend, Wash.: Bay Press, 1983).

[5] B. Eljera, "A Bloody Year for Asian Americans," *Filipinas* (October 1999): 19.

[6] E. Guillermo, "What Joseph Ileto Stands For," *Filipinas* (October 1999): 32.

[7] S. Welch, *Sweet Dreams in America: Making Ethics and Spirituality Work* (New York: Routledge, 1999), xi, xvi.

Foucault's perceptive analysis of the microphysics of power, to be sure, but I have chosen to name my stance hopeful realism, rather than follow along the lines of his stance of "hyper and pessimistic activism."[8]

UNFINISHED DREAM AS A THEOLOGICAL
AND POLITICAL STANCE

Indeed, the virus of hate and the instruments of marginalization die hard in "the land of the free and the home of the brave." This is a sobering fact that we cannot simply wish away with a magic wand; we have to name it no matter how painful and agonizing. Are we condemned to this plight? Is this our "manifest destiny"? Or, is our "*new* manifest destiny" to struggle and make our dreams a reality?[9] Contributors to this anthology have chosen the latter path.

History Is Not Closed: God Is Not Finished Yet

It is easy to fall into cynicism and despair and to give up the America of our dreams. Cynical realism or hedonistic carnivalism is the more logical outcome in the face of the pervasiveness of the forces of closure or the culture of death. However, the contributors to this volume have chosen a different posture: they have not given up the America of their dreams. To speak of unfinished dreams is not simply to state a painful fact of history, it is also to say no to those who want to give a closure to history. It is to state an ontological belief that history is open. It is a refusal to let the forces of closure in whatever circumstances have the final word. Of course, we can allow the forces of closure to have the final word. But we can choose, and I say we must choose, not to let these forces claim the final word in the way we live our lives.

At this point I am reminded of the debate between Walter Benjamin and Frank Horkheimer, both of the Frankfurt School of Philosophy, in 1937. Horkheimer, out of his historical materialist position, argued that any notion of an unclosed past and an open future is idealistic. He stated, "What happened to those human beings who have perished does not have any part in the future. They will never be called forth to be blessed in eternity."[10] Horkheimer thus operated on the presupposition of a closed history. In contrast, Benjamin wanted to work out a notion of history that does not ignore our unity in history with past generations, especially those who were crucified by the idolatrous forces. He refused to see history as closed and finished. For him, the work of the past is not

---

[8] M. Foucault, "On Genealogy of Ethics: An Overview of Work in Progress," in *Foucault Reader*, ed. Paul Rabinow (New York: Pantheon Books, 1984), 343.

[9] See F. F. Segovia, "Aliens in the Promised Land: The Manifest Destiny of U.S. Hispanic American Theology," in *Hispanic/Latino Theology: Challenge and Promise*, ed. A. M. Isasi-Díaz and F. F. Segovia (Minneapolis, Minn.: Fortress Press, 1996), 30.

[10] As cited in H. Peukert, *Science, Action, and Fundamental Theology: Towards a Theology of Communicative Action* (Boston: MIT Press, 1984), 206; see also D. Lane, *Keeping Hope Alive: Stirrings in Christian Theology* (Mahwah, N.J.: Paulist Press, 1996), 119-23, 200-210.

closed, not even to a historical materialist. He believed that we can keep past history open and unclosed. In response to Horkheimer, Benjamin argued that the corrective for the idea that history is closed "lies in the reflection that history is . . . a form of emphatic memory *(Eingedenken)*. What science has 'settled,' emphatic memory can modify."[11] Furthermore, emphatic memory gives us an experience that "prohibits us from conceiving history completely non-theologically" or "forbids us to regard history completely without theology."[12] Emphatic memory helps us to read history theologically.

I am in agreement with the main direction of Benjamin's ideas, but I would like to reverse his order. Reading history theologically demands emphatic memory. One cannot do authentic theology without embracing the spirit of emphatic memory, especially if the sufferings of the victims are not to be in vain. Emphatic memory or the hermeneutics of remembrance (hermeneutics of retrieval) opens up the past and reconnects the living with the dead. The history of suffering is not closed; it is open to us through emphatic memory or through remembrance. Through our emphatic memories we open the past to establish our solidarity with those who have gone before us. This is what Christian Lenhardt calls "anamnestic solidarity."[13] But we do so because we believe that the future is open. When emphatic memory or remembrance opens up the past and our solidarity with the dead, it also opens up the future. The past is opened not only for its own sake but also in relation to the future. Those who have gone before us have a future, and this future is tied to our acts of remembrance and solidarity.

As people of faith and as theologians, however, we do not stop with the declaration that history is open. History is open, but the belief that history is open cannot survive the onslaught of the forces of death unless it is rooted in the more fundamental belief that God is not yet finished with history. More pointedly, history is open because God is not finished with history. To use a religious idiom of the black church in North America: "God ain't finished with us yet!"[14] God's act of creation is continuing still. The fate of the victims is not sealed in the graveyard, and those who have suffered have not suffered in vain.

Naming the Unfinished Dreams: Ultimate Defiance and Hopeful Realism

It is upon the conviction that God is not yet finished that I lament and speak of unfinished dreams, and it is upon this conviction that I find the reason for our hope. Contributors to this volume have resolved to name the unfinished dreams, not only because they cannot be hidden anymore but also as a testimony of

---

[11] As cited in Peukert, *Science, Action, and Fundamental Theology*, 207.

[12] Ibid. See also Lane, *Keeping Hope Alive*, 202, quoting Rolf Tiedemann, "Historical Materialism, . . . " *The Philosophical Forum* 15 (Fall-Winter 1983-84): 79.

[13] As cited in Peukert, *Science, Action, and Fundamental Theology*, 208; see C. Lenhardt, "Anamnestic Solidarity: The Proletariat and its *Manes*," *Telos* 25 (1975): 133-155.

[14] E. Oglesby, *Born in the Fire: Case Studies in Christian Ethics and Globalization* (New York: The Pilgrim Press, 1990), viii.

defiance and hope. The unfinished dreams and nightmares must be named, if we are to take full account of our defiant hope and vision. We have to bite the bitter pill of the durability and pervasiveness of the forces of closure, says Derrick Bell, not as a sign of submission but as a sign of "ultimate defiance."[15]

I know that it is hard to live in hope when we are overwhelmed with events that continue to test our hopes. But paradoxes happen, and they happen still, for when our experience seems to be at its bleakest, hope sprouts and blooms. We see this in communities of racial and ethnic minorities that have dared to hope amid terrible situations and in individuals whose lives show that they are prisoners of hope. We, too, can help cultivate this hope in our place and in our time. "Because we don't bring this true hope with us from birth and because our experience of life may perhaps make us wise but not necessarily hopeful," says Jürgen Moltmann, "we have to *go out* to learn hope. We learn to love when we say yes to life. So we learn to hope when we say yes to the future."[16]

If Moltmann can say that we learn to hope when we say yes to the future, I believe it is equally fitting to say that we can learn to hope when we say yes to life. When we love life, we cannot help but be prisoners of hope. Loving life necessitates that we give ourselves to the radical demands of hope. This hope demands, for the sake of life, that we give up neither hope nor the courage to act on that hope.

Unfinished Dreams, Eschatological Imagination, and Vision

Suffering and marginalization may give birth to cynicism and fatalism, but they can also propel eschatological imagination and vision. To speak of unfinished dreams is not simply to denounce that which is not right, but also to announce or to open up our imagination to alternative possibilities that are not simply given by the logic of the present. These two dimensions are inextricably interwoven. The denunciation of the "what is" propels the annunciation of the "what might be," and the annunciation of the "what might be" propels the denunciation of the "what is." Eschatological imagination is a protest, following Dermot Lane, "against the premature closure of our understanding of the present and a plea for openness towards the future."[17]

Perhaps, to the dismay of those who expect grand solutions from the marginalized, contributors to this volume, as it will be obvious to the readers, do not have a grand utopian blueprint for an alternative tomorrow, and I do not know of any one of them who is attempting to develop one. If utopia means an ideal community to which we can point where a new world is already realized, then we do not have a utopian vision or a grand utopian blueprint. But we can have an "atopia," following Sallie McFague, which is "an imagined world both

---

[15] D. Bell, *Faces at the Bottom of the Well: The Permanence of Racism* (New York: Basic Books, 1992), 14.

[16] J. Moltmann, *The Source of Life: The Holy Spirit and the Theology of Life* (Minneapolis, Minn.: Fortress Press, 1997), 39.

[17] Lane, *Keeping Hope Alive*, 2.

prophetic and alluring from which we can judge what is wrong with the paradigm that has created the present crisis on our planet."[18]

This atopian thinking or eschatological imagination does not come simply by striking a magic wand or with the help of some supernatural genie in a lamp. Nor does it come simply by sitting and imagining a better world in some meditation center. The cultural creativity that R. B. J. Walker speaks about applies to eschatological imagination:

> The challenge of cultural creativity is not only a matter of creating visions of a better world but of reconstructing the conditions under which the future may be imagined. Cultural creativity does not occur in abstraction. It arises from concrete everyday practices, from people able to make connections with each other and engaging in dialogue about the meaning of their experiences.[19]

Eschatological imagination names the unfinished dreams of a people and longs for an alternative tomorrow. It comes out of the experience and reflection of liminality and of being at the interstices.[20] The experience of liminality or in-betweenness on the part of ethnic and racial minorities has spawned eschatological imagination and vision. Our experience of living in different worlds has convinced us that we can live differently, and the exploration of this different way of dwelling constitutes our common search and struggle. The essays in this volume testify, in varied ways, to the common longings of racial minorities for a new and better tomorrow.

To be sure, our longings for a new and better world are informed by our particular experiences and perspectives, but particularity is not identical with exclusivism. In fact, the awareness that we people of color have of our particular perspectives and experiences of being excluded propels us to enlarge our dreams and visions. If America, for people of color, is still an unfinished dream, it also is an unfinished dream for white America—and for all Americans! A full flowering of racial colors is our vision for all. We can discern this vision in various theological motifs such as Pentecost and the eucharist. Pentecost is not Babel. Pentecost points to a society in which various cultures and race celebrate and honor their differences. This colorful future is not a mere pluralism or a multicolored world, but a world in which image representations, difference, and power dynamics are taken into serious account.

Unfinished Dreams: Remembering the Dis-membered

It may seem that hoping is only associated with the future and memory with the past. This is not exactly true. In fact, those who are impassioned by

---

[18] S. McFague, *The Body of God: An Ecological Theology* (Minneapolis, Minn.: Fortress Press, 1993), 198.

[19] R. B. J. Walker, *One World, Many Worlds: Struggles for a Just World Peace* (London: Zen Books Limited; Boulder: Lynne Reinner Publishers, 1988), 169.

[20] See J. Young Lee, *Marginality: The Key to Multicultural Theology* (Minneapolis, Minn.: Fortress Press, 1995), 152-53.

eschatological imagination are also those who are deeply immersed in the memories of the past, specifically painful memories that wounded the community. Those who hope and envision a better world are also those who have not forgotten or lost the sense of memory. Thus, Fumitaka Matsuoka can speak of "visionary memory," a vision that is propelled by the retrieval of the painful memories.[21]

The point I raise here resonates with the ideas of Benjamin noted earlier, but there is a specific twist to this act of remembrance that gives it a sharp edge. Opening up and rereading the past involves, for Benjamin, a reading of history against the grain. By this he means that we need to reread the past from the perspectives of the victims, what contemporary theologians refer to as dangerous memories. To speak of unfinished dreams is to affirm our solidarity with the victims of previous generations and to declare to the world that their memories are not forgotten.

The powers-that-be of any society will do everything within their means and might to make marginalized communities lose their memories as an effective way of controlling them. Yet the dangerous memories must not be forgotten; they must be exhumed. Janice Mirikitani exhumes the painful past of former Japanese-American internment camp victims through a poem that gives voice to the experience of her own mother. When told by the hearing commissioner that her time was up, her mother (through Mirikitani's prophetic poetry) protested:

> So when you tell me my time is up,
> I tell you this:
> Pride has kept my lips
> pinned by nails,
> my rage coffined.
> But I exhume my past
> to claim this time.[22]

To exhume the past—this is the challenge that Mirikitani poses for us, for there is no visionary memory that forgets the pains of the past. To forgive and move forward is not to forget. Rather, it is to re-member the dis-membered; it is to make whole those who have experienced brokenness.

This discourse on unfinished dreams not only names the pains of the present but also names the past memories of unfinished dreams in order to carry them forward to the future. What was buried is exhumed not simply for its own sake, for there is no joy in exhuming the unfinished dreams of the previous generations as such. The buried is exhumed because it is necessary in forging a new and better tomorrow.

---

[21] F. Matsuoka, *Out of Silence: Emerging Themes in Asian American Churches* (Cleveland, Ohio: United Church Press, 1995), 117.

[22] J. Mirikitani, *Shedding Silence: Poetry and Prose* (Berkeley, Calif.: Celestial Arts, 1987), 35.

Unfinished Dreams: Living between Memory and Hope

If the discourse on unfinished dreams is one of memory *and* hope, then it is neither memory on the one hand nor hope on the other. Rather, and more appropriately, to speak of unfinished dreams is to live between memory and hope or to live in the tension of memory and hope. Living between memory and hope is living in the betwixt and between. It is not a life thrown into an either-or situation, but one that is both this and that, as well as moving beyond.[23]

Living between memory and hope is a life laden with pain, but it is also a creative and grace-filled life. It goes against the grain to talk of celebration when speaking of unfinished dreams. Yet, it is not solely a note of lament or of hope, but also a call to celebration. Daring to say that something is not yet finished is itself a manifestation that the power of the longed-for-but-not-yet is already experienced in the present in the form of a foretaste. In a situation of marginalization, struggle itself is an experience of liberation. And, if we are to sustain ourselves in the long and arduous journey, every inch of victory must be celebrated in anticipation of that which is yet to come. As Virgilio Elizondo puts it: "The prophetic without the festive turns into cynicism and bitterness, or simply fades away. On the other hand, the festive without the prophetic can easily turn into empty rituals or even degenerate into drunken brawls."[24]

As one who is fully aware that the fulfillment of our dreams is not to arrive soon, when I speak of unfinished dreams I am naming a mode of living in which the journey is understood as constitutive of the destination. Too often we think of the process as a means to an end or of the journey as a means of getting to the destination. Too often we think of action not as an experience to be lived for its own sake but as a means to a greater end. But there is something terribly amiss with this notion: it fails to realize that the process itself is constitutive of the goal, as the journey is constitutive of the destination. To put it differently, the destination is already in the journey. Or, to use the words of Nelle Morton, "the journey is home."[25]

Finding a home in our journey is liberating; it is healing. It liberates us from the dead weight of the past and from making our goal or destination a procrustean bed that crunches us into its image, that makes us oblivious to the greatness of the most banal and momentary. When our destination becomes a procrustean bed that prevents us from seeing that our destination is already embedded in the journey, as the flower in the bud, the spring in the freezing winter, or the butterfly in the chrysalis, we experience a great loss—the loss of not seeing greatness in the banal, the eternal in the momentary, the world in a grain of sand.

---

[23] P. C. Phan, "Betwixt and Between: Doing Theology with Memory and Imagination," in *Journeys at the Margin: Toward an Autobiographical Theology in American-Asian Perspective*, ed. Peter C. Phan and Jung Young Lee (Collegeville, Minn.: Liturgical Press, 1999), 113.

[24] V. Elizondo, *Galilean Journey: The Mexican-American Promise* (Maryknoll, N.Y.: Orbis Books, 1983), 120.

[25] N. Morton, *The Journey Is Home* (Boston: Beacon Press, 1985).

Celebrations of some points in the journey are nourishing, but, more than this, the journey is home. Yes, the journey must be celebrated as home, and we must consider it home, because in our historical existence the future that we desire is always given to us in the form of promise. We do not have the foresight to predict the final endtime of our journey, much as we ache to know, for that is not accessible to us. Our calling is to do the best that we can and to live fully in our time. I hesitate to say that these times are more challenging than other periods of history, but they are *our* times and *our* challenge.

Underrepresented minority scholars in the United States are finding a home in their journey, a journey characterized by dreaming and struggling. "My journey is not over yet," says Andrew Sung Park, "but I am at home; for home is everywhere God is and I am. And home is not only the place to relax, but also the place to struggle, challenge and grow."[26] Park's point resonates with Fernando Segovia's notion of "alien" but becoming "strangers no longer." Speaking from a U.S. Hispanic-American perspective, Segovia states that there is no doubt that we will continue to remain aliens, but "we have ceased to behave as aliens, keeping our place and struggling in silence; instead, we have embraced our place as aliens, found our voice as aliens, and lifted that voice up as aliens."[27]

Unfinished Dreams: Waiting in Hope

Without hope, one cannot truly wait. Only those who hope can truly wait. Robert McAfee Brown calls this kind of waiting a waiting in hope—in contrast to waiting casually, waiting in doubt, and waiting in dread.[28] Those who wait in hope are not just expecting something external to themselves that is to come. Those who wait are already being grasped by this hope as they wait.[29]

Waiting in hope is not the kind of casual waiting we commonly think of, nor is it an aimless and idle waiting, much less a waiting in dread. The waiting that is generated by a deep sense of hope is an active waiting—not just for the sake of letting the time pass quickly or breaking the boredom of waiting, but rather in anticipation of that which one awaits. The activity that is generated by waiting in hope consists not in killing time but in redeeming the in-between time or the time being from being just another time. Waiting in hope redeems and gives significance to the time being. This time being, for those who wait in hope, is not to be written off or to be grimly avoided, but to be embraced as an occasion for faithful living. The time being is our time, a precious and momentous time, a time to be reclaimed for creative and active living.

It amazes and humbles me to be in touch with the lives of people, who, when there is no other choice but to wait, have responded to the situation creatively in

---

[26] A. Sung Park, "Church and Theology: My Theological Journey," in Phan and Young Lee, *Journeys at the Margin*, 172.

[27] Segovia, "Aliens in the Promised Land," 30.

[28] R. McAfee Brown, *Persuade Us to Rejoice: The Liberating Power of Fiction* (Louisville, Ky.: Westminster John Knox Press, 1992), 41-52.

[29] P. Tillich, *The Shaking of the Foundations* (London: SCM Press, 1949), 152.

order to transform the given situation. Marginalized races in the United States have waited and have been told to wait for decades. Instead of being reduced to cynicism, they have produced a waiting that is transformative. There is no denial that this waiting is forced upon them, with no choice except to wait in order to survive, but they have reclaimed this waiting as a strength, as a waiting that creatively transforms the situation.

I am reminded of a cartoon that appeared in South Africa around the time of its first national election, upon the collapse of the apartheid regime. It depicted a white person complaining that he had been waiting for thirty minutes in the polling place, while a black person responded that he had been waiting decades. When I speak of unfinished dreams, I refer to this type of creative and active waiting. To dare say that something is unfinished is to wait actively. I am aware that it is difficult to wait for a long time and stay awake. Like Jesus' disciples who could not stay awake while in Gethsemane during his final hours (Mk 14:32-38), there is also a temptation to sleep while waiting. Staying awake is a struggle; to struggle is to stay awake. Giving voice to the unfinished dreams is a form of keeping us awake while we continue to wait.

CHILDREN OF UNFINISHED DREAMS, CHILDREN OF PROMISE: AGENCY AND COLLABORATIVE PROJECTS

Children of unfinished dreams and children of promise, this is how I would name racial minorities in the United States in general and the contributors to this volume in particular. Our presence in "the land of the free and the home of the brave" can be attributed to different factors. Many came as immigrants from other lands, others due to slave trades and as refugees, and some found their lands engulfed by U.S. expansionism, which began in 1810.[30] Whatever the circumstances, historical events have led us into the belly of the empire, and so began our common plight—a plight of unfinished dreams and continuing struggle.

Living in the belly of the empire has given us the privilege of sharing the cornucopia of blessings from our new place, but these blessings do not make us oblivious of our being insiders-outsiders. The dominant group constantly reminds us of this. Realizing that the current social arrangement is not eternal and that it belongs to the realm of the alterable, we have committed ourselves to the task of making our dreams come true. We have given a voice to our unfinished dreams and have accepted the challenge of active agency. We are aware that some racial minorities have broken through the glass ceiling of corporate America, but this is only because others have broken their silence and have let loose their stammering tongues. We are grateful to these monuments of the past, especially for those who have paved the way for us, but true gratefulness happens when we transform the monuments of the past into movements of

---

[30] J. González, *Mañana: Christian Theology from a Hispanic Perspective* (Nashville, Tenn.: Abingdon Press, 1990), 31.

today—movements of transformation and movements that weave together our scattered voices and visions.

So, we, the contributors to this volume, have woven together our multiple voices with the hope of creating a chorus of voices. We have woven together our voices because it is only in so doing that we gain the power to challenge hegemonic discourses and practices. Putting together a collaborative book project is only a small dimension of our common struggle. Nonetheless, it is a significant undertaking, especially since it brings together voices from various racial minorities.

Moreover, such a collaborative project is especially significant when we think of the distinctive pressures that minority scholars have to undergo in the predominantly white academic institutions. Struggling to survive in the academy is more than enough to sap one's energies. Isolation, especially if the presence of a minority scholar in an institution is only a token, contributes to the situation. If we are not only to survive but also to thrive, we minority scholars must be engaged in a "conspiracy," that is, to "breathe together" as we seek to expand breathing spaces not only for people of color but for people of all stripes.[31] Being able to put a collaborative project together is an indication that we have moved beyond the survival stage of our academic careers.

Much remains, however, to be done in collaborative ventures, and I look forward to more such ventures among minority scholars. A poem written by a Taiwanese girl, entitled "Sleep My Child," speaks deeply of a resolute hope and a commitment to forge a better tomorrow in our trying times:

> To bed now, my child!
> It is already very late.
> Tomorrow, we still have work to do,
> Tomorrow, we still have to go to school.
>
> Child! Why are you not yet asleep?
> I know:
> You still have much to say.
> I know:
> You still have many things you want to do.
>
> But,
> Tomorrow . . .
> I know when you all grow up,
> You will surely know what it is that I want to say.
> Sleep then, my child![32]

---

[31] D. Messer, *Conspiracy of Goodness: Contemporary Images of Christian Mission* (Nashville, Tenn.: Abingdon Press, 1992), 148.

[32] Lin Lin, "Sleep My Child," in *Li Poetry Magazine* 93: 43, cited in C. S. Song, *Theology from the Womb of Asia* (Maryknoll, N.Y.: Orbis Books, 1986), 106-7.

What is tomorrow in the heart of a girl? Small or big, she believes that there is a tomorrow and that there must be a tomorrow. But this tomorrow does not come by itself. The mother in the poem reminds her child of the work that must be carried out. Blessed are those who dream dreams, but we also need blessed people who are willing to help make our common dreams come true. I bring this project to a close knowing full well that "tomorrow, we still have work to do." Indeed, tomorrow's work is waiting, for our dreams are still unfinished. May this work inspire us to engage in more collaborative and transformative projects in the years to come.

Contributors

Victor Anderson
The Divinity School, Vanderbilt Univ.
Nashville, Tennessee

Miguel A. De La Torre
Hope College
Hope, Michigan

Eleazar S. Fernandez
United Theological Seminary of the
    Twin Cities
Minneapolis, Minnesota

Diana L. Hayes
Theology Department, Georgetown
    Univ.
Washington, D.C.

Dwight N. Hopkins
The Divinity School, The Univ. of
    Chicago
Chicago, Illinois

Ada María Isasi-Díaz
The Theological School, Drew Univ.
Madison, New Jersey

Daisy L. Machado
Brite Divinity School, Texas
    Christian Univ.
Fort Worth, Texas

Fumitaka Matsuoka
Pacific School of Religion
Berkeley, California

Andrew Sung Park
United Theological Seminary
Dayton, Ohio

Peter C. Phan
Catholic Univ. of America
Washington, D.C.

Marcia Y. Riggs
Columbia Theological Seminary
Decatur, Georgia

Fernando F. Segovia
The Divinity School, Vanderbilt
    Univ.
Nashville, Tennessee

Linda E. Thomas
Garrett-Evangelical Theological
    Seminary
Evanston, Illinois

Emilie Townes
Union Theological Seminary
    of New York
New York City, New York

Index

Adams, Elisa Bonita, 232
"Aesthetic Age" of Vasconcelos, 65–69
African Americans and black theology, vii,
76–77, 113–116, 130; alienated consciousness and, 38–41; American
exceptionalism and, 223–224; Asian
Americans and, 68–69, 158–159, 163;
"Beloved Community," moral vision of,
90–97; Christianity as source, 37, 48–
50; Civil Rights Movement, 68–69, 87–
97, 195; Clinton, William Jefferson, 103;
conjuration/conjuring culture, 48; ecology and the environment, 83–84, 115;
gender, 79–81; historical and narrative
issues, 37–51, 138; historical black
churches, 37–41, 89–90; human liberation as source, 48–49; integration, 88–
90; *The Melting Pot,* Israel Zangwill,
239–241; *mestizaje/mulatez* concept,
inclusion in, 206; multiple sources, 48–
51; race and race discrimination, centrality of, 58–60, 73–77, 130, 138; self-
referential inconsistency, dilemma of,
37–38; sexual orientation, 81–83; slave
narratives as source for black theology,
38, 40–50, 98–100, 107–108, 224;
"twosomeness" of worldview, 124; white
America, identification with, 176;
womanist theology and, 72–86, 98–116
AIDS epidemic, 206
alienation, 229–230, 277
Althusser, Louis, 140
amalgamational model of integration, 155,
244
America. *See* United States/America
"American Creed," 257, 259, 267
American Dream: Christian studies, as context for, 228–231; deconstruction of, 241–
245; the deferred dream, 87–97; exaltation of, 232–241; Filipino Americans and,

172–174, 175–178, 179; national identity and, 224–226, 228; race discrimination and, 64–65; significance as theme, viii;
theology of exile, diaspora, mixture, and
otherness as basis for critiquing, 228–229,
261–267; unfinished dream as theological and political stance, 269–280;
Zangwill, *The Melting Pot,* 232–241,
244–245, 255, 259, 262
American exceptionalism, 223–224
anagnorisis, 230
Anderson, Victor, 37–51
Anglocentric/Eurocentric complexion of
U.S., 3–9
apartheid, 205
Appleby, Joyce, 223, 224, 227
Aristotelian philosophy, 132, 234
Asian Americans: African Americans and,
68–69, 158–159, 163; Cambodian
diaspora and experience of killing fields,
120–121, 124–128; Chinese immigration, 6, 120–121, 122–124, 127–128,
153; Filipino Americans (*see* Filipino
Americans); *han,* 157, 158, 163, 164,
165–166; identity and value systems,
119–128; immigration bars to, 6; Japanese internment in World War II, 120–
122, 127–128, 275; Korean Americans
(*see* Korean Americans); liberation theology, view of method in, 129–151; maternal figure as rewritten by Maxine
Hong Kingston, 122–124; model minority, viewed as, 154; race and race discrimination, views on, 152–166; transmutation,
theology of (*see* transmutation, theology
of); value systems and identity, 119–128
assimilation, 58, 60–62, 155, 209–210, 244,
246–252, 255–256, 259–261, 262–263
Austin, Stephen, 225
Ayrton, Edith, 233

Of Related Interest

Decolonizing Biblical Studies
A View from the Margins
Fernando F. Segovia
ISBN 1-57075-338-5

"In this fascinating volume the leading cultural biblical critic
Fernando Segovia skillfully weaves together his pioneering
studies that chart the methodological and hermeneutical
paradigm shift underway in biblical criticism. . . . It should be
read and widely used by all who care about the present and
the future of biblical criticism."
—*Elizabeth Schüssler Florenza*

Teaching the Bible
The Discourses and Politics of Biblical Pedagogy
Fernando F. Segovia and Mary Ann Tolbert, editors
ISBN 1-57075-202-8

"An absolutely indispensable compendium of resources for
charting the changes in the discipline of biblical studies, for
exposing the operations of power in the past and present
interpretations and uses of the bible, and for discovering a
variety of postmodernist and postcolonial pedagogies in the
reading and teaching of the bible in a radically pluralistic age."
—*Abraham Smith*

Toward a Theology of Struggle
Eleazar S. Fernandez
ISBN 0-88344-982-X

"Not only Christians, but all those who seek to speak, write,
and enact real hope for suffering peoples, will be challenged
and enriched by Fernandez's work."
—*Mark Lewis Taylor*

Please support your local bookstore, or call 1-800-258-5838.
For a free catalogue, please write us at
Orbis Books, Box 308
Maryknoll NY 10545-0308
Or visit our website at www.orbisbooks.com
Thank you for reading *A Dream Unfinished*.
We hope you enjoyed it.